Deleuze, Japanese Cinema, and the Atom Bomb

Thinking Cinema

Series Editors
David Martin-Jones, University of Glasgow, UK
Sarah Cooper, King's College, University of London, UK

Volume 1

Deleuze, Japanese Cinema, and the Atom Bomb

Deleuze, Japanese Cinema, and the Atom Bomb

The Spectre of Impossibility

David Deamer

Bloomsbury Academic
An imprint of Bloomsbury Publishing Inc

B L O O M S B U R Y

NEW YORK • LONDON • OXFORD • NEW DELHI • SYDNEY

Bloomsbury Academic
An imprint of Bloomsbury Publishing Inc

1385 Broadway
New York
NY 10018
USA

50 Bedford Square
London
WC1B 3DP
UK

www.bloomsbury.com

Bloomsbury is a registered trade mark of Bloomsbury Publishing Plc

First published 2014

Paperback edition first published 2016

Library of Congress Cataloging-in-Publication Data
Deamer, David.
Deleuze, Japanese cinema, and the atom bomb : the spectre of impossibility / David Deamer.
pages cm.– (Thinking cinema ; volume 1)
Includes bibliographical references and index.
ISBN 978-1-4411-7815-2 (hardback)
1. Motion pictures–Japan–History–20th century. 2. Nuclear warfare in motion pictures. 3. Motion pictures–Philosophy. 4. Deleuze, Gilles, 1925-1995. I. Title.
PN1993.5.J3D43 2014
791.430952'09045–dc23
2014004627

ISBN: HB: 978-1-4411-7815-2
PB: 978-1-5013-1773-6
ePub: 978-1-4411-4589-5
ePDF: 978-1-4411-4909-1

Typeset by Fakenham Prepress Solutions, Fakenham, Norfolk NR21 8NN
Printed and bound by CPI Group (UK) Ltd, Croydon, CR0 4YY

in memory, Lee
for Jill and Nyah

Contents

List of Tables

List of Images

Acknowledgements

Thanks to David Martin-Jones for inviting me to write this book, and for unfailing dedication throughout the process. Rob Lapsley, David Martin-Jones, Anna Powell and Henry Somers-Hall have inspired my thinking, unthinking and rethinking of Deleuze and the cineosis over the years this project has taken to coalesce, and for this I owe each much gratitude, as well as for commentaries on versions and drafts.

There have been many other people whose insight, conversation, support and conviviality helped realize this book: Jeff Bell, Linnie Blake, William Brown, Ian Buchanan, Clare Colebrook, Felicity Colman, Colin Gardner, Ullrich Haase, Joanna Hodge, Wahida Khandker, Craig Lundy, Patricia MacCormack, Philippe Mengue, John Mullarkey, Simon O'Sullivan, Patricia Pisters, Xavier Aldana Reyes, Richard Rushton, Mark Sinclair, and Daniel W. Smith. Such encounters and opportunities couldn't have happened without the existence of the visiting speaker programmes, symposiums and conferences of the Human Sciences Seminar (Department of History, Politics and Philosophy, MMU); the English Research Institute / Centre of Research English (Department of English, MMU); *A/V* (Institute of Humanities & Social Science Research, MMU); and *Deleuze Studies* (Edinburgh University). My thanks to the friends and colleagues who make it happen.

I owe thanks to Yamane Kazuyo (Kochi University and Director of IFLAC: The International Forum for the Literature and Culture of Peace, Japan); Ishida Satoko and Suzuki Akiko (Shochiku); Sue Zlosnik and Jess Edwards (Department of English, MMU); Berthold Schoene and Helen Malarky (Research Institute, MMU); Rachel Hayward (Cornerhouse cinema, Manchester); Alan Hook, Rachael McConkey, Vee Uye, and Ana Miller (Trauma film screenings and seminars, MMU); Sarah Cooper (Thinking Cinema); Katie Gallof, Mary Al-Sayed, Tanya Leet, Charlotte Rose, Claire Cooper (Bloomsbury); Dominic West, Richard Crane and Kim Storry (Fakenham); Krishna Stott (Bellyfeel, Manchester); David, Aleks and all the baristas (Caffè Nero, Oxford Road, Manchester).

* * *

Some aspects of the work in a few sections of this book first appeared elsewhere either in earlier stages of development or somewhat differently framed. *Children of the Atom Bomb* (Chapter 1) was previously discussed in terms of recollection-images (not affection-images) in '"Watch out! Recollection": the "spectre of impossibility" in Kaneto Shindo's *Children of the Atom Bomb*', *A/V* 6 (Manchester Metropolitan University, 2007). An exploration of *Godzilla* (parts of the end of Chapter 1 and a sub-section at the beginning of Chapter 2) was given a first outing in respect to the imprint (rather than the binomial) in 'An imprint of *Godzilla*: Deleuze, the action-image and universal history', David Martin-Jones and William Brown (eds), *Deleuze and Film* (Edinburgh University Press, 2012). Nietzsche's universal history (moments in Chapters 2, 4 and 5) was also experimented with in that essay; as well as, in less developed form and in respect to the Stoics, Heidegger and Artaud, in 'Cinema, chronos / cronos: becoming an accomplice to the impasse of history', Jeff Bell and Claire Colebrook (eds), *Deleuze and History* (Edinburgh University Press, 2009). The methodology of the explication of the co-ordinates of the time-image cineosis through Deleuze's temporal syntheses of *Difference and Repetition* (Chapter 5) was first rehearsed (in greater depth, if not with some of the nuances here) in 'A Deleuzian cineosis: cinematic syntheses of time', *Deleuze Studies* 5:3 (Edinburgh University Press, 2011). Thanks to the editors, Edinburgh University Press and Manchester Metropolitan University for permission to plunder these texts.

* * *

A note on Japanese names and terms: Japanese names have been rendered with family name first followed by given name. This is to respect both Japanese naming conventions (as well as more recent English language Asian cinema scholarship). When a film character is first mentioned the name of the actor will appear in parenthesis afterwards, except in the limited cases where the name has not been verifiable or not deemed necessary (as in the case of the voices in *anime*). Accents on English rendering of Japanese words has not been used (except in quotes from other writers) as these vary according to year, convention, taste and source.

Introduction: Event, Cinema, Cineosis

The great post-war philosophers and writers demonstrated that thought has something to do with Auschwitz, with Hiroshima, but this was also demonstrated by the great cinema authors.[1]

Event, cinema, cineosis

Seventeen seconds past 8.15 a.m. on 6 August 1945, the Japanese city of Hiroshima was destroyed by a 9,700-pound uranium bomb. Unleashed by the United States of America, the bomb detonated at an altitude of 1,900 feet; ground zero temperature was 5,400°F. Three days later, at 11.02 a.m., a second plutonium bomb was exploded over Nagasaki, the force 40 per cent greater than that of Hiroshima. Hundreds of thousands of people – soldiers and civilians; men, women and children – were instantaneously vaporized, torn apart by imploding infrastructure, burned alive in raging firestorms, drowned in rivers (appearing, at first, to offer escape) and poisoned by radioactive fallout.[2]

Japanese cinema – so critical narratives have a tendency to proclaim – has continually failed the nuclear event. Kowtowing to political suppression and mass psychological repression, Japanese cinema turns away from Hiroshima and Nagasaki. The few films that do make it to the screen are seen, with rare exception, as reflecting a pervasive Japanese victimology. The Japanese film industry has 'not produced a particularly large or especially distinguished body of film work on the bomb', has not examined 'Hiroshima, Nagasaki, and the bomb … in any constructive or convincing manner'.[3] This book challenges such an outlook. We will discover a Japanese cinema of the atom bomb worthy of such a name, a cinema composed of many masterpieces. The films explored will include those by well-known directors – Kurosawa Akira, Shindo Kaneto, Oshima Nagisa and Imamura Shohei; popular and cult classics – Honda Ishiro's *Gojira / Godzilla* (1954) and Otomo Katsuhiro's *Akira* (1988); contemporary genre flicks – Miike Takashi's *Dead or Alive* (1999) and Kiriya Kazuaki's *Casshern* (2004); rarely screened documentaries – Ito Sueo's

Hiroshima, Nagasaki ni okeru genshibakudan no koka / The Effects of the Atomic Bomb on Hiroshima and Nagasaki (1946). These films, and others encountered in this book, will be seen to capture the nuclear event in a myriad of ways: from manifest depictions of the atomic attacks (their genesis, aftermath and legacy), through oblique re-figurations in imaginary times and spaces, to traces interpolated into other story-worlds. The nuclear event will appear in documentary and fictional modes; in action cinema and contemplative melodramas; in science fiction, horror, and yakuza movies; through realist and modernist narrative encodings. The Japanese cinema of the atom bomb will be revealed as a heterogeneous assemblage of films.

To make this argument I deploy the film-philosophy of Gilles Deleuze. Deleuze, in his *Cinema* books, invents a cineosis, a taxonomy of filmic concepts, of cinematic signs.[4] These signs describe cinema as a field of differential images, giving onto different conceptions of history and diverse philosophical encounters. Each film in this book will be explored through one of these images and signs. In so doing I am allowing two series (cinema and cineosis) to flow alongside one another, until film snags upon sign, sign upon film, causing a break in these flows, a break that allows writing to begin. The trajectory of this book, accordingly, will be unashamedly taxonomic, following the procession of filmic concepts as enunciated in *Cinema 1* (1983) and then *Cinema 2* (1985). Using this trajectory will allow for many different types of analysis and connections between movies, connections that do not rely upon historical succession or categories such as auteur or genre – but which will still permit such relations when and if required. Such a procedure will create the conditions to extend or transform a reading already in play and to re-encounter a film anew, will foreground how different filmmakers – at different times, under different conditions – have depicted, imagined and displaced the Japanese nuclear event: its happenings, its germinations, its aftermaths; its affects and effects; its historical co-ordinates; its physical and psychological consequences; its repressions and remembrances.

Through such a cineotic encounter of the twenty-five films in this book, the Japanese cinema of the atom bomb will be revealed as a heterogeneous assemblage. The ultimate aim in this revealing, it must be emphasized, is not to evaluate one film or type of film in respect to another; nor is it to evaluate the films in respect to the real of the Hiroshima and Nagasaki atomic attacks. Rather, this book explores how each film – in its own way – creates the nuclear event; creates the nuclear event as an image, as an image in respect to history, as an image in respect to thought.

Cinematic territories and critical processes

In consequence, *Deleuze, Japanese Cinema, and the Atom Bomb* pioneers a number of new territories and processes for cinema studies – with all the exhilaration and risk such an enterprise engenders. (1) There are but few engagements with Japanese films of the atom bomb; and those that do exist appear in essay form or part of wider critical projects. This book is thus the first devoted to the Japanese screen and the nuclear event, to a territorializing of the domain through the films thereof. Such a territorializing, or organization, is provided by way of Deleuze's film-philosophy. (2) Accordingly, this book is also the first dedicated to an encounter with Japanese film through a Deleuzian framework. The Japanese cinema has been examined through many theoretical paradigms over the years, including (as we will see) culturalist, psychoanalytic and Marxist: we aspire to contribute toward an expansion of the approaches to this cinema. Such novelty is not purely for novelty's sake. The Deleuzian cine-methodology – or more specifically, the way in which I will enunciate and employ Deleuze's film-philosophy – is fundamental to the project of the book, to seeing the Japanese cinema – and the Japanese cinema of the atom bomb – as a heterogeneous assemblage of films. (3) So, on the one hand, this book is the first to explicate and designate a complete Deleuzian cineosis. There have been previous accounts of Deleuze's film taxonomy; the most developed being that of Ronald Bogue's wonderful *Deleuze on Cinema* (2003). However, Bogue declares 'obviously, the tally [of signs] is insignificant … Deleuze is no ordinary system builder … his taxonomy is a generative device meant to create new terms for talking about new ways of seeing.'[5] We agree with such a statement of purpose, but we do not see this as precluding a rigorous unfolding of the semiotic logic, an enumeration of the signs. This, as Deleuze would have it, is a fundamental aspect of understanding their 'differentiation' and 'specification'.[6] (4) On the other hand, this book breaks new ground in deploying the cineosis. Elucidatory accounts, such as those of Bogue and D. N. Rodowick's magisterial *Gilles Deleuze's Time Machine* (1997), incline toward an opening-up of the *Cinema* books in the context of Deleuze's philosophical project – using cinema in general and any-film-whatsoever as conceptual examples. By contrast, writers who use the *Cinema* books for their own ventures (exploring a genre, filmmaker, national cinema, and so on) tend to select and employ one sign, image or limited number of either for the task in hand. This book navigates its way between these two approaches, and is thus the first to deploy the complete cineosis in respect to a specified cinematic domain. Such a methodology is fundamental to a deterritorializing of the Japanese cinema of the atom bomb, describing the assemblage of films as heterogeneous.

Over the five chapters that compose the body of this book we will thus unfold the Deleuzian cineosis and use it to explore Japanese cinema and the nuclear event. In Chapter 1, we will encounter perception-images, affection-images and action-images. These concepts will designate the essential co-ordinates of the earliest films: how, in the immediate aftermath of the atomic bomb, Japanese cinema perceived the attacks through scientific objectivity; and how, by the end of the occupation period, the focus shifted to the people of Hiroshima and Nagasaki, the drama of men, women and children affected by the nuclear event. The chapter will conclude by looking at mainstream Japanese film and the means by which it masked the attacks through the creation of an action-cinema of monster movies. Such indirect depictions, it may seem, appear to dehistoricize the Japanese cinema of the atom bomb – accordingly, Chapter 2 focuses upon the links between action-image films and history (in both direct and indirect depictions of the nuclear event), discovering different types of action-image and different types of historical conceptualization. Such a passage from direct to opaque depictions creates a logic of disappearance, so Chapter 3 looks at a withdrawing of Hiroshima and Nagasaki from the Japanese screen, and how the atomic attacks can appear (consciously, unconsciously) as trace images. These traces will be explored in rural dramas, yakuza movies, horror films and the avant-garde through the cineotic components of impulse-images and reflection-images, signs which describe cinematic symptoms and filmic figures (such as metaphors, allusions and allegories) as moments of the shock of history. Chapter 4 extends the exploration of such moments to indirect and direct depictions of the nuclear event, a reversal where we encounter traces as images of thought for characters. Using Deleuze's concepts of the mental-image, we investigate flashbacks, recollections, dreams, hallucinations and other associated signs in samurai movies, arthouse films and contemporary dramas. Finally, in Chapter 5, we explore a crisis in cinema. Chapters 1 through 4 described how films attempt – through various means – to produce images that can be encompassed within rational co-ordinates of history and thought. In the concluding chapter we discover a cinema concerned with escaping such encompassings, a Japanese cinema of the atom bomb sustaining ambiguities and uncertainties in science fiction, documentaries and modernist dramas. Here we encounter time-images: a cinema of indeterminate images of history and thought.

In this way the Japanese cinema of the atom bomb will be revealed as a heterogeneous assemblage of films: employing different codes of narration across all genres, composed with varying intensity, creating diverse modes of historical conception and images of thought. Cinema is not seen as representation, as representations that can only ever fall short of and fail the event they must re-present. Films are images which create an event, which create history and thought as an event. Together, the twenty-five films explored in this book compose a perspectival archive of the nuclear attacks on Hiroshima and Nagasaki.

This introduction explores the ground and procedure for such a project. A central thread will be to address the viability of using Deleuze, a contemporary French philosopher, for the study of Japanese films, and the charge of Eurocentrism this move may engender. The ambition will be to suggest ways the *Cinema* books can be said to elude such Eurocentrism – and how my own project can follow such escapes. This claim will necessitate foregrounding the work of critics whose work on both world and Japanese cinemas resonates with that of Deleuze, as well as providing an overview of the concerns of the *Cinema* books within Deleuze's wider philosophical project. It will also require a general mapping of Japanese atom bomb films, their place within Japanese cinema and key critical discourses thereof. It is with such a mapping that we will begin.

The spectre of impossibility

How can a film capture, express, depict such an event as the atomic attacks on Hiroshima and Nagasaki? How can cinema do justice to the *pika* (atom bomb) and *hibakusha* (atomic bomb-affected people)?[7] How can the Japanese nation make movies that explore the moment of the nuclear event, that explore the antecedents, the aftermaths? Abé Mark Nornes describes the Japanese screen as being haunted by 'the spectre of impossibility'; in the face of such horror, the possibility of 'representation' can seem beyond reach.[8] Such a response echoes that of critical theorist Theodor Adorno, who declared, in the wake of the Second World War and Auschwitz, the writing of poetry as barbaric.[9] How can poetry, art, film, represent such torment and misery, and do it justice? Adorno would later disavow such a proscription, stating 'perennial suffering has as much right to expression as the tortured have to scream.'[10] We should not sneer at such a reversal, but rather understand it as telling, as symptomatic, as the very crisis at the heart of the matter. John T. Dorsey and Naomi Matsuoka put it this way: 'the problems faced by artists who try to depict the horrors of twentieth-century reality are intimidating, beginning with the basic questions of whether they can do so, and if so, whether they should.'[11] Every film that attempts to create images of the atom bomb, of any social or personal trauma, of its genesis, happening and consequences must answer these questions. Dorsey and Matsuoka outline two fundamental ways in which these problems have been negotiated. There are filmmakers who simply document and record, 'regarding themselves as reporters, as witnesses, or as preservers of the records and documents.'[12] Then there are filmmakers who 'see a clear lesson in such events' and accordingly 'try to highlight that lesson in the depiction of what would otherwise seem either a manifestation of absolute evil or of meaningless destruction like that of a natural disaster.'[13]

Whatever the case, as E. Ann Kaplan and Ban Wang comment, 'narratives and images designed to represent traumas are viewed with suspicion, for they seem to have the seductive power to gloss over the horrendous fact and to distort the literal truth of trauma.'[14] 'To represent or not to represent: that is the question.'[15] Yet to resist and renounce such attempts make the traumatic event 'untouchable and unreachable.'[16] Art and cinema become 'impoverished as a tool of critical historical analysis.'[17] Even so, dangers are prevalent. Kaplan and Wang expand upon Dorsey and Matsuoka's tendencies, identifying 'four main positions' for the viewer, correlates of 'differing narrative strategies': (1) where the film works to present a 'comforting "cure"'; (2) where the film attempts to '"shock" and "vicariously" traumatize'; (3) where the film 'exploits' the event, the viewer becoming 'voyeur'; and (4) where the film transforms the viewer through a dialectic of 'empathetic identification' and 'cognitive distance' as a 'witness.'[18] It is the last position that Kaplan and Wang see as being the most valuable. This kind of film, which they align with the codes of modernism (or as they put it, 'anti-narrative') offers a way to both critically explore historical trauma as well as escape the inherent dangers of mainstream cinema – the three other spectatorial positions.[19] They give some ground. 'To a mind less indoctrinated and more inclined to read against the grain,' they comment, 'mainstream narrative or imagistic interpretations of trauma … merit more than a simplistic negative judgement.'[20] However, a certain hierarchy of value remains; Kaplan and Wang believe exploring historical trauma through cinema is something best left not to mainstreamers, but modernists.

Yet this solution is not without its impasses. The modernist-mainstream distinction is made more complex with films from cultures other than that of the viewer or critic. More significantly, perhaps, it does not allow for reasons external to cinema. Proscription and political censorship can force the use of 'imagistic interpretations', for instance. A covert mainstream narrative may be the only way to get a film made. A modernist film may never be seen by the masses, and such engagements become tangled up in issues of class, coterie and elitism. Indeed, techniques once modernist may become, in time, mainstream (as in the case of Hollywood's use of Soviet montage). Furthermore, such divisions deny variations in spectatorship, risk positing the viewer as a homogenous universal mind outside of space and time, geography and history, gender, class, race and age. As Adam Lowenstein has written, in 'Holocaust cinema, "modernism" often trumps "realism"' and 'in the case of Hiroshima and Japanese cinema, "realism" trumps "allegory" as the critical discourse's preferred representational mode'.[21] In the latter instance this occurs 'without sufficient sense of what allegory might mean in this particular context'.[22]

It is at this point we can foreground a key aspect of Deleuze's film-philosophy, to shift the argument and to anticipate a different approach. In *Cinema 1*, Deleuze puts it this way: 'it is not a matter of saying that the modern cinema … is "more valuable" than the classical cinema'; rather 'no hierarchy of value applies'.[23] Perhaps a critical study should begin with an affirmation of cinema as a heterogeneous assemblage of forms and varying intensities; perhaps a critical study should begin by focusing upon 'directors [who] were able to invent and get screened, in spite of everything'.[24] Perhaps an exploration of Japanese cinema and the atom bomb can arise through an engagement with filmmakers who have – each in their own way – found the will and means to overcome the many spectres of impossibility.

Heterogeneity and intensity

The first Japanese film to explore the nuclear event was Ito Sueo's *The Effects of the Atomic Bomb on Hiroshima and Nagasaki* (1946). Lasting nearly three hours, the film is composed of documentary footage of the devastated cities and surviving *hibakusha*. Never screened to the public, at least not till many decades after its completion, the film was confiscated by American officials during the initial phase of the occupation. From the very beginning, then, Japanese cinema was haunted by a very powerful incarnation of the spectre of impossibility: prohibition. The occupation, lasting from 1945 to 1952, was dominated by an American leadership led by General Douglas MacArthur as Supreme Commander for the Allied Powers (SCAP). SCAP created the Civil Censorship Detachment (CCD) to enforce prohibitions covering any mention of war and the atom bomb.[25] When sovereignty was returned to the Japanese people, the situation improved – but only slightly. The 1951 San Francisco Peace Treaty made Japan an ally and a vital staging ground for the Korean War (1950–3). The financing of atom bomb films was not something the Japanese mainstream cinema industry would encourage.

Nevertheless, films were made – by independent studios, sometimes funded by political organizations; for example, Tasaka Tomotaka's *Nagasaki no uta wa Wasureji / I'll Not Forget the Song of Nagasaki* (1952) and Shindo Kaneto's *Gembaku no ko / Children of the Atom Bomb* (1952). These movies exhibit an elegiac tone, very different to the objective documentary style of *Effects*. *Children*, furthermore, attempted – for the very first time – to render on-screen the moment of the *pika* and its effect on human bodies. *Nagasaki* and *Children* focus upon the *hibakusha*, and their overcoming of the nuclear legacy. Such films in the elegiac mode would also be produced for a younger audience – Kimura Sotoji's *Nagasaki no ko / Children of Nagasaki* (1957) and *Semba Juru / A Thousand Paper Cranes* (1958).

At the same time, the immediate post-occupation period also saw films with strident socialist perspectives. Sekigawa Hideo's *Hiroshima* (1953) was another adaptation of Osada Arata's novelistic testament on which *Children of the Atom Bomb* was based, funded by the leftist Hiroshima City Council who had also financed Shindo's film (and which they believed had failed politically). Sekigawa depicts the horrors of the *pika*, the experiences of the *hibakusha* in the hours, days and weeks after the bomb; and laces the narrative with critiques of both the Japanese and American military and government. Another director, Kamei Fumio, developed and accentuated such political encounters, making a number of documentary-esque films, including *Ikiteite yokatta / Still, It's Good to be Alive* (1956), *Sekai wa kyofu suru / The World is Afraid* (1957) and *Hiroshima no koe / Voices of Hiroshima* (1959). Similarly, Imai Tadashi's *Jun'ai monogatari / A Story of Pure Love* (1957) exposed the rejection and betrayal of the *hibakusha* by Japanese society.

By 1960, films of direct depiction of the nuclear event and its immediate aftermath were no longer being produced. It wouldn't be until the 1980s that such movies returned to the Japanese screen. This second and more dispersed cycle began with two *anime* (Japanese animations) based upon *manga* (Japanese comic) publications: Masaki Mori's *Hadashi no Gen / Barefoot Gen* (1983) and Hirata Toshio and Sakai Akio's *Hadashi no Gen 2 / Barefoot Gen II* (1986). These films focused upon the experiences of a young boy caught up in the nuclear attack, and the story of his survival in the aftermath of the bomb. The decade closed with Imamura's *Kuroi ame / Black Rain* (1989) – an echo, of a kind, of the social-realist features of the 1950s, films which can be seen as prefiguring the Japanese New Wave of which Imamura was one of the leading proponents. The New Wave, a modernist film movement at its height during the 1960s, promoted film techniques such as multiple narrative strands, the interweaving of time-frames and extreme self-reflexivity, and such procedures accordingly permeate *Black Rain*. Kurosawa's contemplative *Hachi-gatsu no kyoshikyoku / Rhapsody in August* (1991) saw the director reflect upon the long-term legacy of Hiroshima and Nagasaki some forty-five years after the event. In the twenty-first century there have been two films from Kuroki Kazuo, *Utsukushii natsu kirishima / A Boy's Summer* (2002) and *Chichi to kuraseba / The Face of Jizo* (2004), completing a loose trilogy beginning with *Ashita / Tomorrow* (1988).

Yet foregrounding these direct depictions of the nuclear event by the Japanese cinema is only part of the story. Many of the essays in Mick Broderick's important edited collection *Hibakusha Cinema* (1996) (primarily focused upon Japanese atom bomb films but extending to novels and non-Japanese movies) also explore depictions that have a more opaque relationship with the atom bomb. These films manifest themselves most significantly in popular mainstream cinema through *kaiju eiga* (mysterious monster movies), such as Honda's *Godzilla* (1954) which kick-started the genre. Godzilla is awoken by atomic bomb testing by the Americans in the Pacific and ravages Japan – the monster somehow connecting with the nuclear event. Other genres, such as science fiction, also explore a post-apocalyptic Japanese environment, projecting it into the near or distant future. Freda Freiberg cites, for instance, Otomo's *anime Akira* and – in a chapter on Japanese film in *Atomic Bomb Cinema* (2002) – Jerome F. Shapiro discusses another *anime*, Miyazaki Hayao's *Kaze no tani no Naushika / Nausicaa of the Valley of the Wind* (1984). It is not, however, just the extensive *kaiju eiga* cycles and sci-fi *anime* that offer up indirect depictions of the Japanese nuclear environment. The Cold War films of the 1950s also, unsurprisingly, have a post-apocalyptic flavour. James Goodwin, again in the *Hibakusha Cinema* collection, focuses upon *gendai geki* (contemporary dramas) such as Kurosawa's *Ikimono no kiroku / I Live in Fear* (1955) as paradigmatic of the genre. More unexpectedly, perhaps, is the inclusion of *jidai geki* (period films). Goodwin mentions the medieval drama *Rashomon* (1950) which 'reflects Kurosawa's response' through its decaying mise-en-scène 'to the unprecedented destructiveness with which the atomic age begins'.[26] Goodwin's remark on *Rashomon*, while little more than an aside, gives a first glimpse of a willingness to explore how the Japanese cinema can capture up the atom bomb as a trace element or a filmic figure (such as a metaphor or allegory). In the case of *Rashomon* – as we will see – this was Kurosawa's way of sidestepping prohibition and proscription during the American occupation. Similarly, Linnie Blake, in a chapter on Japanese atom bomb cinema in *The Wounds of Nations* (2007), identifies how images of the *pika* and *hibakusha* pervade Japanese horror films and in so doing reopen the prematurely bound wounds of the past, thereby offering a kind of healing. For instance, Nakata's J-horror *Ring* (1998) has images and references open enough, for Blake, to be interpreted against the background of Hiroshima and Nagasaki. With *Ring* and *Rashomon* we approach – in different ways and at different historical junctures – limit situations for the continuum of expression which registers a dissipation of the intensities of affect of the atom bomb in Japanese cinema. With trace expressions of the *pika* and the *hibakusha*, Hiroshima and Nagasaki continually break through into other story-worlds, constituting ambiguous filmic rememberings.

This overview of the post-Pacific War Japanese cinema's response to the atom bomb is, without doubt, incomplete – and will be fleshed out in the body of this book. However, even from this sketch, it is clear that the mapping has two striking features. First, the films include some of the key Japanese directors of the last sixty years, as well as some widely acknowledged masterpieces. Second, the films would seem to be self-evidentially heterogeneous. Across genres – documentary; *kaiju eiga*; sci-fi; *jidai geki*; *gendai geki*; J-horror – and through different modes – scientific-objectification; elegiac; social-realist; realist; modernist – spectres of impossibility are overcome in any number of ways upon the Japanese screen. Yet the response by cineastes, in both regards, is curious.

Atom bomb cinema and film studies

The four most prominent texts on the history of Japanese cinema available in English say little about Hiroshima, Nagasaki and film. For instance, Joseph L. Anderson and Richie's monumental *The Japanese Film* (1959; expanded 1982) has little over a page; and Richie's later *A Hundred Years of Japanese Film* (2001) even less.[27] Noël Burch's *To the Distant Observer* (1979) contains just a few scattered references and Sato Tadao's *Currents in Japanese Cinema* does most at three or so pages.[28] This is disproportionate, to say the least, given the momentous nature of the event. There is a reason. All of these writers see atom bomb films as being of little or no importance in the overall narratives they construct around the history of Japanese cinema. These writers have all produced excellent, diverse and perceptive commentaries on the Japanese screen. Yet the resistance to engaging with films of the atom bomb can just as well be viewed as another aspect of the spectre of impossibility.

When an intensive engagement in this area does surface, it is predominately antagonistic. The earliest history in English is a short essay from Richie, '"*Mono no Aware*": Hiroshima on Film' (1961).[29] Richie sets out to provide an overview of the films released between 1945 and 1960 (although there is no mention of Ito's suppressed *Effects*). Coloured by the films of Tasaka and Shindo, Richie evokes the Japanese term *mono no aware* (translated as 'sympathetic sadness') to describe the elegiac mode of address of the nascent atom bomb cinema.[30] These films are thus seen as regarding the nuclear event through 'a feeling for the transience of all earthly things', and so invoke 'a near-Buddhistic insistence upon the recognition of the eternal flux of life upon this earth'.[31] For Richie, the subsequent overtly political, social-realist films are anti-American, and are the reason why direct depictions of the atom bomb cease being produced at the end of the 1950s; any director proposing such a project would be labelled as communist – not a great position to be in (for a mainstream director or a major studio) during the early days of the Cold War and the Japanese treaty of economic and military dependence with the Americans. Furthermore, Richie sees this socio-political stance as being in bad faith, as being essentially un-Japanese. The *mono no aware* attitude is the authentic mode, true Japanese cinema.[32] Accordingly, Richie's essay subsumes these elegiac atom bomb films into Japanese cinema in general, and sees them as only minor works unable or unwilling to explore the nuclear event as a consequence of the Japanese war effort. Variations on such a narrative – as we will see throughout this book, in respect to any number of subsequent critiques – tend to permeate criticism of the Japanese cinema of the atom bomb.

Many of the essays in *Hibakusha Cinema* echo such antagonisms, or at the very least are highly ambivalent. Opening with Richie's '"*Mono no Aware*"', Nornes goes on – in 'The Body at the Centre' – to describe Ito's *Effects* as failing the *hibakusha*, focused as the film is on the devastation of the cities and wounds of the bomb's living victims. Linda C. Ehrlich sees Kurosawa's atom bomb films of the 1990s, in 'The Extremes of Innocence', as products of a master losing his edge in his old age. Maya Morioka Todeschini in '"Death and the Maiden"' and Dorsey and Matsuoka in 'Narrative Strategies of Understatement' believe Imamura's *Black Rain* to lack his former New Wave vitality and political verve. These films by Imamura and Kurosawa fail in respect to an ideal which existed sometime in the past, and for Ito, ideals which were yet to come.

Interestingly, the essays in *Hibakusha Cinema* which do escape such antagonisms and ambivalences tend to focus upon more indirect depictions of the nuclear event. Chon A. Noriga celebrates monster movies in 'Godzilla and the Japanese Nightmare' as exploring the vicissitudes of the Cold War arms race. Freda Freiberg in '*Akira* and the Postnuclear sublime' describes how the *anime* is exemplary of an ecstatic postmodern catharsis of a post-apocalyptic Japanese imagination. Shapiro's *Atomic Bomb Cinema*, perhaps the most recent overview, similarly affirms Japan's nuclear movies by focusing upon such opaque expressions. While not a book devoted to Japanese films (the first seven chapters cover the American cinema), it does reserve its final section for the Japanese response to Hiroshima and Nagasaki. Shapiro begins by reflecting upon and then rejecting Richie's reading of the *mono no aware* concept as incomplete, exploring it through Kawai Hayao's translation as 'sorrow ... directed at something disappearing', claiming it can only be understood in relation to its counterpart, *urami*, the 'continuation of a process ... born out of the spirit of resistance'.[33] In this way, Japanese atom bomb films exhibit the conjunction of *mono no aware* and *urami* and follow a trajectory that explores the 'restoration of balance and harmony through playfulness'.[34] These films are thus no longer laments of victimization, as Richie would see it, but also attempts at overcoming the horrors of the past. Yet what we discover with Shapiro, just as with Richie before, is a tendency to homogenize the Japanese cinema of the atom bomb. Richie may well dismiss these films while Shapiro lauds them – but both see such movies as representations embodying a concept within a singular Japanese cinematic tradition. Such an analysis is achieved through exclusion. It may well be that Richie had not heard of the suppressed *Effects*, but the active exclusion of the social-realist films of the late 1950s sets up an unproductive paradox: the un-Japaneseness of films from Japan – films emerging from Japanese directors and the Japanese film industry which are considered by European and American critics as not being truly Japanese. Shapiro must have known about Ito's documentary, but his procedure is to exclude any movies, including the social-realist films, that may trouble his argument. Such a procedure of affirmation through exclusion can be seen in exemplary and overt form in Lowenstein's 'Allegorizing Hiroshima' (2008), which explicitly validates such indirect engagements with, and traces of, the atom bomb. For Lowenstein, the allegorical approach allows traces of the nuclear event to disrupt filmic continuums and nuclear images to retain their power, while direct depictions necessarily tame the traumas of history and thought.

What we encounter in these narratives is the mechanism of homogeneity. Homogeneity is never simply the assertion that everything is the same; rather there is always a (sometimes clandestine) exclusion, a cutting away that allows the appearance of homogeneity to be all the more acceptable. Furthermore, it is never enough to merely expose that which is excluded: to reintegrate it into a new unity; to sustain a duality of inclusion in a too-delicate balance; or allow that which was excluded to dominate. Each of these processes retains the secret structure of homogeneity, displacing, sustaining or reorientating it. Rather, a dismantling of homogeneity requires something other: the propagation of multiplicity. I want to argue that the Japanese cinema's response to the atom bomb is heterogeneous, the films are riven with differences. This is not to say that Richie, Shapiro and the other critics do not offer up insightful engagements with the films they explore. Indeed, this book will use their readings, sometimes by way of collaboration, sometimes as a point of departure. It is only to say that the homogenous approach tends to limit thinking about Japanese cinema and the atom bomb, tends to exclude and essentialize. Indeed, it seems to me that this homogenizing approach to writing about Japanese films in the wake of Hiroshima and Nagasaki has its origin in critical responses to the Japanese screen in general.

A certain tendency in critical responses to Japanese cinema

Anderson and Richie's *The Japanese Film* – which, while showing signs of age, has yet to be surpassed in scope – was the first book in English to explore Japanese cinema. Research began, the authors assure us, as early as 1947 – work carried out in Japan under terrible conditions: not only the immediate aftermath of the Pacific War, the early years of the occupation and the horrendous social and economic situation; but also the problem of the availability of films. Many of the movies discussed are non-extant, preservation not being a priority in the early years of the cinema. Then there is the destruction of films stored in Kyoto due to the Kanto earthquake (1923); censorship-burnings by the Japanese militaristic government (mid-1930s onwards); and the American firebombing of Tokyo during the war (where all the major studios had been located after Kanto). Still, Anderson and Richie viewed over five hundred films; used Japanese research material, including the definitive four-volume *Nihon eiga hattstsu shi / History of the Development of the Japanese Film* (1957) by Tanaka Jun'ichiro; and interviewed many players in the industry. The book itself – with its wonderful chapter titles ('Slow fade-in', 'Establishing shot') – takes a dual approach: a linear history describing the films; then elements such as content (genres and themes), techniques and key directors. In essence, the book is a critical evaluation of the cinema, directors and industry. Kurosawa comments in the Forward: 'as a creator, I am particularly pleased that the authors of this book … take a firm stand for what they believe right and good.'[35] This procedure extracts – toward the end of the volume – nine directors that embody the essence of Japanese cinema. This allows Anderson and Richie to retroactively measure all films in conformity to this essence. Richie went on to extend this approach in a series of histories, including *Japanese Cinema* (1971); *Japanese Cinema: An Introduction* (1990); and, most recently, *A Hundred Years of Japanese Film*. Paul Schrader comments on the first of these books, that the 'volume emphasised a cultural point of view: the struggle of Japanese filmmakers to be Japanese in a non-indigenous medium'.[36] For Richie, Japanese cinema is other to Western cinema. American and European film tend toward a 'representational style', while the Japanese film tends toward the 'presentational'.[37] Representation 'is realist and assumes that "reality" itself is being shown', while the presentational has 'no assumption that raw reality is being displayed'.[38]

What can be made of such a generalization? It is clear this methodology is in good faith. Anderson and Richie are arguing for Japanese cinema to be considered as distinctive, against the neo-colonialist assumption that movie-making belongs to Hollywood and Europe. Japanese cinematic style was, for Anderson and Richie, Japanese from the very beginning. This is a crucial aspect of their project and constitutes an attack on the entrenched view held by many critics of the time that the films of the West set a standard for 'other' cinemas, standards these 'other' cinemas could only dream of achieving, and then only under the exceptional situation of the Romantic notion of the director of genius (who, most likely enough, had studied American movies). Perhaps it is only now that we can begin to see problems with some aspects of this approach. Indicative is Schrader's comment. It seems strange to assert that film is a non-indigenous medium for the Japanese, as if the technology dropped from the sky and landed in the lap of a now-swordless samurai. Japan had cinema from the very beginning. The *Cinématographe Lumière* arrived in 1897; and later that year the first movie camera was imported into Japan by the Tokyo photographer Shiro Asano.[39] Two years after this the Association of Japanese Motion pictures was formed.[40] To call the medium non-indigenous could be sustained, I guess, if we were to say the same of, say, Russia, Germany or Italy. The problem is that this culturally unique argument encourages a binary and wholesale othering: the West and (othered) East. It addresses the hierarchy but not the mechanism of the hierarchy. Ironically, it is also as problematic for 'Western' cinema as it is for 'Eastern' cinema. It is as if the radically different early experiments such as American classical realism, British social-realism, French Impressionism, German Expressionism, and Soviet montage can be grouped together, homogenized.[41] This is not to mention early Eastern adoptions and experiments such as Indian 'naturalism'.[42] In truth, the early days of cinema saw diverse experiments that the above list falls far short of recounting. Richie acknowledges some of these discrepancies, yet insists on the representation–presentation dichotomy. These concerns are brought to the fore by David Desser, who writes: 'this is a problematic area in regard to Japanese cinema, which by certain Western standards is already "radical" juxtaposed to the Hollywood classical style.'[43] Desser cites two 'overwhelming, if implicit, assumptions':[44] first, that Japanese cinema is seen as a 'closed system'; second, as a 'unified text'.[45] For Desser, the work of Burch is exemplary in this regard.

In *To the Distant Observer* – a wonderful series of essays and interjections, sidesteps and notes – Burch writes that 'the specific traits of a Japanese "theory" must be sought … in the practice of her arts'.[46] This seemingly anti-Western imperialist approach is, without doubt, admirable (although, as we will see a little later, under the terms of its own argument severely compromised). Burch intends to explore 'the modes of representation common to, and distinctive of, most Japanese films within given periods, and with the highly refined styles generated by these modes in the work of a handful of auteurs'.[47] Here, already, we begin to see the problem (one common to the other writers we have already looked at) – a norm based upon a select number of directors. For Burch, the 'golden age' of Japanese cinema is the 1930s and early 1940s. He is at pains to point out that the commonly held belief among Western critics is that the 'golden age' is the immediate post-war period of the late 1940s and early 1950s, which saw the international recognition of, most prominently, Kurosawa Akira, Mizoguchi Kenji and Ozu Yasujiro. The reason for this is 'the relative compatibility of those films with the ideology of representation and signification which informs the dominant culture (and of course the dominant cinema) of the West.'[48] The 1930s and 1940s, for Burch, instead have 'a fundamental incompatibility' with Western modes of representation.[49] 'This period', continues Burch, 'is *terra incognita* outside of Japan, and indeed to younger Japanese audiences.'[50] Why is early Japanese cinema so different? Chinese, Indian and Egyptian films were, for instance, from the very start, tangled up in American cultural and British political imperialism. Burch claims, 'in two thousand years of recorded history, no part of Japanese territory had ever been occupied until the 1945 defeat. Japan was never subjected to the semi-colonial status.'[51] As Burch concludes, Japan's 'cinema, of course, is but a minor consequence of this crucial fact.'[52] Desser summarizes Burch in the following way: the Japanese cinema (1) 'reproduces the essential characteristics of traditional Japanese culture, which began in the middle 600s, refining itself in the twelfth through the seventeenth centuries'; (2) 'has undergone no significant changes since its pertinent traits were defined'; and (3) 'is a unified text reproducing these pertinent traits in a unified manner (and any deviation from these traits makes such films "unJapanese").'[53] This is a similar narrative, as we have seen, in Richie's dichotomy of the representational and presentational.

Such approaches risk closing down thinking about a film. While there can be no objection to the reading of Japanese movies through Japanese culture, such a reading depends upon an *a priori* homogenization. When transformations occur, such as after the war, this narrative additionally risks seeing this as loss, the perversion of an ideal form, rather than as potentially generative and creative. Conversely, I would like to claim that readings can still be effective by considering Japanese cinema in the context of world cinema – the cinema of the world – as geo-historically heterogeneous. National cinemas have differences within, and also connect transnationally. Such a proposition allows us an escape from the binary oppositions that lead to hierarchy and exclusion. One theoretical approach for this, I want to argue, is the Deleuzian cineosis. Yet such a Deleuzian encounter, as we will now see, is also not without risk.

Deleuze and world cinema

If a significant danger for the European film theorist is the essentializing of

Japanese cinema, then the seemingly obverse approach is equally problematic. This is the universalizing theoretical model (for example, disciplines such as structuralism, Marxism, psychoanalysis). However, essentialism and universalism are not as diametrically opposed as might first be thought. For example, Burch writes that *To the Distant Observer* is part of 'the modern search for a Marxist approach to art … and which involves a detour through the East'.[54] In this way 'the larger theoretical implications of Japanese practices are to be derived through a reading conducted from outside the culture which has produced them'.[55] Is not this also the case with Richie? Could not the dichotomy of representation and presentation be seen as a Western theoretical model imposed from the outside into a Japanese environment?

Yet by using Deleuze do I not risk just this, imposing a Western philosophical method onto the Japanese cinema? For David Martin-Jones this problem is a factor of the *Cinema* books themselves.[56] In *Deleuze and World Cinemas* (2011), Martin-Jones lists the fourfold reason for this: (1) the emphasis on American and European films; (2) the ahistorical nature of the books; (3) the use of the Second World War as the division between the movement-image and the time-image; and (4) the universal ideas of time that arise from that division. I want to briefly explore these points in turn, not so much to refute them – as they are all defensible – but rather to suggest a line of escape from each by reading the *Cinema* books as a taxonomy of difference promoting heterogeneity.

Problems in the *Cinema* books begin, for Martin-Jones, with 'the geographically limited selection of films' which 'represent the dominant Western cinemas of the USA and Europe, along with the one or two directors from outside the West'.[57] His list of 'outside' directors provided is indeed limited: 'Ozu, Glauber Rocha, Youssef Chine and Yilmaz Gûney'.[58] Yet the situation is rather more ambiguous. There are approximately 800 films mentioned across *Cinema 1* and *Cinema 2*, some in passing, some in detail, some a number of times. Of these, approximately 250 are from the USA and 234 from France (170 excluding co-productions). It might thus be more accurate to describe the filmic selection as Franco-American. Yet Deleuze does engage at length with cinema from outside the American-European axis: there are 31 Japanese films explored. Indeed, some European countries get less of a look-in than Japan. There are only 26 films from the USSR (of which one is by Kurosawa) and 23 from the UK (28 including American co-productions). Furthermore, discussions on Japanese cinema get more book-space than both British and German cinema – perhaps equal to that of Italian and Soviet film. However, this is not just a question of space, but also of significance. The study of Mizoguchi and Kurosawa in *Cinema 1* is an essential contribution to the creation of the action-image, decentring any simple alignment of American cinema and realism. The exploration of Ozu at the beginning of *Cinema 2* – which Deleuze will return to throughout that book – is a lynchpin of the argument for the time-image alongside Italian neo-realism and the French New Wave. In short, there is little sense of there being a Euro-American axis to the *Cinema* books; discussions tend to focus on certain moments in film history without proposing any dominant mode. Also, in addition to the directors Martin-Jones mentions, we find the aforementioned Mizoguchi and Kurosawa as well as Ichikawa Kon from Japan, and Michel Khleifi, Borhane Alaouié and Ousmane Sembène from the Middle East and Africa. Deleuze also discusses a number of directors who, while beginning in Europe, went on to make a significant number of films elsewhere – Luis Buñuel's association with the Mexican film industry during the 1950s and 1960s, for example. Deleuze's selection, as Martin-Jones indicates, probably has much to do with the availability of film products at French cinemas before the age of video, DVD and the internet, an availability which has significantly democratized and simplified film research.[59]

The second problem, for Martin-Jones, is the 'ahistorical exploration of films'.[60] Deleuze himself repeatedly stressed his books were not a history of cinema; however the taxonomical approach does not mean the project is as ahistorical as Martin-Jones might contend. Indeed, the argument that the books are ahistorical initially appears undermined by Martin-Jones' third problem, 'the central positioning of the Second World War as dividing line between movement- and time-images'.[61] Yet it is just this universal historical anchor point that is the foundation of the ahistorical approach, according to Martin-Jones. Nevertheless, Deleuze also proposes other events which are, in different contexts, as – or more – significant as the war. He refines his claim for different countries in Europe inventing their time-images at different moments: 'why Italy first, before France and Germany? It is perhaps for an essential reason, but one which is external to cinema.'[62] His – albeit brief – analysis discusses specific political and economic dimensions in these three countries. Deleuze also argues: 'mutation of Europe after the war, mutation of an Americanised Japan, mutation of France in '68.'[63] In *Cinema 2* Deleuze, again briefly, discusses the creation of time-images through the rise of African third world political cinema; and with respect to 'black American cinema's black-powerism' and 'female authors, female directors' through the 'historical and political' movements of different 'minority communities'.[64] The Second World War is not the only transformation point – and in any case, the Second World War was never only a European war, hence our designation in this book (with respect to the focus upon Japan) as the Pacific War.

The crucial point for Martin-Jones is that these problems all dovetail in 'the apparently universalizing conclusions … concerning time'.[65] This refers to the way in which Deleuze divides cinema into two meta-categories: movement-images and time-images. The former tend towards creating linear temporal flows, the latter put such linearity into crisis. We have, in essence, the cinema of linearity and the cinema of simultaneity. Yet this is only the broadest of ways of describing movement-images and time-images. Not only do movement-images designate a number of temporal organizations (progressive, cyclical, succession, memories, dreaming), but so do time-images (another kind of succession, co-existence and the eternal return). Further, at every level of a film (frame, shot, montage, sequence and the film in-itself) and across the work of directors, genres and national cinemas, all the various images and signs of movement- and time-images are present. We can only talk of one image or sign dominating at a certain level. This heterogeneity, this clamour of images and signs competes with the tendency to divide cinema into the two meta-categories: 'we can choose between emphasising the continuity of cinema as a whole, or emphasising the difference between the classical and the modern.'[66] It is often believed, no doubt due to the physical division of *Cinema 1* and *Cinema 2* into two books, that Deleuze tends towards the latter understanding. Yet the discussion on movement-images continually anticipates and creates time-images; and *Cinema 2* not only describes more movement-images but returns to the movement-image throughout. This is not to say that Deleuze is emphasizing continuity. Rather, Deleuze is exploring a paradox. Which account do we choose? Deleuze articulates both positions: 'what has seemed fundamental to us in this system of images and signs is the distinction between two kinds of images with their corresponding signs, movement-images and time-images', and 'there are many possible transformations, almost imperceptible passages, and also combinations between the movement-image and the time-image.'[67] Deleuze will, in addition, read some filmmakers and some films from both the standpoint of the movement-image and the time-image.

Yet despite these escapes, Martin-Jones' problems haunt the *Cinema* books – Deleuze is a European philosopher. Can any European escape Europe? Can you take the Eurocentrism out of a European? We can only really choose to emphasize Deleuze's putative Eurocentrism or not; and only be aware of and mitigate against the dangers of using Deleuzian film theory outside of European and American cinema. In *Deleuze and World Cinemas*, Martin-Jones goes on to write a book that takes every precaution. In this way it remains one of the key stimuli for my own project. Where I differ from Martin-Jones is that I believe this opportunity is created in the *Cinema* books themselves by way of the taxonomic project, the twofold semiotic of heterogeneous images and signs.

I would like to assert that Deleuze's philosophy can be seen as one of the inspirations for the emerging discipline of engaging with film through a specific understanding of all cinema as a heterogeneous world cinema. Lúcia Nagib, in 'Towards a Positive Definition of World Cinema', puts forward three ways to avoid Eurocentrism:[68] (1) 'World cinema is simply the cinema of the world. It has no centre. It is not the other … It has no beginning and no end, but is a global process'; (2) 'world cinema is not a discipline, but a method, a way of cutting across film history according to waves of relevant films and movements'; and (3) 'world cinema allows all sorts of theoretical approaches, provided they are not based upon the binary perspective.'[69] In the *Cinema* books Deleuze employs a number of philosophies, the approach is heterogeneous and self-disturbs every binary it may appear to reify; the method cuts up cinema and connects films in any number of different ways, many contradictory; and there is no centre, there is no norm with which to posit an 'other'. Nagib's essay and its conclusions draw on a number of sources. One is Ella Shohat and Robert Stam's seminal *Unthinking Eurocentrism* (1994) which, while not engaging with Deleuze to any great degree, does use *Cinema 2* and Deleuze and Félix Guattari's '"minor" esthetic' – which appears in *Kafka* (1975) and *A Thousand Plateaus* (1980) and is picked up in the *Cinema* books as modern political cinema – in respect to Brazilian *Cinema Novo* and the films of Rocha.[70] The point is, however, that Deleuze's *Cinema* books can be seen and used in such a way that escapes the very Eurocentrism of which they can be accused. I choose to read *Cinema 1* and *Cinema 2* as an instantiation of Nagib's approach to world cinema. I do not claim Deleuze is alone in this, nor the primary or most successful exponent: just one voice among many who have attempted, no matter how incompletely, no matter how prone to failure, to keep alive difference in cinema – the affirmation of all cinema as world cinema. Indeed, with regards to Japanese film, which is the focus of this book, we can identify at least two precursors who also anticipate Nagib.

Japanese cinema as world cinema

Sato, for instance, sees Japanese cinema from the very beginning as heterogeneous, with influences both from within Japanese culture and from elsewhere. When cinema came into being in Japan the industry soon polarized into two mega-genres: the *jidai-geki* and the *gendai-geki*. Yet these two types of film are not simply different on the basis of genre, but also with regard to their theatrical influences, geography and audiences. *Kabuki* theatre usually has two male protagonists, the primary being the *tateyaku*, a samurai who follows the *bushido* code of honour above personal feelings; the secondary, the *nimaime*, a handsome, if foolhardy male who expresses individual love and kindness towards the female. *Kabuki*, however, was challenged in the late nineteenth century by *Shimpa*, which while reconstituting the *tateyaku* and *nimaime* roles, recast them in contemporary settings. 'As period drama [*jidai-geki*] evolved from *Kabuki*, so contemporary drama [*gendai-geki*] evolved from *Shimpa*.'[71] *Tateyaku* performances were seen in *jidai-geki*; while *nimaime* performances were seen in *gendai-geki*. Period films were shot in Kyoto, which still retained much traditional architecture; and contemporary dramas in Tokyo, which was more modern and international in style. As the leading men and geo-historical settings were different, the two genres tended to polarize audiences, men preferring the period dramas and nostalgia of the *bushido* code, women preferring the more progressive contemporary dramas where the male characters could follow their hearts and women received more screen-time. These two genres, furthermore, were also later affected by the *Shingeki* theatre with 'texts and techniques directly imported from the West … [which] primarily aimed at realism and became the mainstream of Japanese drama from the 1930s onwards'.[72]

Simultaneously there was the direct influence of foreign films which, according to Sato, 'have been imported since the early days of Japanese cinema and their influence on Japanese filmmakers were considerable'.[73] Sato comments, 'in the 1920s some Japanese films were modelled after German expressionist films, and films from Denmark' and 'in the 1930s [there was] respect for the psychological realism of French films'.[74] While Soviet movies of the 1920s and 1930s were censored or banned, 'Eisenstein's montage theory came to exert a strong influence on the leftist "tendency films" (*keiko eiga*) popular around 1930, and resulted in a fad for an extreme style of editing'.[75] Most significantly, according to Sato, the movies 'that had the most profound influence on the Japanese public and film-makers were the pre-war American films'.[76] For Sato, then, Japanese cinema is riven with difference, is open to change, is part of world cinema. It cannot be subsumed under any unitary concept, under any single cultural aspect. It is vital, alive, multifaceted, on-going, in process.

Desser is also exemplary in this respect. *Eros Plus Massacre* (1988) sets out to explore the Japanese New Wave as an approach in Japanese cinema where the idea of the mode 'transcend[s] genres, schools, movements, and entire national cinemas'.[77] 'Japanese cinema', for Desser, is 'part of a system, a system called "Japan"', which demonstrates 'how Japanese cinema reflects, is worked on and works upon, Japanese culture'.[78] The Japanese film is not a closed system, nor does it have an internal unity, but rather is a system within the systems of world cinema.

With Desser and Sato we find different approaches, different conclusions, but in each the willingness to consider Japanese cinema as heterogeneous, in a relationship with world cinema, as a heterogeneous cinema of the world. Neither sees the Japanese film as a closed system. Rather the methodology is to make connections. In this way their work prefigures Nagib. Furthermore, one a Japanese writer, one a 'Western' writer, neither adopt a 'West'–'other' dichotomy and hierarchy – and their sharing this view allows for the claim that the heterogeneous approach can be considered as one possibility for an escape from the accusation of Eurocentrism. The Deleuzian methodology, I have maintained, can also be aligned with the Nagibian procedure, can also be used to accentuate heterogeneity. The key to this is the taxonomical system, the regimes, the domains, the images and signs of the twofold cineosis.

A Deleuzian cineosis

The *Cinema* books describe a taxonomy of cinematic signs. What is a cinematic sign? We might begin by saying the way in which images are framed, shot and edited; the way they use colour or black and white; the way they use silence and sound, voice, effects, music – in other words, all the material elements of composition available to the filmmaker. However, the cinematic signs themselves are not simply the 'technical' dimension of the images but rather the way in which these material elements are perceived and engender feeling, reaction and thought in the spectator.[79] Deleuze goes on to build a vast semiotic system. In all, there are some thirty component signs at play in the movement-image grouped into some ten domains; and some nine signs at play in the time-image grouped into some three domains. This twofold cineosis is a series of created concepts which, taken together, have a certain consistency. These concepts allow us to read and think, or better still, reread and rethink the cinema and its films in myriad ways.

This 'thinking cinema' is fundamental. Indeed, Deleuze's cineosis is inspired and given its co-ordinates through philosophy, most overtly through the work of Henri Bergson. In *Matter and Memory* (1896) Bergson describes a world where the material body experiences perceptions and affects and performs actions in respect to memory-images. However, this material dimension interacts with pure memory, a beyond of the memory-image. We can elucidate these two dimensions by referring to Deleuze's later commentary on his founding philosophical text, *Difference and Repetition* (1968). Deleuze writes that the book was an attempt at 'putting into question the traditional image of thought'.[80] By this traditional, or classical, image of thought Deleuze means thinking 'according to a given method' which 'determines our goals'.[81] The method is that of 'the process of recognition' where we 'designate error', we '"want" the true' and we 'suppose that the true concerns solutions'.[82] Deleuze thus proposes 'a new image of thought – or rather, a liberation of thought' from 'those images which imprison it'.[83] This new image of thought goes 'beyond the propositional mode', involves 'encounters which escape all recognition' which 'tears thought from its natural torpor and notorious bad will, and forces us to think'.[84] Bergson's world of matter and Deleuze's classical image of thought inspire the taxonomy of the movement-image; while Bergson's pure memory and Deleuze's new image of thought inspire the taxonomy of the time-image.

However – and this is crucial – the signs of the movement-image and the time-image are both, in-themselves, an expression of Deleuze's new image of thought.

This double articulation of the cineosis can be explained by turning to *What is Philosophy?* (1991). In this book Deleuze and co-author Félix Guattari claim that thought takes 'three great forms – art, science, and philosophy'.[85] These three forms of thought have a common purpose, they are 'always confronting chaos, laying out a plane, throwing a plane over chaos'.[86] However, the three forms of thought are 'distinguished by the nature of the plane and by what occupies it'.[87] Each of the domains has its own kind of plane, its own consistency; similarly, each plane is occupied in different ways. Art thinks through sensations, science thinks through functions and philosophy thinks through concepts.[88] The movement-image and the time-image are a nexus of technical functions, cinematic sensations and philosophical concepts. As functions and sensations, the movement-image describes a classical image of cinematic thought while the time-image describes a new image of cinematic thought. As concepts, however, the cineosis in its entirety is a new thinking of cinema.

What, then, is this cineotic thinking challenging? My response: a hierarchy of cinematic forms. In 1969 Jean-Louis Comolli and Jean Narboni published 'Cinema/Ideology/Critique' in *Cahiers du cinéma* and so announced the journal's 'Maoist phase', its 'red years'.[89] In the wake of the release of Costa-Gravas' *Z* (France | Algeria, 1969), Narboni, as Emilie Bickerton puts it, accused the film of 'offering a brand of sterilised militancy … repackaged for thrills. *Cahiers* immediately shredded the film's political credentials.'[90] Comolli and Narboni thus inaugurated their cinematic classification and hierarchical system (films of form types A, B, C, D, E, F and G) which described the different ways in which film reified political ideology, in line with the structuralist / Marxist / psychoanalytic approach of the time. This categorization – used to delineate which kind of films troubled the dominant ideology – went on to inform not only the journal's editorial policy, but also the movies that could be examined in the publication. The *Cahiers*' 'Maoist phase' saw readership drop 'from 14,000 issues bought in 1969 to 3,000 in 1973'.[91] There is something wonderfully perverse in this will to exclude all cinema from a cinema magazine, film in-itself and on the whole not being worthy of the theory that it engendered. This tendency towards taxonomy, hierarchy of form and condemnation no doubt pre-existed the theorizing of Comolli and Narboni, yet they created a very powerful model which was picked up elsewhere. Colin MacCabe, in 'Realism and the Cinema' (1974), posits that there is only really one type of cinema, classical realism. While the form can be made progressive or be subverted, there is only the possibility of what he calls revolutionary texts, films which go beyond the limits of realism. And then David Bordwell's 1979 essay 'Art Cinema as a Mode of Film Practice', which repeats, in another way, the binary between classical realism and arthouse cinema and lays the groundwork for his cataloguing of cinema types through national cinemas and industries. All in order to describe broad trends in cinema, to hierarchize and (even those who know not what they do) condemn the classical realist mode of composition. In this context the *Cinema* books seem to be both a continuation of the will to categorize and at the same time an untimely attempt to resist, in general, hierarchy of form and, in particular, the *a priori* negative critique of classical realism.

The assumptions Comolli and Narboni, MacCabe and Bordwell make about classical realism were the co-ordinates of film studies in general at the time, and the division of the good and the bad based upon modes of composition an accepted, almost universally unreflected upon, norm. Many of these preconceptions are still with us today – and even when certain types of classical realism (such as a genre like horror cinema) are acclaimed, it always seems to be by exception (this genre does what another cannot). For Deleuze, a good or bad film has nothing to do with its mode of composition. A good film is not one which obeys certain formal criteria, but rather one which can be appropriated. A film is machinic.[92] Cinema is composed of little machines, that compose slightly bigger machines, and bigger machines still. And little film machines can be joined with other little machines – philosophies, theories, books and other films – for productive readings, 'a productive use of the … machine'.[93] Cinema is not, with Deleuze, to be treated as a representation. The principle is not to discover 'the' meaning, the 'truth' of a film, be that at a 'surface level' or somehow 'buried' deep within. The task of a Deleuzian encounter with film is to put it together with other machines: 'it is at the level of interference of many practices that things happen.'[94] Writing about cinema should be 'a montage of desiring-machines'.[95]

This, then, is the point of using the cineosis – to use a film to create an adventure in cinema, in history, in philosophy. Each of the thirty-nine little sign machines, each of the thirteen image-domain machines avail themselves to different filmic, historical and philosophical conceptions: the film theories of Jean Mitry, Pier Paolo Pasolini, Sergei Eisenstein; the historical conceptions of Nietzsche and Bourdieu; the philosophies of the Stoics, Heidegger, Artaud. In this way, using the cineosis is an 'exercise that extracts from the text its revolutionary force'.[96] As Deleuze says in 'The Brain is the Screen' (1986), 'there's nothing more fun than classifications or tables. They're like the outline of a book, or its vocabulary, its glossary … it's an indispensable work of preparation', yet 'it's not the essential thing, which comes next…'[97]

Deleuze, Japanese cinema, and the atom bomb

In writing this book, I followed the procedure of allowing the Japanese cinema of the atom bomb to flow alongside the Deleuzian cineosis, until a film snagged upon an image or sign, or an image or sign resonated with or sought out a film. In so doing, a number of questions arose, questions that gained force, accumulated and diversified as the project progressed. These questions concerned the filmic image, the relation of the image to history, and the way in which the image and history capture and engender thought.

Accordingly, Chapter 1 explores the very earliest of atom bomb films in consort with the primary co-ordinates of Deleuze's movement-image. The aim is to explore the fundamental ways in which the nuclear event of Hiroshima and Nagasaki is captured in Japanese film as a special image. To do this I begin with Bergson's sensory-motor process, from which Deleuze creates the primary co-ordinates of the movement-image: perception-, affection- and action-images. These concepts are used to discuss how each film creates its own image of the *pika* and the *hibakusha* – the claim being that certain films do so in radically different ways. I will therefore explore Ito's documentary *The Effects of the Atomic Bomb on Hiroshima and Nagasaki* as a perception-image; Shindo's elegiac *Children of the Atom Bomb* as an affection-image; and Honda's monster movie *Godzilla* as an action-image. In Ito's documentary the *pika* forms the centre of the film, while in *Children of the Atom Bomb* the centre is the *hibakusha*; the former tends toward the cold-eye of scientific objectivity, the latter toward an emotional engagement. With *Godzilla* we encounter something very different, the disappearance of the *pika* and the *hibakusha* and the creation of a monster and heroes. This is an action-image, an indirect depiction which seemingly appears to sacrifice real history.

The second chapter of the book thus develops the question of film, history and action-images. For Deleuze, the action-image is doubled, composed of two forms. On the one hand, the large form describes how characters are created to rectify a situation. On the other hand, the small form explores how a situation is revealed through the behaviours of a character. By way of Nietzsche's analysis of historical practices in 'On the Uses and Disadvantages of History for Life' (1874), Deleuze sees both action-images as being thoroughly historical, each form having its own horizon of history. The large form corresponds to universal history creating laws that describe vast historical co-ordinates. The small form corresponds to a history as it happens, instead focusing upon how events impact individuals and the masses. The *Godzilla* films, in this way, can be explored through the large form and universal history and be found to capture up hundreds of years of conflict between Japan and the USA. In contrast Shindo's *Daigo Fukuryu-Maru / Lucky Dragon No. 5* (1959) and Masaki's *Barefoot Gen* – both films of the small form – can reveal a history as it happens, to the people. Accordingly, we will discover the action-image to be a heterogeneous domain, one thoroughly historical, through which particular films create very different images of the *pika* and the *hibakusha*, the atomic event, its antecedents and its legacy.

So far, each of the films explored sits on an intensive line from direct to indirect depiction. Chapter 3 focuses upon this aspect of Japanese atom bomb cinema and extends it toward disappearance, the *pika* and *hibakusha* becoming trace elements, appropriated by Japanese genre cinema, the yakuza flick, the horror film and the sci-fi movie. We encounter the *pika* and *hibakusha* as symptoms or figures, metaphors and allusions. The argument here is that such traces are interactions of the forgetting and remembering of the bombing of Hiroshima and Nagasaki. In order to carry out this analysis it will be necessary to expand the conceptual framework of the movement-image. This will be done by exploring how Deleuze generates more images by aligning Bergson's sensory-motor schema with the semiosis of Charles Sanders Peirce from *Pragmatism and Pragmaticism* (1903). The focus will be upon impulse-images and reflection-images. Shindo's *Hadaka no shima / The Naked Island* (1960) is an impulse-image, describing a rural island as a symptom of the nuclear event and creating a cyclical conception of historical trauma. Miike Takashi's *Dead or Alive* and Tsukamoto Shinya's *Tetsuo* (1989) will be explored through reflection-images as instances of the Japanese cinema displaying echoes of the *pika* and the *hibakusha* as filmic metaphors and allusions. Reflection-images, in this way, encounter a return of the repressed memory of the atomic event, as the shock of history in story-worlds of genre and arthouse films. And it is this shock of history that will be reintegrated in direct depictions of the atomic event, such as Kuroki Kazuo's *The Face of Jizo* (2004).

Deleuze describes the way in which the movement-image captures memory as images of thought occurring through what he names mental-images. There are three types: relation-images, which display thought on-screen through symbols; recollection-images, which depict memory on-screen through flashbacks; and dream-images, which create on-screen hallucinations, nightmares and dreams. Deleuze discusses these images by way of a return to Bergson's *Matter and Memory*, and sees films of the mental-image as being the very consummation of movement-images, a repetition of perception-, affection- and action-images in the domain of thought. In Chapter 4 we will encounter such mental-images of the atom bomb in the films of Kurosawa: *I Live in Fear*, *Rashomon*, *Yume / Dreams* (1990) and *Rhapsody in August*. These films are exemplary in exploring how memory becomes a fundamental problem of the Japanese cinema of the atom bomb.

Yet the consummation of the movement-image through mental-images also announces its crisis and prepares the way for the regime of time-images. Just as the taxonomy of the movement-image is inspired by Bergson and Peirce, the taxonomy of the time-image is inspired by the syntheses of time in Deleuze's *Difference and Repetition*. Chapter 5 begins by describing the way in which time, for Deleuze, is composed of three heterogeneous elements: the present, the past and the future; and rather than time being seen as a linear trajectory, presents, pasts and futures create complex interweavings. In this way we encounter a Japanese cinema of the atom bomb which disrupts the special images of the *pika* and the *hibakusha* and concomitantly – through a return to Nietzsche – the co-ordinates of history. Kiriya Kazuaki's science-fiction epic *Casshern* (2004) creates a future world in which the dropping of the atom bomb may or may not have occurred. Oshima Nagisa's *Daitoa senso / The Pacific War* (1968) and Imamura's *Nippon Sengoshi – Madamu onboro no Seikatsu / A History of Postwar Japan as Told by a Bar Hostess* (1970) undermine the documentary form to explore the path toward and legacy of the nuclear event, each in its own way destroying the certainties of historical narration. To conclude, we will discover how two direct depictions of atomic attacks on Japan disrupt image and history through narrative and memory – Imamura's *Black Rain* and Sekigawa's *Hiroshima*.

After Deleuze, we can see these films of the Japanese cinema of the atom bomb as a nexus of heterogeneous images. Each film, in its own way, is a masterpiece – and each film explores the nuclear attacks of Hiroshima and Nagasaki as cinematic image, image of history and image of thought in its own way. These images swarm: a monstrous force dominates the skyline, decimates the landscape. Now a city on fire. Naked bleeding bodies. Shattered stumps of buildings. Streets, empty of human life, still, no movement. Shadows burnt on walls. A makeshift hospital. Skin falling from flesh, empty eye sockets. At the epicentre of these cinematic images, Hiroshima, Nagasaki, the *pika*. Surrounding and inhabiting these images, the *hibakusha*, dead and alive. These images, by way of assemblage, form little machines. A film is a horde of images, images surrounded by images. The images of the *pika* and the *hibakusha* had to be discovered by cinema and they had to be forgotten. Again and again. And each time, in their own way, these images had to be composed, had to become little machines that could overcome the spectre of impossibility.

1

Special Images, Contingent Centres

The special image or contingent centre is nothing but an assemblage of three images, a consolidate of perception-images, action-images and affection-images.[1]

Movement-images

Each atom bomb film overcomes the spectre of impossibility in its own way; each, in its own way, creates a singular encounter with the nuclear attacks on Hiroshima and Nagasaki. This chapter explores this proposal by focusing upon some of the earliest films of Japan's post-war and post-occupation nuclear cinema. Each film will be considered in relation to Deleuze's movement-image, which describes a cinematic nexus of perception, affect and action. These three avatars of the movement-image dominate in different types of the earliest atom bomb films: documentary, contemporary drama and monster movies. Accordingly, each film creates its own contingent centre, its own special image of the *pika* and *hibakusha*.

Shot in 1945, the very first Japanese film of the nuclear holocaust was Ito Sueo's documentary *The Effects of the Atomic Bomb on Hiroshima and Nagasaki* (1946). Cameras capture, with scientific precision, scenes from the immediate aftermath of the *pika*, devastated city ruins devoid of life, *hibakusha* receiving treatment in makeshift hospitals. Shindo Kaneto's *Children of the Atom Bomb* (1952) is an elegiac melodrama, creating an emotional response to the atomic attack. Produced soon after the end of the occupation, Shindo's focus is a kindergarten teacher returning to Hiroshima to find out what happened to the young children once in her charge. Very different again is Honda Ishiro's *Godzilla* (1954), the first Japanese atom bomb movie to snare the imagination of a mass audience. *Godzilla* signals, for the Japanese screen, the move from direct expressions of the nuclear event (as in *Effects* and *Children*) to indirect depictions. In this way, the atomic nightmare is not just experienced, not just survived, but resolved. Furthermore, the logic of the film permits the monster to return: rise (and fall) again and again; to enter into monster mêlées with other imaginary beasts sequel after sequel throughout the years that follow.

These very different early Japanese atom bomb films will each be explored through one of the three primary co-ordinates of Deleuze's movement-image: perception-images, affection-images and action-images. Perception-images describe the creation of a special image, a contingent centre (usually, though not necessarily, a character) and its concomitant relation to all other images in the film. Affection-images channel emotion through and around this special image, on a face, across an object or within the mise-en-scène. Action-images describe the way in which this contingent centre defines or is derived from a determined situation and how that situation can be reconfigured by acts of individuals. In using these three co-ordinates of the movement-image, each film will be seen to create its own special image of the *pika* and the *hibakusha* – centres contingent upon the mode in which each film operates. Ito's *Effects* is dominated by images of pure perception organized around the *pika*, science-images of the devastated cities and surviving *hibakusha*. Accordingly, the film will be explored from the perspective of the perception-image. Shindo's *Children of the Atom Bomb* focuses upon the experiences and emotions of a central character and will be explored from the perspective of the affection-image. Honda's *Godzilla* allows characters to act upon the indirectly determined situation of the nuclear event; in consequence, this film will be explored from the perspective of the action-image.

The aim of each of these engagements is primarily twofold. The first objective is to foreground, through perception-, affection- and action-images, the diversity of the films describing the nuclear event of Hiroshima and Nagasaki – the assertion being that the Japanese cinema has responded to the atomic bomb in any number of different ways, and that these films constitute a heterogeneous assemblage. The second aim, parallel to and generative of the first, is to explore the difference in-itself of each of the films. In other words, each film in-itself is also – before being dominated by a single type of image – an assemblage of types. Not only does this difference in-itself of a film account for variations in previous critical responses, but it also allows for the production of new perspectives. These new perspectives should not be considered the truth of the film, ultimately revealed, never to be surpassed. Rather, they could be seen as another variation: a twist here, a reversal there, the extension or reworking of an idea – a resolute seizing or desperate grab at something just within or beyond reach. In this way, this first chapter lays the groundwork for the rest of the book, where such cinematic encounters with the special images of the atom bomb will be explored through different philosophies of history and thought.

In order to begin this exploration of the heterogeneous assemblage of films that compose the Japanese cinema of the atom bomb, it will first be necessary to enunciate in detail the fundamental co-ordinates of the movement-image. Accordingly, this chapter will commence with an account of the sensory-motor process of Henri Bergson's *Matter and Memory* (1896) from which arise the concepts of perception, affect and action.

Bergson, sensory-motor process

Images are matter. 'The word', writes Bergson 'is of no importance.'[2] Yet in reconceptualizing matter as image, Bergson reconceives the relationship between the forces external to an organic body and the forces internal to that body as being of one and the same kind: 'we consider matter before the dissociation which idealism and realism have brought about between its existence and appearance.'[3] The image, then, is both the thing and the representation, the extension of the thing into representation and representation into the thing: 'by "image" we mean a certain existence which is more than that which the idealist calls a representation, but less than that which the realist calls a thing – an existence placed halfway between the "thing" and the "representation".'[4] Everything that is matter is an image, this atom, this cell, this organ, this body, this environment. Bergson is describing a universe of scale, a fractal universe of recursive images: 'every image is within certain images and without others.'[5] A universe where at and between every level all images are a centre that act upon each other and have a force between one another to a varying degree. All images are forces operating at scale and distance. At different scales, some images aggregate, construct centripetal consistency: a molecule here, a body there, here a planet, there a solar system: contingent centres, special images. In this way every image is always a multiplicity, is always composite and, at one and the same time, has integrity – and again, is a component in a vaster image.

The human body, for instance, is an assemblage of component images at a number of levels, atoms, molecules, cells, organs. It has a globalizing integrity, a whole body defined by its wrap of skin – yet it is also in an environment, fed by light, oxygen, water, food; and expelling waste. Zoom in, it is all just forces of molecules continuous with the molecules that surround it, distant moments in empty spaces. Zoom out, the body is but one of millions upon millions; ants on an anthill, swarming over the face of the Earth. For Bergson, the logic which proceeds from these observations means that from every perspective, everything is an assemblage of images interacting with other assemblages of images.

Images, then, capture both inorganic and organic life, which at the molecular level is composed of forces. Some images pass through other images; some images are reflected by other images, giving a certain consistency, that is, creating 'outlines'.[6] It is here that the relationship between images and perception is announced.

Perceptions are images acting upon other images. At the simplest level, these perceptions are collisions. If we introduce sensory receptors in organic life we find that in visual perception light waves collide with, say, a light-receiving device: the retina. The concept of perception as a collision impacts upon hastily formed notions of the difference between the senses. A visual perception is not different in kind from that of, say, tactile, olfactory or sound perception: all are collisions. 'If we follow, step by step, the progress of external perception from the monera to the higher vertebrates,' writes Bergson, 'we find that living matter, even as simple as a protoplasm … is open to the influence of external stimulation, and answers to it by mechanical, physical and chemical reactions.'[7] These influences are reactions, at the most basic simple reflections and an exchange of forces. However 'as we rise in the organic series, we find a division of physiological labour. Nerve cells appear, are diversified, tend to group themselves into a system'; there is thus only a 'difference of complication' between the monadic cellular animals and the multifaceted life forms.[8] In other words, actions are only possible because of the sensory input of a perception, but these actions can become more diverse in more complex life due to the intensive forces at play within the organism, which form 'centres of indetermination' where 'the degree of this indetermination is measured by the number and rank of their functions'.[9] These intensive forces are affects and are, in effect, engendered by perception. The crux being this: that the interval between a perception and an affect and an action can be of a variable length of time: instantaneous or emerging after a prolonged period. For Bergson, 'I find that [affects] always interpose themselves between the excitations that I receive from without and the movements which I am about to execute'.[10] Variable affect hands back perception to the world as action.

The body, then, is an image mapping a dynamic of extensive and intensive forces. The body is an image that distributes outside (extensive) disturbances through the body (as intensive turbulence) to component parts of the body to bring forth an (extensive) reaction. The body is situated in the world, and the world image is a component of the universe which in turn contains a multitude of images, of which one is the human-qua-itself, and so on. This is the sensory-motor schema. In its finitude, the sensory-motor schema is movement. Extensive movement received → intensive movement of sensory data, dissipated or directed → the emission of extensive movement.[11] A movement of images as perception → affect → action: an organic process.

Cineosis and cinema

One of the most memorable moments in Japanese – and world – cinema is the first appearance of Godzilla. Aging palaeontologist Dr Yamane (Takashi Shimura) is leading a scientific search party from Tokyo through the interior of Odo Island in the wake of the (yet unseen) monster's devastating attack. Three images describe the power of the encounter: framed in a long shot, standing in for the collective sight of the search party, Godzilla emerges from behind a hill; then a cut to the face of Emiko (Kochi Momoko), Dr Yamane's daughter. As the monster's grinding metallic roar permeates the warm afternoon air, Emiko's face traverses a series of emotions, from wonder to shock to fear; finally, Ogata (Takarada Akira) drags the now-supine Emiko to her feet and together they flee. Here, in a short cinematic sequence, can be seen Bergson's organic sensory-motor process: perception, affect and reaction. Accordingly, for Deleuze, this process can be used to describe the cinema, a cinema of movement-images: perception-images (Godzilla seen behind the hill); affection-images (the face expressing emotion); action-images (flight, escape). Taken together these filmic moments create a logic of succession for the characters and for the viewer.

Perception-images create relationships between images, engendering a centre to which all other images relate. These images tend towards wide shots: a landscape, the Earth from space. Affection-images describe the sensation of perception on the features of a character, for instance, faces expressing emotion. These images tend towards close-ups: the face, an eye or insect. Action-images bring to fruition expressed affect; deliver affect back to the world as a reaction to perception. Here we tend to encounter medium shots: bodies hip to head. These types of images are not limited to the visual. Sound images can appear in wide shot (the murmurings of a crowd) or in close-up (the ticking of a bomb).

Figure 1.1 Perception-image – Godzilla's first appearance, *Godzilla* (Honda, 1954)

Figure 1.2 Affection-image – Emiko's face, *Godzilla* (Honda, 1954)

Figure 1.3 Action-image – Ogata and Emiko escape, *Godzilla* (Honda, 1954)

Already it is clear these designations are contingent: is not an extreme wide shot of the Earth from space also the Earth in extreme close-up – an affective perception-image? Any image of the movement-image is thus a composite of perception, affect and action. Yet at the same time, and in the context of the other images that surround it in the film, each image tends towards being a perception-image, affection-image or action-image, is dominated by its perceptual, affective or reactive dimensions. Further, every film of the movement-image, while a composition of component images, has one image type in ascendancy. In this way a film can be said to be a perception-image, an affection-image or an action-image film. The relations between the movement-image and its three primary avatars can be described as in Table 1.1.

Table 1.1 The primary coordinates of Deleuze's movement-image after Bergson

movement-image	a consolidate of perception-, affection- and action-images
perception-image	creates a centre, an image to which all others relate
affection-image	expresses affect – emotion – upon the surface of a central image
action-image	allows a central image to react to the world upon the world

Godzilla is a composition of movement-images yet is dominated by the action-image. Perception and affect pass immediately into action. Exploring this film through the concept of the action-image has philosophical consequences. In overcoming the spectre of impossibility and attempting to embody co-ordinates of the nuclear situation as a monster, Honda is making possible actions to be logically performed against it – and for those actions to triumph. Further, the sensory-motor system also forms an assemblage with the spectator and the rapid succession of images (environment and monster → face → reaction in world) captures the viewer in a logical and cohesive continuity of movement. The viewer becomes locked into the philosophical structure of the film: concerned with what happens next. The film continues to deliver the next image and then the next image in quick succession. In Shindo's more contemplative *Children of the Atom Bomb* everything is slowed down. It is not action that dominates, but affect. The school teacher embarks on a journey to Hiroshima. In visiting the children, the surviving members of her crèche, the spectator is taken on an emotional journey. Rather than the driving succession of action-images, there are meditative images that reflect upon the world. In contrast, Ito's *Effects* confronts the viewer with images of almost unbearable horror, but transforms them so we are able to gaze upon them as images of scientific enquiry, through perception-images. Rather than creating affective or active engagement, *Effects* casts a cold-eye upon the nuclear event.

Each of these films, then, can be read as a perception-image, an affection-image or an action-image film. Each film creates a different type of spectatorship, a different type of response. Each film is a different cinematic, historical and philosophical moment, a different overcoming of the spectre of impossibility; each has its very own special image of the *pika* and the *hibakusha*.

I. Perception and the centre

The Effects of the Atomic Bomb on Hiroshima and Nagasaki (1946)

Ito Sueo remembers his first encounter with the Japanese nuclear event. 10 August 1945: 'I was in the Culture Film Unit', recollects Ito, a Tokyo-based documentary filmmaker with Nippon Eigasha (Nichiei).[12] 'We talked about the damage from the atomic bombs … news of which had been coming in from the Domei Tsushinsha desk. They said that this disastrous scene ought to be recorded … I agreed.'[13] Such is the origin of one of the most controversial films ever made, *The Effects of the Atomic Bomb on Hiroshima and Nagasaki*. The proposed aim of the documentary was to 'appeal to the world by communicating the inhuman facts through the International Red Cross', an exigent plea for the cessation of the continued use of such weapons against the Japanese population.[14] However, at noon (Tokyo standard time) on 15 August everything changed. 'The enemy has recently used a most cruel explosive', announced the Emperor in the radio broadcast of the Imperial Rescript.[15] 'Should we continue to fight,' Hirohito declared, 'not only would it result in the ultimate collapse and obliteration of the Japanese nation, but also it would lead to the total extinction of human civilization.'[16] With Japanese surrender, so ended the Pacific War. Yet the filmmakers at Nichiei believed a film should still be made, a document recording what had happened.[17] On 7 September, Ito set out by train to recce Hiroshima and Nagasaki. Upon his return to Tokyo formal funding had been achieved through the hastily convened Japanese Special Committee to Study the Damage of the Atomic Bomb, created by Monbusho (the Education Ministry). On 15 September, amid the intensifying confusion of the Allied invasion, members of the Nichiei documentary crew and a Monbusho team of scientists arrived in Hiroshima. Filming commenced.

Effects is divided into two sections, the first set in Hiroshima, the second, Nagasaki. The Hiroshima section begins with a series of maps of the city, descending in scale, before giving way to a succession of shots of the destruction. These images zero in on the ground beneath the hypocentre: from 15 kilometres to ten kilometres; then eight, five, four, two, one; then 800 metres, 300 metres. Each shot brings with it more and more devastation. At the hypocentre, a truck halts carrying Monbusho scientists; they leap to the ground and begin to survey the site. The scientists are filmed examining the ruins of the cityscape. Screen titles name them and their institutions. Intertitles create sub-sections of film on heat, on the blast, and so on. Yet such empirical progression will not constitute the only organization of images. There are tracking shots from the back of a jeep: shattered concrete, twisted iron, sun-bleached bones. Horizontal pans capture the encompassing desolation of the broken city. Vertical tilts explore the open carcases of the remaining buildings. These flowing images glide through, across and within the devastation. It is as if the camera adopts a transcendent attitude, becomes a ghostly entity. Still, the camera will cease to move and cease to track movement: it will focus on rock and bone – skulls with empty eye sockets staring out of the grey rubble towards the unflinching eye of the camera. Shots of atomic bomb shadows, shadow imprints when vegetation, objects and humans were vaporized by the *pika*: solid objects which disappeared, instantaneously. These organizations of the visual field are accompanied by a soundtrack composed of elegiac music interspaced with interminable moments of silence. Sometimes there is the voice of a narrator, giving geographic details and historical exegesis, detailed scientific and medical information. From the devastated city, the film enters a makeshift field hospital. This passage from exterior to interior is achieved through the delivery of a body. In the hospital the camera is placed before one shocking image of a human after another. Images are spliced together unsystematically. These bodies display for the camera the effects of the atom bomb on flesh. Men, women, girls and boys – tattoos from patterned clothing seared onto the skin, keloid-scarred faces with melted eyes, terrible wounds cracking open charcoaled skin. Then a repetition, with a difference: from Hiroshima to the devastation and carnage of Nagasaki. Once again a shattered city, once again a chaos of human butchery: image upon image, succession, flows and discrete cells of horror. Scientists survey the scene, measure out units of ruin. Doctors display *hibakusha* wounds for the camera.

Effects is a cinema of horror. Yet, despite the acknowledged importance of the film as document, for many commentators the way in which the *hibakusha* are imaged seriously compromises the project. Not only does the film record,

Figure 1.4 500 metres from the centre, the remains of Urakami Cathedral in the ruins of Nagasaki, *The Effects of the Atomic Bomb on Hiroshima and Nagasaki* (Ito, 1946)

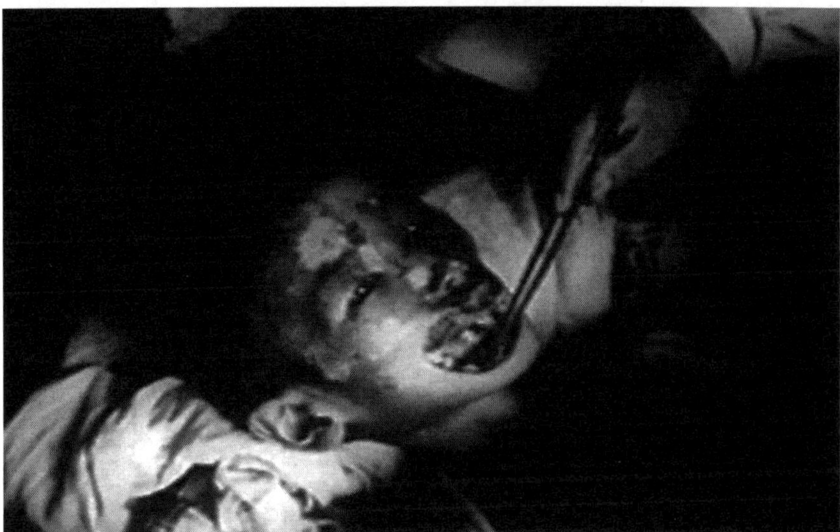

Figure 1.5 Young *hibakusha*, keloid-scarred, flesh burnt from face, *The Effects of the Atomic Bomb on Hiroshima and Nagasaki* (Ito, 1946)

as Ito puts it, an 'inhuman' act, but the documentary itself is seen as callous, barbaric, and inhuman.[18] It is as if the film is an extension of the bomb, reifying the event, complicit in such ruthless terror. Some even believe the film not to be Japanese, but to be an American military conspiracy. How can the film be Japanese, describing with a cold-eye such horror inflicted upon its own people?

Inhuman effects

In 'When the Human Beings are Gone…' (1994), a *zadan* (conversation among peers) between Kogawa Tetsuo and Shunsuke Tsurumi, Kogawa begins by asserting that while *Effects* was conceived as a film with a humanitarian outlook, it was first hijacked by the bureaucratic remnants of the fascist Japanese government and then again by the invading American military.[19] In this way the film became 'an accumulation of facts'.[20] The technique used to depict the ruins of the cities by Monbusho scientists 'was applied to human beings … so that human bodies were reduced to just another kind of data'.[21] While *Effects* cannot but reveal 'the sheer facts in all their monstrosity', the film has a 'callousness'.[22] For Kogawa, this is a factor of the film being 'thoroughly edited and revised by the Americans'; the original framing and shooting of images thus 'suited the Americans just fine'.[23] The film as conspiracy: 'from the very beginning, the Americans requested that the film be made in this fashion, in the manner of a scientific record.'[24] This discourse on *Effects*, the responsibility for the tone of images, both visual and sonic (the voice-over narration in the film is in English, and not Japanese), can be seen in microcosm in discussions of its title. Kyoko Hirano in 'Depiction of the Atomic Bombings in Japanese Cinema during the U.S. Occupation Period' (1996) reports that Nichiei's producer, Iwasaki Akira, 'felt that the title given to it by the Americans … was callous'.[25] The title, it seems, was originally composed in English and then translated into Japanese as *Hiroshima, Nagasaki ni okeru genshibakudan no koka*. As well as meaning 'effect', '*koka*' can also be rendered as 'result', and Kogawa comments that 'from the beginning [the US military] openly used the word *koka* … as the title indicates, [the Japanese *hibakusha*] are mere research material'.[26] The Iwasaki quote originally appeared in a chapter of Hirano's *Mr. Smith Goes to Tokyo* (1992), the term 'inhuman' used instead of 'callous'.[27] This semi-synonymic exchange in a critique of translation itself reflects the problem and power of interpretation between languages.[28] Monbusho, aware of such sensitivities, catalogued the film in 1967 using the word '*eikyo*', 'influence'.[29] In 1994 a Japanese language version was finally produced, this time using the more neutral term '*saigai*', 'disaster'.[30] These retranslations of the title, the arguments and problems surrounding them, indicate that many Japanese commentators believe the film predisposed toward an American imperative.

Tsurumi, Kogawa's interlocutor in the *zadan*, sees this problem of authorship somewhat differently. Tsurumi comments 'there was this word that popped up many times, "epicentre." – "Epicentre" – "epicentre" – "epicentre"… One could feel that one was gradually getting closer to the "centre," and to knowing what the centre actually represents.'[31] Yet the absence of any depiction of the *pika* means that the whole idea of a unitary centre to the film – a unifying perspective or narrative trajectory – is a ruse. Rather, for Tsurumi, *Effects* 'reveals the changing conditions in the beginning of the Occupation period – August, September, October 1945, all different'.[32] Accordingly the film can be seen to express 'the state of mind of the Japanese, that of the Americans, and so on'.[33] The film has a 'multiplicity of perspectives'.[34] One perspective 'is the scientific … the one interested in the epicentre'; another is – near the end of the film – an 'attitude of social morality'; yet another is the original motivation for the documentary, 'the desire to make the tragedy known to the world'.[35] Ultimately *Effects* is, for Tsurumi, a film 'with many centres' and 'the perspectives are constantly shifting'.[36]

Abé Mark Nornes, however, believes the film to be a purely Japanese project. For instance, it was only in October, towards the end of shooting, that the occupation forces arrived in Nagasaki. Ito, in an interview with Nornes, recalls being summoned to report to the US Military Nagasaki Communications Office, and having a conversation with an American official conducted with 'a pistol laying on the desk'.[37] The film stock was confiscated. Nornes writes: 'Nichiei filmmakers had exposed 26,000 feet of film about all aspects of the bombing … but they were on the verge of losing everything.'[38] Yet there was to be a reprieve. The US Strategic Bombing Commission arrived in Japan with the brief to record the results of the fire bombings (of Tokyo and other Japanese cities) as well as the nuclear attacks. Daniel McGovern, an ex-Hollywood – now military – cinematographer, was part of the commission. Learning of Ito's film, McGovern reasoned with General Headquarters (GHQ) that it was futile for the Americans to reshoot. The job was done, the footage just needed editing. McGovern, furthermore, proposed 'the only individuals qualified to do this work are the cameramen who exposed the film … the individuals who were members of the Japanese research party'.[39] GHQ acquiesced. Ito later reported that McGovern let the Japanese work without interference.[40] 'Ironic and unfathomable though it may be,' writes Nornes, *Effects* 'is, in all its inhumanity, a Japanese film.'[41]

Despite this attribution of authorship to the Japanese, the idea of the film being 'inhuman' prevails. For Kogawa this inhumanity is articulated by the Americans, the victor's disregard for Japanese life underpinned by modern 'Western' scientific technology and research attitudes. For Nornes this inhumanity is rather a function of the documentary process employed by Ito, capturing the 'explicit point of view' of the Japanese Monbusho scientists.[42] 'The filmmakers', according to Nornes, 'consistently reinforce … [this point-of-view] with scenes of the scientific teams walking through the rubble, making measurements … treating horrific injuries, and conducting autopsies.'[43] In this way 'the narrator stands in for the scientists, speaking for them in the strange unnerving technical language of specialists'.[44] This approach has cinematic antecedents. *Effects* can be seen as the final Pacific War period documentary of the Meiji era *kagaku eiga* (science film).[45] These war period documentaries were influenced by Nazi *kulturfilm*, but in Japan had 'a penchant for the accumulation of data without processing it for larger meaning'.[46] A short such as *Bakufu to dampen / Bomb Blast and Shrapnel* (1943) is exemplary, consisting of images of blasts and their effects on different types of material. The *kagaku eiga* prioritized above all 'the direct representation of reality'.[47] *Effects*, similarly, prioritizes an uncompromising depiction of the 'reality' of the atom bomb, the difference being the bomb and blast are absent – the only presence that of the materials of concrete and flesh. Instead of the bomb and blast, there is the 'originary space in the air', 'the ultimate reference point', a 'powerful magnetic, imaginary point we call the epicentre'.[48] So, for Nornes, the inhumanity of the film is a result of the documentary implicitly giving 'voice to the point of view of the bomb itself'; it 'expresses no need to give human meaning to the bomb'.[49]

Effects is inhuman because it fails to place the *hibakusha* at the centre of the film, fails to make the *hibakusha* the special image. The people are but images among other images, rubble, skulls, broken buildings, twisted metal, scientists with rulers and chalk, doctors with lab coats and stainless steel implements. Yet, perhaps it is in just this way that the film is able to depict the unimaginable brutality of the nuclear event. The indifferent *pika* knows no distinction between a human body and a stone cathedral. In order to explore such a reconsideration of the film, *Effects* can be read through Deleuze's cineotic concept of the perception-image.

Perception-images

Deleuze calls the perception-image a 'type' of image in general which can be 'represented' in the material practice of the cinema by a 'particular' sign (the way in which an image is framed, shot, edited and so on).[50] In this way the sign 'represents a type of image, sometimes from the point of view of its composition, sometimes from the point of view of its genesis'.[51] The genetic sign of the perception-image is where 'each image varies for itself, and all images act and react as a function of each other'.[52] This genetic organization describes a series of images without an on-screen centre. When organized around a centre, the second sign of the system, the sign of composition, is formed where 'all [images] vary principally for a single one'.[53] This, for Deleuze, is the true meaning of the objective and subjective in cinema: the latter creates a subject, the former does not; yet composition arises out of the genetic. Deleuze is describing how a molar organization results from a molecular process. As Anna Powell succinctly glosses, 'molecularity is distinct from the "molar" macro order of ideological, social and psychic schemas'.[54] The molecular is the genesis of the formation of the relation between a subject and the world, and, as Deleuze and Guattari comment, 'molar organisation has the function of binding molecular process'.[55]

As well as such a dyadic decomposition, Deleuze also subjects the perception-image to a triadic unfolding: the signs of which are the solid, the liquid and the gaseous. Deleuze transposes this terminology from Bergson's *Matter and Memory*: 'we have no reason … for representing the atom to ourselves as a solid, rather than liquid or gaseous'.[56] As Deleuze puts it, 'we start out from a solid state, where molecules are not free to move about (molar or human perception)'; then 'we move next to a liquid state, where the molecules move about and merge into one another'; and finally 'we … reach a gaseous state, defined by the free movement of each molecule'.[57] The triadic system is a continuum of signs: solid, liquid and gaseous perception. In this way, the dyadic and triadic systems overlay one another, each being decompositions of the monadic system. These levels of the perception-image can be illustrated as in Table 1.2.

With solid perception cinema creates a 'central and privileged image' at the heart of the film.[58] The central image would be the main character, fashioned through shot-reverse shot coupling, static framing and invisible montage (wide shot, medium shot, close-up, cutting on movements). This is a subjective image in that it creates a subject. Liquid perception marks the transition of the solid to the gaseous, of the gaseous to the solid. This is where the camera in movement constructs flowing images in long takes, continually reframing environments and bodies. Multiple characters can form centres from the periphery, and a shot can transition from the camera-eye to a point-of-view shot without a cut. Finally, the perception-image can be purely objective in the sense of all images interacting with each other without creating any special on-screen anchor points. Gaseous perception is acentred: 'everything is at the service of variation and interaction'.[59] Gaseous perception in this way is the genetic element of the perception-image, where the creation of a central subject or subjects remains unconstituted. As Deleuze puts it, 'the programme of the … gaseous image [is to go] beyond the solid and the liquid: to reach "another" state of perception,

Table 1.2 Perception-image

perception-image		
molar composition		molecular genesis
solid perception	liquid perception	gaseous perception

which is also the genetic element of perception'.[60] In short, while the molar solid has a unitary centre and the molarized liquid multiple centres, the molecular gaseous has no such on-screen centre; there is instead a 'universal interaction of images which vary in relation to one another, on all their facets and in all their parts'.[61] Yet, as Deleuze points out, if a character or alternative does not emerge in the actual images of the film, there is still a centre of a kind in the gaseous. The perception-image is a movement-image, and a common-sense perceptual framework asserts itself. This is a factor of on-screen 'camera-consciousness', a centre very different from a human one.[62]

We encounter here a crucial aspect of the Deleuzian cineosis, the actual and the virtual. Cinema is a practice of creating and linking images, 'multiplicities, each of which is composed of actual and virtual elements'.[63] On the one hand, actual images, the on-screen visuals and accompanying audio: the trajectory of images that compose the film. On the other hand, the virtual: something far more 'ephemeral'.[64] The virtual is a process which connects an actual to an actual: actual on-screen images are framed, shot and edited together, and what is out-of-field of the frame and the shot, and the edit in-itself, are virtual connections. All cinema is composed of actual images and all cinema operates through virtual connections. While purely virtual processes do not exist just as 'purely actual objects do not exist', they have 'mutual inextricability' and there is a difference: 'the relationship between the actual and the virtual is not the same as that established between two actuals.'[65] Movement-images are generally dominated by actual-to-actual movements, through the flow of on-screen images (cutting on an action, the flow from long shot to medium shot to close-up). In this way virtual connections are overwhelmed, become invisible. The actual on-screen images dominate. Yet some types of movement-image allow the virtual to arise – expose what is beyond the frame, expose the artificial linkage between images, open up a space for indeterminacy of and amid actuals. And such indeterminacy is the characteristic of an exposed virtual and a space for thought. The genetic sign of the perception-image, molecular perception, is one such movement-image. Gaseous perception is an organization of images where the virtual can arise from, within and between the actual images, and these virtuals can cohere, become a coagulation of thought, a virtual centre.

Nonhuman perception

All three signs of the perception-image are encountered in *Effects*. Solid perception organizes a linear progression of images: Hiroshima then Nagasaki; cities then people. Again, from the very beginning of the film, where Hiroshima is captured in the series of scaled maps then frozen images, zeroing in on the epicentre and from the epicentre outwards, the film unfolds. Yet, for all this, no central on-screen image emerges; there is no character created to act as an anchor point for all other images. This function cannot be located with the narrator, the voice-over being just one element of the soundtrack (which includes music and silence) and which itself dissolves into a kind of drone or hum of lists, facts, jargon. Such a dissolving is also apparent in the visual field. Liquid perception: shot from the back of jeeps the camera flows over the devastated infrastructure; positioned in the foothills of the surrounding mountains the camera sweeps across the broken city. The moments in which the movement of the camera will uncover, through its reframings, instants of horror: a sea of rubble, and then a skull. Is there, in this, the creation of special images, a series of multiple centres? In the broadest of terms, we encounter two: Hiroshima and Nagasaki. Yet these fragment; each explores the remains of a city, then the *hibakusha*, and within these domains, fragmentation continues, becomes the organizing principle. It is as if, within each frame, across each shot and throughout the trajectory of the film, what was solid becomes liquid becomes gaseous. The very form of the film – despite attempts to organize it through molar composition – becomes molecular. Gaseous perception: the shots of the *hibakusha*, image upon image, one after another. The depiction of the shattered cityscapes: rubble as the molecules that once composed buildings and the lives that inhabited them. Bricks, rocks, skulls, possessions: scattered remnants of civilization. Shadows: bodies, vegetation, and objects, all made gaseous. Each on-screen image, in this way, is its own actualized moment. Yet each moment of horror and between each moment of horror, a virtual opens up, creates a single virtual image: the reference point is always that of the *pika*.

It is in just this way that *Effects* can be encountered so differently by Kogawa, Tsurumi and Nornes. For Kogawa, *Effects* has a solid organization; the event of the *pika* may not be depicted, but no matter, it is the camera that takes its place, the camera an extension of the atom bomb. The bomb, designed and deployed by the USA, is now a camera, and the camera is an American conspiracy. For Tsurumi, there are multiple centres. *Effects* captures many perspectives:

American, Japanese, Monbusho, Nichiei, military, scientific, medical, journalistic, ethical, aesthetic. The film is one of liquid perception. Nornes, however, sees *Effects* as a film organized through the gaseous with the *pika* a virtual centre: an 'assemblage of matter-images' which has a 'corresponding assemblage of enunciation'.[66] Accordingly, such a gaseous organization means the film 'remains open' in respect to its actual on-screen images.[67] Ronald Bogue puts it very well when he writes that the gaseous is 'a locus of generative differentiation such as a seed or ovum'.[68] In such a way, although the film is organized by gaseous perception with a virtual centre, moments of liquid and solid perception are composed. *Effects* thus allows for not only Nornes' reading, but for those of Tsurumi and Kogawa.

However, in considering *Effects* as a film dominated by the sign of gaseous perception, we also turn away from the inhumanity of the film. Gaseous perception, as the genetic sign of the perception-image, precedes a creation of molar entities, of characters, of a human centre (solid perception) or centres (liquid perception). It is thus curious to designate a molecular organization inhuman – as its very condition is generative of and prior to the human. We could, instead, posit the nonhuman (which in turn refers us to the virtual centre, the bomb). Both these prefixes, in- and non-, are negations. It seems, in this discussion, we cannot escape the negative connotation of something not being human. We cannot help but anthropomorphize, it seems. We believe the human to be the fundamental position from which we must enunciate everything, the fundamental position from which every image must emerge. Yet in the sense we mean it here, nonhuman is not a negation. Deleuze puts it this way: the 'non-human, the cine-eye' is 'the eye of matter, the eye in matter'.[69] It is an image which 'prefigures the human subject'.[70]

In re-evaluating *Effects*, in turning away from the inhuman toward the nonhuman, we accordingly reorientate the discussion of the film. The spectator is confronted with images of almost unbearable horror but is able to gaze upon them objectively, mediated as they are through a distancing by way of gaseous perception-images. This is in-itself horrifying to a human subject as viewer. This is the method Ito uses to overcome the spectre of impossibility; the atom bomb itself, never depicted, is the contingent centre of the film, the special image present through virtual connections. This black hole is the horizon of the on-screen images of devastation, both environmental and human, images which traverse its edge and describe its presence, the crater described by its carnage, which circumscribes the nonhuman atom bomb.

This gaseous perception-image that is *Effects* is captured by Nibuya Takashi in 'Cinema / Nihilism / Freedom' (1994), who comments that 'the absolute indifference of the camera/film is violently exposed, nullifying the good will or passions of the photographers'.[71] This is not to be taken as a negative critique. Rather, it is the indifference of the universe to the human, to human good and to human evil. This is the indifference of the atomic bomb. Capturing the nuclear event in this way through the camera-eye engenderers a kind of vertigo in the mind of the spectator; the human body becomes nothing but a speck of dust. This is the way in which the universe can horrify humanity, by displacing it as centre.

From *Effects* to affects

It will take a very different type of film to explore the human dimension, to focus instead upon the affects on the Japanese people of the nuclear holocaust. This will not simply be a case of giving more screen-time to the *hibakusha*, but rather giving the people a voice; not only depicting their wounds, but exploring their emotions and feelings, their experiences. Indeed, Nornes can only validate *Effects* on the possibilities of what it could have been, or what it would become. In the 1980s prints of the film became available in Japan and 'in an act of real resistance … Japanese citizens' re-edited the film, inserting new sequences. They 'made their own films … which resist the power of the epicentre … by redirecting us to a space all but forgotten (or simply avoided): the point of view of the victim … Substituting the point of view of the *hibakusha*.'[72] This re-appropriation of the film by Japanese *hibakusha* is instructive. These films would create human centres by composing a molar image, solid perception or liquid perception, and, concomitantly, extending perception-images into affection-images. Nornes posits this as the 'completed' project, something the original film was unable to achieve.[73] Thus, while Nornes believes Ito's *Effects* to be 'the origin of *hibakusha* cinema', it must be designated so only in its genetic condition, as a seed for the people's films to come, as an ovum for films which resist the logic of the epicentre.[74] The designation *hibakusha* cinema should accordingly be reserved for films which put the *hibakusha* at the centre of the film – and this type of film could only emerge after the end of the occupation.

II. Affect and indetermination

Children of the Atom Bomb (1952)

From Hiroshima, close-up, captured with the fluid moves of the camera tracking the ruins of a building – to a vast wide shot of an idyllic island framed between a still sea and dappled sky. So begins *Children of the Atom Bomb*. On the island, Miss Ishikawa (Otowa Nobuko) is leading a group of young children in their mid-afternoon calisthenics. After bringing the class to a close, she wishes them all a happy summer holiday. She cycles home along a dirt path that tracks the coastline, passing rural smallholdings where fishermen mend nets, to the house of her aunt and uncle. As she helps her aunt tidy away a quilt, they quietly discuss her own plans for the summer – to visit Hiroshima, her home town, which she escaped in the immediate aftermath of the atom bomb.

Miss Ishikawa travels by ferry, leaving early so as to arrive before sunset. As the small boat chugs through the calm waters of the Setonaikai Inland Sea, she stands silently on deck. In the distance Hiroshima appears. On the soundtrack, sorrowful horns play in a minor key accompanying a voice-over: 'This is Hiroshima where the world's first atom bomb victims died on August 6, 1945. Her beautiful rivers still flow, just as they did that fateful day. Her beautiful sky is just as big as it was that fateful day. The children of that day are now grown. And the devastated city rebuilt.' Shots of the ports, cranes, factories; and then the suburbs; the boat passes under bridges, buildings get bigger, brick and concrete. The city appears, surrounded by mountains. Boys are wrestling on a beach. Kids play in a high school rec yard. The camera pans across the city: new homes, new metropolitan buildings – interspaced between zones of destruction and on-going construction. Now among rubble by a dead tree, Miss Ishikawa lays some flowers against a makeshift rock memorial: 'father, mother, Haru, it's me Takako.' She walks away, and then turns to look once more at the remains of her family home. Cut to her face in close-up. A flashback: it is a morning like any other; her father (Shimizu Masao), mother (Hosokawa Chikako) and sister all getting ready for the day. Before she runs from the house, greeting the family servant Iwakichi (Takizawa Osamu) on the way out, young Takako pulls a page from the wall calendar. It is 6 August 1945. Cut back to Miss Ishikawa among the ruins. Another flashback, of a kind: images of clocks counting down to 8:15 a.m.; children play with butterfly nets, splash in the river; men and women arrive for work. A plane traverses the clear sky, silently. White light. Images of *hibakusha*, bleeding in the rage of the atomic light, crawling in the dirt, trapped under collapsed buildings. Voices screaming, a choir chants a lament. The mushroom cloud. White heat: the shadow of a man, vaporized, sitting on a stoop.

Shindo's *Children of the Atom Bomb* was released on 6 August 1952, Hiroshima city's atomic bomb memorial day.[75] A film such as this could only have been made after the end of the Allied occupation. As Monica Braw reports in *The Atomic Bomb Suppressed* (1991), while the occupation forces instructed the post-war Japanese government to rescind their control of the press and media so 'liberal tendencies would be further encouraged', these freedoms were, in reality, tightly restricted.[76] This was the 'secret' work of the American Civil Censorship Detachment (CCD).[77] There were many, complex motives for the effacement of the nuclear event from the Japanese media and arts. 'The security of the United States, which, the CCD said, demanded secrecy about the bomb'; 'fear of criticism'; and 'the campaign of impressing war guilt on the Japanese' were all factors.[78] 'But above all,' for Braw, 'there was the concern about the reputation of the United States. An often-stated reason for the suppression was that the material gave the impression that the United States was inhumane or barbaric in using the atomic bomb.'[79] Accordingly, the CCD 'reviewed all domestic productions at the stages of synopsis, screenplay and completed film' to ensure no violations of the secret code.[80] A planned production by Shochiku to be called *Hiroshima* had its synopsis examined by the CCD in January 1948, and was cancelled in May of the same year.[81] Similarly, an independent film *No More Hiroshimas* was terminated in June 1949.[82] Hiroshi Shimizu's *Hachi no su no kodomotahic / Children of the Beehive* (1948), which was originally to feature a nuclear attack before focusing upon war-orphaned children, was allowed – but only after purging all images of the atom bomb.[83] *Nagasaki no kane / The Bell of Nagasaki* (1950), directed by Oba Hideo and written by Shindo, suffered a similar fate. The first draft of the script, sent to the censors in April 1949, contained a horrific depiction of the atomic bombing. It was immediately rejected. Oba and Shindo were not to be put off, and a second draft was submitted at the end of April. Instead of removing the scene, however, the script now commenced with an opening on-screen declaration: 'We might say the atomic bomb had been given to the Japanese as a revelation of science who preferred savageness, fanaticism, and intolerant Japanese spirit to freedom, culture and science.'[84] Nice try. Again, the script was rejected. A third version submitted in June 1949 was accepted. The depiction of the atomic bomb, however, was, as Hirano puts it, 'merely suggested', with the mushroom cloud appearing momentarily at a distance.[85] As Hirano comments, 'to portray the bombing and its aftermath more realistically and to show the full emotional impact of its tragic victims, Japanese filmmakers had to wait until the termination of the occupation'.[86] It is thus tempting to believe that the expunged depiction of the bomb Shindo had originally intended for *The Bell of Nagasaki* was restored in *Children of the Atom Bomb*. Whatever the case, it is clear that Shindo had been preparing to shoot *Children* for some time. Funding was already in place from the Teachers' Union of Hiroshima, and the lead role had been cast. Filming began just a few days after the end of the occupation.

Mono no aware and *higaisha ishiki*

Despite the historical significance of this first depiction of the *pika* as experienced at the epicentre, this moment is not the focus of the film. Rather, the movie concentrates upon Miss Ishikawa. After the flashback/thought sequences, she finds herself at the skeletal remains of Czech architect Jan Letzel's domed exhibition space, the Hiroshima Prefectural Hall. It is then she has an unexpected encounter with Iwakichi, her family's former servant. He is begging at the roadside, in rags, nearly blind and with half his face keloid-scarred. Initially he attempts to run away, ashamed. However, she eventually persuades him to allow her to stay with him the night. During their conversations Miss Ishikawa discovers Iwakichi's grandson, Taro, is now at an orphanage, the parents dead. She offers to take boy and grandfather back to her island. Iwakichi refuses, giving any number of poor reasons. This encounter inspires her to track down the surviving children of her wartime crèche. In this way, *Children* creates images organized around a human centre: Miss Ishikawa. As a survivor of the nuclear attacks on Hiroshima, she is a *hibakusha*. Her return forms a series of encounters with other *hibakusha*. In so doing, the film explores the experiences, emotions and feelings of a number of survivors of the nuclear attack on the city.

According to Hirano, the film was a 'box-office success'.[87] However, as Richie reports, 'upon seeing the film … the Union complained … saying that it was not satisfied, that Shindo had turned the story into "a tearjerker and had destroyed its political orientation"'.[88] Richie, although he sees *Children* as the most artistically satisfying of the early post-occupation atom bomb films, concurs. There is, however, some ambivalence in his response. That the story fails to present the 'political orientation' anticipated by the union is not considered a problem, as this would have been anti-American, aligned with the stance of the Japanese Communist Party to which the Teachers' Union was affiliated.[89] Correspondingly, Richie does lament that the film fails to address what Richie sees as the true cause of the nuclear attack – Japanese military aggression and the Japanese people's complicity with the state. Yet, that *Children* eschews political commentary opting for an emotive narrative trajectory reflects, for Richie, the authentic Japanese attitude toward the nuclear event. 'From the first films on,' he comments, 'Hiroshima was not an "atrocity" but a "tragedy"', depicted in an 'elegiac' mode.[90] Speaking for the Japanese, Richie puts it thus: '"this happened; it is all over and finished, but isn't it too bad? Still … what we feel today we forget tomorrow; this is not as it should be, but it is as it is"'.[91] This attitude is captured by the Japanese term *mono no aware*, which 'indicates a feeling for the transience of all earthly things; it involves a near-Buddhistic insistence upon recognition of the eternal flux of life upon this earth'.[92] *Children*, in this way, exhibits '*mono no aware* par excellence', depicting how the Japanese people display a 'passivity' after any terrible event. There is an all-encompassing '"it can't be helped" philosophy through which the Japanese for centuries have attempted to make life endurable'.[93] For Richie, the 'elegiac regard … has remained as the single constant element' to Japanese atom bomb cinema.[94] Shindo's film is seen by Richie as a lyrical portrait of Japanese passivity, an ahistorical lament of endurance.

Isolde Standish, writing some forty years later, reaches similar conclusions. In *A New History of Japanese Cinema* (2005), Standish reads the film in the context of post-occupation Japanese war cinema. There is, in these films, a depiction of the Japanese as 'mere victims of the times in which they live'.[95] Here we encounter *higaisha ishiki*, the post-war 'victimisation complex', which is 'exemplified' in stories 'recounting the experiences of children', as in Shindo's film.[96] For Standish, 'loose plotlines … coincidence and fate are the causal elements that forward the flow of the narrative'.[97] We can see these elements in *Children*, which has Miss Ishikawa accidentally encounter Taro's grandfather, which in turn leads to the search for the surviving students of her crèche. Accordingly, the binding element is Miss Ishikawa, who is constructed to 'define our understanding of the events depicted' and 'provide the narrative continuity that links the various … "slice-of-life" micro-plots'.[98] Yet Miss Ishikawa, for Standish, is not simply a centre created by Shindo to navigate the children's stories (taken from Osada Arata's book upon which the film was based). Rather, 'the image of the teacher as a socially respected profession' both 'mediate[s] the spectators' point of view' and at one and the same time, testifies to 'the truth of the events recorded'.[99] Miss Ishikawa is the centre, and the centre constructs truth. For Standish, this truth is that of passive fatalism.

Children of the Atom Bomb, in this way, is an exemplary film of the post-occupation period, imbued with the *mono no aware* and *higaisha ishiki* attitudes (passivity and victimhood) with respect to the Pacific War and the nuclear event. Yet there is something troubling about this movement between the general and the particular without any attention to difference. In other words, the film is not exhausted by this analysis. *Children* may well be impregnated with *mono no aware* and *higaisha ishiki*, passivity and victimology. However, in my view, this is only inasmuch as these 'essential' Japanese characteristics and post-war tendencies are that which Shindo sets out to explore and understand, ultimately in order to discover – or rather, create – an alternative response to the horrors of the nuclear event. Such a reading of *Children* can be unfolded through Deleuze's concept of the affection-image.

Affection-images

Films of the movement-image organize themselves around the sensory-motor response: a character sees, feels and reacts and the act changes the world. The movement-image can therefore be decomposed into three component images: the perception-image, the affection-image and the action-image. One type will rise to dominance. It can be said of every shot, sequence and film – this is a perception-image, this is an affection-image, this is an action-image. Yet every image remains a combination of types. Accordingly, the same decomposition of the perception-image necessarily traverses affection-images and action-images. Just as perception-images had a dyadic molar and molecular organization, so will the other images; and just as the perception-image had a triadic organization of signs, so too will affection-images. These monadic, dyadic and triadic levels of the affection-image can be illustrated as in Table 1.3.

Table 1.3 Affection-image

	affection-image	
molar composition		molecular genesis
icon	dividual	any-space-whatever

The icon is the first sign of composition. Here affect appears in the close-up of a face. As an affection-image, intermediary between perception and action, the icon has a relation with both. On the one hand the face reflects the world it apprehends, the expression of an affective quality. On the other hand the face can express an affective power, desire orientated towards an action-to-come, affect as precursor. The icon is thus an external expression of the internal intensities engendered by perception and prior to action. The quality of the face is expressed in direct conjunction with a perception, 'fixed on an object', and has immobility, a face caught in 'wonder'.[100] The power of the face is expressed – correspondingly – through mobility, the face passing from one state to another, 'each part taking on a kind of momentary independence'.[101] Qualities and powers thus interpenetrate: powers are a series of qualities; and a quality is a compound of powers rendered as a singularity. Such is the close-up of a face.

Deleuze initiates his analysis of the icon with 'an example which is not a face', the clock; for the clock similarly expresses polarities of power and quality: 'on one hand it has hands moved by micromovements … on the other hand it has a clock face as receptive immobile surface.'[102] Such an example, for

Figure 1.6 The icon – Miss Ishikawa's face as an external expression of internal intensity, *Children of the Atom Bomb* (Shindo, 1952)

Deleuze, corresponds to Bergson's definition of the affect: 'a motor tendency on a sensitive nerve.'[103] Deleuze writes: 'even if we are only shown … [the clock] once, or several times at long intervals: the hands necessarily form part of an intensive series which … prepares a paroxysm'; filming a clock anticipates the disruptive event of zero-hour.[104] The paroxysm par excellence is the atom bomb, so it is unsurprising filmmakers have exploited these powers and qualities of the affect: as the time approaches 08:15 (Hiroshima) or 11:02 (Nagasaki) the clock marks the coming of the nuclear paroxysm. In Masaki's *Barefoot Gen* there is a shot of a clock prior to the atomic blast. In Imamura's *Black Rain* a clock is shown on three occasions: anticipating the event, destroyed as the bomb detonates, and after, as detritus with the hands now shadows. In Kuroki's *The Face of Jizo* stopped clocks are salvaged as objects of memory. In *Children*, as the moment of *pika* draws near in Miss Ishikawa's memory-imagination, there is a series of different clock faces. Each reads 08:14, one minute prior to the nuclear event. Shindo continues the sequence by focusing upon a single clock face, filming the micromovements of the second hand as the time approaches 08:15. Correspondingly, the soundtrack is stripped of every element except a heightened tick-tock: time in close-up. These clock images are interspaced with human activity: a woman washing, a man in an office, children playing, a baby at the breast; faces of Japanese people. These faces are icons of power and quality, designed to affect the spectator, an anticipation of the nuclear event.

When qualities and powers can no longer be differentiated, the icon dissolves and becomes the dividual. There are no longer individualized faces, instead individual and group are aligned. This is the second sign of composition, 'beyond all binary structures', exceeding 'the duality of the collective and the individual'.[105] The dividual involves 'directly uniting an immense collective reflection with the particular emotions of each individual'.[106] In other words, the dividual describes neither an individual apart from the mass, nor the mass as a deindividualized whole – it captures the in-between. The dividual occurs in exemplary fashion in *Children*. At the moment of the *pika*, Shindo inscribes the effects of the atom bomb as affect across a singular complex entity: naked young female bodies. This sequence – in its choreographed theatricality, in its cinematic reflexivity – is disorientating: beautiful young women, naked, smeared with charcoal, painted with delicate traces of blood. It is with the dividual we can thus begin to see what is essential to the affection-image: indetermination. The icon, while it circumscribes a particular human centre and expresses affect upon the surface of that centre, remains an external rendering of internal intensity. Affect, then, may be determined in respect to the reflected perception (quality) and action-that-comes (power), yet what is internal to the character is indetermination in-and-of-itself. The human is a centre of indetermination. The dividual accentuates this indeterminacy. It dissolves individuation, collapses powers and qualities, and relinquishes the co-ordinates of the face. Indeterminacy of expression now appears on the surface as actualized images. In *Children*, these naked women palpably depict the *hibakusha* – yet they correlate qualities and powers of shock, exploitation, sexuality, theatricality, cinematic reflexivity, the bomb: the dividual marks the expression of indetermination upon determined images.

This sequence of the film, the icon-montage of clocks and faces, the dividualized *hibakusha* women, are moments of thought that belong to Miss Ishikawa, images engendered by her surroundings, the ruins of the devastated cityscape of Hiroshima. In this way these signs of composition, the icon and the dividual, emerge from any-space-whatevers, the genetic sign of the affection-image. For Deleuze any-space-whatevers are 'spaces which we no longer know how to describe … deserted but inhabited … cities in the course

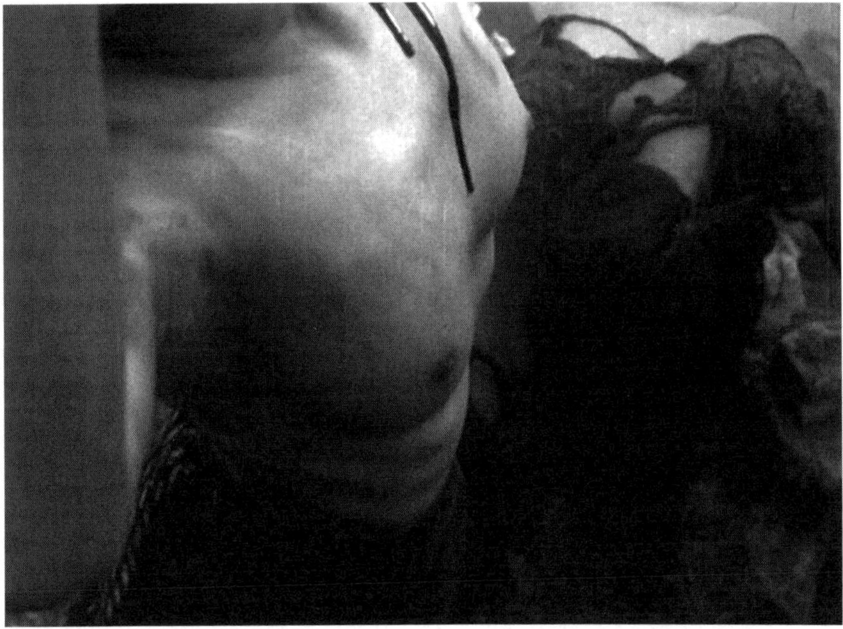

Figure 1.7 The dividual – the expression of indetermination upon determined images, *Children of the Atom Bomb* (Shindo, 1952)

Figure 1.8 The any-space-whatever – Miss Ishikawa traversing a gaseous mise-en-scène, *Children of the Atom Bomb* (Shindo, 1952)

of demolition or reconstruction'.[107] As the genetic sign of the affection-image, any-space-whatevers correspond to the genetic sign of the perception-image. This is gaseous perception, images without an actual centre, without a human body at the centre. If gaseous perception 'tends towards a perception as it was before men (or after), it also tends towards the correlate of this, that is, towards an any-space-whatever released from its human co-ordinates'.[108] In other words, just as we discovered a nonhuman perception, we discover nonhuman affect. Affect expressed by the any-space-whatever, where faces and bodies are subsumed and at its purest disappear within a gaseous mise-en-scène. In this way, the any-space-whatever 'no longer has co-ordinates, it is pure potential, it shows pure Powers and Qualities, independently of the states of things or milieux which actualise them'.[109] Indetermination saturates the mise-en-scène.

In *Children*, any-space-whatevers are the vestiges of the family home which precede the flashback-thought sequence and the skeleton of Hiroshima Prefectural Hall which supersede it. These are backgrounds which are traversed by the movements of the centre that is Miss Ishikawa, backgrounds which she perceives and upon which her actions are performed: a turning toward, a turning away, a walking through. Accordingly, *Children* describes how the any-space-whatever is the very ground of affect, the powers and qualities of the mise-en-scène, the genesis of the composition of dividual images and icons of expression.

A centre of indetermination

Yet *Children* is dominated by the sign of the icon, by faces. Faces shot in close-up, a nexus of qualities and powers, external expressions of a centre of indetermination. Iwakichi's keloid-scarred face, with its quality of shame; or the serial powers of anger, injustice and despair. The face of Miss Ishikawa's old friend (and reason for the return to Hiroshima) Morikawa (Saito Miwa); a face expressing stoicism – despite being rendered sterile by the atom bomb her life remains focused upon children, she works as a midwife, is waiting to adopt a child, and knows what has become of the three surviving members of the crèche. Sanpei's stupefied face at the moment of the death of his father; Toshiko's face imbued with the promised deliverance of her Christian faith, praying, as she prepares for her own death; Heita's face, full of joy and hope – a reflection of his now-crippled sister's marriage to the steadfast ex-soldier who willingly keeps his pre-war vow. And Taro's face: a face describing unbound love for and dependency upon his one remaining family member, his grandfather Iwakichi. All these characters, all these faces traversed by such qualities and powers, are centres, icons. But they are also elements which orbit a greater centre: Miss Ishikawa. It is Miss Ishikawa that binds all these qualities and powers. *Children* is a film of faces, a film expressing affect through the faces of the *hibakusha* – and as axis, the icon that is Miss Ishikawa.

As we have seen, the icon is the external expression of the internal intensity which constitutes the human as a centre of indetermination. In other words, the transformation of external perception into external action occurs through internal intensity. Expressed on the face as quality (orientated toward perception) and power (orientated toward action), internal intensity is thus selection: the selection of an object perceived, the selection of responsive action (be it instantaneous, delayed, or indeed the unconstituted). Miss Ishikawa – as a *hibakusha* returnee – perceives the any-space-whatevers of Hiroshima and perceives Iwakichi as others pass unseeingly through the mise-en-scène and by the old disfigured beggar. Miss Ishikawa reacts to these perceptions by seeking out encounters with Sanpei, Toshiko and Heita; with

Iwakichi's grandson Taro. These perceptions and reactions of Miss Ishikawa are captured, in *Children*, as qualities and powers expressed through her face. It is this that makes the film a 'tearjerker'; it is this that makes the film an emotional journey. Yet, these qualities and powers are also external markers of the selection of perceptions and possibilities of action. The centre of indetermination thus corresponds to choice: choice in the selection of images perceived, choice in the actions-to-come. Choice, be it unconscious or conscious – or some temporal becoming from one to the other – is the correlate of the icon. Ann Kibbey, in *Theory of the Image* (2005), explores the icon after C. S. Peirce, describing it as having 'no inherent relationship to what it signifies'.[110] It is a 'likeness', it has a 'resemblance' to something, yet is somehow at a distance.[111] Peirce writes: 'a pure icon can convey no positive or factual information.'[112] The relation between icon and world, for Kibbey, is thus 'provisional, problematic, possible … – a hypothesis rather than an assertion of fact'.[113] For Peirce, 'good examples of icons were not direct visual analogies, not things that could be said to look like other things in the way that a portrait resembles a person'.[114] Instead, icons are diagrams and algebraic equations. Miss Ishikawa's face is a diagram or algebraic equation, an external expression of internal intensity, indetermination and choice.

It is at this point that we can return to the analyses of Richie and Standish. Aligning the film with the concepts of *mono no aware* (Richie) and *higaisha ishiki* (Standish) only goes so far. With *Children*, the problem is framed in how Miss Ishikawa as a centre of indetermination relates to elegiac passivity and atom bomb victimhood. Miss Ishikawa's journey through the film is one of choices, beginning with the decision to return to Hiroshima in the first place. In this way, Miss Ishikawa as icon, the qualities and powers that traverse her face, are external expressions of indeterminate internal intensities made determinate through choices made. Furthermore, her interactions with the other *hibakusha* she encounters orientate their relations to the *mono no aware* and *higaisha ishiki* attitudes. If Sanpei and Toshiko are repulsed by and resigned to fate – one with the loss of his father, the other with her own impending death – the episode with Heita, where the crippled sister and the soldier marry, provides an answer. Hope for the future. The crucial aspect is not simply that Miss Ishikawa chooses hope over despondency, chooses to carry on, after Heita, to once again try and persuade Iwakichi to come to her island with his grandson. But that she chooses choice. As Deleuze puts it, choosing choice (instead of believing there is no choice) is the 'true choice'; it is that which appears to 'restore everything to us.

It will enable us to rediscover everything, in the spirit of sacrifice, at the moment of sacrifice.'[115]

In this regard, Iwakichi represents for Shindo the opposite path, that of passivity and victimhood: 'Damn war. Stupid war. Atom bomb. Maggots. The dead are all maggots.' Drunk, he commits suicide, burning himself alive in his rough wooden shack. This is not just self-pity. In so doing, he sets up the conditions for Taro to be free to go with Miss Ishikawa. He sacrifices himself for another. Yet in just this way Shindo provides a critique of such sacrifice – this sacrifice of death. Iwakichi embodies the worn-out, brutalized, subservient patriarchy of Japan. He believes he has no choice. He is shamed, for the loss of everything, the war, his son, his son's wife, his face, his occupation, his grandson Taro to the orphanage.

Children thus explores a series of polarities: passive acceptance of fate and active intervention; victimhood and resistance; reactionary sacrifice of death and revolutionary sacrifice in life. As Kibbey puts it, 'the icon can be a means of changing the world, of imagining different relations than those that exist'.[116] In this way, Noël Burch believes the film to be 'militant', playing 'a considerable role in the campaign which resulted in Japan's solemn renunciation of nuclear weapons'.[117] The movie has a 'grandiloquent lyricism' and 'semi-documentary nature', making it 'one of the most effective films of the period'.[118] *Children,* through Miss Ishikawa, is a film that champions intervention, resistance, revolution and life.

Children and monsters

Children of the Atom Bomb is an affection-image film, a film that expresses affect. It is dominated by the sign of the icon: faces expressing internal intensities, qualities and powers embodied by the *hibakusha*; women, men and children affected by the atom bomb. These emotions, expressed on faces on-screen, are thus the fundamental way in which the spectator encounters the film. *Children* is, in this way, a very different type of cinema to *The Effects of the Atomic Bomb on Hiroshima and Nagasaki*. *Effects* is dominated by perception-images, the sign of gaseous molecularity. Images capture the devastated cities and *hibakusha* through a cold-eye, a camera-eye that stands in for the indifferent *pika*. *Children* and *Effects* create two diverse perspectives on Hiroshima and Nagasaki, each tending towards one of the extremes of the dyadic poles of depiction of the nuclear event, the *pika* and the *hibakusha*, the nonhuman (molecular perception) and the human (molar affect). Already, then, the Japanese response to the atom bomb can be seen as heterogeneous, overcoming the spectre of impossibility in two very different ways.

Yet, there is a third moment to the sensory-motor process, a third domain of movement-images: the action-image. Perception-images create a centre. Affection-images express emotion, make the centre one of indetermination and choice. Action-images extend emotion and choice into behaviour. See, feel, act: the three primary domains of the movement-image. The question that must now be confronted is this: what would a Japanese film of the atom bomb dominated by action-images be like? Action-images tend to create characters that are engendered by a determined situation to bring about a change in the world. Thus, it might initially seem that the Japanese cinema will be presented with an insurmountable problem. How can this situation – the atomic bombing of Hiroshima and Nagasaki – be encompassed by an individual who can take on the nuclear event and resolve it?

Yet this is not really the problem it may at first seem. A solution appears in the very earliest of post-occupation Japanese atom bomb films. It occurs through substitution: direct depictions of the nuclear event become indirect. *Effects* and *Children* depict the events of August 1945 and its aftermath. Perception-images and affection-images appear perfect for this undertaking: perception-images for a looking-on, a capturing of an event; affection-images for charging such images with emotion, with qualities and powers. Action-images extend affect into action, extend emotion into acts, attempt to master the situation – and the genre of films that take special delight in overcoming the spectre of impossibility in such a way is the *kaiju eiga*, the monster movie. Yet such opaque expressions cannot but raise the question of betrayal. Surely such dramatizations distort the event, fall far short of the horror of the *pika* and betray the suffering of *hibakusha*?

III. Action and resolution

Action-images (large form)

The action-image is realism. For Deleuze, 'what constitutes realism is simply this: milieux and modes of behaviour'.[119] In other words, the action-image creates a determined spatio-temporal situation and characters that can perform actions within that situation. While the perception-image inclines toward a wide shot seen by the camera or character, in the action-image the wide shot exists as a situation to be acted upon.[120] Similarly, affective backgrounds (any-space-whatevers) become 'actualised directly in determinate, geographical, historical, social space-times'.[121] Concomitantly, while perception-images create characters as a centre and affection-images then express emotion through that centre, the action-image takes these forces and uses them to act on the world. In this way, affects 'appear as embedded in behaviour'.[122] As we will discover, the action-image is (perhaps) the most complex of all Deleuze's images. Realism is a domain composed of many action-image avatars: reversing, transforming, unfolding and nascent forms. For now, however, we are concerned only with the most prevalent, that of the large form. Even here, things are far from simple. The large form action-image is composed through laws, is organized through a dyadic polarity and a triadic series of signs, and is subject to a number of variations.

Situation → action → resolved situation: SAS'.[123] This is the trajectory of the large form action-image, and – according to Deleuze – it operates through five laws, as expressed in Table 1.4. The first law, S(→S'), 'concerns the action-image as organic representation in its entirety'.[124] Organic representation is structural because 'the places and moments are well defined in their oppositions and their complementarities'.[125] In other words, the action-image creates conflicts in a determined space-time. It does so through alternate parallel montage, a 'succession of shots' which takes up the situation (S) and encodes the conflicting forces in the narration to propel the film toward conclusion, the resolved situation (S').[126] Deleuze's second law traces such an encoding through the creation of characters: S→A. If the first law was dependent upon parallel montage, here, another aspect of alternate montage comes to the fore: convergence. As Deleuze puts it: 'very quickly two points emerge from this milieu, then two lines of action which will alternate … from one to the other and form a pincer'.[127] The third law, for Deleuze, 'is like the reverse of the second'; while

Table 1.4 The five laws of the large form action-image: situation → action → (new) situation (SAS')

S (→S')	the initial situation (to final resolved situation)
S→A	from situation to action
A (→S')	action in-itself (preparing the new situation)
A^P	the proliferation of action – preceding the final action
→	the gap in-itself, between the initial and final situation, encompassing action

alternate convergent montage is necessary for the passage from situation to action, 'at the very root of the duel, there is something which rebels against any montage'.[128] This is the logical conclusion of convergent montage. Characters must clash at A; and A – the final showdown – must necessarily come very close to S'. It is this final action that generates the resolved situation. A is, in effect, A(→S'). Deleuze's fourth law is where 'the duel is … not a unique and localised moment' but rather 'polynomial', and so it is 'difficult to mark out its boundaries'.[129] This is A^P, a proliferation of duels. At its most extreme, this formulation complicates the lines of action, A in-itself retroactively fragmenting. Finally, all the laws 'dovetail'.[130] The space-time between the first and final moments of the film constitutes a gap, or passage → of action. It is through → that the protagonist discovers capabilities equal to that of the situation. This is the fifth law.

As the large form action-image is a movement-image, however, it also exists in relation to perception-images and affection-images. The perception-image, as was seen above, has three levels: the image in-itself as a monadic entity; molar composition and molecular genesis as a dyadic polarity; and a triadic series of signs which describe these two poles and the transition between them. With the perception-image the signs described different modes of objective and subjective perception. With the affection-image, the signs described varying distributions of qualities and powers. With the large form action-image, the signs will describe intensities of relation between situation and action across the five laws. The monadic, dyadic and triadic levels of the large form action-image can be illustrated as in Table 1.5.

Each sign negotiates the five laws according to the distribution of molar and molecular forces. The milieu is concerned with a highly determinate situation, and this determined situation creates clear lines of force. These actions are in turn concerned with describing the situation without ambiguity, the actions emerging from it purely sustaining an environment. With the binomial, there is a tendency towards action for-itself, the duel in its conclusive and polynomial aspects: a film of conflicts. Finally, the genetic sign accounts for 'a much more complex behaviourism' where the action-image takes 'into account internal

Table 1.5 Action-image (large form)

action-image (large form)		
molar composition		molecular genesis
milieu	binomial	impression

Table 1.6 The three varieties of the action-image (large form)

SAS'	the resolved situation is improved with respect to the originary situation
SAS	the resolved situation is static with respect to the originary situation
SAS''	the resolved situation is worse with respect to the originary situation

factors'.[131] Emotion permeates characters (and is thus closest in relation to, and extends, the affection-image). This emotion, a factor of the milieu, is the internal duel, and exists for action and resolution.

As well as five laws and three signs, Deleuze specifies three varieties of the large form action-image. These varieties, notated in Table 1.6, describe the ways in which the final situation is resolved. There is the (most common) SAS' variation. Here the character has risen to the challenge and rectified the world. With the SAS variation, things remain unchanged despite the actions which have been performed. Here the actions of the character may be about 'surviving in an impervious milieu', which may well be a triumph in-itself.[132] This may be where the situation offers no challenges and so the character 'must compensate for an over-benevolent milieu by inventing for himself the trial … which enables him to give himself up to a fundamental duel with himself'.[133] The SAS'' variation describes a worsening of situation, where 'the individual, an abandoned being … no longer knows what to do'.[134] We enter a 'descending spiral' where the individual 'falls lower and lower'.[135] It could be a tale of failure, the story of a crack-up.

Taken together, the three signs of the large form action-image distribute the five laws across their series, describing different intensities of the link between situation and action – and the three varieties pronounce, against the original situation and through action, the status of the resolution. The action-image, in short, discovers myriad ways to describe and then resolve a situation through the acts of individuals. With regard to the Japanese cinema of the atom bomb, our concern is thus how action-image movies describe and then resolve the nuclear situation. In this way, we encounter the opaque expression of *Godzilla*.

Godzilla (1954)

The mainstream Japanese film industry, writes Richie, has 'naturally used Hiroshima, Nagasaki, and the bomb', however, 'not … in any constructive or convincing manner'.[136] The fundamental reason for this is that popular cinema ('ordinary story-line films') 'must dramatize and this means that they must distort'.[137] Symptomatic of this is the *kaiju eiga*, and paradigmatic, for Richie, is *Godzilla*. However, far from being a betrayal of the horror of the *pika* and the suffering of the *hibakusha*, I believe the large form action-image of *Godzilla* allows cinema to create the fundamental conditions for the nuclear event. The nature of these dramatizations and distortions must be explored – before reversing Richie's critique – through Deleuze's laws, signs and variations of the large form action-image.

First law, S(→S'): a Japanese trawler, the *Eiko*, is in the ocean off the east coast of Japan. After a hard day's work hauling fishing nets, the crew kick-back, enjoy a balmy evening on deck. As a guitar is gently strummed, the peaceful dusk is shattered by the sound of an atomic explosion, a blinding flash of white light and an intense wind. The *Eiko* catches fire and sinks. The co-ordinates of this opening scene give the film a determinate spatio-temporal placement creating the initial situation: Japan and the nuclear nightmare. Second law, S→A: in order to pass from the initial situation to the resolved situation, the forces inherent in the milieu will need to unfold, engender collectives and individuals. These forces will be dual, opposing and parallel – describing the confrontation between different bodies through behaviours. In *Godzilla*, these parallel forces are embodied by the Japanese collective represented by Ogata and the monster. As the trawler goes down, it sends out an SOS which is relayed to the coastguard, who in turn telephone Ogata. The collective is synthesized into a particular body, that of the action-hero. As the film progresses, this 'moving from the collectivity to the individual and from the individual to the collectivity' will continue as the character base expands and contracts.[138] By contrast, Godzilla is at first concealed. Rescue boats disappear: a newspaper headline reads 'Floating mines? Volcanic eruption?' Odo Island is hit by an inexplicably violent and devastating storm. As the Japanese collective investigate, the monster appears from behind a hill. The true horror of what Ogata must eventually confront is finally revealed.

Third law, A or A(→S'): the final confrontation will occur at the end of the film and will resolve the situation. Ogata and Godzilla meet on the sea floor of Tokyo Bay. The hero deploys the oxygen destroyer and the monster is defeated. Ogata claims Emiko, the girl, as his own – and all is now right with Japan. The threat to the very existence of the collective has been eliminated, and the future promise of life is embodied in the triumphant coupling of the hero and his woman. Fourth law, A^P: in order to reach this final confrontation at A, the film has had to pass through any number of duels. The concluding binomial is the terminus of a polynomial series. On the one hand, there are the violent encounters between Godzilla and the collective of the Japanese Defence Force in Tokyo. On the other hand, Ogata must traverse a series of duels within the Japanese collective. He has to show that the way to deal with the monster is through violence, not to somehow tame it, as recommended by Dr Yamane; and he has to convince Dr Serizawa (Hirata Akihiko), through rhetoric and force, to allow the use of his terrifying new weapon, the oxygen destroyer. The cost will be great: the elimination of all marine life from the waters around Japan.

Fifth law, →: engendered by the situation, standing in for the collective and prevailing in the many duels he must fight, Ogata becomes capable of the final confrontation and resolution. Inversely, it might also be said, Godzilla has been incrementally prepared for defeat; its victories, each more devastating than the one before, appear as a kind of lizardy hubris. The resolution is thus an ethics. What is evil and what is righteous have been defined, no matter how much of what might be considered evil (through a different organization of images) the righteous must propagate.

While the formal arrangement of images in *Godzilla* is organized through the five laws of the large form action-image, there can be different intensities of the link between situation and action. These intensities are described by the three signs. With the milieu, the tendency is towards highly determinate situations which directly engender character behaviour. With the binomial, the film is orientated towards duels and action permeates the whole film. With the impression, the genetic sign, situations are mediated through an internalization, traversing an intensive line before action can begin. *Godzilla*, an opaque depiction, appears to be of the binomial.[139] On the one hand, the defined milieu creates forces that spiral down to form multiple binomial tessellations. On the other hand, while the situation imprints upon both the monster and the characters, actions are externalized rapidly, according to the defined roles that correlate each. *Godzilla* tends, in this way, to a series of duels. Finally, the film can be considered in regard to the variations of resolution: SAS (static), SAS' (improved) and SAS'' (devolved). The trajectory of the film appears unmistakably that of the SAS' variation, that of the improved situation: Godzilla is defeated, the Japanese collective triumphs and Ogata gets the girl.

Such are the laws, signs and variations of *Godzilla*, such are the distortions and dramatizations of the film. The question is, after Richie, if the narrative manipulations and indirect depiction of the nuclear event can be viewed as a convincing and constructive contribution to Japanese atom bomb cinema.

Emperor Godzilla

Richie was writing in 1962. Twenty-first-century writers have been inclined to take *Godzilla* far more seriously. Chon A. Noriega puts it most succinctly: 'Godzilla (the bomb).'[140] *Godzilla* 'link[s] the "thinkable" monster with the "unthinkable" nuclear environment.'[141] It is in this way that Honda overcomes the spectre of impossibility. It is in this way that a film about the nuclear event of Hiroshima and Nagasaki can be distributed to screens as mass popular entertainment. *Godzilla* performs a sleight of hand. As Samara Lea Allsop comments, 'the use of a Jurassic creature … as an allegory for nuclear warfare would seem comical … were it not based on a disturbing reality'.[142] The film, for Allsop, is ultimately an attack on America's decision to deploy the atom bomb. Yet it is not simply this *kaiju eiga* narration and dramatization that is rehabilitated by these later critics, but also that of the film's narrative distortions. Jerome F. Shapiro believes that while 'the most common way to look at *Gojira* is as a condemnation of America's use of nuclear weapons against Japan', this kind of response is 'much too simple'.[143] Rather the film describes 'the restoration of balance and harmony. *Gojira* suggests that men have become too powerful because they make war; consequently, society is no longer in harmony with the natural order of things. Thus, the world is dangerously unbalanced.'[144] In this way, the very distortions of such a realist narration (its duels; its situation → action → new situation trajectory; its triumphant resolution) are what are essential to the film. For Shapiro, 'something must counterbalance the male element'.[145] In a wonderful reading, Emiko is transformed from a connective device into 'the central character'.[146] She is at the heart of the film, the axis around which the three men spiral: the father (Yamane), the fiancé (Serizawa) and the lover (Ogata). For Allsop, it is the use of Serizawa's invention that is key: 'as it becomes clear that the Oxygen Destroyer would be the only means to defeat the monster, Dr Serizawa laments his discovery of the terrible invention and claims that its destruction would be similar to an atomic bomb.'[147] Accordingly, 'this scene is arguably an attempted representation of the conflicting views of those who created the world's first nuclear bomb.'[148] Allsop's observations are astute, yet this reading seemingly creates contradictions. If the oxygen destroyer is the atom bomb, what is Godzilla? It also draws attention to the monster being awoken by a nuclear event in the first reel. Noriega provides an answer: *Godzilla* displays a 'cyclical logic'; Godzilla is not simply an embodiment of the atom bomb, but an effect of the bomb and ultimately destroyed by atomic technology, thereby representing the 'circuitous logic of the arms race'.[149] For all these critics, then, *Godzilla* is an important contribution to the Japanese cinema of the atom bomb. Accordingly, dramatization and distortion are not to be condemned. They are the very power of the movies. The question is solely that of which type or kind of distortion and what is at stake in each dramatization. Or in our Deleuzian terminology, the question is of the organization of images and signs.

Despite the differences in the readings of the film by Noriega, Allsop and Shapiro, they all agree on one point – and simultaneously concur with Richie: *Godzilla* 'wags a warning finger' and 'echoes the "never again"' attitude.[150] Shapiro's restoration of balance and Noriega's circular logic of the arms race may well be more complex versions of Allsop's anti-nuclear interpretation – but it is the same message they all see *Godzilla* propagating. For Richie this is not enough: 'this very popular reading … is good as far as it goes', but elides any 'digging into the whole half-forgotten mess in order to finally come to terms with it'.[151] What is needed is something else. 'One meets [Japanese] people', comments Richie, 'who affirm that they are glad that they lost the war; one also meets a smaller number who are inclined to take a philosophic view and to maintain that what happened to Hiroshima is partially the fault of the Japanese … This Japanese attitude, needless to say, never reaches the screen.'[152]

However, it seems to me that *Godzilla* can be read in just such a way. *Godzilla* can indeed be seen as an excavation of the conditions for the nuclear event. Furthermore – contra Richie; contra Noriega, Allsop and Shapiro – the movie, rather than being one which condemns the use of the atom bomb on Hiroshima and Nagasaki, can be seen to explore the necessity of the attacks. Such a reading is made possible due to the movie's opaque engagement with the nuclear event through an analysis of the large form action-image organization.

The initial situation (S) – the American H-bomb test with which the film begins – is the condition for describing a conflict inherent in the closed system of the Japanese nation. The conflict which emanates from this situation diverges into and explores a binomial between the monster ($S \rightarrow A_1$) and the Japanese collective ($S \rightarrow A_2$). Godzilla ($S \rightarrow A_1$) is seen by the people of rural Odo Island as the return of an ancient Japanese energy, a Japanese monster, one that returns from time to time to rule over the nation. The monster is mythical, stories of

Figure 1.9 Emperor Godzilla – the legend becomes real, *Godzilla* (Honda, 1954)

which are told late at night round fires or while tucking little children into their beds at dusk. Yet the legend becomes real. It is here we encounter the cultural resonance.

Emperor Hirohito, in his New Year message of 1946, concluded with a statement which would foster the conditions for post-war Japanese democracy. The links between the emperor and the people 'do not depend upon mere legends and myths. They are not predicated on the false conception that the emperor is divine and that the Japanese people are superior to other races and fated to rule the world.'[153] Godzilla, in this way, can be seen not as the atom bomb, but as an embodiment of the concept of the divine emperor, a monstrous incarnation of totalitarian power capturing up the forces of the state religion, Shinto ('Way of the Gods'), the fascistic Japanese war machine and the militaristic war government. The defeat of the monster (at A), in this way, is an overcoming of legend and myth. This overcoming occurs through the diverse polynomial aspects of the film (A^P) in respect to the Japanese collective ($S \rightarrow A_2$). Ogata versus Yamane and Serizawa: these and other duels function as a democratic regime (with all its flaws and inequities). This trajectory thus operates to validate democratic processes that recognize the connections between the individual and the collective. It is this democratic process which authorizes the use of the oxygen destroyer. And the oxygen destroyer is the atomic bomb. This is the ethical judgement (→) of the film. *Godzilla* ultimately validates the use of the atomic bomb on Hiroshima and Nagasaki, for bringing to an end the Japanese emperor system, and for creating the conditions for a triumphant future democracy for Japan (SAS').

Never again

For Damian Sutton, however, films of the large form action-image that conclude with such a glorious fulfilment (SAS') are problematic. Such an ending might well be what both character and viewer hope for; we may demand that the hero/heroine 'gets the girl' or the guy, and that 'a new, different and more equitable society might emerge as a reflection of their union'.[154] Yet if this happens we no longer have a 'tale to tell, no warning to give'.[155] Sutton's assertion comes in the wake of an exemplary elaboration of the way in which the three large form action-image variations unfold the social field (socius). 'The socius', for Sutton, 'is always coming into being'; it 'will be organised and will become an organism; and we have the capacity to change the organism'.[156] This has a fundamental political dimension. For Sutton, after Deleuze, there are 'three routes for political change': the 'cancerous, the empty and the full body' of the final socius – each of which corresponds to a variation of the large form: SAS'', SAS, and SAS'.[157] These variations are 'what gives the ethical image its capacity for political reflection, and what gives it the ability to tell a story about how a socius might reorganise'.[158] The cancerous is a 'tyrannical reconstruction', the empty a 'formless body politic' and the full depicts 'revolution as fulfilment'.[159] The full dissolves the conflict embodied by the initial situation, and so closes down the dynamics of the critique, the ethical process of the film (→). In order to sustain an 'ethical image', writes Sutton, 'the gap cannot, must not be filled'.[160] The cancerous and the empty, 'the more intriguing aspects of the SAS/SAS'' tragedies', keep the ethical image open.[161]

With *Godzilla*, of the alternatives of the variations, only the full (SAS') is actualized: the triumphant ascendancy of the democratic regime over the mythic domain of the emperor system. The cancerous (SAS'') would have entailed Godzilla reigning over Japan; the empty (SAS) would mean a stasis in the initial situation, an on-going crisis between the conflicting forces. With the final SAS' variation, that of fulfilment, the ethical image is presented as complete, the judgement is final: the justified use of the atomic bomb. Yet there are those words spoken at the very end of the film, after the death of the monster, after Ogata joins Emiko for the promise of the future. 'I don't think that was the only Godzilla,' Dr Yamane fearfully predicts, 'another Godzilla may appear somewhere in the world.' And so it will be. *Godzilla* remains an origin which will be taken up in subsequent films, over a sequence of sequels, reimaginings and alternative versions. We thus encounter a particularly intricate organization of the large form action-image. Each film will have its own modality (one of the three variations), yet being a part of a series, this will always be of the empty form, the SAS variation. The monster will always return. 'In this sense,' comments Sutton (in another context) 'a whole narrative tradition … becomes an ethical and political image.'[162] The *Godzilla* films, as a series, thus necessarily unfold a vast SAS variation, an empty image sustaining the ethical process.

It is in such a way that paradoxes are exposed in the 'never again' attitude *Godzilla* supposedly propagates. This attitude is the message of the film, according to Richie, and refers to the use of the atomic bomb. When Richie writes that *Godzilla* substantiates the 'role which Japan has … adopted, that of "the new Switzerland"', he is alluding to the 1947 'Peace Constitution.'[163] Yet Article Nine of the constitution was an acknowledgement of the monstrous forces that Japan saw within itself. Accordingly the nation swore to 'forever renounce war as a sovereign right of the nation and the threat or use of force as a means of settling international disputes … The right of belligerency of the state will not be recognised.'[164] If *Godzilla* declares that never again must Japan suffer the horrors of the atomic bomb, it is only upon the condition that never again will the nation allow the rise of the monstrous forces of the emperor system, of state Shinto and the fascist-militarist complex. Yet Godzilla will indeed arise again, and again. Thus, while – in respect to the Deleuzian reading and Richie's critique – we can say that the film does indeed dig 'into the whole half-forgotten mess', in this there must not be a 'finally', there must be no coming 'to terms with it.'[165]

Horizons of history

Each Japanese atom bomb film overcomes the spectre of impossibility in its own way; each, in its own way, creates a singular encounter with the nuclear attacks on Hiroshima and Nagasaki. This chapter has explored this proposal by focusing upon some of the earliest films of Japan's post-war nuclear cinema:

Ito's documentary *The Effects of the Atomic Bomb on Hiroshima and Nagasaki*, Shindo's elegiac drama *Children of the Atom Bomb*, and Honda's monster flick *Godzilla*. Each of these films has been considered through Deleuze's movement-image and its three primary co-ordinates: perception, affect and action. These three movement-images dominate in different types of films. Accordingly, each type of film creates its own contingent centre, and each particular film has its own special image of the *pika* and *hibakusha*.

Effects propagated perception-images. At the centre of the film was the *pika* – the effects of atomic bomb were captured with a nonhuman eye, the camera-eye describing the indifference of the nuclear event toward the human. *Children* operated through the affection-image. Here the *hibakusha* appeared as special image, and the atomic attack was depicted from the perspective of humanity, disparate responses to the atom bomb and its aftermath. In this way *Effects* and *Children* describe extreme poles of the nuclear event: the *pika* and the *hibakusha*. *Godzilla* does something entirely different. While *Effects* and *Children* are direct depictions of the nuclear event, *Godzilla* overcomes the spectre of impossibility that haunts the Japanese cinema of the atom bomb through an opaque expression. Yet far from this being a betrayal of the horror of the *pika* and the suffering of the *hibakusha*, this approach allows for an exploration of the fundamental conditions for the nuclear event. The large form action-image is generated through the creation of determined spatio-temporal situations and defined lines of force. It is a structural and organic representation directed toward an ethical image, toward evaluation and judgement. *Godzilla*, in other words, can be seen as exploring causes for the events which *Effects* will describe and *Children* will lament. In this way, the large form action-image is not only structural, but creates a determined conceptual image of history within which it can generate its conflicts, distribute its duels, and pronounce its triumphant resolutions, its cancerous milieus and its stymied and interminable situations. *Godzilla* will spawn a series of large form action-image films riven with differences and repetitions that – over the years – will decentre the nuclear event and the Pacific War to encompass a widening historical horizon. These films will explore the continual death and rebirth of the nation-civilization and the endless battles between imperial Japan and colonialist USA which the cycles see as the conditions for the nuclear event. The large form action-image, in this way, is indicative of how Deleuze's cineosis is generative of cinematic images of history. It is this aspect of the movement-image we will begin to explore in the next chapter.

2

Horizons of History

The film of monumental and antiquarian history … to this is opposed a type of film that is no less historical.[1]

Action-images

Cinema is ineludibly historical. Every film, in its own way, captures spatio-temporal forces – socio-historical moments – as it traverses the process of production and consumption. This chapter begins an exploration of these forces within the Japanese cinema of the atom bomb. The focus will be upon films which describe determined situations and character behaviour, realist cinema, the action-image: from *kaiju eiga* (monster movies) and science fiction to social realism and family dramas. Each film will be considered in respect to the mode of historical conception that arises from its organization of images: a universal history from the large form action-image; and – by way of a reversal – a people's history from the small form action-image. According to its creation of special images of the *pika* and *hibakusha*, be they direct or indirect, each of these action-images will be seen to have its own horizon of history.

Even the most opaque depictions of the Japanese nuclear event, such as the *kaiju eiga*, cannot escape the mesh of historical forces permeating the image. In *Godzilla* the eponymous monster becomes a manifestation of Japanese fascism and militarism, a horrific incarnation of the mythic emperor that will ultimately require and validate the nuclear solution. Over the next twenty-one years *Godzilla* would inspire fourteen sequels, these films becoming known as the Showa cycle (after the official name of Emperor Hirohito and the era corresponding to his reign). However, by the time of the final film of the series, Honda's *Mekagojira no gyakushu / Terror of Mechagodzilla* (1975), Godzilla is transformed. The monster is now the saviour of the nation. The extension of the Showa cycle – in this way – reconfigures and re-evaluates the horizons of Japanese history, the conflicts with the USA and the final solution of the atomic bomb. Such indirect depictions of the nuclear event become even more fantastic through the liberation of *anime* (Japanese animation). Otomo Katsuhiro's *Akira* (1988) and Miyazaki Hayao's *Nausicaa of the Valley of the Wind* (1984) are exemplary. Beginning and ending with spectacular atomic events, *Akira* creates incredible devastations and mutations in twenty-first-century neo-Tokyo, capturing history in an alternative present and projecting that present into the future. *Nausicaa*, by contradistinction, invents a medievalized post-apocalyptic society, the nuclear event a thousand years in the past. Yet *anime* need not be reserved for such imaginary future scenarios. Masaki Mori's *Barefoot Gen* (1983), for instance, depicts the nuclear event with horrifying contemporary historical resonances. The film tells the tale of a little boy and his family before, during and after the atomic attacks on Hiroshima. In this way, the film has more in common with social-realist witness testimonies such as Shindo Kaneto's austere *Lucky Dragon No. 5* (1959). Focusing upon the story of a trawler caught up in Cold War American H-bomb testing in the Pacific, the film explores a real event appropriated for the opening spectacle of the original *Godzilla* movie. From inventively thrilling monster mêlées and sci-fi epics to factually based witness experiences, from opaque to direct depictions, these films – each in their own way – all create their own historical mapping of the nuclear attacks on Nagasaki and Hiroshima.

Fundamental to this mapping is the mode of historical conception that arises from each film's organization of images: the universal history of the large form action-image and the people's history of the small form. The large form describes the way in which situations engender actions, creating a history that parallels moments of the past, eternalizes traditions and judges outcomes. The small form describes how actions reveal situations, creating a people's history of the event, a history concerned with the stories of individuals and the masses. Thus, on the one hand, Masaki's *Barefoot Gen* and Shindo's *Lucky Dragon No. 5* are films of people's history: a child's survival over a few weeks in July and August 1945; the nuclear legacy impacting upon a group of fishermen and their community. On the other hand, the Showa *Godzilla* series is of universal, reflective history – capturing up the historical moment of the nuclear event and creating reiterations and parallels between temporal domains, subsuming the atomic bombing within immense historical forces. Finally, *Akira* and *Nausicaa* negotiate a trajectory between these two historical conceptual frameworks, each performing a critique of one form through the other: *Nausicaa* from the perspective of people's history, *Akira* from that of universal history. Each of these action-image events thus creates its horizon of history in a very different way.

In order to explore the action-image, the small and large forms, universal and people's history, this chapter will commence with an account of Friedrich Nietzsche's analysis of historical practices in *Untimely Meditations* (1873–6). This account, as we will see, proves to be the inauguration of Deleuze's interweaving of the images and signs of the cineosis with a multitude of forms of historical conceptualization.

Nietzsche, history

Nietzsche's 'On the Uses and Disadvantages of History for Life' (1874), the second of his *Untimely Meditations*, describes contemporary nineteenth-century historical practices. There are, as Nietzsche sees it, three 'species' of such practice: the monumental, the antiquarian and the critical.[2] Each aspect is a way in which the past is captured in the present for the future. Why three? As Craig Lundy comments: 'such questions ("why three…?", "which one accounts for…?") are mostly superfluous, insofar as Nietzsche's purpose … is to provide examples of how history can either engender or inhibit life. His discussion … is thus a contingent and incomplete one.'[3] Nietzsche's three 'historicals', as Lundy calls them, become Deleuze's touchstone for his exploration of cinema and history.[4] This exploration begins, in *Cinema 1*, with the large form action-image, which Deleuze sees as 'bring[ing] together the most serious aspects of history as seen by the nineteenth century', the three aspects analysed by Nietzsche.[5] As the cineosis is elaborated, however, Deleuze will reflect and expand upon these three categories. Furthermore, Nietzsche's own description of the historicals is merely the starting point for the development of his own argument, a philosophy of history that Deleuze will echo in *Cinema 2* with respect to time-images. This is to anticipate many themes we will return to in the chapters to come. For now, however, we are concerned with only the action-image.

What is history? 'This is a universal law,' writes Nietzsche, 'a living thing can be healthy, strong and fruitful only when bounded by a horizon.'[6] Nietzsche invokes – in order to contextualize his analysis of such horizons – Viennese dramatist Franz Grillparzer: 'All human beings have at the same time their own individual necessity, so that millions of courses run parallel beside one another in straight or crooked lines.'[7] If these humans were to record events from the perspective of their own lives, we would encounter history captured by actors in or witnesses to events, a history as it happens. For Grillparzer these courses would 'assume for one another the character of chance' and thus seemingly 'make it impossible to establish any all-embracing necessity prevailing throughout all events'.[8]

Yet history can become reflective – can free itself from the anchor of the time in which the historian lives. Such a reflective history is needed to organize the chaos of human experience, to frame its narrative and generate 'generalisations'.[9] There are, for Nietzsche, three such reflective horizons: the historicals. Monumental history 'pertains to him as a being who acts and strives'; antiquarian 'as a being who preserves and reveres'; and critical 'as a being who suffers and seeks deliverance'.[10] With monumental history, man 'learns from it that the greatness that once existed was in any event once possible and may thus be possible again'.[11] It 'makes what is dissimilar look similar' and 'it will always have to diminish the differences of motives and instigations.'[12] Antiquarian history venerates the past to conserve it and constructs group customs. For Nietzsche, 'by tending with care that which has existed from of old', the antiquarian 'wants to preserve for those who shall come into existence after him.'[13] This is a history of traditions – and a history under perpetual threat from the new. The critical, Nietzsche's third type, analyses the past, 'bringing it before a tribunal, scrupulously examining it and finally condemning it'.[14] It designates good and evil, the incorruptible and the corrupt, the healthy and the sick – in service of any kind of desire. It conjoins the histories of the possible and of tradition through judgement. There is no self-evident *telos* in Nietzsche's account of the historicals; there is no direction or ultimate aim manifest in such historical reflection. History, for Nietzsche, is not a movement of progress – or indeed an inexorable regression. Rather, it is the weft and weave of civilizations, of people, of ideas – a nexus of superimpositions: pasts in the service of a present for a future. Depending upon the situation, humans turn to 'a certain kind of knowledge of the past, now in the form of monumental, now of antiquarian, now of critical history'.[15]

For Deleuze, these horizons of history – history as it happens and the three aspects of reflective history – become powerful forces within the cinematic environment. Forces created through – as we will now see – films of the action-image.

Cineosis and cinema

On 1 March 1954, some 2,000 miles from Japan and 40 miles off the coast of Bikini Atoll in the Marshall Islands, a Japanese fishing boat – the *Daigo*

Fukuryu Maru – was caught in American H-bomb testing. A few months later this disaster would appear in the opening moments of Honda's *Godzilla*, the script by Kayama Shigeru rewritten by Murata Takeo and Honda in order (among other things) to incorporate the event. This moment in the film causes the awakening of both the monster and action-hero, seeding the duel between the two that propels the narration toward conclusion. Shindo Kaneto, five years after *Godzilla*, would remember the *Daigo Fukuryu Maru* and make *Lucky Dragon No. 5*. This film would portray the incident from the perspective of the crew, describing the impact of the disaster upon them and their community. With *Godzilla* and *Lucky Dragon No. 5* we can explore how an event can be captured up in cinema through both universal history and people's history. For Deleuze, this occurs through an organization of action-images, which are described as having two fundamental forms.

On the one hand, some films tend toward making the actions of the characters a direct consequence of the situation and through such actions allow a modification of that milieu. On the other hand, some films focus upon the actions of characters which – through their exploits, conflicts and achievements – reveal the situation, the environment, social relations. These two poles of the action-image are the large form and the small form respectively. The large form relates to the laws of reflective history: the monumental, the antiquarian and the critical. The small form relates to a history as it happens.

As we will see, the small form's history as it happens will be able to create direct engagements with the atomic bomb. This is because it has no need to resolve the initial situation. It can allow itself to describe what happened and how people responded, such as with Shindo's *Lucky Dragon No. 5*. Similarly, Masaki's *Barefoot Gen* will use this small form to describe the atomic bombing of Hiroshima from the perspective of a child; it will concern itself with the lives of Japanese civilians in the days leading up to the *pika*, and the experiences of the *hibakusha* in the aftermath. The small form, accordingly, allows a people's history.

Things are very different with the large form. Deleuze analyses this action-image – intially – with respect to Hollywood. 'The American cinema constantly shoots and reshoots a single fundamental film, which is the birth of a nation-civilisation.'[16] The crucial point, for Deleuze, is that this is not only the condition of movies properly called historical – the epic, period pictures and war films – but that 'all the other genres were already historical, whatever their degree of fiction.'[17] Gangster flicks, westerns, adventure and action films, and later horror and science fiction, all had 'the status of pathogenic or exemplary historical structures'.[18] These structures are that of reflective history (a nexus of monumental, antiquarian and critical). Yet reflective history is not unique to Hollywood. Indeed, it is this conceptual foundation of universal history which 'it has in common', for example, 'with Soviet cinema'.[19] However, whereas Hollywood operated through 'organic representation', the large form of the early Soviet cinema unfolds a 'dialectical development'.[20] Instead of the birth of the nation, we encounter the 'advent of the proletariat'.[21] In Japan, popular post-war cinema is closer, without doubt, to the organic structures of the Hollywood model. The occupation and post-occupation period was, after all, flooded with American film – and Japanese cinema responded in kind.[22] The Showa *Godzilla* cycle is exemplary of such a response. Yet these films are not so much concerned with the genesis of the nation, but rather the nation's death and rebirth. And it is this death and rebirth that would be explored – time after time – through each of the *Godzilla* sequels, through each film's repetitions and differences. Furthermore, the indirect depictions of the *Godzilla* cycle are not only able to explore the forces inscribed within the immediate Japanese social situation at the end of the Pacific War, forces which resulted in the atom bomb, but also how these forces were generated by the monumental, antiquarian and critical horizons of history.

I. History from above

Terror of Mechagodzilla (1975)

A mountain-top crumbles. Disturbed stone and earth, uprooted trees and vegetation tumble down sheer rock face. Metal blast doors are exposed, gliding open to reveal the presence of a dark chamber. Slowly at first, but with increasing velocity, a giant silver form emerges from the concealed silo. Against the backdrop of a clear blue sky a giant metal head appears, crown hooked, ears rampant, with yellowy blank eyes, snarling silver jaws. The wide articulated neck gives way to sheet metal circumscribing a vast chest, arms terminating in missile-launcher fingers. Jagged plates jut from a spine becoming the thick girth of a metallic tail. Kneecaps, spiked. Feet spurt jets of burned propellant. Thrust, acceleration, flight: the robotic war machine Mechagodzilla has arisen!

To Tokyo: Mechagodzilla towering over the 1970s steel, concrete and glass infrastructure. Rays, missiles, stomping: the city reduced to rubble. Then Godzilla appears. The monster mêlée begins. Body to body, Godzilla rips the head from Mechagodzilla. But the metal behemoth still functions.

Such is the cliff-hanger finale of *Terror of Mechagodzilla*. Its resolution will not only conclude the film but also the fourteen episodes of the Showa *Godzilla* cycle that came before. *Terror of Mechagodzilla* alludes to previous films in the series from its opening sequence. As the titles roll, there is a montage of moments from the preceding movie, *Gojira tai Mekagojira / Godzilla vs. Mechagodzilla* (Fukuda Jun, 1974). Mechagodzilla as doppelgänger, shedding the Godzilla-skin that has sheathed it, exposing a body fashioned from silver-sleek space titanium, revealing the ruse of its previous identity. The true Godzilla in agony, its flesh a pincushion of missiles, blood pumping from a wounded neck. Then triumph: Godzilla rendering its enemy inoperable by twisting head from body; Mechagodzilla debris plummeting into the ocean below. The music accompanying these images, furthermore, is a re-orchestration of Ifukube Akira's metallic-roaring score from the original *Godzilla* movie. There is, in this way, a sense of finality, of conclusion, to *Terror of Mechagodzilla*. Perhaps this is as it should be, for over the course of the Showa series everything has changed.

In the original movie Godzilla was a monstrous force inherent to the nation, yet one opposed by and in conflict with the Japanese collective. In the *Mechagodzilla* diptych, Simians are now the enemy: an alien monkey-people clothed in human bodysuits. Their plan is to claim Earth as their own.

Figure 2.1 The final Showa duel – Godzilla versus Mechagodzilla, *Terror of Mechagodzilla* (Honda, 1975)

Beginning with Japan, they must first defeat Godzilla, the nation's protective force. In *Godzilla vs. Mechagodzilla* the Simians created their metallic doppelgänger. Yet Godzilla won out, stymieing the alien invasion. In *Terror* the Simians are at it again. Commanded by their leader Mugal (Mutsumi Goro), the aliens have rescued the remains of Mechagodzilla from its watery grave and are repairing it with the help of embittered human scientist Dr Mifune (Hirata Akihiko). Crucial to the Simians' strategy is Mifune's beautiful daughter, Katsu (Ai Tomoko). Resurrected by the aliens as a cyborg after her tragic death, Mechagodzilla's brain is installed within her. Thus, when Godzilla severs Mechagodzilla's head it has little effect. Katsu, meanwhile, has fallen in love with action-hero Ichinose (Sasaki Katsuhiko), a member of the Japanese Marine Biology Institute. Katsu will sacrifice herself for Ichinose and her lost humanity, rendering the headless Mechagodzilla inoperable. In this way, Godzilla can now destroy its enemy. As the film concludes, Ichinose carries Katsu's body out onto headland overlooking the ocean at the same time as Godzilla is returning to its watery home. Godzilla and Ichinose catch each other's eye in mutual understanding, before the monster disappears beneath the waves. So ends the Showa cycle.

What we see in *Terror of Mechagodzilla* is Godzilla as saviour and a representative of the human Japanese collective and its individuals. Reciprocally, we encounter a monster of equal and opposing nature, a monster similarly representative of its own individuals and collective, one that is Simian-alien. From the origin of *Godzilla*, such transformations, realignments, substitutions and externalizations are the *fait accompli* of a series of incremental reconfigurations that have occurred over the course of fifteen films. And such reconfigurations are not simply structural; they simultaneously impact the cultural resonances of the original movie.

Godzilla, a film of the Japanese cinema of the atom bomb, was one of opaque expression. The monster was emperor, a mythic and legendary divine force capturing up the desires of state Shinto and the militaristic-fascistic war government. Against Godzilla was arranged the Japanese collective, and at its centre the action-hero Ogata: the move from one to the other negotiating the path from collective to individual and individual to collective – the democratic regime. The film thus described how democracy became capable of overcoming fascist-totalitarianism, a becoming that in turn validated the atomic bombing of Hiroshima and Nagasaki. The four reconfigurations of the Showa cycle – across the fifteen films, concluding with *Terror of Mechagodzilla* – thus generate a number of questions. Does the transformation of the monster constitute a rehabilitation of the emperor system, a realignment of Godzilla with the Japanese collective establishing a rapprochement with the nation's fascistic and militaristic past? What is substituted for the enemy within, to what do these now externalized forces refer? These questions must be interrogated. In the first instance, this will require us to explore the Showa cycle through the large form action-image in order to apprehend the way in which the four reconfigurations are enacted. In the second instance, we will need to consider how these reconfigurations map Japanese cultural history. Finally, we must account for the way in which such history appears in its universalist conception. Only then will we be able to approach the ultimate question: what becomes, in the wake of *Terror of Mechagodzilla*, of the atomic bombing of Hiroshima and Nagasaki?

The four Showa reconfigurations

The large form action-image is constituted by five laws which designate the cinematic trajectory situation → action → new situation. These laws describe the way in which the initial situation decomposes into two conflicting lines of force, a conflict which in turn is resolved in the final moments of the film. Such a conflict is revealed as polynomial, a series of duels which the hero has to negotiate in order to become capable of creating the final situation. The three signs of the large form describe different intensities distributed across these laws: the milieu, where devolved actions unfold from a well-defined situation; the binomial, a revelling in action for-itself through a proliferation of duels; and the imprint, a situation internalized as emotional conflict. Lastly, the modal variations of the large form designate the status of the final resolution: triumph (SAS'); stasis (SAS); and disintegration (SAS"). Such are the laws, signs and modes of the large form action-image. As was seen in the previous chapter, *Godzilla* abided by these five laws, and the film embodied the sign of the binomial, action in-itself, with the final moment one of triumph (SAS'). The conflict in the initial situation gives rise to Godzilla and Ogata, who as representative of the Japanese collective has to negotiate a number of duels (action in-itself, the binomial as polynomial) in order to defeat the monster, and this defeat constitutes a moment of collective victory. In the final moment of the film, nevertheless, there was voiced the possibility of more Godzillas: thus the anticipation of the return of the monster, thus the Showa cycle. This extension of the *Godzilla* movie has an effect with regards to the mode of variation. The film can no longer be seen to resolve itself through triumph (SAS'). Rather, the extension re-orientates film to one of an interminable situation (SAS). It was at this point we concluded Chapter 1.

However, we have seen with *Terror of Mechagodzilla* that the extension of the Showa cycle will not simply be a series of repetitions, but also distribute difference. In other words, the extension will constitute a series of reconfigurations which occur through the laws, signs and modes of the large form action-image.

For instance, while the milieu of each film always describes a moment of the greatest crisis, such critical instants are open to variation. In both *Godzilla* and its sequel, *Gojira no gyakushu* / *Godzilla Raids Again* (Oda Motoyoshi, 1955), it is atom bomb testing in the Pacific – a theme returned to near the end of the series in *Gojira tai Megaro* / *Godzilla vs. Megalon* (Fukuda Jun, 1973). In *Kingu Kongu tai Gojira* / *King Kong vs. Godzilla* (Honda Ishiro, 1962) and *Kaijuto no kessen: Gojira no musuko* / *Son of Godzilla* (Fukuda Jun, 1967) the crisis is an atomic accident. Yet not only nuclear nightmares inspire conflict. In *Gojira, Ebira, Mosura: Nankai no daiketto* / *Godzilla vs. the Sea Monster* (Fukuda Jun, 1966) it is domestic terrorism. In *Mosura tai Gojira* / *Mothra vs. Godzilla* (Honda Ishiro, 1964) and *Gojira tai Hedora* / *Godzilla vs. Hedora* (Banno Yoshimitsu, 1971) it is environmental pollution. The most pervasive crisis, however, is that of alien invasion, beginning with *San daikaiju: Chikyu saidai no kessen* / *Ghidorah, the Three-Headed Monster* (Honda Ishiro, 1964) and concluding the cycle with the *Mechagodzilla* diptych. These conflicts are structured by the first law of the large form action-image, S(→S'), from initial to final situation. Yet across the Showa cycle each film becomes an episode of what appears to be the interminable situation: Japan in a state of permanent crisis from nuclear threat, terrorism, pollution or invasion. The first law thus also describes the trajectory of the entire Showa cycle, from *Godzilla* to *Terror of Mechagodzilla* and across the thirteen films in between, creating an immense cinematic event. And it is through this cycle-event that the remaining four laws of the large form will operate, re-inscribing the sign of the binomial through an exponential expansion of duels – and powering the Showa reconfigurations.

The sign of the binomial is constituted through a domination of the third and fourth laws (action in-itself and the proliferation of duels). However, these laws are presaged by the second, describing how the conflict inherent in the situation bifurcates into two opposing forces. In *Godzilla* these forces were defined as the monster and the Japanese collective; from *Godzilla Raids Again* onwards things are more complex. In this second film of the cycle (another) Godzilla is discovered locked in mêlée with Anguirus, a horned, fanged and tusked quadruped dinosaur. It is their antagonism that coheres into a singular destructive force that constitutes the danger to the Japanese collective, a pattern that continues with the third film of the series, *King Kong vs. Godzilla*. In *Mothra vs. Godzilla* this procedure will mutate. A benevolent monster is introduced, Mothra, a butterfly-like creature seen across its entire lepidopteran lifecycle. Mothra becomes aligned with the Japanese collective, sharing the aim of saving Japan. The introduction of Mothra is an essential element in the transformation of Godzilla, which is played out in *Ghidorah*. In this fifth film the arrival of a space monster on Japanese soil allows Mothra to persuade Godzilla to join forces with it against the invading alien force. The alien attack movies are thus instrumental in Godzilla becoming aligned with the Japanese collective and, furthermore, will go on to introduce a devolved opposing force to the human collective representative of the invading monster. In the *Mechagodzilla* films it is Simians escaping from a planet teetering on the event horizon of a black hole. In *Kaiju daisenso / Invasion of the Astro-Monster* (Honda Ishiro, 1965) the aliens are from Planet X, a moon orbiting Jupiter. In *Kaiju soshingeki / Destroy All Monsters* (Honda Ishiro, 1968) the aliens, all-female Kilaahks, are from a planet located in the asteroid belt beyond Mars. In *Chikyu kogeki meirei / Godzilla vs. Gigan* (Fukuda Jun, 1972) it is insectoid aliens from Nebula-M, once again disguised as humans. As the Showa cycle continues, Godzilla will be called upon on behalf of and in consort with the Japanese collective to confront any number of monsters – including Gigan (a giant cyborg monster with a chainsaw protruding from its belly) and Megalon (an armoured bug-like creature with rampant proboscis, bulging yellow eyes and drills for arms) in turn representative of these alien invaders.

These polynomial duels (A^P) that traverse the fifteen films of the Showa cycle act as the cogs and workings of the reconfigurations that create the dual substitutive strata of destructive forces external to the nation. This ultimately aligns Godzilla with the Japanese collective and transforms it from destroyer to saviour. The final battle of *Terror*, where Mechagodzilla is defeated by Godzilla and the Simian horde crushed by the Japanese collective, is thus the binomial (A) that allows the final resolution of the entire series.

Such a resolution, furthermore, also reconfigures the mode of this large form action-image. The interminable situation (SAS) of the series-extension that was superimposed upon the triumphalism (SAS') of the Japanese collective over the monster in *Godzilla* is thus overturned. *Terror of Mechagodzilla* reasserts triumphalism, a resolution all the more illustrious in that it has taken the entire Showa cycle to bring it to fruition. This resolution is that of the simultaneous victory of both the Japanese collective and Godzilla. Such a conclusion refers us to the fifth law of the large form action-image, the gap (→), which extracts the central character in respect to the collective, and describes how that character becomes capable of resolving the milieu. Across the Showa cycle this character is – ultimately – revealed as being Godzilla.

The Showa cycle thus appears to take as its very subject the rehabilitation of the monster and its rapprochement with the Japanese people. Given the initial alignment, in *Godzilla*, of monster with the emperor, such rehabilitation and rapprochement appears to constitute a shocking historical revisionist forgetting of the horrors of Japan's fascistic and militaristic past. Can this be the case?

Filmic extension as historical archaeology

In 1937 the Japanese Central China Expeditionary Force advanced upon Nanking. At its approach half the population fled. Lord Russell of Liverpool's history of Japanese war crimes, *The Knights of Bushido* (1958), describes the features of the monster that awakened in the hearts of the Japanese military during the Pacific War and the creation of the Greater East Asia Co-Prosperity Sphere.[23] Russell reports eye-witness accounts from the war tribunals, the people of Nanking were 'hunted like rabbits, everyone seen to move was shot'.[24] Russell reports 'indiscriminate killing' of 'both sexes, adults and children alike' until 'the gutters ran with blood'.[25] War crimes included the 'rape of girls of tender years and old women'.[26] For Russell, 'the evidence given before the Tokyo Tribunal by eye-witnesses of the abnormal and sadistic behaviour displayed by the ravishers defies description'.[27] Russell puts the death toll in the first six weeks at around two hundred thousand Chinese civilians and military. This was just the beginning. From Nanking and China, Japan went on to annex French Indo-China, British Malaya, the Dutch East Indies, the Philippines, Thailand and Burma. Along the way were death marches, enforced industrial servitude, sexual slavery, cannibalism, vivisection and mutilation. These are the forces and desires that the original *Godzilla* movie embodied in the monster – it was these forces and desires the film opposed by way of the Japanese collective; thus the destruction of Godzilla at any cost, a validation of the use by the Americans of the atom bomb on Hiroshima and Nagasaki. What tale, then, does the extension of the Showa cycle tell through its reconfigurations?

For Chon A. Noriega the transformation of Godzilla directly reflects changes at the time the films were being made: 'The Limited Test Ban Treaty in 1963, which prohibited atmospheric nuclear tests, resolved the problem behind Godzilla ... By 1965, Toho Studio's president had decided to tailor Godzilla to its primary audience: Children.'[28] The transformation occurs, for Noriega, in *Ghidorah*. In this first alien invasion movie of the Showa series, space monster King Ghidorah arrives fresh from the destruction of the civilizations of Venus to take on the Earth, and Godzilla joins forces with Mothra to save Japan. 'The film transformed Godzilla into a hero, especially among Japanese children', comments Noriega, the image of the monster 'soon adorning their clothing, lunch boxes, toys, and candy'.[29] These children were 'a generation removed from World War II. The realities Godzilla reflects became "history" rather than lived experience.'[30] In this way, the origins of the monster of Nanking and the solution of the atomic attacks on Hiroshima and Nagasaki fade. The extension of the Showa series constitutes, for Noriega, a waning of the coordinates of *Godzilla*, an active forgetting of history.

There is, however, another way to consider this transformation. Rather than seeing the series as simply reflecting a changing present and instituting the erasure of history through distance from the original movie and nuclear event, the Showa extension can be read as a digging into the past, as an archaeology. In this way, the films become not less historical, but more so. *Ghidorah* is no decisive break, dividing the cycle into a before and after. The polynomials instead perform a series of transformations over the entire cycle. *Ghidorah* is but one vital moment among a multitude.

The third film, *King Kong vs. Godzilla*, is another. Just as in *Godzilla*, the giant lizard is awoken by a nuclear incident, the crisis is caused by American intervention – this time a UN submarine under US command. Yet at one and the same time the Japanese are themselves intervening in the South Pacific, forces of capitalism conspiring to capture King Kong for exploitation through advertising revenue. There is a mirroring here: the Americans have awoken the Japanese monster par excellence; and the Japanese have awoken the quintessential American monster. These mutual awakenings result in an equivalence and correlation: King Kong and Godzilla become twin forces of destruction. In parallel to this great binomial fought on Japanese soil, the collective has the

Figure 2.2 Japan and the USA – Godzilla versus King Kong, *King Kong vs. Godzilla* (Honda, 1962)

task of solving the problem of the two monsters, the hope being that they will somehow exhaust and destroy each other. This resolution remains unfulfilled, both survive their final battle. Indeed, this film is the first to foreground and openly declare the generalized condition of the on-going Showa cycle, that of the interminable situation.

With *King Kong vs. Godzilla,* Japanese Godzilla is counterbalanced – both as a destructive force and as an ethical image – by the giant American ape. With *Ghidorah*, Godzilla is transformed from a devastating oppositional force to the representative of the Japanese collective as protector of the nation. With *Invasion of the Astro-Monster*, the opposing force is augmented with an alien collective. Such reconfigurations ultimately play out in the concluding diptych of the *Mechagodzilla* films, where it is as if American King Kong has fragmented, decomposed into the invading US-Simian collective, lots of little apes and a war machine.

The Showa *Godzilla* cycle, in this way, can be said to describe a permanent crisis between the civilizations of America and Japan. A crisis of flashpoints occurring over a one-hundred-year period; a period which began with the arrival of the US in Japanese waters in 1853 and concluded with the atomic bombing of Hiroshima and Nagasaki. As the Showa series extends it thus performs an archaeology of *Godzilla*, of Japanese history in respect to the effects of the nation's conflicts with the USA. This archaeology constitutes a contextualization of the nuclear attacks on Hiroshima and Nagasaki through the domains of monumental, antiquarian and critical history, a universal history engendered through the situations and polynomials of the large form action-image of the Showa *Godzilla* cycle.

Kurofune and *sonno-joi*

Monumental history is embodied by the first and second laws of the large form action-image.[31] This aspect of universal history 'favours … analogies and parallels', and these may occur 'between one civilisation and another' and/or between 'the principal phenomena of a single civilisation'.[32] These conflicts are described through the deeds of great figures – the passage from situation to restored situation embodied in action. In this way there are two tendencies – first, that historical events chart the collision of two embodied forces (parallel montage). Secondly, that this structure is repetitive: these forces clash continually, form peaks and describe homogeneous phenomena (convergent montage). The antiquarian, for Deleuze, 'runs parallel to the monumental', and corresponds to the third and fourth laws of the large form action-image.[33] The duel, A in-itself, is taken as the foundation of the present. But of course duels are polynomial and in this way antiquarian history selects events – no matter how different – that form a coherent mapping of a civilization. These duels are the archival data of a nation that essentialize traditions. Finally, 'the monumental and antiquarian conceptions of history would not', for Deleuze, 'come together so well without the ethical image which measures and organises them both'.[34] This organization equates a critical history with the fifth law of the large form action-image where the gap (→) between situation and restored situation marks the very co-ordinates of the story being told. This is 'a matter of Good and Evil', where 'a strong ethical judgement must condemn the injustice of "things", bring compassion, herald the new civilisation'.[35] Across any large form action-image, then, there will be a nexus of such universal, reflective historical forces. These correspondences appear as in Table 2.1.

The aspects of universal history that emerge from the large form action-image configure the extension of the Showa cycle. This configuration is simultaneously an archaeology of the initial situation of *Godzilla* and a revealing of the internal

Table 2.1 The five laws of the action-image (large form) and universal history

S (→S') S→A	the initial situation (to final resolved situation) from situation to action	monumental history
A (→S') A^P	action in-itself (preparing the new situation) the proliferation of action	antiquarian history
→	the gap in-itself	critical history

conflict of the old and the new inherent within Japan opened up by an external American intervention.

On 2 July 1853, four *kurofune* (black ships) entered Edo (now Tokyo) Bay. Each was six times the size of any Japanese vessel, mounted with 61 guns and held nearly 1,000 men. Abe Mashiro, *daimyo* (domain lord) of Fukuyama and head of the ruling Tokugawa power structure, ordered the boats to turn back. A letter of refusal came from Commodore Matthew C. Perry along with a set of white flags. As Marius B. Jansen puts it, Perry indicated that 'failure to meet his demands … would bring on a war that Japan would most assuredly lose, and in that case the white flags of surrender would be useful'.[36] His demands were for a treaty regarding the hospitality and return of sailors washed up on Japanese territory. Perry eventually left Edo vowing to return for an answer. This he did in February of the following year. Negotiations lasted twenty-three days during which Perry disclosed the real reason for the treaty: trade. Hayashi, the chief negotiator, reminded the Americans that they had originally requested much less than this. A compromise was reached. The Americans could purchase supplies, but only for their ships. Perry 'saw this as an opening', while the Japanese 'a formula that permitted … [them] to maintain they had denied trading privileges'.[37] Whatever the outcome, these negotiations opened Japan's eyes to the world and the Pacific arena became the stage for a conflict between American colonialism and Japanese imperialism. Japan took Okinawa in 1879, and a section of Manchuria in 1894. In 1898, the US seized the Philippines, Guam and Hawaii. In 1904 Japan went to war with Russia and took control of the Sakhalin and Kurile Islands, and in 1910 occupied Korea.

This external intervention, however, awoke an internal division at the very heart of the Japanese nation. One of the most significant dates in Japanese history is 1600 AD when Tokugawa Ieyasu won the battle of Sekigahara – a battle for control of the Japanese islands. This began what is now called the Edo period, which saw the Emperor become a figurehead (the transcendent spiritual power of the nation) while material control of Japan lay with the Shogun – a military dictatorship. Under the Tokugawas, Japan entered *sakoku* (seclusion) and a strict hierarchical social system took root. The Tokugawa base of government – the *bafuku* – was set up at Edo, the *daimyo* (regional lords) becoming vassals. This hierarchical social system coalesced into a rigid stratification of society: nobility (the court), *daimyo*, samurai, farmers, artisans and merchants. Social mobility ossified, position allocated from birth. Yet this oppressive shogunate regime introduced a 250-year period of national stability, a stability guaranteed by the Emperor who embodied the spiritual essence of the Japanese people. In this way, the division of power between court and military dictatorship founded a stasis on which the modern Japanese state was based. The first Japanese encounter with the Americans thus heralded a break in this *sakoku*-stasis and ultimately led to the fall of the Tokugawa regime.[38] The Shogun signed the treaty with the Americans against the wishes of the Emperor. These events led to a fissure opening up between *daimyo* that supported the shogunate and *daimyo* aligned with the court. Chief among the anti-treaty, pro-Emperor *daimyo* was Tokugawa Nariaka. Nariaka's chief advisor was the samurai-scholar Toko Fujita, and together they set up an academy for the dissemination of anti-foreigner literature. Toko wrote a charter for Nariaka, the foremost policy being *sonno-joi*: 'reverence to the Emperor, expel the foreigners'.[39]

These duels – between *daimyo* representatives of the Emperor and Shogunate – constitute a conflict between the 'old' and the 'new' formed in the wake of the crisis of American intervention and the subsequent encounters between America and Japan in the Pacific arena. An antiquarian history – the stasis of the Edo period – is thus overlaid with a monumental history: on the one hand the conflict between the 'old' as *sakoku* and the 'new' as a global awakening occasioned by the black ships; on the other hand, the on-going external crisis between the Americans and Japanese. These are the monumental and antiquarian forces captured up in the five laws of the polynomials that structure Showa *Godzilla. Godzilla* will end with the triumph of the new over the old, the Americans over the Japanese; aligning the monster with the antiquarian forces of the old Japan and championing the Japanese collective as world citizens represented by American democratic principles.

As the Showa series extends it may appear such conclusions are reversed, Godzilla transformed and realigned with the Japanese people, an external force introduced to occasion such a transformation and substitute one for the other. However, this extension can instead be seen as a digging into the historical forces that inspired the initial situation of the film. This archaeology is a critical history, one which shows the historical conditions leading up to the atomic bombing of Hiroshima and Nagasaki. Each film is a layer of earth, each stratum peeled away to reveal another: the Showa series as excavation, a universal and reflective history of vast and complex internal and external historical forces.

What is the ethical judgement of such a universalist historical archaeology? It is certainly not a rehabilitation of the monstrous forces of Nanking and a reconstitution of the links between the fascist-militarist war machine and the

Japanese people. Rather, it is the very conditions for the ultimate collapse of such links and such forces upon the universalist historical horizon. Showa *Godzilla* describes the death, and discovers the birth, of modern Japan during the 1853–1945 period. This death is constituted by the atomic bombings of Hiroshima and Nagasaki, a historical necessity occasioned by the transformation of Japanese society into fascist-militarism. Yet the birth was conceived very differently, both inside and outside Japan. The Russo-Japanese War (1904–5) – in which Imperial Japan declared war upon and triumphed over Imperial Russia – was celebrated in Europe: 'in England … there was a "Learn from Japan" movement that called for a rebirth of patriotism and loyalty.'[40] Japan, writes Jansen, 'was now a major world power', seen in terms of the established European and emerging American powers.[41] Yet over the years since the *kurofune*, Japan had also learned from these nations. The murderous genocides and political, economic and cultural interventions of European imperialism in Africa, South America and Asia; the homicidal annihilations of Manifest Destiny through the on-going westward spread of European-America into the lands of the native Americans and the peoples of the Pacific. In Japan, *sonno-joi* came to express the need to create a zone of Japanese influence in Asia and the Pacific, the Co-Prosperity Sphere, free of European and American interference. The archaeological monumental and antiquarian histories of the Showa cycle establish a new critical history of the atomic bombings of Hiroshima and Nagasaki as constituted in *Godzilla*. They declare not only an end to the Japanese fascist-militarist imperial war machine, but excavate the universal-world conditions that sustained it.

From above, from below

There are three cycles of *Godzilla* films: the Showa series (1954–75); the Heisei series (1984–95) (comprising another seven films); and the Millennium series (1999–2004) (comprising a further six films). In the Heisei and the Millennium cycles the forces of extension and archaeology begin again. Each cycle takes *Godzilla* as its origin, but passes over the films of the other series. In turn, each extension functions as its own archaeology: its own meta-cycle of death and rebirth of the Japanese nation. Each cycle extends the binomial of the large form action-image and performs an excavation of the forces of monumental and antiquarian history exploring the ethical judgement of the nuclear event of Hiroshima and Nagasaki. The popular success of these opaque film-cycles perhaps answers the question as to why, in Japan, there have been no attempts to harness the large form action-image for direct engagements with the atom bomb. The *Godzilla* movies have proved themselves equal to the task. Or perhaps it is because the *Godzilla* cycle has so effectively colonized the large form action-image that Japanese filmmakers have had to find other forms, other types of images and signs, other ways to explore the nuclear event – ways which will allow different horizons of history, other types of historical engagement.

Yet we need not immediately look away from realism for such responses. If the action-image describes the relation between situation and action, there could be said to be two primary ways in which this can occur: as well as the trajectory situation to action, as in the large form, a reversal, the trajectory action to situation. This is the small form. Such a reversal will allow filmmakers to create another realist cinema. Instead of developing milieux in need of resolution through the actions of characters, we can begin with characters, people who will reveal the situation. Similarly, just as the large form corresponded to a mode of historical practice, so will the small form. Instead of universal history, we see a history as it happens, a people's history. Rather than history from above, history from below. To begin exploring these reversals, we can do no better than to turn to Shindo Kaneto's *Lucky Dragon No. 5*. *Godzilla* began with a defined moment: the destruction of a small Japanese trawler out in the ocean. This moment gives birth to Godzilla, the *Godzilla* cycles and to the *kaiju eiga*. Yet this moment was a real event, one that would be made into a film of the small form action-image by Shindo, a very different type of action-image, creating a very different historical horizon.

II. History from below

Lucky Dragon No. 5 **(1959)**

Manakichi Kuboyama (Jukichi Uno) is dying: bathed in sweat, convulsing in agony, drifting in and out of consciousness. Around him his wife, daughters, mother, the crew members of the *Daigo Fukuryu Maru* and medical staff. In flashback: the rolling waves; from the sky, a rain of tan-coloured ash insubstantial as snowflakes falls through the complex interweaving of the ship's masts, ropes and tied sails. Aikichi dies, the acute radiation syndrome from the ash-detritus of the hydrogen bomb finally claiming him. His funeral will be attended by friends, family, and those that have cared for him during hospitalization in Tokyo. Now Aikichi is just ashes himself. His wife will carry his remains home, to Yaizu, a long journey across the country by train. Travellers will take their turn to quietly pay respect, low bows, best wishes, bouquets of flowers. His death has been announced over the radio, on TV, as newspaper headlines. The nation will mourn. Doves will be loosed into the sky.

This passing of Manakichi constitutes the final sequence of *Lucky Dragon No. 5*. Shot in black-and-white and produced by Shindo's newly formed independent film company Kindai Eiga Kyokai, the story is based upon real events. In 1954 an American hydrogen bomb – codenamed Bravo, and part of the test series Castle – was exploded near the landmass of Bikini Atoll. It was, at the time, the most powerful explosion ever created, fifteen megatons, some 1,000 times greater than the Hiroshima bomb. A trawler, the *Daigo Fukuryu Maru*, was fishing for tuna in the area. On the horizon, a white flash, the mushroom cloud. Later in the day, ash fell from the sky, the entire crew becoming exposed to nuclear fallout. Over the weeks that followed all became ill. The government intervened and complaints were made to the Americans. The Bikini Atoll affair, as it became known, became international news. After six months, with nearly all the crew in recovery, *Daigo Fukuryu Maru*'s radio operator Manakichi Kuboyama died. *Lucky Dragon No. 5* depicts these events.

However, Shindo's 'well-intentioned' film 'had to falsify on several counts', according to Richie.[42] For example, 'the director thought it necessary to place the fishing vessel much closer to the bomb test than it actually was so that the film might include some spectacle'.[43] Furthermore, Shindo 'had to disregard completely the fact that the fishermen repeatedly had been warned to stay out of the area; had been told why; and yet they still insisted upon entering it. To have acknowledged this fact would have weakened the impact, the whole meaning, of his film.'[44] The same kinds of objections regarding falsification were voiced by Richie – as was seen in Chapter 1 – with regards to *Godzilla*: cinema distorts, films dramatize. While it has since been revealed that, contra Richie, the *Daigo Fukuryu Maru* was well outside of the danger area when the bomb was dropped, the essential point is that no film can faithfully reproduce a historical moment or moments, moment for moment: this is an impossibility. The only question is rather of the type of dramatization, the kind of distortion. In *Godzilla*, the *Daigo Fukuryu Maru* became the *Eiko*, and in the first few minutes of the movie it was destroyed in the H-bomb test that awakens Godzilla. This fleeting event provided a spectacular beginning for the film: the ship ravaged by fire, flames against the night sky and reflected upon the water, slowly sinking beneath the waves. It was this event that described the situation, marked both the rise of Godzilla and the involvement of the man who would defeat the monster; it was the moment which generated the internal and external conflicts of the entire Showa series. *Lucky Dragon No. 5* distorts and dramatizes – or rather, captures – the real event in a very different way, and for a completely different purpose.

Nets and provisions have been loaded. The *Daigo Fukuryu Maru* sets out from the fishing port of Yaizu in Shizuoka Prefecture. Wives and children wave the crew off. As the ship pushes on through Japanese territorial waters, we see men landing tuna, sharks and swordfish: mallets clubbing, knives gutting. This opening section takes up over a third of the screen time of the film. Shindo captures the rhythm of the sea. This is a powerful evocation of the working life of these fishermen. The trials they have to go through to make their living and to feed their community. The disappointment when fish stocks elude them. The ancient rituals they perform for good luck. The economic basis for the decision they will make to push on out towards the Marshall Islands. Their renewed joy as once again there is catch. How they relax at night: drinking, competing at *go*, playing their musical instruments and singing sea shanties. In short, the film is concerned with the lives of these men as a collective.

After they witness the atomic explosion, everything changes. The fishermen return to port burnt black, an external sign of the internal sickness to come. Their friends stop them in the street. Their wives are concerned, their children afraid. In this way, the event at sea effects the whole community – the catch

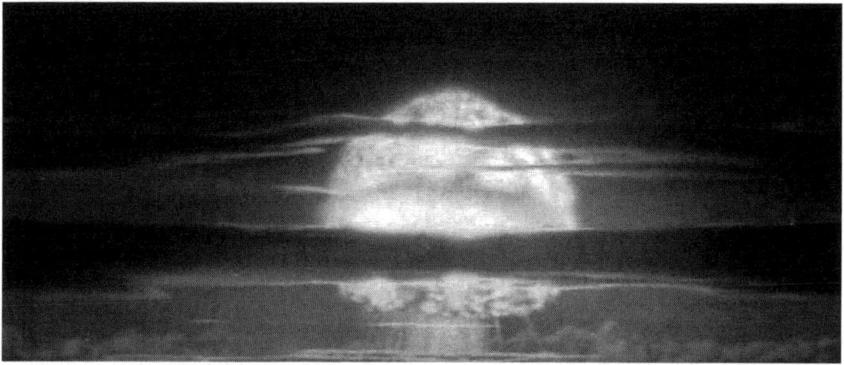

Figure 2.3 H-bomb on the horizon, *Lucky Dragon No. 5* (Shindo, 1959)

Figure 2.4 The crew of the *Daigo Fukuryu Maru* witnessing the H-bomb, *Lucky Dragon No. 5* (Shindo, 1959)

itself is feared contaminated. The men get ill. No longer able to work, transferred to Tokyo, all will eventually recover, except Aikichi. It is only in the closing moments of the film that Shindo focuses upon an individual, and even then he finds a way to describe the social aspects of the situation. Filmed in widescreen, the mise-en-scène is always crowded with family and hospital staff surrounding the dying man.

This is a very different type of film to *Godzilla*. The nuclear event is no spectacular inauguration to the film. The milieu is not described to create forces and engender actions in order to rectify the situation. Rather, we begin with actions in-themselves; it is through the behaviours of the characters that the situation is revealed. And when the nuclear explosion happens, it is the event that modifies behaviours. In short, this is no film of the large form action-image. Similarly, we are no longer concerned with universal history. In *Lucky Dragon No. 5* we discover the small form action-image and, after that, the horizon of a people's history.

Action-image (small form)

The small form action-image is composed of progressive, linear action, played out through the main character or characters. It is through such actions, and the way the characters perceive and are affected, that the situation of the world is revealed. Thus, the small form attempts to uncover the social situation as a function of characterization. Once the situation is revealed, the actions of the characters can reflect this new – disclosed – universe. Thus, on the one hand, it is not the situation that must change, but the actions of the characters. The crucial question, on the other hand, is of the situation which is not initially given in-itself, and the degree of inference of that situation which traverses the polarity of the molar to the molecular across three constitutive signs. In the small form the molar signs of composition are the index of lack and the index of equivocity; while the molecular genetic sign is the vector. The monadic, dyadic and triadic levels of the small form can be illustrated as in Table 2.2.

The signs of composition describe how an action specifies a situation through an 'index.'[45] An index is something that points to the situation, and, for Deleuze, it describes two poles of an ellipsis – that of lack or (the 'more complex') equivocity.[46] An index of lack reveals a situation through a deduction (be it reasoned or obvious) of characters' actions; the index of equivocity functions by leaving deduction open. In essence, then, in the small form situations are revealed thorough the actions of characters. Sometimes the situation is unambiguous, what was lacking is ultimately disclosed. Sometimes, however, it is left unclear how the actions relate to such situations and the situation itself can remain obscure. The genetic sign of the small form action-image is the vector, where lack and equivocity interact. Actions reveal situations through lack, but there are multiple actions and multiple situations which are 'simultaneous' and homogeneous.[47] In such a way, the degree of inference of the revealed situation traverses the trajectory of the molecular vector to the molar indices of lack and equivocity.

Lucky Dragon No. 5 is a film of the small form action-image. In the first instance, the formal structure of the film describes an action → situation → new action formula. Action: the behaviours of the fishermen of the *Daigo Fukuryu Maru*; their relationships, their working lives, the problems that they encounter. Situation: the American hydrogen bomb tests in the Pacific – which appear as if from nowhere, out of the blue. New action: the men of the *Daigo Fukuryu Maru* function in a different way – everything has changed, their relationships with their families, their community and the world at large. In the second instance, there is the question of the type of sign. With *Lucky Dragon No. 5* the revealed

Table 2.2 Action-image (small form)

action-image (small form)		
molar composition		molecular genesis
index of lack	index of equivocity	vector

situation, that of the atom bomb, is immediately and unequivocally given at S. This is an index of lack. In other words, through action (A and A'), the situation (S) is revealed; it is as if S traverses the succession of images which constitutes the behaviours of the characters, retroactively (A←S) and reactively (S→A'). In this way, both the actions and the new actions are a well-defined index of an unambiguous situation. *Lucky Dragon No. 5* ultimately explores how the nuclear situation inherent in the Japanese social scene permeates the lives of the collective.

As we saw earlier in this chapter, the historical conceptualization that aligned with the small form was described as a recording of events as they happened by a witness or actor. Deleuze identifies this process as a '*habitus*', where the actions of characters describe a particular situation.[48] In other words, rather than the large form action-image with its vast historical sweep, its parallels and elision of difference, we have a more intimate situation. There is, instead, a people's history. One way to explore such a concept of people's history through *habitus* is in reference to the work of Pierre Bourdieu, who reinvigorated and popularized the term. As Julien Vincent puts it, Bourdieu 'was hostile to any philosophy of history and indeed to any sociological concept or statistical category constructed "from above"'.[49] Against universal history and its laws of the monumental, antiquarian and critical, Bourdieu focused upon cultural patterns and economic trends as process. In this way, it has something in common with the Communist Party Historians' Group in the UK; historians – such as Eric Hobsbawm, Christopher Hill and E. P. Thompson – who focused upon the role of the masses, the common people, in history. Indeed, Bourdieu translated Thompson's *The Making of the English Working Class* (1963) into French. His work can be characterized as attempting to address 'the question of history "from below"'.[50]

Bourdieu, *habitus*

We can begin by approaching Bourdieu's conception of history through its technical aspect, although we will be able to simplify the method a little later. This technical aspect can be captured through the formula: practice = [(*habitus*) (capital)] + field; where practice is a function of *habitus*, capital and field.[51] The *habitus* is the past of each individual, and of the collective to which that individual belongs. It operates unconsciously in the present. *Habitus*, therefore, shapes perceptions, affects and actions. As Bourdieu puts it in *Outline of a*

Theory of Practice (1972): 'each individual system of dispositions may be seen as a structural variant of … [the] group.'[52] Individual *habitus* is related to group *habitus*; '"personal" style', for Bourdieu 'is never more than a deviation in relation to the style of a period or class.'[53] Capital refers to the resources distributed throughout social space-time. In this way, it encompasses a number of aspects: economic capital (money), cultural capital (learning, qualifications), symbolic capital (status), social capital (group networks) and so forth. Finally, field describes the external social spaces of the present, institutions such as the family, the law, the education system. Bourdieu sees the field as game-like, commenting: 'the social fields, which are the products of a long, slow process of autonomization … are therefore, so to speak, games.'[54] In other words, each has a unique internal logic, its own rules. The human is born into these games with resources and dispositions 'unaware'.[55] Practice, then, is not a universal law, but rather a function of a specific nexus of geo-historical co-ordinates, co-ordinates that can evolve and change over time. The critical point would be to become conscious of such practices in the present; uncover the dispositions, resources and games, explore and define their relations.

We can simplify matters by aligning Bourdieu's formula with Deleuze's small form, practice as action; and action an index of *habitus*, capital and field as situation. This nexus can be tabulated as in Table 2.3. Pursuing this association, the poles of molar composition and molecular genesis could, in turn, be seen as the degree to which on-screen actions (practice, behaviours) can reveal or disclose the situation (history as a nexus of *habitus*, capital and field). The molar would allow practice to be reasonably identified and in turn allow new actions to unfold. No doubt there are many ways in which the molar can become molecular: people cut off from or escaping their past; the present destroyed by ill fortune or re-orientated by revolution; a field in which the rules of the game are fractured. The point is the molecular would be much harder to define, involve various different changes in *habitus*, capital and field, and generate

Table 2.3 The action-image (small form) and people's history

A	practice (unaware)	[(*habitus*) (capital)] + field
S	revealed *habitus* revealed capital revealed field	past: human and the collective resources distributed throughout social space-time the social field: game
A'	practice (conscious)	revealed [(*habitus*) (capital)] + field

a dispersed series of new actions. Similarly, we can move from these dyadic poles to the triadic signs of the small form action-image, and in so doing map the degrees to which practice reveals history through the material on-screen images of a film. Thus, the index of lack would describe a solid perception of the state of affairs, practice would be functional with regard to easily defined historical co-ordinates, which once revealed would unambiguously determine the reconfiguration of the actions of the characters. With the index of equivocity, practice would be unable to clearly reveal the state of affairs; perhaps one of the elements of *habitus* or capital or field remains a void. Accordingly, the situation remains ambiguous, undecidable; the new actions may or may not be the correct response. With the vector it would be as if the terms of the formula could be applied differently to different groups. Each of the formulae would play out in their own way, could be in-themselves each pole of the index, yet it would be in their correspondence that situations would be described: history as a series of competing narratives, or vectors, multiple responses which nonetheless describe a homogeneous milieu. Each film of the small form action-image will tend toward one of the three signs, and in so doing reveal a particular variation of history from below – people's history.

With *Lucky Dragon No. 5* the historical nexus of *habitus*, capital and field is revealed through the practice of the twenty-three crew members of the *Daigo Fukuryu Maru*. They are described throughout the film *en masse*, as a group with a common purpose, who emerge from a common history. They are working men, family men, traditional seafarers. And when, toward the end of the film, Aikichi is individualized as an extraction from the collective, this is done so as a variation of group experience. Their *habitus*, in this way, is clearly circumscribed. Similarly, they share common resources, their capital is the environment of the sea and a trawler that has seen better days. The field in which they operate is catch and trade as barter across the sea and Yaizu community. Their practice, then, is defined with precision through the images Shindo projects on-screen. The event of the hydrogen bomb, in this way, disrupts everything – and the film is an attempt to describe that disruption in relation to the modifications undergone by practice. The *habitus* fractures, their group dispositions are broken open with respect to family and community relations. The effects are also seen in the domains of capital and field. Their economic situation is devastated. This crisis will be further disrupted by the Americans' talk of compensation, depicted as a cynical response laden with – as we will see – certain terms and conditions. Finally, field; the rules of the game are fundamentally changed. From their embedded co-ordinates as fishermen, they become patients in the hospital system and pawns in political machinations. Shindo conveys this masterfully: as the crew members are captured in these domains they disappear from the screen – once active participants in the milieu (A) they are reconstituted as passive victims (A'). The film instead focuses upon the relevant officials. In a key scene, Japanese doctors face American politicos, either side of a table. The Americans want to help; in order to do so they must run their own tests. A Japanese doctor sees through this ruse: accuses them of wanting to use the crew for medical research – you have never once apologized for what has happened to the *Daigo Fukuryu Maru*, just as you have never apologized for the atomic attacks on Hiroshima and Nagasaki. The Americans remain silent.

Lucky Dragon No. 5 reveals itself to be a film of lucid rage, an index of the on-going nuclear situation in post-war Japan for people living and dying in the present. The small form action-image and its corresponding enunciation of a people's history, in this way, are proven to be able to powerfully describe the horizon of the Japanese nuclear legacy. Such a conception of image and history will subsequently be brought to bear directly upon the atomic attacks of Hiroshima and Nagasaki.

Barefoot Gen (1983)

The atom bomb explodes over Hiroshima. The mushroom cloud unfolds like a red rose over the city below. Then silence. A white light washes over the streets, flooding homes, public buildings and open spaces, lapping into doorways, and up over balconies, drowning men, women and children. A little girl stands on the road, her contours black lines. Holding a red balloon, she looks up into the sky. The balloon bursts. Vivid colours frame her. Her pretty orange dress becomes rags. Now naked, her hair is burnt away, her eyes melt from her face. Her body cooked brown. A soldier turns towards the light, his uniform is ripped open, his body twists in a slow-motion spiral to the ground. An old man, his head torn from his neck, hair and beard burnt away. A young woman with a baby wrapped to her back; as their clothes burn, the baby tumbles. Pure instinct, the mother's arms – already skinless – reach for the now blood-red object. Buildings are dismantled: Hiroshima Castle, then the Prefectural Hall. The city is sucked up through the stalk of the mushroom cloud, up into its arterial-red gills, as the margins roll and grow. The screen goes red. The thunder rumbles on. The mushroom cloud dwarfs the city. The screen goes black.

Such is the moment of the *pika* in Masaki's *Barefoot Gen*. Susan J. Napier's analysis of the formal structure of the film is beyond reproach: *Barefoot Gen* 'is obsessed with action and with the temporal … particularly with two temporal moments, the period of time leading up to the bombing of Hiroshima and the period immediately following it.'[56] The cataclysm divides the film absolutely. As I will show, *Barefoot Gen* is, in this way, a film of the small form action-image.

At the beginning of the movie, Japanese planes bomb Pearl Harbor: '8th December 1941 – Japan began the Pacific War against the USA and UK.' Two years later, B29s carpet-bomb Japanese cities. Then, the image of Fat Boy: 'at the same time … the Manhattan Project was in progress … the atomic bomb was almost ready.' Cut to a Hiroshima street, early morning. A warden shouts: 'The air raid threat is over! All clear.' A family emerge from a shelter: first Gen; next his younger brother Shinji; his older sister Eiko; then his father and pregnant mother. As Gen stands in the dawn light, his stomach rumbles: 'I'm hungry.'

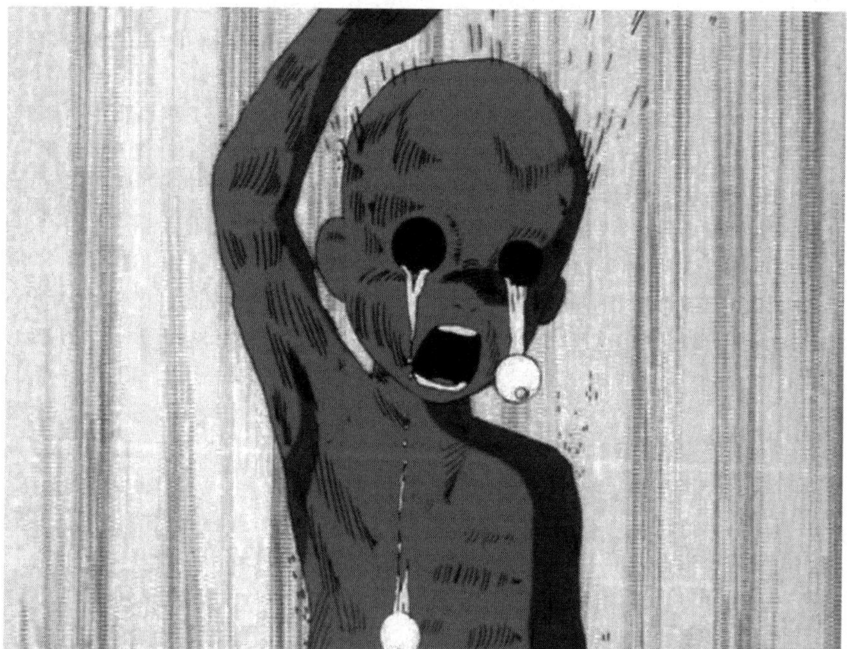

Figure 2.5 A little girl at the moment of the *pika*, *Barefoot Gen* (Masaki, 1983)

Hunger: this is the pervasive condition of the family and the community, circumstances that are described through each of the characters' daily activities. At the market an officer declares he is off to the front for the glory of Japan. The crowds follow his unit singing a patriotic song. Gen and his brother sing along – though with the subversive innocence of kids they do so with an alternative lyric: 'Isn't it a horrible place, the military? With tin bowls and tin chopsticks. We're not Buddhas, just one bowl of rice is not enough.' The government canteen is distributing soup, thick, for once, with vegetables. But the father has run out of ration tickets. 'What a society. You can't buy food even if you have money.' So it goes on; at home there is one potato which the boys fight over, before Eiko reminds them their mother is pregnant. The next morning, another air raid warning, and the family leave the house for the shelter. 'Isn't it strange,' says Gen, 'all the cities have been bombed, but they have not touched Hiroshima.' Later in the day, their mother collapses. 'Fatigue and malnutrition' is the doctor's diagnosis. That night the boys raid a priest's compound and steal a carp for her. The next morning – the third day – another air raid, but once again the plane passes silently overhead, it is over before it began. Gen heads off to school. Silently, another plane traverses the sky. Then, the atom bomb explodes.

Afterwards, Gen awakes. The city is gone. Bodies burnt to a crisp. Naked zombies, dripping flesh, eyeballs hanging, entrails dragging behind them as they stumble through the rubble. A horse on fire gallops through the carnage. Gen runs to his house. With his mother now, they watch his father, sister and brother as they are burned alive under the collapsed structure. 'Mum it's hot,' cries little Shinji. Horrors multiply. With the cataclysm, the situation is revealed, made manifest ('all the cities have been bombed, but they have not touched Hiroshima'); and in so doing, the functional behaviour of the characters are reconfigured. In the move from action to new action, hunger becomes starvation; hard times become harder still; and Gen is transformed from a dependent child into someone who must provide for his mother and his newly born sister.

Action → situation → new action: a very powerful film of the small form action-image. Once again this formula has allowed, as it did with *Lucky Dragon No. 5*, a direct depiction of the Japanese nuclear situation; as will the structure accordingly dovetail with a people's history. Perhaps such similarities are a factor of both films being based upon real events – *Barefoot Gen* is autobiographical, by way of a source text, a Japanese *manga* from 1973 by Nakazawa Keiji. Yet there are significant differences between the films: one is black-and-white, live-action and social-realist, focusing upon the collective; the other a vibrantly coloured *anime*, a family drama which extracts a child as centre. Another difference occurs in reference to the signs. For while *Barefoot Gen* may initially appear, as *Lucky Dragon* before it, to be of the index of lack, such a designation will ultimately undergo a transformation – a transformation which will in turn reveal a secret and radical horizon of history.

Index of lack

With *Barefoot Gen* the situation seems to be an index of lack, the situation of the atom bomb immediately determined at S (at the centre of the film). The nuclear event appears as a caesura, instantaneously changing everything: A (before the bomb) becoming A' (after the bomb), focusing in upon one character, reconfiguring his behaviours. It may thus appear that *Barefoot Gen* describes a passive acceptance of fate. Yet, this is not the case. If actions cannot rectify the situation, they can react to it, adapt. Napier, in this way – and once again

Figure 2.6 Naked *hibakusha* zombies, *Barefoot Gen* (Masaki, 1983)

– says almost everything. While *Barefoot Gen* 'fits into the "victims' history" model' of Japanese cinema of the atom bomb, it only does so as critique.[57] 'The overall tone of the film', for Napier, 'is very far from the mood of passivity and powerlessness that pervades [victims' history films] … in many aspects [it] is a … powerful anti-war film with a strongly activist subtext.'[58] The term 'victims' history' refers to the way in which the Japanese people are depicted as 'helpless victims of a corrupt and evil conspiracy between the government and the military'.[59] Napier describes this view as emerging through the collaboration of the occupied nation's government and the Allied forces 'to create an image of a postwar democratic Japan that would free the Japanese from an inescapable fascist and military past'.[60] The idea was to scapegoat the war on the military and government, allowing the people to be 'liberated from the dark shadows of war guilt and recrimination'.[61] One of the key ways in which this is achieved is through a zero-sum formula: Pearl Harbor ↔ Hiroshima/Nagasaki, allowing 'the atomic bombing to cancel out responsibility for Pearl Harbor'.[62] The crucial aspect is that the refiguring of the Pacific War as simply the Asian aspect of the Second World War erases the civilian euphoria of the military triumphs of the China War which morphed seamlessly into the wider world conflict. On the face of it, this is exactly the case with *Barefoot Gen*, which sets the initial historical horizon as the Japanese attack on Hawaii.

Yet, writes Napier, 'the film's narrative, pacing and imagery refuse to uphold such a one-note interpretation'.[63] Accordingly we can discover ways in which *Barefoot Gen* escapes such victimology. For instance, even at such a late stage in the war, the Japanese people in general are supportive of the on-going military endeavour. The parade at the beginning of the film makes this clear. In the second half of the film, a few days after the nuclear attack, the Emperor surrenders on behalf of the nation. Gen and his mother are collecting the skulls of their family from the burnt ruins of their home; in the street, people are crying that the war has ended, that Japan will not continue to fight. There is a palpable echo of shame. Gen's mother, however, presents an opposing position. She cannot believe anyone would want the war to continue. Earlier in the film Gen asked his father when the war will end. His father replied: 'It won't be long. Japan will lose the war.' Gen then asked: 'Why do we continue to fight?' The father comments: 'Our leaders are making mistakes and the army is out of its mind.' Then: 'I'm not patriotic. And I'm proud of it. A war which kills so many people can't be right … the only war worth fighting is one that saves lives.' As Napier puts it, 'the narrative momentum in these early scenes is of resistance rather than acquiescence'.[64] If such a move may appear as cynical post-war hindsight, this is to miss the point. As Deleuze comments with respect to the small form: 'it was necessary to start from modes of behaviour to infer from them the social situation which was not given an in-itself, but which itself referred back to struggles and modes of behaviour which were always in action or in transformation.'[65] In this way the *habitus* 'indicated … differences within a single civilisation. Thus one moved from the behaviour to the situation in such a way that, from the one to the other, there was the possibility of a "creative interpretation of reality"'.[66]

In this way we return to the formula of Bourdieu. *Habitus*: the community appears with a common purpose, to support the war effort, and emerges from a common history. The canvas is broad, working men and women, and their children. Yet Gen's family, despite being a part of the community, appear set apart through their resistance. A film of victims' history would have depicted the people in general as passive, accepting their fate. Instead, *Barefoot Gen* shows how the people were supportive of the fascist-militarist government and the war effort. Furthermore, rather than a consistent civilian front, there are variations, differences which manifest in the capital the community has at its disposal. Common resources are divided along feudalistic lines, the military, the priesthood and the people: status means everything. The upper echelons of society have food in abundance (the priest has fish as decoration); the military are given food (albeit of poor quality); while the people undergo strict rationing. Yet they are all operating within the same field; the community of *Barefoot Gen* describes the external social situation of the present, institutions such as the family, the law and the education system. Their practice, then, is defined with precision through the images Masaki projects on-screen. The event of the nuclear bombing of Hiroshima disrupts everything – and the film is thus an attempt to describe that disruption in relation to the modifications of practice: social hierarchy collapses, institutions are destroyed and the already perilous economic situation is devastated. In this way, the atomic attack appears as a year zero, one which brings with it horror, but which ultimately fulfils the prophecy of Gen's father and will bring to an end the insanities of Imperial Japan.

Index of equivocity

However, things may be far more complex than this analysis allows. There is a reason to consider the film as instead obeying the index of equivocity. For Deleuze, this sign does not simply reveal a situation that was initially absent (index of lack), but instead allows the situation to appear as having another facet, a 'double centre'.[67] Deleuze puts it thus: 'it is as if an action … concealed a slight difference, which was nevertheless sufficient to relate it simultaneously to two quite different situations.'[68] These two situations can be 'worlds apart … one … real and the other apparent or illusory'; however, the two situations reflect upon each other.[69] In short, if the index of lack references a simple situation, the index of equivocity discovers a secret complexity: situation$_1$ and situation$_2$.

Gen and his little brother/accomplice Shinji have stolen a carp to feed their pregnant mother. However, Gen fears that the priest ('Mr Carp'), from whom the fish was filched and who discovered them in the act, will tell their parents. Despite being able to convince the incensed priest, after a sound beating, that this carp will save the life of their mother and their unborn sibling, they later spy him approaching their house. The boys hide out as long as they are able, before heading home. As they walk back through the night, Gen says 'be prepared for punishment', and the camera pans vertically to capture the night sky. A star twinkles. But Gen is not punished for the theft. Mr Carp has celebrated the boys to their parents as loving sons and even left a treat of dumplings for them. Their parents and sister look on in admiration. The next morning, however, delivers the atom bomb. Gen is in the street, talking to a school friend. They are looking up into the sky. There is a twinkle in daylight, one that exactly mirrors the twinkle of the star the night before. A B29 appears. What is the connection between these two moments of twinkling? Why such a resonance?

In the first instance, there is the act of theft itself, and its immediate response. Gen and Shinji head off to commit the crime dressed as soldiers, marching as if to war. The crime, however, is revealed as being in good faith, sanctioned both by the priest (as representative of state Shinto) and the family (as representative of the community). Indeed, the crime is reconfigured so that it is no longer a crime. It is instead a necessary action performed in order to feed their mother and her child. As Gen's father has said, 'the only war worth fighting is one that saves lives'. Here, then, it is as if we encounter a justification for Imperial Japan's ambitions, the Japanese Greater East Asia Co-Prosperity Sphere, created to secure the nation's interests as well as expel the Americans and Europeans from Asia; and a justification for Pearl Harbor, the response to the pre-Second World War American embargo on Japan. In the second instance, there is the difference between the two responses to the theft, one real and one illusionary. The twinkling of the star negotiates the opposition of the two situations. On the one hand, there is that of the priest/family. On the other there is the atom bomb. The 'punishment' that Gen was expecting – indeed, that he believed he deserved – is displaced from the one to the other. In this way, the nuclear attack is positioned not as a zero sum game, a response to the bombing of Pearl Harbor, but rather as punishment, a punishment far in excess of that for which Japan enacted its imperial project. *Barefoot Gen* is thus a very different film from *Lucky Dragon No. 5*. While both describe a people's history, *Lucky Dragon* sees the Japanese unequivocally as passive victims of American aggression, figured through the disappearance of the collective from the screen and the death of Aikichi. With *Barefoot Gen* the circumstances are very different. Gen is selected through the deaths in his family, becoming the centre of the film. Furthermore, the film designates an impasse: an active revolutionary resistance to Japanese state belligerence that continues the war; and an active reactionary cry against the American deployment of the atom bomb in response to Japan's natural imperial rights. In *Barefoot Gen*, the moment of the *pika* in history is, as Deleuze puts it in respect to the index of equivocity, an 'irresolvable image'.[70]

III. History and the future

From composition to genesis

As we have seen thus far, the action-image has two fundamental formulae. Some films tend toward the actions of the characters resolving the situation. This is the large form action-image, the signs of composition being the milieu and the binomial. Some films tend toward the actions of characters revealing the situation. This is the small form, the signs of composition being indices of lack and equivocity. As Deleuze puts it, the 'Small and Large do not merely designate forms of action, but … ways of conceiving and seeing a "subject", a story or a script'.[71] This has involved a distribution of intensities across the molar signs and concepts of history to which both refer. The large form through its laws and variations, connective to monumental, antiquarian and critical history;

the small form as a linear unfolding describing a people's history, a history as it happens. Accordingly, realism, the action-image, has proven to be a fecund procedure for the creation of cinematic images of the Japanese nuclear event: from the opaque depictions of the Showa *Godzilla kaiju eiga* cycle through to the direct depictions of *Barefoot Gen* as family drama and the social-realism of *Lucky Dragon No. 5*. On the one hand we have the nuclear event captured up in vast historical forces. On the other, we have the nuclear event, be it the attacks on Hiroshima and Nagasaki or Cold War atomic testing in the Pacific, portrayed with respect to individual and collective experience. From Showa *Godzilla* to *Barefoot Gen* and *Lucky Dragon No. 5*, it is as if we pass from wide shot to close-up – a movement which indicates an essential polarity. From large to small, from universal history to people's history, the tendency appears to be that of a vast stratification of impersonal historical forces – or, the forces of history revealed in the ways they act upon individuals and groups.

No doubt, this complementarity of molar action-images could be said to offer an implicit critique of one form by the other. When *Lucky Dragon No. 5* films the *Daigo Fukuryu Maru* disaster, can we not but see this as a response to the opaque depiction of the sinking of the *Eiko* at the beginning of *Godzilla*. Yet the indirect approach of the Showa *Godzilla* cycle allows a complex exploration of historical forces on a scale which *Barefoot Gen* and *Lucky Dragon No. 5* cannot equal. From the perspective of the universal, such a people's history must appear limited in scope. From the perspective of people's history, however, the exposition of such laws and generalizations elides the horror of the *pika* and the suffering of the *hibakusha*. Such an opposition of molar action-images and their attendant conceptions of history would seem, accordingly, to demand a Japanese cinema of the atom bomb that exposes and makes explicit such critiques: to answer the implicit demands of one form and one conception of history by the other.

Such demands begin to be answered by the genetic signs of the action-image: the imprint of the large form and the vector of the small. The action-image, realism, which created the complementarities of the large and the small forms, is generated by a simple relation, that of situation and action. The moment of genesis thus contains within itself the seeds of composition for both molar forms. Accordingly, the genetic sign of the small form will appear as a kind of deformation of the large form, and the genetic sign of the large a kind of deformation of the small. Similarly, with regard to historical horizons, it is possible to accentuate the way in which universal and people's history impact one another;

the way in which one inhabits or inhibits the other, and in so doing performs a critique. Two Japanese atom bomb films from the 1980s put these genetic forces into flow in an exemplary manner: Miyazaki Hayao's *Nausicaa of the Valley of the Wind* and Otomo Katsuhiro's *Akira*. Both *anime*, each has something of the small and the large; each explores aspects of universal and people's history. And to do so, these films adopt a new perspective – no longer is the present explored in respect to the past; the present and the past are instead appraised from a future state. Accordingly, the small form is allowed to deform the large, the large to deform the small; and each foregrounds the critique of the historical conception of that which it deforms.

Nausicaa of the Valley of the Wind (1984)

Nausicaa of the Valley of the Wind is set some thousand years in the future, a now-mythical nuclear war having caused the collapse of twentieth-century civilization. The atomic legacy is the Toxic Forest, a primeval jungle that has infested much of the planet, creating plants the size of trees, trees the size of castles: incredibly beautiful, yet deadly to humans. A double injunction: Ohmu (giant armoured slug-like creatures with fiery red eyes and golden tentacles) protect the forest; and the plants thereof ejaculate poisonous spores into the atmosphere, allowing it to proliferate and advance, swallowing cities and towns. The Valley of the Wind is one of the last places on Earth relatively immune to such infestation. A powerful sea breeze, from which the valley gets its name, sweeps across its fields and over the desert to the forest beyond, keeping the spores at bay. Or for the most part: discovering infestations is a continual chore, a task that every man, woman and child treats with the utmost importance. But people are happy there, among the medieval windmills and watermills, orchards and farmsteads.

Yet everything is about to change. The Valley of the Wind becomes the staging ground for a war between Tolmekia and Pejite, two relatively technologically advanced city states. These warring states are locked in a conflict with a long-forgotten cause, both out to destroy the other. Furthermore, a nuclear weapon has been discovered, a remainder of the millennia before, and Tolmekia and Pejite believe whoever controls it will triumph over its rival and the Toxic Forest. It is such a situation that threatens the very existence of the Valley.

Figure 2.7 'Amazing … no wonder the world was incinerated.' One thousand years after the *pika*, *Nausicaa of the Valley of the Wind* (Miyazaki, 1984)

Philip Brophy can be seen to describe *Nausicaa* as if being of the large form action-image. While the film 'subverts the narrative binary of warring sides', focusing instead upon the people of the Valley of the Wind, in so doing it 'introduces a far greater force for them to combat: the … Earth'.[72] The film, in essence, describes the human-versus-nature conflict: Tolmekia, Pejite and the Valley are each in their own way attempting to survive the encroachment of the Toxic Forest. Brophy is correct to see the conflict between the warring states as a background. However, *Nausicaa* does not in this way reconstitute a binomial. Contra Brophy, Valley and Forest are not in conflict; the narrative line of the film gradually reveals that maintaining a balance between the two is essential to the survival of all species on the planet. There is no binary opposition between the Earth and humanity, just the illusion of one. The Toxic Forest is in reality a surface mass of vegetative processes that are purging the earth of its radioactive legacy. It is Nausicaa's task to reveal the situation as being an eco-system. The film, accordingly, appears to be of the small form action-image. Yet if this is a film of the small form, it is a very special one, that of the genetic sign, the vector. Here actions give rise to 'successive situations' each 'equivocal in itself' and together forming a 'broken line'.[73] There are thus different zones in which the action unfolds: the Toxic Forest, the Valley of the Wind, the desert that separates them, Tolmekian and Pejite spaces, and – most secret of all – underneath the

Toxic Forest, where life begins again. As well as horizontals there are verticals: ground, underground and air – the sky describing the thick clouds of spores, the wind from the sea, and the trajectories which carry the Tolmekian and Pejite ships. This ecosystem is not only spatial, but also temporal: the present, the past and the future – there is a process revealed, and the Toxic Forest and its creatures have as much right to exist as do the humans with their villages and cities. The film's trajectories, then, consist in linking these 'heterogeneous elements' which will 'interconnect directly'.[74]

It is such an interconnection, or eco-system, of horizontal, vertical and temporal heterogeneous elements that allows *Nausicaa* to be considered a film of the vector. This vectoring refers us to the film's conception of history. For the dimensions of *Nausicaa* sanction two series that describe a breaking open of the line: simultaneous, in background and foreground, operating at different scales. In the background: the warring states. Tolmekia and Pejite are the inheritors of binomial forces locked in an endless battle for supremacy, the situation of a war lasting one thousand years, each with the desire to assert its identity over the other. Such a configuration describes the laws of the large form creating monumental and antiquarian conceptions of history. Yet neither of these forces emerges as being in the right; the ethical judgement is stymied. Or rather displaced, occurring in the foreground through the central character of Nausicaa who must reveal the co-ordinates of the eco-system: the evil of the conflict described by the warring states, the righteousness of the balance between Valley and Forest, civilization and nature, humanity and Ohmu. It is the actions of Princess Nausicaa that will reveal this more fundamental situation, this more fundamental truth as an outcome of a broken line. We thus no longer have a simple linear form, where the situation is discovered through an index. The vector is enacted through and between series. While both background and foreground describe an index of lack (the uncovering of a determined state of affairs), the relation between foreground and background forms an index of equivocity (the alternatives between the conflict of the warring states and balance between Valley and Forest). It is the simultaneity and scale of these series that retains the characteristics of both indices and relates them through the vector.

Nausicaa describes – through such a space – a nexus of various group dispositions, different modes of economic, geographical and social capital, as well as diverse social fields across and between Tolmekia, Pejite and the Valley. Yet it is the revelation of Nausicaa that at one and the same time both creates a people's history as well as allowing this history from below to critique the vastness of a history from above, a universal history that threatens as an encompasser. *Nausicaa* reveals the simultaneities of these two heterogeneous series at differing scales. This vector therefore elides the successive linearity of temporality – a before and after: peace emerging from the exhaustions of war, harmony after the ravages of conflict. The vector is instead successive in its spatiality: a becoming conscious of the possibility of breaking open the temporal line. It is this that allows the critique of universal history which would condemn Japan and the world to the repetition of the same. *Nausicaa*, set in the future and offering a displaced view on the present in the context of the past, sees it as possible for Japan – and indeed the world – to escape a cycle of destruction heralded by the nuclear attacks on Hiroshima and Nagasaki and threatened by the Cold War between the USSR and USA. Japan – as a people – can lead the way in such revelations. Such a truth is revealed in the opening moments of *Nausicaa*.

Outside, in the night, the wind blows across the hills, grasslands, orchards and fields of the idyllic valley. The old and blind wise woman in service of dying King Jihl, Oh-Baba, expounds on the tapestry set on the ancient stone wall of the throne room. Even though she can no longer see the images depicted, she remembers them intimately. 'See that man …? After one thousand years of darkness, he will come, clad in blue, surrounded by fields of gold to restore

Figure 2.8 Nausicaa, Ohmu tentacles holding her aloft, *Nausicaa of the Valley of the Wind* (Miyazaki, 1984)

mankind's connection with the Earth that was destroyed.' Nausicaa, the young daughter of Jihl, who has not noticed the detail of the tapestry before nor heard the story, listens entranced. Oh-Baba tells Nausicaa that Lord Yupa, a ronin warrior and old friend to her father, is searching for the man in blue. To find him is his destiny. Laughing at the aged seer's mythic view of the world, he instead claims to be searching for the secret of the Toxic Forest, to understand it, and so know if humanity has any chance of survival. 'I want to know the truth.' The man in blue will be revealed as Nausicaa; the field of gold as Ohmu tentacles holding her aloft. Nausicaa does not restore balance; she reveals it as being an already-here. Nausicaa is not harbinger of a new Earth emerging from a death and rebirth, but reveals it as an always possible. In so doing she averts a repetition of the nuclear event.

Akira (1988)

Tetsuo, somehow, has unleashed the power of Akira. It is a power he is unable to control. Screaming with agony, his flesh begins to mutate, his cells multiply at an exponential rate. The tan skin and pink muscle of what remains of his right arm, now reconstructed in metal, bubbles and boils. His shirt is ripped open as his chest expands; his body becomes a bloated bulk of seething meat; his epidermis

Figure 2.9 Becoming *pika* – Tetsuo mutates with the power of Akira, *Akira* (Otomo, 1988)

unable to contain his boiling fat. Forty feet tall, more foetus than the young man he once was, Tetsuo stumbles forward. The screen cannot contain him. Tendrils shoot from his fingers, incorporating the elements of the world around, people and objects. The structure of Neo-Tokyo stadium begins to crumble at his touch, his weight destroying the infrastructure. A light emerges from the centre, a perfect sphere blindingly white. It expands, wrecking all in its path, enveloping the seething mass of Tetsuo, swallowing the stadium, then city blocks. Forces reach equilibrium, before collapsing in upon themselves, leaving an immense crater. Shock waves spread out, and what remains of the city collapses in clouds of dust. So ends *Akira*.

Akira can be compared and contrasted with *Nausicaa* point for point. It too is a film set in the future offering a displaced view on the present in the context of the past. However, it is a film that uses the large form action-image and universal history to explicitly critique the small form and people's history. In so doing it describes a very different image of the legacy of the nuclear attacks on Hiroshima and Nagasaki: the impossibility of escaping such cycles of destruction due to the monstrous nature of human desires.

The ending of *Akira* echoes the opening of the film: World War III, '1988.7.16 Tokyo', a massive white light envelops the city, wiping it from the face of the Earth. Skip forward thirty-odd years – society is in free-fall, traditional Japanese

Figure 2.10 World War III, '1988.7.16 Tokyo', *Akira* (Otomo, 1988)

values have fragmented, the youth are out of control, unconditional respect for those in power completely erased. Neo-Tokyo is composed of zones, ranging from the steel and glass of the affluent areas to the crumbling graffitied concrete districts reserved for the poor. From this milieu two teenage characters are extracted, Kaneda as captain of a biker gang and Tetsuo, his lieutenant, always in Kaneda's shadow. As the film progresses their paths will bifurcate, Tetsuo becoming involved in secret government experiments, Kaneda in terrorist activities with a revolutionary organization. Freda Freiberg writes that the film 'employs the most sophisticated filmic techniques (fast-paced editing and multiplicity of camera set-ups) of the action cinema'.[75] Yet ultimately it exceeds the norms of such a form, employing 'a confusing plethora of characters; a disjointed, almost incoherent, narrative which incorporates in its frenetic, hysterical course … SF, teen movies, action thriller, horror and social satire elements'.[76] Violent action-image sequences dominate, duels form discrete sequences, dispersing the violence across a vast cast of characters and groups: the military, the government, the revolutionaries, scientists, a Shintoesque religious cult and the gangs of disenfranchised youth. Each sequence places one group against another, the conflicts played out through increasingly violent episodes, the violence encompassing – toward the end of the film – every image, permeating the mise-en-scène of every frame.

Akira is thus clearly a film of the large form action-image, but of a very special type. The SAS' formula undergoes a fracturing, becoming S1 → A1 → S2 → A2 → S3 and so on. Passing through this are the divided and opposing forces of Kaneda and Tetsuo, each of whom seems to extract and embody the violence that traverses the milieu. Orphans, abandoned, disenfranchised, dislocated – one bullied as a child, the other a loner, both looking for revenge against society. In this way, these two characters embody the violence in the milieu, which traverses their bodies, is imprinted upon their forms. *Akira* is a film of the genetic sign of the large form action-image. This is the impression, 'the inner, but visible, link between the permeating situation and the explosive action', that which 'appears on the outside' of the character as an imprint of 'what happens inside' – thus the mutation of Tetsuo at the end of the film.[77] The imprint is not just internal to, not just traversing the exteriority of the characters; it encompasses objects which relate that character to the world. The emotional object central to the film is Akira. Kaneda asks 'what the hell is this Akira thing?' His girlfriend Kai responds 'the ultimate energy'. Akira is a cypher, used to overcome the spectre of impossibility and embody the atom bomb. 2019, 1988, 1945: the nuclear events that cyclically destroy Japan.

For Freiberg, the moment of the Akira-Tetsuo *pika* which concludes the film is not simply carnage as spectacle, it also has a spiritual dimension: 'it is not the end of the world. In fact, he appears to become one with the cosmos, to be liberated from the torments of the flesh and the world into a kind of divine spiritual essence.'[78] Similarly 'Kanada survives the holocaust … and returns to the real world, but not before experiencing the most exhilarating journeys through time and space … we experience with him the erasure of the boundaries between the past and the present and future, between exteriority and interiority, between fantasy and reality, between body and spirit.'[79] *Akira* is, in this way, 'frightening but cathartic – a release and relief'; the final devastation will 'destroy the oppressive society' as well as 'enable its rebirth.'[80] Freiberg's analysis is inspired by that of Alan Wolf: 'in Japan the underside of the imported modernization narrative is the myth of cyclical rebirth, of endless eternal desire and suffering.'[81] Japan has 'the ability to stay, survive, be reborn … the ultimate symbol of that truth is the historical experience of the atomic bomb and the devastating destruction of Japan.'[82]

This analysis is only half the story, however. The film may well be of the large form and of universal history, yet in fracturing these co-ordinates and exploring the impression it offers a critique of the small form and people's history. *Akira*, in this way, describes the people as the molecular elements of an aggregated history. The monstrous form of Tetsuo which ends the movie is merely the externalization of what was in him and the society of which he was part from the very beginning. 'Even the most repressive and the most deadly forms of social production are produced by desire within the organisation', write Deleuze and Guattari in *Anti-Oedipus*.[83] 'The fundamental problem of political philosophy is … why do people still tolerate being humiliated and enslaved, to such a point, indeed, that they actually want humiliation and slavery not only for others but for themselves?'[84] Deleuze and Guattari respond by echoing Wilhelm Reich, who 'refuses to accept ignorance or illusion on the part of the masses as an explanation of fascism … no, the masses were not innocent dupes; at a certain point, under a certain set of conditions, they wanted fascism.'[85] Rather, 'desire produces reality'.[86] In *Akira*, the sign of the imprint of the large form describes the genetic conditions which englobe the small form; ultimately such an englobing sees people's history as being encompassed by universal history.

In this way, *Akira* is not simply the catharsis that Freiberg celebrates. Rather, it attacks the notion that people's history breaks from universal history, an escape from the cyclical movement of universal history. Rather, it is the fundamental building blocks of such. Universal history simply extracts the laws.

The final image of *Nausicaa* is of a green shoot in the soil purged of radioactivity deep beneath the Toxic Forest. This symbol of hope concludes many films of the Japanese cinema of the atom bomb (including that of *Barefoot Gen*). *Akira* ends – just as it begins – with a nuclear event. If there is a message of hope here, in the inevitability of cycles of destruction, it is that the laws of universal history see Japan as being able to survive. *Nausicaa* believes such survival as impossible. *Nausicaa* resists and explicitly critiques the laws of universal history, it is a film about escaping a cycle of atomic events; *Akira* believes such cycles inevitable, a consequence of human fascist, totalitarian desire which founds the laws of universal history.

Traces: Symptoms and figures

In describing the large and small forms of the action-image, Deleuze is exploring tendencies, just as in all his categorizations. The signs of composition of the large and the small attempt a purity of image and historical conception. Showa *Godzilla* designates a universal history through the signs of composition of the large form, while *Barefoot Gen* and *Lucky Dragon No. 5* express a people's history through the signs of composition of the small form. The genetic signs explicitly illustrate how any specification of forms is always in process and always remains an interaction. Thus *Akira* and *Nausicaa* extend these formulae to create complex overcomings of the spectre of impossibility.

Yet the vector and the imprint do not exhaust an extension of the action-image. Rather, they are merely the first indication of how SAS' and ASA' organizations can transform each other in a number of different ways. Deleuze will go on to name these transformations reflection-images, as well as discovering a type that precedes the very division of the action-image into its two forms, the impulse-image. The next chapter will explore these images, encountering new ways in which the films of the Japanese cinema of the atom bomb can overcome the spectre of impossibility. These forms, I will contend, are essential to extending the heterogeneity of the assemblage beyond direct and indirect depictions of the nuclear event. It will be as if the atomic attacks are disappearing from the Japanese cinema, but in so doing leaving a trace. In a sense, this is when the action-image no longer wants to depict the atom bomb, but still the atom bomb wants to be depicted through the movement-image. It is as if the atomic attacks become filmic symptoms and cinematic figures, a moment in which the *hibakusha* and the *pika* return, a moment marking a return of history as a shock, a return of the nuclear event of Hiroshima and Nagasaki.

3

Traces: Symptoms and Figures

We call the sign of such deformations, transformations or transmutations Figure. There are here all kinds of aesthetic and creative evaluations.[1]

Impulse-images and reflection-images

Traces of atom bomb imagery appear in Japanese films as symptoms and figures. There could be said to be cinematic symptoms: films which, while not depicting the *pika* or the *hibakusha*, appear permeated with the nuclear legacy. There could be said to be cinematic figures: the *pika* or the *hibakusha* as filmic allusions and metaphors, appropriated imagery of atom bomb. It is as if the nuclear event is haunting Japanese screen-images and the cinematic horizons of Japanese history. This chapter discovers these traces in yakuza flicks, horror movies, the avant-garde and contemporary dramas. Accordingly, these films will be explored through Deleuze's cineotic concepts of the impulse-image and the reflection-image, where impulse-images diagnose symptoms of the world and reflection-images create, deploy and reflect upon transformational filmic figures.

Japanese cinema proves fertile ground for such traces, which arise in varied circumstances. In Chapters 1 and 2 we saw how the nuclear event could be described not only directly, but also indirectly through monster and sci-fi movies. As I will demonstrate in this chapter, such a trajectory creates a logic of disappearance – films where there is but a trace of the nuclear event. For example, Shindo Kineto's *The Naked Island* (1952) can be seen to describe the legacy of the nuclear situation through the mise-en-scène of life on a small, barren Japanese island; whereas Tsukamoto Shinya's avant-garde *Tetsuo* (1989) alludes to the atomic attacks through the metamorphosis of bodies in a claustrophobic urban environment. In Miike Takashi's *Dead or Alive* (1999) the reference appears far more explicit: a gangster and a cop go head-to-head, and an image of the *pika* is used to figure excessive violence. We can see these traces in ghost movies – such as Kobayashi Masaki's *Kaidan / Kwaidan* (1964) and

Nakata Hideo's *Ringu / Ring* (1998); and the arthouse – with Hosoe Eikoh's *Heso to genbaku / Navel and A-bomb* (1960) and Teshigahara Hiroshi's *Tanin no kao / The Face of Another* (1966). It may well be impossible to designate the nature of some of these traces: are they conscious or unconscious on the part of the filmmakers, a profound moment or a black joke? These may be questions we want to ask; but the more productive aspect, it seems to me, is to think of these traces as symptoms and figures of filmic historical memory appearing against a backdrop of cinematic forgetting. In this respect Kuroki Kazuo's *Face of Jizo* (2004) is exemplary, returning us by way of the trace to direct depictions of the nuclear situation, reflecting upon the very processes of forgetting and remembering through its own appropriation of the symptoms and figures of genre movies and the experimental cinema.

These very different films will each be explored through the movement-image avatars of the impulse-image and reflection-image. Impulse-images explore naturalism, which Deleuze sees as a nascent form of the action-image, where primal forces inhabit the mise-en-scène and characters. Shindo's *The Naked Island* is just such an impulse-image, describing the day-to-day life of a family living in harsh conditions on the Setonaikai archipelago, the film symptomatic of a post-apocalyptic environment. Deleuze's reflection-image examines the creation of cinematic figures. First, there are figures of attraction – cinematic metaphors and synecdoches – which can be seen in a genre film such as *Dead or Alive*, where nuclear imagery is appropriated to describe the annihilation of the antagonists' world. Second, there are figures of inversion – cinematic allegories – which create a resonance of the atomic bomb in other narrative trajectories, seen in films of the avant-garde such as *Tetsuo*. Third are discourse-images. Here we encounter self-reflexivity. If the preceding figures have been useful for exposing traces of the atom bomb in Japanese cinema, the discourse-image is perfect for exploring the very mechanism of the trace. Kuroki's *Face of Jizo* tells the story of a *hibakusha* woman haunted by the ghost – or memory – of her father, a haunting that confronts the repression of the *pika* by American and Japanese forces during the occupation period.

The aim of all these filmic engagements is, as always, twofold: to explore the heterogeneity of Japanese atom bomb cinema; and to exploit the difference in-itself of each film. This third chapter expands the types of film discussed, as well as extending the domain of the assemblage. We explore how the contingent centres of the *pika* and the *hibakusha* (Chapter 1) with their linkages to the horizons of history of the nuclear event (Chapter 2) become traces in the wider contours of Japanese cinema, and how the cinema of the atom bomb will itself reflect upon such traces as forgetting-remembering in history and memory. We move, in this way, from perception-, affection- and action-images (Chapters 1 and 2) to impulse-images and reflection-images. The impetus for such a move is the semiosis of Charles Sanders Peirce as described in his Harvard lecture series *Pragmatism and Pragmaticism* (1903). Accordingly, this chapter will begin with a reconsideration of the movement-image cineosis, made necessary by such an expansion in taxonomy.

Peirce, semiosis

With the doubling of action-images and the promise of the impulse-image and reflection-images, Deleuze's movement-image expands well beyond the primary co-ordinates of Bergson's sensory-motor system of perception, affect and action. The desire for new images is not difficult to explain; the more images, the better Deleuze can account for and explore different cinematic forms. The mechanism Deleuze utilizes to extend the movement-image taxonomy is the semiosis of Charles Sanders Peirce.[2] Peirce's system is explicated as a fundamental aspect of his pragmaticist doctrine, in *Pragmatism and Pragmaticism*, as a 'method of reflexion having for its purpose to render ideas clear'.[3] This method is a logic; and this logic is 'only another name for semiotic … the quasi-necessary, or formal, doctrine of signs'.[4] On the one hand, there is a basic correspondence between Peirce's semiotic logic and Bergson's sensory-motor schema which allows Deleuze to create resonances between the two.[5] On the other, there is the generative power inherent in Peirce's semiosis, which inspires Deleuze to create the extensions of the movement-image.[6]

The fundamentals of Peirce's system concern the constitution of signs, which appear to be composed of three categories. These became known as firstness, secondness and thirdness. Firstness is feeling. It indicates contemplation without reason. The famous example Peirce gives is that of experiencing the colour red. 'Category the First is the Idea of that which is such as it is regardless of anything else. That is to say, it is a Quality of Feeling.'[7] Secondness is reaction. It is how one state of mind is broken into by another, either from within or without: the cry of a child rousing a parent. 'Category the Second is the Idea of that which is such as it is as being Second to some First, regardless of anything else and in particular regardless of any Law … it is Reaction as an element of the Phenomenon.'[8] Thirdness is representation. It mediates between two other states. 'Category the

Third is the Idea of that which is such as being a Third, or Medium, between Second and its First. That is to say, it is Representation as an element of the Phenomenon.'[9] An encounter with fire, between the feeling of heat (firstness) and the pain registered by touch (secondness) there is a rule, flames burn skin. Thirdness – representational thought – for Peirce, is relational, law-like. These three categories generate the sign – firstness, secondness and thirdness: feeling, reaction and thought. A sign is a complex entity, but a complex entity that can – as Peirce has shown – be broken down into categories.

However, while existing in-itself, a sign is also – necessarily – part of signification, part of the process he calls semiosis. As Peirce writes, 'a sign … is something which stands to somebody for something in some respect or capacity'.[10] There are thus three states of the complete sign: the sign can simply be the sign in-itself; the sign also has a relationship with its object; and the sign has a relationship with its interpretant, the receptor of the sign. As Peirce has already delineated three categories of the sign (firstness, secondness and thirdness) they must correlate with these states. Thus Peirce delineates the three trichotomies of signification, which can be tabulated as in Table 3.1. Each element is called a sign division, and can be named and similarly defined. The first trichotomy describes how 'the sign in itself is a mere quality, is an actual existent, or is a general law'; the second how 'the relation of the sign to its object consists in the sign's having some character in itself, or in some existential relation to that object, or in its relation to an interpretant'; and the third 'its interpretant represents it as a sign of possibility or as a sign of fact or a sign of reason'.[11]

The delineation of such elements within the processes of signification also allows for the creation of new combinations of divisions. Peirce calls the original combinations genuine signs: firstness composed of qualisign, icon and rheme (111); secondness composed of sinsign, index and dicisign (222); and thirdness

Table 3.1 Peirce's semiotic schema by division

sign / category	sign in-itself	sign and object	sign and interpretant
firstness (111)	qualisign (1)	icon (1)	rheme (1)
secondness (222)	sinsign (2)	index (2)	dicisign (2)
thirdness (333)	legisign (3)	symbol (3)	argument (3)

composed of legisign, symbol and argument (333). However, these genuine signs, or rather thirdness (333) and secondness (222) – not firstness (111) which is indivisible – can have degenerate forms. Genuine secondness (222) can have a strong and a weak form. The weak form is the firstness of secondness (211). The strong form is secondness of secondness: genuine secondness (222) itself, and relatively degenerate secondness (221). Genuine thirdness (333) can split into a strong form as well as weak and weaker degenerate forms. The weakest degenerate is the firstness of thirdness (311). The weak degenerate form is the secondness of thirdness; thus we have a double, what we might call the firstness

Table 3.2 Peirce's semiotic schema by class

category \ sign		sign in-itself	sign and object	sign and interpretant	Example (from Peirce)
111	firstness (genuine)	qualisign (1)	icon (1)	rheme (1)	feeling of red
211	degenerate secondness	sinsign (2)	icon (1)	rheme (1)	individual diagram
221	relative degenerate secondness	sinsign (2)	index (2)	rheme (1)	spontaneous cry
222	secondness (genuine)	sinsign (2)	index (2)	dicisign (2)	weathercock / photograph
311	degenerate firstness of thirdness	legisign (3)	icon (1)	rheme (1)	diagram, apart from its individuality
321	degenerate firstness of secondness of thirdness	legisign (3)	index (2)	rheme (1)	demonstrative pronoun
322	degenerate secondness of thirdness	legisign (3)	index (2)	dicisign (2)	cry identifying individuals by tone
331	relative degenerate firstness of thirdness	legisign (3)	symbol (3)	rheme (1)	common noun
332	relative degenerate secondness of thirdness	legisign (3)	symbol (3)	dicisign (2)	proposition
333	thirdness (genuine)	legisign (3)	symbol (3)	argument (3)	syllogism

of the secondness of thirdness (321) and the secondness of the secondness of thirdness (322). Strong thirdness has three values of thirdness: genuine thirdness (333) itself, as well as a relatively degenerate firstness of thirdness (331), and a relatively degenerate secondness of thirdness (332).[12] These ten classes, or full signs, can be tabulated as in Table 3.2 (which also lists the divisions that compose them, their genuineness or degeneracy, as well as given examples for each from Peirce).[13] It is this semiosis, its procedures of unfolding, which will inspire Deleuze to extend the movement-image taxonomy, generating new forms of movement-images.

Cineosis and cinema

Tsukamoto Shinya's *Tetsuo* concludes with one of the most powerful images in modern Japanese avant-garde cinema. Composed of metal detritus and human organic matter, an immense erect phallus dominates the screen. This pulsating penis-machine has its origins in the duel between two men infected by a metal virus. Now integrated as part of this obscene engine, their mission will be to 'fuck the world'. Such an audio-visual image captures up and overlays milieux, fulfilled- and potential-actions with qualities of affect, and in so doing creates a complex sign. This sign, in turn, is an allusive image, an allegorical moment, an image of thought that refers us to an atomic missile poised to penetrate Japan. *Tetsuo* creates an interweaving of perception, affect, action and thought – a nexus that demands to be accounted for as a movement-image in its own right. It is such a demand, according to Deleuze, that the Peircian semiosis can answer in resonance with the Bergson sensory-motor schema.[14]

Deleuze describes Peirce's categories this way: first the image affects us; secondly, we act upon the image; thirdly, the image enters into thought. Now, it will be noticed that this trajectory, while bearing a resemblance to that of Bergson, does not completely align. Peirce's topography begins with how an image affects, whereas Bergson begins with perception; and Peirce's account passes beyond action, seemingly the final category in Bergson's schema. In order to reconcile the differences between the two frameworks Deleuze invokes corresponding terms for each of the other's categories. He labels the Bergsonian perception-image as having 'zeroness' in reference to Peirce, and Peircian thirdness as describing a 'mental-image' in reference to Bergson.[15]

Zeroness, for Deleuze, can be introduced into the Peircian schema as there is a silence in Peirce's approach: 'in his phenomenology, he claims the three types of image [firstness, secondness, thirdness] as a fact, instead of deducing them.'[16] Peirce's categories are possible only inasmuch as feeling (affect), reaction (action) and thought (relation) depend upon an initial perception. Peirce takes perception for granted. Yet Peirce's account is instructive. Perception does not really exist in-itself, rather 'perception is strictly identical to every image'.[17] Deleuze writes that 'the perception-image will therefore be like a degree zero in the deduction which is carried out as a function of the movement-image'.[18] In essence, after Peirce, the perception-image disappears from the movement-image taxonomy. Yet as we will see in a moment, paradoxically, this disappearance will become another aspect to the generative process of mapping Peirce and Bergson.

Relation, according to Deleuze, can be thought of as 'the closure of deduction'.[19] In Bergsonian terms this can be seen as the 'memory-image'.[20] For Bergson, the memory-image underpins the sensory-motor schema (perceptions → affects → actions). This response is recognition in the mind/body but 'set in motion … by an initial impulse'.[21] Simply put, our bodies obey laws based upon a repetition of the perception → affect → action trajectory. With regards to the movement-image, Deleuze names this cinematic avatar the mental-image. The creation of mental-images, in this way, constitutes another aspect of the generative process of mapping Peirce and Bergson, which can be notated as in Table 3.3.

The alignment of Peirce's fundamental categories with Bergson's sensory-motor schema sets the conditions for the creation of a number of other movement-images. This occurs through the Peircian logic of combination of sign elements, the generation of degenerate images. Deleuze writes that 'between firstness and secondness [affection-images and action-images], there is something which is like the "degenerate" affect, or "embryonic" action', the impulse-image.[22] Similarly, the reflection-image arises as an intermediary between the action-image and the mental-image, a prefiguration of thought in action.[23] In essence, the impulse-image corresponds to Peirce's

Table 3.3 The fundamental co-ordinates of Peirce's semiosis with Bergson's sensory-motor schema in respect to Deleuze's movement-images

Peirce	**Bergson**	**Deleuze**
[zeroness]	[perception]	[perception-image]
firstness	affect	affection-image
secondness	action	action-image
thirdness	memory-image	mental-image

weak secondness; while the reflection-image corresponds to Peirce's weak and weakest thirdness. Furthermore, the action-image, which corresponds to strong secondness, and the reflection-image and the mental image, both of thirdness, can all be unfolded. The action-image, as strong secondness, is double. We thus have the large form and the small form action-image.[24] As reflection-images and mental-images are both of thirdness, each can be unfolded into three component images: reflection-images into attraction-images, inversion-images and discourse-images; mental-images into relation-images, recollection-images and dream-images.

Accordingly, we thus appear to have eleven movement-images, ten of which correspond to Peirce's ten classes (with zeroness making the eleventh). These images can be tabulated as in Table 3.4. Finally, however, we must return to zeroness, the disappearance of the perception-image. In Chapter 1 it was seen how perception-images have three levels: the image in-itself as a monadic entity; molar composition and molecular genesis as a dyadic polarity; and a triadic series of signs which describe these two poles and the transition between them: the solid, liquid and gaseous. As 'perception is strictly identical to every image' it becomes a 'function of the movement-image'.[25] Each movement-image will also have three signs, corresponding to the poles of composition and genesis, each appropriate to its own image and named accordingly. This gives us ten movement-images (corresponding to Peirce's ten classes) and thirty constituent signs.

These new movement-images allow us to explore more and different forms of cinematic experience. Mental-images – as we shall see in Chapter 4 – account for films dominated by images of thought such as flashbacks (recollection-images), dreams (dream-images) and symbols (relation-images). This chapter is concerned with impulse-images and reflection-images. Reflection-images, coming between the mental-image and the action-image, explore the way in which action-images are transformed by figures of thought. We thus confront the Japanese cinema capturing up iconography of the *pika* and *hibakusha* as filmic metaphors (figures of attraction) and cinematic allegories (figures of inversion). Such movies create traces of the nuclear event in Japanese films; and the Japanese cinema of the atom bomb will respond to such attraction- and inversion-images by making them trace the very subject of the narrative through self-reflexivity (figures of discourse). We begin, however, with the impulse-image, which – as much as the reflection-image – circumscribes the action-image perimeter (coming as it does before action and after affect). Such

Table 3.4 Deleuze's full extension of movement-images after Peirce

Peirce		Bergson	Deleuze
000	[zeroness]	[perception]	[perception-image]
111	firstness (genuine)	affect	affection-image
211	degenerate secondness	action	impulse-image
221	relative degenerate secondness		action-image (small form)
222	secondness (genuine)		action-image (large form)
311	degenerate firstness of thirdness	memory-image	attraction-image (reflection-image)
321	degenerate firstness of secondness of thirdness		inversion-image (reflection-image)
322	degenerate secondness of thirdness		discourse-image (reflection-image)
331	relative degenerate firstness of thirdness		dream-image (mental-image)
332	relative degenerate secondness of thirdness		recollection-image (mental-image)
333	thirdness (genuine)		relation-image (mental-image)

impulse-images allow us to explore cinematic naturalism, affective pre-conscious behaviours as symptoms of the world. Kaneto Shindo's *The Naked Island*, in this regard, is exemplary – describing a mise-en-scène and characters permeated by the legacy of the Japanese nuclear event.

I. Symptoms and chronos

The Naked Island (1960)

Before dawn, the sun yet to rise from behind the hills, a *cho* traverses the sea in near-silence. A man, Senta (Tonoyama Taiji), stands aft operating the *ro* that powers the boat forward. A woman, Toyo (Otowa Nobuko), sits toward the prow. Upon reaching the stone dock, husband and wife leave the boat and walk down a path, each carrying a yoke roped with two empty pails. From a small stream they fill the pails with fresh water using large wooden ladles. They then make their way back to the *cho*, the pails now full and heavy, each yoke bowed across their shoulders. Toyo operates the *ro*, and as they navigate the sea heading towards a small rocky atoll, the sun breaks across the horizon. On this nameless, waterless hump of land, their two young boys, Taro (Tanaka Shinji) and Jiro (Masanori Horimoto), are keeping lookout. When they see their parents returning home, they go to work. One prepares a table and lights the fire, the other feeds the animals. Husband and wife make the arduous climb up the steep hill, both laden with the cumbersome pails. Upon reaching the small wooden shack in a clearing at the top, all sit, and eat in silence. After the meal, the father goes to the fields, where he begins decanting water carefully onto the soil between the sweet potato plants. The only sound is that of the wood on wood, and water seeping into the parched earth. Later, his wife will return from taking their older son, Taro, to the mainland school by *cho*. Together Senta and Toyo will tend the crops in silence, as Jiro swims in the warm waters of the Setonaikai Inland Sea.

Oshima Nagisa, the doyen of the Japanese New Wave, declared that Shindo's *The Naked Island* confirmed 'the image foreign people hold of the Japanese' – the film exploring, as it does, a primeval way of life in the same geo-historical moment as 1960s Japan.[26] Critic Michitaro Tada took a similar view, commenting, at a French film première, that Europeans seem to 'think that the Japanese are as foolish and without questions about their circumstances of their lives as the characters'.[27] According to Michitaro, 'the West' prefers

Figure 3.1 'The difficult land' – Senta walking the fields, yoke strung with pails, *The Naked Island* (Shindo, 1960)

'approaching the Japanese as a primitive people rather than a technologically sophisticated one'.[28] Critics from 'the West' have (inevitably, as both Oshima and Michitaro would see it) been more generous. Susanne Rostock has written that the film 'makes the minutiae of everyday life extremely powerful'.[29] 'Until I saw it, I didn't fully understand how deeply relevant filmmaking could be … I realised you could actually change a person's whole perception of life in a 90-minute movie.'[30] Richie, in *One Hundred Years of Japanese Cinema*, sees the film as a cultural document, writing: 'it escape[s] much of the sentimentality which conversations about how awful life is would have made inevitable. We observe the social conditions which make the islanders' labour necessary and we draw our own political conclusions.'[31] Yet in the filmography at the end of the book Richie curiously presents an opposing view: 'we watch the little people lead their awful lives' – at one and the same time substantiating the fears and echoing the critiques of Michitaro and Oshima.[32]

Perhaps the most interesting take on the film comes from Acquarello, who believes *The Naked Island* should be seen within the 'framework of the unforeseen residual legacy of the atomic bombing and the cultural (and societal) toll of the Pacific War'.[33] The film is a 'bittersweet, poetic elegy' that 'can be regarded as an oblique representation of *hibakusha* cinema'.[34]Accordingly, the film 'serves as an allegory for a humble way of life irrevocably transformed by a landscape poisoned by nuclear exposure – a naked island – the uncalculated, indirect fallout of a seemingly distant and alien war'.[35] Is it just that Acquarello's reading of *The Naked Island* is affected by Shindo's direct depictions of the atom bomb? We have already seen that Shindo wrote the script for Oba's 1950 film *The Bell of Nagasaki*, directed *Children of the Atom Bomb* two years later and *Lucky Dragon No. 5* at the end of the 1950s. The atom bomb is also a subject Shindo would return to after *The Naked Island* in the stories of a dying *hibakusha* woman in *Haha / Mother* (1964) and, of a troupe of actors in Hiroshima on the day of the attack, *Sakura-tai chiru* (1988). Yet Acquarello observes 'Shindo's continued re-examination and personal reconciliation with the legacy of the atomic bombing are not solely limited to overt representations of the annihilating tragedy' and cites the famous medieval horror stories *Onibaba* (1964) and *Kuroneko / The Black Cat* (1968) as examples of how the nuclear event permeates his films.[36] This is a view shared by Adam Lowenstein. In 'Allegorizing Hiroshima' (2004), he offers a reading of *Onibaba* 'as a means of refiguring how cinematic representations of Hiroshima are legislated' on the Japanese screen.[37] The Japanese cinema of the atom bomb should not only be considered an assemblage of direct and indirect depictions, but also one that includes films that display traces of the nuclear event.

Doing so sees *The Naked Island* not so much as an overcoming of the spectre of impossibility, but rather as a haunting; as if the film is symptomatic of the Japanese nuclear legacy. We can in this way turn to the Deleuzian cineosis, which designates the symptom as a sign of the impulse-image, where the impulse-image describes cinematic naturalism. Furthermore, such an exploration of *The Naked Island* will allow us to discover a new horizon of history, one in which the atomic attacks on Hiroshima and Nagasaki become the curse of time.

Naturalism (Zola)

What is naturalism? The images of *The Naked Island* make little attempt to abbreviate the events being portrayed. Long takes predominate; slow pans reframe and follow movements. Shindo says these shots abide by the law of the 'natural sequence'; moments are not decomposed (filmed from different angles and scales, then recomposed in the editing suite).[38] And no moment is too small to be examined. Shindo captures the rhythm of work, and in so doing makes this the focus of the film, an image of the dignity of labour opposed to the forces of the contemporary Japanese industrial capitalist societal state. Even if there is nostalgia, there is no sentimentality, for the work is hard, endless, a battle: each necessary element torn from the landscape with extreme effort. As Shindo has said of the film, 'labour stems from survival'.[39] Beyond or before choice: this is what life is. Thus the renunciation of dialogue; not a word is spoken during the film. It is as if there is nothing to say – this is as things are, should and will be. It is as if the renunciation of dialogue casts events in an unending present, no past or future except that of the same. This is Shindo's cinematic naturalism.

Deleuze cites Émile Zola, French novelist and critic, as being the essential naturalist in literature. The forward to Zola's early novel *Thérèse Raquin* (1867) and (several years on) the essay 'The Experimental Novel' (1880) are manifestos for the style. At the heart of naturalism is the prerogative that life should be described in consort with the natural sciences: 'we have no longer any right to romance.'[40] Zola contrasts the naturalist project to 'idealist novelists' who 'base their works on the supernatural and the irrational, who admit … the power of mysterious forces outside of the determinism of phenomena.'[41]

Such idealism is, for Zola, 'metaphysical chaos'.[42] Rather, naturalism is the analysis of humanity as an organism which functions through 'heredity and surroundings'.[43] Concomitantly, naturalism also distinguishes itself from realism. 'The Experimental Novel' takes as its foundation Claude Bernard's *An Introduction to the Study of Experimental Medicine* (1865). Bernard, for Zola, was not only 'battling to put medicine in a scientific path' but also attempting to show that science could 'disengage itself little by little from empiricism'.[44] Here Zola aligns empiricism with realism, which, as Belle M. Sherman points out, equates to '"haphazard observation" in contrast with a scientific experiment undertaken to prove a certain truth'.[45] Yet both idealism and realism have a place in the naturalist project. On the one hand, 'empiricism invariably preceded the scientific condition of any branch of knowledge'.[46] On the other, the idea is harnessed in the service of experiment. The naturalist author thus tests characters and world, is someone who 'accepts proven facts, who points out in man and in society the mechanism of the phenomena over which science is mistress, and who does not interpose his personal sentiments, except in phenomena whose determinism is not yet settled, and who tries to test, as much as he can, this personal sentiment, this idea *a priori*, by observation and experiment'.[47] Naturalism thus mediates a path between, moderates and corrects the risks of idealism and realism.

Shindo's *The Naked Island* is the naturalist film par excellence. The travails of the family describe in intimate detail life on the surface of the Inland Sea, and in so doing explore the fundamental relationship between the human and the world. Shindo's instigation of Zola's test, in this way, is the death of the elder son. After the funeral, his mother expresses a moment of almost unendurable pain. She upends a pail of precious water on the crops, begins ripping up cherished plants. Falls in the dirt and mud, crying. Then, gathering herself, she stands, sets right the pail, and goes back to work. In the original cut, the film finished with a statement in *kanji* script: 'life goes on'. Shindo's producer advised this be dropped from the final edit: the audience will understand.[48] 'We are', writes Zola, 'experimental moralists, showing by experiment in what way a passion acts in a certain social condition.'[49] Naturalism 'experiments on man', it 'dissects piece by piece this human machinery … through the influence of the environment.'[50]

Impulse-images

Naturalism, for Zola, comes between realism and idealism; and for Deleuze the impulse-image comes between 'the realism of the action-image' and 'the idealism of the affection-image'.[51] The affection-image 'is developed in the Any-Space-Whatevers / Affects pair' while the action-image is 'developed in the Determined Milieux / Modes of Behaviour pair'.[52] The affection-image captures faces and bodies in order to express qualities and powers, and these qualities and powers can also be expressed as pure indeterminate backgrounds. The action-image creates determined situations, and these determined situations either spiral down to a body for defined actions (the large form) or are revealed by the body through behaviours (the small form). Between the affection-image and the action-image, writes Deleuze, 'we come across a strange pair: Originary Worlds / Elementary Impulses'.[53] While elementary impulses describe the molar organization of impulse-images – through symptoms and the fetish – originary worlds create the molecular genetic organization. The monadic, dyadic and triadic levels of the impulse-image can be illustrated as in Table 3.5.

Originary worlds will present backgrounds that are neither determinate nor indeterminate but rather a conjunction of the two, one within the other: 'although it may resemble one … the originary world is not an any-space-whatever', rather it 'appears in the depths of determined milieux'.[54] But 'neither is it a determined milieu' – instead the determined milieu ultimately 'derives from an originary world'.[55] Thus, while this genetic sign of the impulse-image may have a coherent space-time, it also has 'a formless character'; Deleuze gives examples such as 'a house' or 'desert' or 'forest'.[56] In this way, unlike the large form action-image where a defined socio-historic situation spiralled down into actions which a character performed, the originary world generates impulses in characters. An impulse is a fragment of the originary world that impales a character that then reacts immediately. Symptoms are the 'first aspect' which 'concerns the nature of impulses'.[57] These impulses 'are "elementary" or "raw"', such as 'impulses to nourishment, sexual impulses'.[58] Deleuze describes these

Table 3.5 Impulse-image

impulse-image		
molar composition		molecular genesis
symptom	fetish	originary world

symptoms as 'prior to all differentiation between the human and the animal'; characters become 'human animals', such as 'the fashionable gentleman a bird of prey, the lover a goat, the poor man a hyena'.[59] In other words, these impulses are symptoms of the originary world. It is as if the originary world erupts through the character. The 'second aspect' of the molar organization concerns 'the object of the impulse' – it is a 'fragment' that connects character to originary world, 'the "partial object" … a haunch of meat, a raw morsel, a scrap, a woman's briefs, a shoe'.[60] The fetish has two poles, 'fetishes of Good and fetishes of Evil' or 'holy fetishes and fetishes of crime and sexuality' which 'meet and interchange … the former might be called relics, and the latter, in the vocabulary of sorcery, "vults" or voodoo objects'.[61] These dual but exchangeable sides of the fetish are indicative of the impulse-image in general: 'they are the two aspects of the same symptom', and of the originary world, the molecular genetic sign from which the molar signs are composed.[62]

What Shindo creates in *The Naked Island* is an originary world, a timeless land in a geographically and historically specific milieu. Shindo makes his aim clear – it is to 'capture … human beings struggling like ants against the forces of nature'.[63] As we have seen, the originary world is populated with 'human animals'.[64] Shindo depicts exactly this, most overtly during the early sequence of the film as the family eat breakfast: shots of the family are intercut with those of the animals eating. Shindo animalizes his characters, insofar as he sees humanity as part of nature, prone to the same forces. These forces also describe 'a world of a very special kind of violence'[65] – not sustained realist violence, conflicts and duels which organize the narration; but a naturalist, impulsive violence. The wife returns from a solitary trip to the mainland and makes her way up the hillside, laborious step after laborious step, but then falls, spilling the water. As she pushes herself to her feet, the husband strikes her to the ground. His violence is primal. The violence emerges as a deep impulse. As Deleuze puts it, 'fundamentally there is an impulse which, by nature, is too strong for the character, whatever his personality'.[66] These are symptoms, the first pole of molar composition, determined by the originary world which the characters inhabit.

The fetish appears in *The Naked Island* as water – and it has a double aspect which again corresponds to, or is extracted from, the originary world. It is the seawater (nearly always present as a background within the frame), undrinkable and separating them from the mainland, and the freshwater needed for their crops. Yet this freshwater is torn from the originary world as a fragment, by hard labour, every last drop precious (hence the violent outburst of the husband when the wife falls, and the significance of his standing aside at her outburst after the death of their son). Similarly the sea supplies small fry, octopus and crabs to eat, and seaweed for fertilizer. And in this way the fetish passes back and forth from relic to the vult: the boys have caught a fish, kept it in a rock pool. The family travel by ferry to Onomichi – a traditional town undamaged by the war – to sell the fish, which results in a meal at a restaurant and new clothes from the market. Then they pass a small electronics store; behind the window a television transmits a programme. As they watch, a young woman in a black leotard performs modern dance against a pure white background. Shindo, to heighten the impact of this moment (the family have never encountered anything such as this before), transposes the body-image on the TV from the vertical to the horizontal: an overt camera manipulation, the only one in the film, further distancing the image from the family's understanding. Here we encounter the vult: the television as a voodoo entity. After this collision with technology, the son will die.

It is this vult that describes the trace of the atomic bomb in *The Naked Island*, and links the mise-en-scène of the originary world to the symptomatic death of the child. The vult, the television, is a voodoo fragment of modern technology. The same technology that gives to the world the ploughshare, generating surplus and trade; generating need and greed, territorial expansion: the war-machine, the atomic bomb. The vult is not torn from a defined milieu, but from the same originary world which lies beyond good and evil, and is handed back to the characters as a symptom. After the nuclear event of Hiroshima and Nagasaki,

Figure 3.2 The vult – a dancer on TV, *The Naked Island* (Shindo, 1960)

the *hibakusha* who survived experienced something beyond comprehension – people were dying, days and weeks after the event. At first no one understood why, at first no one knew about the residual effects of the bomb, about radiation sickness. No one understood, at first, what the symptoms were symptoms of. In *The Naked Island*, after the child is buried, the mother and the father stand atop the atoll. In the night sky, above the hills of the main island, fireworks explode and light pours down upon the town below.

The vult and the symptomatic death of the child, however, are not the final conclusion of *The Naked Island*. Shindo rather returns to the delicate balance of the originary world of the family's island, to the non-ending toil of fetching water and growing crops. The family carry on. They endure. This is the task, the naturalist vision of *The Naked Island*: a film describing endurance, enduring the originary world, its fetishes (vults and relics), and its symptoms. Such endurance describes the way in which the naturalism of the impulse-image captures the Japanese nuclear event within its own horizon of history.

Horizons of history (redux)

To discover the concept of history sustaining the impulse-image, it will first be necessary to consider the way in which it acts as intermediary between the realism of the action-image and the idealism of the affection-image. Such a consideration, moreover, will also allow us to ascertain the relations between movement-images and the practice of history in general.

'The history of modern historiographic thought', according to Harriet Gilliam, can be described through the polarity of and exchanges between realism and idealism.[67] Furthermore, such a history of history 'displays the pattern, roughly, of a circle – common origin, differentiation, attempted reconciliation'.[68] Gilliam's point of departure is Leopold von Ranke's *History of the Latin and Teutonic Peoples* (1824), which set the 'tendency of early historiography' by 'evaluating, analysing, and collating documentary sources in order to make a rigorous judgment of their impartiality and trustworthiness'.[69] Such a procedure birthed historical realism, which saw itself as a 'scientific methodology emphasising the objective and the tangible'.[70] Historical idealism arose in antagonism to such empiricism. The charge was that realism 'substituted a static, abstract ordering of events for the movement and uniqueness of individual historical existence'.[71] Instead, idealism 'insisted that only by an effort of sympathetic imagination could the past be recaptured and held that history is the subjective'.[72] The idealist sees facts as events which must necessarily be interpreted.[73] These events are, in the words of R. G. Collingwood, 'the outward expression of thoughts'.[74] Thus the extreme poles between the two conceptions of history: the realist and the idealist. Ernst Cassier, however, writes that 'the great historians avoid both extremes'.[75] Instead realism and idealism form a complex interweaving of the objective and subjective, of empiricism and imagination. Gilliam's aim in reconstructing this history of history is similarly an attack on the view that there are such '"pure" and extreme instances of the two theoretical positions'.[76]

Such an analysis refers us to a general description of the relationship between the movement-image and its historical conceptions, the extended and modified movement-image cineosis conceived in the wake of the Peircian semiosis. We began our exploration of the cineosis and history (in Chapter 2) with respect to the large form action-image. Deleuze aligned the large form with Nietzsche's critique of universal history, which annulled difference, preserved and judged the past. This was realism as a nexus of monumental, antiquarian and critical history. As we have seen above, Deleuze contrasts the realism of such action-images with the idealism of affection-images. While Deleuze does not directly explore the connection between the affection-image and historical idealism, he does discuss affect in terms of the human as a centre of indetermination, an expression of internal intensity and choice. Furthermore, Deleuze's affection-image has as one of its co-ordinates the philosophy of Søren Kierkegaard, who in turn articulates a conception of historical idealism in *Concluding Unscientific Postscript* (1846). Kierkegaard writes: 'world-historically, the individual subject certainly is a trifle, but the world-historical is, after all, an addendum; ethically the individual subject is infinitely important'.[77] Thus 'only by paying sharp attention to myself can I come to realise how a historical individual acted when he was living, and I understand him only when I keep him alive in my understanding'.[78] Such an account aligns with Gilliam's analysis of historical idealism. The affection-image and the large form action-image, in this way, describe the extreme poles of historical idealism and historical realism.

What then of the other elements of the cineosis? In the wake of Peirce, movement-images were extended into images of thought (mental-images), as well as having intermediaries either side of the action-image (impulse-images between affect and action; reflection-images between action and thought). At one and the same time, the perception-image became zeroness, functional with respect to all other images giving each its triad of signs. In order to understand the way in which each of these movement-images relates to history in the aftermath of Gilliam's analysis, we must first reconceive their distribution. The extreme poles of the movement-image should not be considered perception-images at one end, and at the other mental-images. Rather, the extreme poles of the movement-image are affection-images (idealism) and large form action-images (realism). We can map the distribution of movement-images in respect to idealism and realism as in Table 3.6.

On the one hand, perception (as degree zero, as disappearing into every other image) must be the condition for both the idealism of the affection-image and the realism of the action-image, as well as the gradations in between. This also reveals something fundamental about the signs of the movement-image which are generated by the zeroness of the perception-image. The triadic sign structure creates gradations. Take, for example, the large form action-image. It is composed of three signs; the milieu, the binomial and the impression. The milieu is concerned with a highly determinate situation, and this determined situation creates clear lines of force that emanate from it. The binomial describes a tendency towards action for-itself, the situation is determined, but captures up individual conflicts. Finally, there is the impression which explores the internal factors of action. The signs of the binomial and the impression are gradations away from the extreme realism of the milieu, toward the idealism of the affection-image. Such a re-evaluation of the perception-image necessarily returns us to Ito's *Effects* with which we began this book: if perception-images do not exist in-themselves, what of our analysis? *Effects*, with its unequivocal socio-temporal placement and its clear lines of force, corresponds exactly to the sign of the milieu of the large form action-image – in other words, a highly objective, empirical, purely historical realist account of the Japanese nuclear event.

On the one hand, thirdness, as we saw above with Peirce, 'is the Idea … between Second and its First'.[79] Mental-images thus traverse the extreme poles of action-images and affection-images – and as we will see in Chapter 4, they

Table 3.6 Movement-images mapped against the extreme poles of idealism and realism

idealism ←			**→ realism**
	[perception-images]		
		action-images	
affection-image	impulse-image	small form	large form
		reflection-images	
	mental-images		

constitute a re-evaluation of affect and action within the domain of thought. Finally, we can consider the remaining images. The small form of the action-image was aligned (as we saw in Chapter 2) with Bourdieu's concept of the *habitus*, as a people's history. Accordingly, lying between the extreme poles of realism and idealism, its historical conception appears as a dialogue between idealism and realism but with a tendency toward, or base of, a realist, functionalist account. Reflection-images – as we will see later in this chapter – create a series of transformations between the forms of the action-image, and will create a network of varying degrees of such realist history. Lastly, the impulse-image occurs midway between the realist domain of action-images and the idealism of the affection-image – and as we saw above with Zola, distinguishes itself from both extremes.

The movement-image, in summary, is conceived as a vast interweaving of images and signs, which take as their poles the extreme idealism of the icon of the affection-image as a pure expression of internal intensity and the extreme realism of the milieu of the large form action-image as pure empiricism. Between these two poles, the images and signs of the mental-image, the reflection-image and the impulse-image mark gradations and reconfigurations of the intermixing of historical idealism and historical realism. Accordingly, each image and each sign of the movement-image should, with regards to its historical conception, be considered as a particular formulation between these two pure horizons of history.

'All the cruelty of Chronos'

We are now in a position to return to Shindo's *The Naked Island* and explore its historical conception of the nuclear event as impulse-image. According to the analysis carried out above, after Peirce and by way of Zola and Gilliam, we see we are somehow poised between realism and idealism, between the action-image and the affection-image, in a particular zone which nonetheless has its own consistency. Deleuze writes: 'what makes the impulse-image so difficult to reach and even define or identify, is that it is somehow "stuck" between the affection-image and the action-image.'[80] For Deleuze, naturalist directors are rare, it is not only 'difficult to reach the purity of the impulse-image', but 'particularly to stay there, to find in it sufficient opening and creativity'.[81] Accordingly, we tend to find films which have naturalist moments, but are dominated by action or affect; and we encounter filmmakers who make action-image films or affection-image films, yet may stray into naturalism. Shindo is exemplary in this regard. *Children of the Atom Bomb* (Chapter 1) is an affection-image with a corresponding idealist conception of history, focused through the intensive expression of the icon of Miss Ishikawa. *Lucky Dragon No. 5* (Chapter 2) is an action-image, of the small form, and thus tends toward a realist conception of history. Yet both have moments of naturalism, the opening sequences of *Lucky Dragon* aboard the *Daigo Fukuryu Maru* and *Children* in the trip by ferry to Hiroshima. *The Naked Island*, however, traverses both these procedures, and the impulse-image dominates: the long takes which depict the labour of the family, their unconscious complex interactions, their silence, and their sparks of naturalistic, impulsive violence.

The historical conception of the impulse-image arises from this naturalism. At the centre of the film, a year passes fleetingly. Autumn: the harvest, Shindo captures traditional Japanese dancing from a festival in the Chuguko region. Winter: traditional ceremonies and the *harukoma* dance performed by the old women of the town. In the fields, the family remove a giant root with great effort: there is work for all times of year, the planting of seeds – stamping them in with a delicate dance of footwork (these dances so unlike the one the family see on TV). Spring: cherry blossom, children playing ball, two butterflies flitting in the air. The crops have grown; wheat is harvested by hand – separated from the stalks, then thrashed, bundled up into sacks, carried by yoke. Taken to the landowner's house as tribute, exchanged for tools at the hardware store, bartered for supplies at the market. This sequence tells us everything about the historical conception of naturalism, the way in which the impulse-image conceives history. In a sense, it is a time before history, a purely cyclical time, endless birth and death and rebirth. This is not the birth and death of historical periods arising from history (action-image), but the vast stratum of time that is the foundation of such periods: an underneath that overpowers history.

Mircea Eliade characterizes this conception of time as belonging to 'archaic and traditional societies' where 'man … feels himself indissolubly connected with the Cosmos and the cosmic rhythms', whereas 'modern societies … insist that [man] is connected only with History'.[82] Yet, in *The Naked Island* this experience of time as outside of history is encroached upon by such historical time. History appears through modern technology, the television as such a fragment, a vult, which momentarily rips the family from their cyclical existence in the originary world. Such technology, as we have seen, is the fruit of civilization, the endless duels of machines of war, imperialist projects, a focal point being the atomic bomb. History, composed of realist determinations and idealist passions, breaks through and disrupts everything. Naturalists, according to Deleuze, in this way 'diagnose civilisation'.[83] Deleuze writes: 'the originary world is … both radical beginning and absolute end', it 'links the one to the other, it puts the one into the other, according to the law which is that of the steepest slope'.[84] Naturalism describes 'all the cruelty of Chronos'.[85] It 'seems to be under an inseparable curse', where 'duration is less that which forms itself than that which undoes itself, and accelerates in undoing itself. It is therefore inseparable from an entropy'.[86] History, be it realist or idealist, and time, be it linear or cyclical, appears as a moment of organization in a universe tending toward complete disintegration. The atomic attacks on Hiroshima and Nagasaki are, in this way, but a moment in the unfolding of the cosmos. This moment is a symptom of entropy and as such must be endured. It is perhaps here, in Shindo's naturalist vision of *The Naked Island*, that we encounter the *mono no aware* attitude in its purest form. After the trauma of death: endurance, a return to the originary world. *The Naked Island* describes an awareness of the impermanence of life which should be conceived, after time has passed, with gentle sadness.

II. Attraction, inversion and *Jetztzeit*

From symptoms to figures; reflection-images (Fontanier)

Despite all this, can *The Naked Island* be considered a film of the Japanese atom bomb cinema? It is neither what we have called a direct depiction (*Effects*, *Children*, *Barefoot Gen*, *Lucky Dragon*) nor an opaque, indirect depiction (*Godzilla*, *Terror of Mechagodzilla*, *Nausicaa*, *Akira*). We have instead approached *The Naked Island* as displaying a trace of the *pika* and *hibakusha*, as a diagnosis of Japan in the wake of the atomic bomb, as symptomatic of the Japanese nuclear environment. We have considered the film as being haunted by the spectre of impossibility. Capturing up the film in these co-ordinates remains tentative – and I am happy enough to leave it this way.

There will be films where the trace appears with more intensity; where images of the *pika* and *hibakusha* act as cinematic metaphors, metonymies and allusions actualized within a yakuza movie, a horror flick and so on. These films, in this way, cannot be said to become a direct or even an indirect depiction of the atom bomb. Or it may be that the film makes the trace the very subject of the film – a film of the Japanese atom bomb cinema reflects upon traces of the *pika* and the *hibakusha* in Japanese society, history, memory. Either way the film is transformed. Deleuze accounts for such transformations through reflection-images. Reflection-images occur through the introduction of figures into a narrative line. Figures are constituted simultaneously in two ways. First, they are 'composed when action and situation enter into indirect relations'.[87] Figures, in this sense, appear as reflections or transformations between the two forms of the action-image, as special images. Second, and as a consequence of the first procedure, these figures become images of thought (and precursors to mental-images proper). There are three aspects to this constitution. As Deleuze puts it, a figure is a sign 'which instead of referring to its object, reflects another; or which reflects its own object, but by inverting it; or which directly reflects its object'.[88] The reflection-image thus decomposes into what Deleuze identifies as figures of attraction, figures of inversion and figures of discourse. Deleuze describes this unfolding by way of the work of the nineteenth-century linguist Pierre Fontanier.

Fontanier was interested in classifying the features of language through a taxonomy of figures. His work became the classic overview and a standard French classroom text, his two books – *Manuel classique pour l'étude des tropes* (1821) and *Des Figures du discours autres que les tropes* (1830) – brought together by Gérard Genette as *Les Figures du discours* (1968). These books explore the sense of language as being composed of either tropes or non-tropes. What is a trope? For Fontanier, a trope is a word, or words, used in any way other than literal. Yet it is not the word or phrase in-itself that is important, so much as the way in which that word or phrase transforms the passage or text in which it operates. Non-tropes, on the other hand, are words or phrases used in a literal way, but which nonetheless affect the sense of the phrase or text in which they appear. Figures are transformative. From this basic division, Fontanier will go on to create a series of sub-categories. Fontanier designates two types of tropes: perfect tropes, 'tropes in a word, or properly speaking'; and imperfect tropes, 'tropes of many words, improperly speaking'.[89] Perfect tropes include metaphor, metonymy, synecdoche; imperfect tropes include allegory, mythology, hyperbole, allusion, paradox and irony. [90] Toward the end of *The Study of Tropes* Fontanier briefly discusses 'other forms of discourse called figures that are not tropes', and this proves the impetus for the second book on literal figures.[91] He lists four types: figures of construction, figures of elocution, figures of style, and figures of thought – each composed of sub-categories.[92] Such is the most basic outline of Fontanier's taxonomy of figures.

Deleuze uses Fontanier's taxonomy in the same way he has appropriated Bergson's sensory-motor schema and Peirce's semiosis, as impetus and inspiration: 'we are not posing any general problem about the relationship of the cinema and language … we are simply noting that cinematographic images have figures proper to them.'[93] Deleuze does not, therefore, simply transpose Fontanier's types and sub-categories into his cineosis intact. Rather, he does so in response to the possible semiotic positions offered by the reflection-image. Deleuze will thus regroup Fontanier's categories into three different images. This regrouping may not be as capricious as it may first seem. It is common in the taxonomy of figures to divide figures of speech (tropes) from figures of thought (literal figures), the rationale being that the former deal with verbal expression, while the latter express ideas. That these two categories are by no means pure has led to the acknowledgement of an overlap, which has in turn been used to create a third category between the two poles, sometimes called figures of amplification. Figures of speech, amplification and thought thus describe a trajectory and difference in degree. Accordingly, Deleuze identifies the three avatars of reflection-images as acting in this way. First: tropes (be they perfect or imperfect) which act through substitution.[94] Second: literal transformations proper, which act through chiastic manoeuvres, where meaning is created through reversals.[95] Third: figures of thought proper, which 'do not pass through any modification' but rather mark out 'deliberation, concession, support, prosopopoeia'.[96] These three aspects inspire attraction-images, inversion-images and discourse-images. The general correspondence can be illustrated as in Table 3.7. Taken together, the three reflection-images create different types of figuration. And it is this difference in degree of reflection-images that can be harnessed to explore the Japanese cinema and traces of the atom bomb: figures of attraction where nuclear imagery is appropriated as cinematic metaphors and allegories; figures of inversion where such figures are amplified through style, the *pika* and the *hibakusha* infusing the narrative trajectory; and figures of discourse where the trace of the atomic attacks becomes reflected upon directly as an image of thought.

We will, in the final two sections of this chapter, explore each of these reflection-images in turn. The concern will be not be simply to recognize and specify such figures, such hauntings of the spectre of impossibility. In the wake of our analysis of the distribution of historical forces across the movement-image,

Table 3.7 Figures: from Fontanier to Deleuze

Fontanier	perfect tropes imperfect tropes	figures of construction figures of elocution figures of style	figures of thought
transition	figures of speech	figures of amplification	figures of thought
Deleuze	figures of attraction	figures of inversion	figures of discourse

our discussion will ultimately extend to focus upon how such films can be said to figure the historical legacy of the nuclear event. We will begin, however, with the first category of reflection-images, attraction-images, which find an extraordinary exemplar in Miike Takashi's yakuza flick *Dead or Alive*.

Dead or Alive (1999)

On waste ground on the outskirts of Tokyo, Ryuichi (Takeuchi Riki) and Jojima (Show Aikawa) face one another, some hundred yards apart: a classic shoot-out at the end of a movie. Jojima, who has just pulled himself from the smashed upturned car on the side of the dirt track, jerks out a dagger buried deep in his ribcage. His left arm is almost severed. With his right hand, and still clutching his handgun, he wrenches the useless limb from the stump of his shoulder. Blood pours from the wound, a muffled scream escapes him as he discards the useless meat and bone. Jojima slowly raises his gun. Ryuichi draws his own firearm in a rapid movement. They pump each other with bullets – eleven shots slam into each of their bodies. Magazines empty, guns are thrown to the ground. The sound of blood dripping to the earth, smoke from the burnt out cars drifts across the azure skies. Jojima reaches slowly behind his back, and pulls free a missile launcher, shoulders the weapon, flicking up the sights. Ryuichi is suddenly wracked with pain. He clutches his chest. When he pulls his hand away, he is holding a glowing ball of energy; he gazes at it in wonder. He stands, and bowls it towards Jojima, who fires the missile launcher. The missile and energy collide – shock waves radiate out, the screen goes white.

Cut to a shot of the Earth, from space, Japan in focus. A sphere of light, the size of a pinprick, appears over Tokyo. It rapidly increases in size, envelopes Honshu, pushing the ocean before it creating a massive tsunami. The atomic event enlarges, burning white, covering the whole of Japan and out over the Pacific Rim.

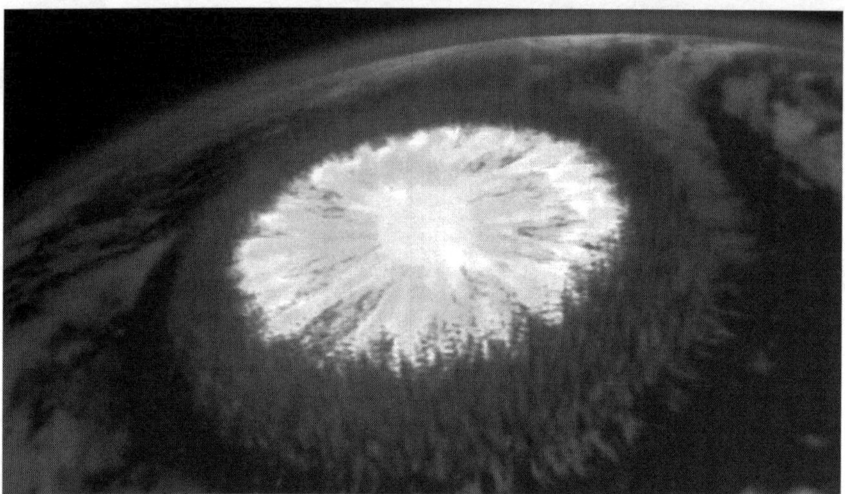

Figure 3.3 The atomic event consumes Japan, *Dead or Alive* (Miike, 1999)

So ends Miike's *Dead or Alive*, a cop versus yakuza flick. What can account for such a use of nuclear imagery? There was no expectation that the film would end in such a way. Furthermore, there appears to be no context for this appropriation. Tom Mes describes this as 'the embellishment of a routine scene', noting the original script designated it as a 'simple shoot-out'.[97] Miike 'exaggerates this climatic skirmish to the point of turning it into a metaphor'.[98] We can concur with Mes, *Dead or Alive* uses the nuclear event as a cinematic trope: 'for each of these two characters the destruction of the other was their entire world … and when they go, naturally that world goes with them.'[99] Yet for Mes, this atomic imagery just does not work – though interestingly enough, not from the perspective of appropriation, but rather for the effect on which it has on the film: 'The climax of *Dead or Alive* is – though a remarkable piece of cinematic invention, let it be said – stylistically out of tune with the rest of the film, ironically making the film's most eye-catching and astonishing moment also its one weakness.'[100]

Perhaps, however, there is another way to consider this use of nuclear imagery, the way in which it acts to transform the film. Before the shoot-out, Ryuchi turns to one of his gang and says: 'This is the final scene.' For Mes, such a statement 'is not so much a self-referential, meta-narrative wink as an acknowledgement by the character that all that's left for him is the clash with his nemesis'.[101] Why such a concern for the integrity of the film-world? Why can this not be seen as a meta-narrative wink? Self-referentiality, it seems to me, traverses the movie from beginning to end. The pre-title opening shot, for instance, has the two antagonists crouching, together, on a jetty at a rundown Tokyo harbour. They look to camera (shades on) and count the film in: 'One … two … one two three four.' It is not enough to say this moment stands outside the film, outside the temporal succession of images that will follow; it is rather a perspective on the movie to come. Miike's first procedure is indeed self-referentiality. His second, intimately related to and a consequence of the first, is excess: if this is only a film, then let us go beyond any artificial limits. After the count-in, what follows is a seven-minute sequence of hyper-rapid montage, guerrilla camera-work and presentational acting styles set to a heavy-metal soundtrack: violence, over-eating, drug-taking, gay and straight sex. Everything is taken to extreme: strippers, corpses, yakuza, cops – every cliché. Yet somehow taken beyond the cliché, through excess, self-referentiality and Miike's third procedure: an indeterminacy of tone. At one moment a semi-naked pole-dancing prostitute gang-member is being drowned in a paddling pool of her own excrement; in the next, we are in a Tokyo university hall witnessing a lecture on Marxism. Misogynist black comedy and pedagogical social critique: each a self-reflection on the film-world as excess. We experience the lecture as a lecture (not as some background moment), and this in turn refers us to the political situation in Japan, ultimately embodied by the two antagonists. Jojima is a cop, but also a family man, his daughter with a heart condition requiring an operation he cannot afford on his public-service salary. Ryuichi is yakuza, but also *zanryu koji* (half-Japanese, half-Chinese), a child of a mixed marriage from Pacific War-era Manchukuo, an ethnic minority unrecognized by the state. The gangster supports his brother, his criminality a sacrifice necessary to send the kid abroad and save him from the racism their community experiences.

Self-referentiality, excess and social commentary: there could, in other words, be much more to the final shot of the film than mere embellishment. To consider this possibility we can turn to the way in which Deleuze accounts for the use of figures in cinema through the cineotic concept of the attraction-image.

Attraction-images

Deleuze's attraction-image explores cinematic figures equivalent to tropes (both proper and improper). The signs of composition develop through two procedures that transform both large form and small form action-images. On the one hand there is what Deleuze calls 'sculptural or plastic representation', the equivalent of perfect tropes.[102] Here 'the action does not immediately disclose the situation'; rather, what is revealed is a 'grandiose situation' (S') which 'encompasses the implied situation' (S).[103] On the other hand, there is what Deleuze calls the 'theatrical representation', the equivalent of imperfect tropes.[104] Here 'the real situation does not immediately give rise to an action which corresponds to it'; rather, 'fictitious' action (A') acts as an 'index to the real action' (A).[105] Deleuze summarizes both moves: 'there is no longer a direct relation between the situation and an action, an action and a situation: between two images, or between the two elements of the image', instead 'a third intervenes to ensure conversion of the forms'.[106] This third is the figure-image. Plastic representations 'are images which represent another image' as in 'metaphors, metonymies, synecdoches'.[107] Theatrical representations 'proceed in a sequence, and it is the sequences of images which has a figural role', as in 'allegory, personification' and so on.[108] From plastic to theatrical: proper tropes to imperfect tropes, these are the signs of molar composition. While Deleuze does not specify a genetic sign, an assumption can be made (we can refer to the way in which, as we will see, the genetic sign of the inversion-image will be generated). This would describe an indeterminacy of theatrical and plastic figures as an overlap in the difference of degree, an overloading of metaphor, metonymy and allegory in a single film. The monadic, dyadic and triadic levels of the attraction-image can be illustrated as in Table 3.8.

Dead or Alive is of the large form action-image. The two antagonists devolve from the confrontation between the Japanese underworld and over-world, organized crime and law enforcement. The nuclear event as the final image is a plastic representation, a fictitious situation encompassing the implied, or real, situation. The atom bomb as metaphor, as Mes saw it. For Deleuze (as for Fontanier) the crucial aspect of such a figure is how it transforms the text into which it is inserted. Ryuichi and Jojima are two characters engendered by complex forces, both historical and contemporary, encircling Japan at the end of the twentieth century: economic triumph and stagnation; fascism,

Table 3.8 Attraction-image

attraction-image		
molar composition		molecular genesis
theatrical	plastic	theatrical-plastic

militarism, imperialism – democracy, capitalism, globalization; nationalism and immigration. Yet Miike is not satiated with procedures inherent to the large form, the bifurcation of these forces into a conflict embodied by characters to produce an ethical image and designate good and evil. Rather, he uses the reflection-image to explore such a distribution through excess, self-referentiality and social commentary. Instead of separating the characters out, Miike prioritizes the logic of convergent montage. Their positions are relative, both do evil, both do good, and these moments can be difficult to define. In the end, they are locked into a trajectory that will not only destroy them but also their families and associates. The confrontation terminates in the final plastic image of the atomic bomb which retroactively transforms the film into a reflection on human belligerence. In the wake of Hiroshima, Nagasaki and the atom bomb, the proliferation of weapons of mass annihilation, the insanity of mutually assured destruction. Such is the trace of the nuclear event in *Dead or Alive*.

Attraction-images of the atomic bomb may appear throughout post-war Japanese cinema, and perhaps nowhere more so than horror and ghost movies. Nakata Hideo's *Ringu* / *Ring* (1998), a film of the small form action-image, has theatrical representations which proceed in sequence. Reiko (Matsushima Nanako), a reporter, is investigating a series of mysterious deaths. The demise of her ex-husband, Takayama Ryuji (Sanada Hiroyuki), can immediately be read in reference to images of the *hibakusha* and the *pika*. When the vengeful ghost Sadako (Ino'o Rie) kills, the moment is rendered through a flash. There is the close-up image of her eye: the eye of the atom bomb. She is the *pika*. Her hair functions as if to hide her face, as if to conceal keloid scars. She is *hibakusha*: when her mortal remains are discovered her skull is still matted with luxurious black hair, which falls away like the effects of radiation poisoning. The video tape that silently infects those exposed to it has a dormancy period, like radioactive sickness after the atom bomb.

Kobayashi Masaki's *Kaidan* / *Kwaidan* (1964), a compendium film of four ghost stories, is replete with such plastic and theatrical representations extending the molar procedures of *Dead or Alive* and *Ring* toward the molecular. In 'Kurokami' / 'The Black Hair' a poor samurai (Mikuni Rentaro) deserts his perfect Japanese wife (Aratama Michiyo) to marry a rich landowner's daughter (Watanabe Misako). When he eventually returns home, he discovers his first wife has died, is now a ghost. In 'Yuki-Onna' / 'The Woman of the Snow' a woodcutter (Nakadai Tatsuya) lost in a snowstorm is spared by a female phantom (Kishi Keiko) – but he must never tell. Later marrying, he reveals this

Figure 3.4 Sadako's eye – the eye of the *pika*, *Ring* (Nakata, 1998)

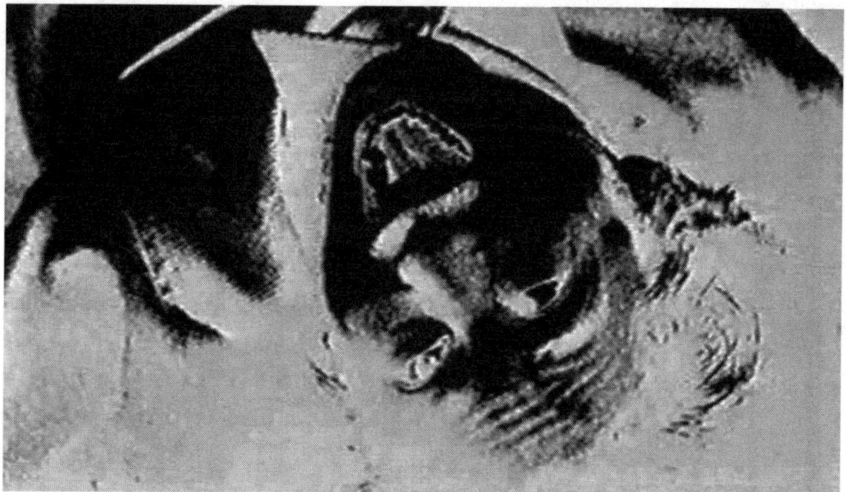

Figure 3.5 The *pika* consumes Ryuji, *Ring* (Nakata, 1998)

secret to his wife, but she immediately changes form to that of the phantom. In 'Miminashi Hoichi no hanashi' / 'Hoichi, the Earless' a blind musician (Nakamura Katsuo) is made to perform songs telling of an ancient battle fought at sea by the ghosts of the dead. To protect himself, Hoichi's body is painted with prayer verses. In the final episode, 'Chawan no naka' / 'In a Cup of Tea', a guard (Nakamura Kan'emon) discovers the reflection of another in his tea. He drinks it anyway. Each of these episodes generates images which can be seen as having a sculptural resonance with the atomic bomb. The tea that can kill evokes stories of the *hibakusha* who quenched their thirst with water – which instantaneously ended their lives. In 'The Woman of the Snow' the ghost appears bathed in light, like the *pika*, and disappears into the night which has become an eye, a figure of the atom bomb (repeated in *Ring*). In 'The Black Hair' the ghost of the first wife is revealed through skull and hair (again, repeated in *Ring*). In 'Hoichi, the Earless' the young man is blind, as if he had looked upon the atom bomb, and the prayers upon his body that are supposed to make him invisible to the ghosts (protect him from radioactive sickness) are partial, he will succumb. Together, across the four episodes, these sculptural figures create a complex theatrical representation of the legacy of the *pika* and the suffering of the *hibakusha*.

The objection will be that we are reading too much into these films. Some may take the view that I see the *pika* and the *hibakusha* everywhere,

Figure 3.6 The eye as the *pika*, *Kwaidan* (Kobayashi, 1964)

Figure 3.7 No protection from radiation sickness, *Kwaidan* (Kobayashi, 1964)

that I see post-war Japanese films as defined by the bomb. Jay McRoy writes that '*Kwaidan* and *Ringu* … draw on a multiplicity of religious traditions (Shintoism, Christianity, etc.), as well as plot devices from traditional literature and theatre'.[109] These stories of the 'woman as "avenging spirit"' use figures such as 'long black hair and wide staring eyes (or, in some instances, just a single eye), as long black hair is often symbolic of feminine beauty and sensuality, and the image of the gazing female eye (or eyes) is frequently associated with vaginal imagery'.[110] Without doubt, we agree. Yet, McRoy's analysis also considers long black hair and the single eye as symbols and associations. Such images are – by their very nature – figures, open to interpretation and, more

importantly, reinterpretation and appropriation. They can function in multiple ways according to different readings by filmmakers and spectators. They are in process, in time. Furthermore (as we will see in Chapters 4 and 5), the eye will be explicitly associated with the *pika* in Kurosawa's *Rhapsody in August*, and the loss of long black hair through radiation sickness, as a threat to beauty, will inspire a scene in Imamura's *Black Rain*. Finally, my use of *Kwaidan* and *Ring* – as we will see below in respect to the trace and history – dovetails with previous critiques of these films in respect to Japanese cinema and the atom bomb in Linnie Blake's *The Wounds of Nations* and Akira Mizuta Lippit's *Atomic Light (Shadow Optics)* (2005).

As was made explicit at the beginning of this chapter, and reiterated in respect to our analysis of *The Naked Island* in the wake of Acquarello, it may well be impossible to tell if such traces are conscious or unconscious on the part of the film, the filmmaker or the spectator – and once again, I am happy enough to leave it this way. This is the nature of what we may call the low-intensity trace. *Dead or Alive*, *Ring* and *Kwaidan* have figures that can be seen to function as attraction-images. They do not, in this way, give us a direct or indirect depiction of the nuclear event. Yet such traces will undergo a strengthening, have higher intensities, leading us back inexorably to the indirect and then direct. It is in just this way that we can deploy the second avatar of the reflection-image, the inversion-image, and encounter traces of atom bomb imagery as literal cinematic figures.

Inversion-images

The inversion-image is an action-image under the aegis of the mental-image which reverses the form. On one hand, there is the large form where 'the action, in effect, is not required by the situation'.[111] As Deleuze puts it, 'the action divides in two: there is the sublime action … which itself engenders another action, a heroic action', but the heroic action is unnecessary, ridiculous even.[112] The second is the small form which is 'reduced … to its most feeble aspect', but through this enfeeblement the sublime emerges.[113] Accordingly, 'we can see how the Small enters into relationship with the Large such that the two Ideas communicate and form figures in interchanging'.[114] The large form undergoes enfeeblement; the small form discovers the sublime.[115] These two transformations are the molar signs of composition. The molecular genetic sign is captured in the gnomic statement that 'the albatross' big feet and its great white wings are the same thing', enfeeblement intertwines with the sublime in an indeterminate action-image (collapsing of forms).[116] The monadic, dyadic and triadic levels of the inversion-image can be illustrated as in Table 3.9.

Figures of inversion will employ traces of nuclear event for their own purposes. This occurs under particular conditions, reversing the way in which the action-image tends to capture up the *pika* and the *hibakusha* in their narrative strategies. We encounter, accordingly, reflections on film style and enunciation – reflections that appear appropriate to the Japanese avant-garde cinema: cyberpunk, arthouse and experimental films.

Teshigahara Hiroshi's *Tanin no kao / The Face of Another* (1966) is such a film of the inversion-image. It transforms the large form action-image through an internalization of the duel, the reversal of the grandiose quest, and the integration of a reflective element. Okuyama (Nakadai Tatsuya) has a severely disfigured face, a result of an industrial accident. Experimental psychiatrist (Hira Mikijiro) fashions Okuyama a mask from flesh-like plastic, modelled upon the face of another person. For a time Okuyama lives a double life, alternating between bandages and the mask. In adopting this new face he comes to believe he has been absolved of all responsibility for his acts, going on to seduce his wife (with his face of another) before attempting to kill her. Such is the internalization of the duel and the grandiose quest transformed and enfeebled. However, it is the reflective device that directly captures up the film in the co-ordinates of the atom bomb.

Table 3.9 Inversion-image

inversion-image		
molar composition		molecular genesis
enfeeblement	sublimation	enfeebled-sublime

Okuyama mentions to his wife that he has been going to the cinema. Teshigahara, at this point, cuts to an image of a beautiful young woman (Irie Miki) walking down the street. It is clear this is the film Okuyama was watching (the aspect ratio changes for the first shot). She is followed by some men wolf-whistling. She turns toward them, revealing one side of her face as horribly keloid-scarred. The woman will eventually commit suicide in the ocean at Nagasaki. The narratives of this film-within-a-film and the main film interweave and act as inversions of one other, yet this relationship is asynchronous. The woman was a victim of the atomic bombing of Nagasaki, she dedicates her time to helping out at an asylum for soldiers suffering war trauma. She is a good person. Yet Japanese society rejects her. She is called 'monster' by kids in the street. Okuyama's trajectory is thus both a reaction to such depictions of *hibakusha* – young beautiful women in melodramatic narratives – and a denunciation of the young woman's fate, constituting revenge upon Japanese society for such rejection.

Face of Another is based upon a book by Abe Kobe, an arthouse film of the inversion-image, enfeebling a grandiose situation, and in so doing creating a powerful critique of an uncaring post-war Japanese society. Hosoe Eikoh's *Heso*

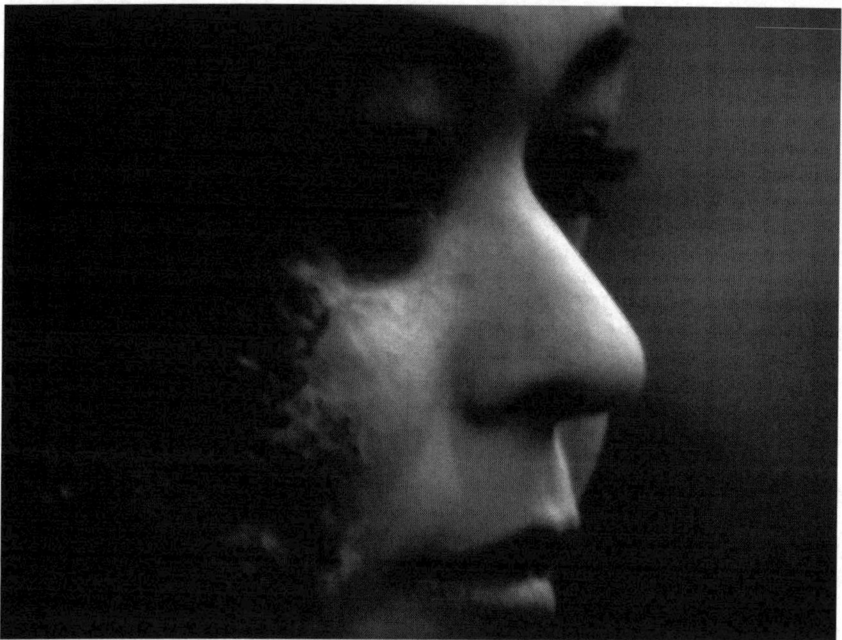

Figure 3.8 The woman with the keloid scar, *Face of Another* (Teshigahara, 1966)

to genbaku / Navel and A-bomb (1960) – a twelve minute abstract short – is also an adaptation, a poem from Yamamoto Taro.[117] Here, however, the transformation of forms is the opposite of that of *Face of Another*. Hosoe creates an experimental cinema of the sublime.

Hooded men stand on a beach. The beach is deserted except for a solitary cow. Naked men carry goats. An image of a headless chicken dominates the screen. Hands fight over an apple placed on a sand volcano. Dancers move across the mise-en-scène. Naked young boys roll in the sand, crawl to the sea. A naked man emerges from the waves to pull a long rope from the navel of a naked boy. The final moment of the film: a mushroom cloud rising up out of the ocean. *Navel and A-bomb*, after this final image, must be read within the context of the nuclear attacks on Hiroshima and Nagasaki (yet in a very different way than the attraction-image used in *Dead or Alive*). The title, the poem (which accompanies the visual image), the mushroom cloud: these offer a perspective on the film. The hands, the apple, the sand volcano: a confrontation of forces that disturbs an originary state, which has the potential to release vast

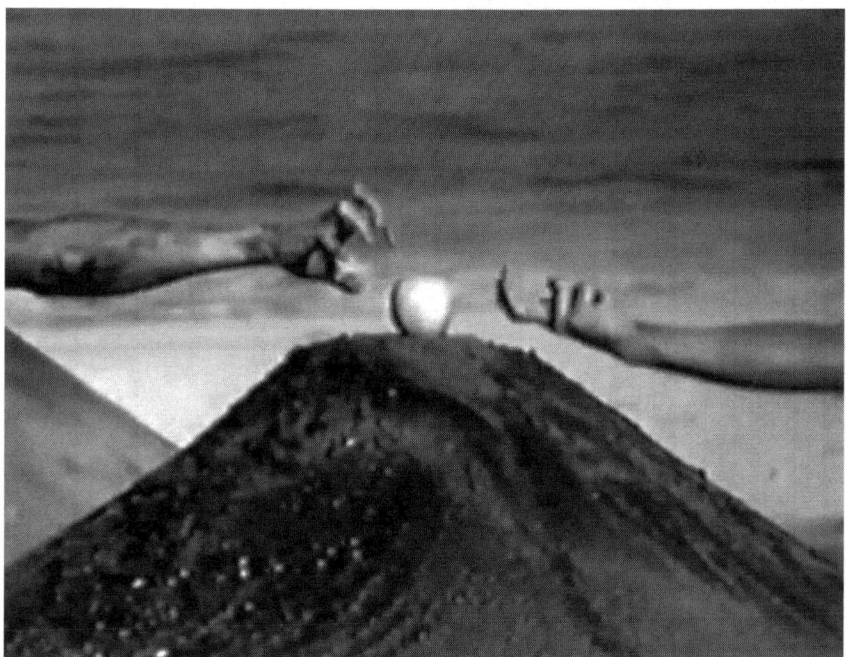

Figure 3.9 Hands fight over an apple atop a sand volcano, *Navel and A-bomb* (Hosoe, 1960)

destructive powers. The fall: the apple. Science: the atomic bomb. America versus Japan: the insane scramble for resources across the Asian Pacific. In an interview, Hosoe said that 'the "navel" represents the original life energy related to humanity's essential life-sexuality', whereas 'the "A-bomb" [is] that which could destroy everything at once'.[118] The elliptic images of the film, in this way, create indices and vectors of the small form, and through inversion, achieve the sublime.

Hosoe's *Navel and A-bomb* and Teshigahara's *The Face of Another* create elusive films of the Japanese cinema of the atom bomb through inversion-images, reactions to mainstream narratives through the cinema of the sublime and the cinema of enfeeblement. Tsukamoto Shinya's surreal cyberpunk masterpiece *Tetsuo* interweaves these themes, interweaves the feeble and sublime, and in so doing creates a powerful and complex inversion-image.

Tetsuo (1989)

Shattered concrete, the reinforcing steel rods once buried deep within now exposed, twisted and broken. The camera explores this devastation, rubble and dust – the smoke clears. The Fetishist (Tsukamoto Shinya) and Salaryman (Taguchi Tomorah) are now fused, the result of a duel between the two, and a series of transformations – the introduction of metal into their bodies, the subsequent reproduction of metal through their organic systems. They form a hybrid metal killing machine – reminiscent of a massive erect penis and distended scrotum. A collection of integrated machinery, a bricolage of every kind of modern industrial metal product, decomposed into its machine parts, and recomposed into the machine. What remains of the Fetishist emerges from the pulsating glands of the penis. On the stem is what remains of the Salaryman: 'I feel great.' 'We can rust the world into the dust of the universe', screams the Fetishist.

So concludes Tsukamoto's *Tetsuo*. Andrew Grossman sees the film as a cinematic rendering of Alvin Toffler's concept of 'future shock', the acceleration of technological innovation resulting in an alienating effect on humanity.[119] Nowhere is this more applicable than in Japan, where the constitutional embargo on warfare (underpinned by an American protection clause) freed up its capital to develop mass-market global products. For Grossman, 'future shock is the inevitable modernist outcome of a post-war Japan too abruptly thrust

Figure 3.10 A pulsating penis-machine, the atomic bomb, *Tetsuo* (Tsukamoto, 1989)

from militaristic imperialism into American egalitarian democracy'.[120] The Salaryman not only integrates with the Fetishist but also begins to assimilate low- and high-tech products – he is the ultimate consumer. If there is an egalitarian narrative to this fetishization, Grossman believes 'Tsukamoto will have none of it, bitterly mocking Japanese pop culture's "diseased" way of fetishising … accelerated future shock'.[121] Grossman extends his analysis through Sandor Ferenczi's binary concepts of the 'alloplastic' and the 'autoplastic'.[122] Alloplasty describes the way in which humanity 'manipulates the external environment to meet their own needs', while autoplasty is the 'more primitive, instinctual behaviours through which species undergo evolutions to fit the demands of the external world'.[123] *Tetsuo*, for Grossman, 'rationalise[s] the ungovernable machines raging in man, machines which are supposedly alloplastic and wilful, but behave more like wild, autoplastic animals'.[124] *Tetsuo*, in this way, is 'a critique of rampant economic modernisation' and its transformational effects on the human centre.[125]

Grossman's reading of the film, capturing up of the concepts of autoplasty and alloplasty as conditions of future shock, is wonderful. However, it seems to me that the film is not only rooted in a present retroactively effected by the shock of the future, but also explores that present as an outcome of the shock of the past. *Tetsuo*, in this way, can be seen as a film of the Japanese cinema of the atom bomb where autoplastic and alloplastic transformations are effects of historical causes.

The film is replete with images that evoke the *pika* and the *hibakusha*, both directly and opaquely. For instance, the opening production title reads 'Regular-size monster series', which refers us back to the *Godzilla* cycle, and its origin, the atomic attacks on Hiroshima and Nagasaki. In this way the film appears to be of the large form action-image. The situation generates the binomial forces of the Fetishist and the Salaryman. Yet very quickly, they come together in a duel that extends across the entire film. This is no film of heroic grandeur. The claustrophobic mise-en-scène is that of urban wastelands, workyards, ironworks, backstreets, and for the most part, a small, cramped apartment. We do not encounter giant monsters, but regular-sized ones. The heroism and triumphalism that underpin *Godzilla* are transformed into a kind of masturbatory adolescent bed-sit fantasy. It is as if Tsukamoto has performed a reversal, an inversion of the large forms of Showa *Godzilla*'s confrontations and the mutations of *Akira* resulting in enfeeblement, revealing the spectacle as impotent.

Yet *Tetsuo* also appears as an inversion of the small form action-image. Driven by the actions of the characters, ellipses permeate the narrative trajectory to such a degree it becomes almost impossible to reconstitute the situation. *Tetsuo* is composed of a whole series of indices and vectors. Moments are revealed (index of lack); others remain ambiguous (index of equivocity). The Salaryman's girlfriend becomes the Fetishist – yet how this transformation occurs remains opaque. The Salaryman is infected by the Fetishist – yet how the experiment by one became a disease for the other is indeterminate. Despite displaying traits of the small form, it is of a very special type. Both Salaryman and Fetishist are transformed from anonymous drones enslaved by capitalism into a horrific machine that can destroy the world. The final image of the film – a singular human/nonhuman rusting phallus emerging from the rubble – is a complex figure of both the *pika* and *hibakusha*. This small form has transmuted into a sublime image.

This is the wonder of Tsukamoto's film. The enfeeblement of the large form and the sublimation of the small form are performed at one and the same time. It is impossible to say which form the film belongs to and which form is inverted. *Tetsuo* – a film with a timespan of just one hour – is a fugue composed of simultaneous voices and themes, all of which interweave: the double fugue, where two (or more) related themes are present from the beginning; and the counter-fugue, where those themes are presented in an inverted form; and where each of these themes can appear at different relative velocities. The result is a contrapuntal composition – becoming molecular.

In this way we can revist the concepts and field that Grossman used to explore the film, autoplasticity and alloplasticity through future shock. The large form action-image describes the alloplastic trajectory, describes how the human engendered by the world can become capable of changing that world; while the small form, where the behaviours of characters change in response to a revealed situation, describes the autoplastic trajectory. If we consider the film as a series of inversions, a double fugue and counter-fugue, we no longer find a film that attempts to rationalize future shock and assert the alloplastic over the autoplastic. Rather, the organic connections between situation and action, action and situation are revealed as being simultaneously nonorganic, the rational is revealed as being concurrently irrational; and the alloplastic and the autoplastic become reciprocal movements between world and body, body and world. Humans created the machinic *pika*, the *pika* created the *hibakusha*. Those that created the bomb are alloplastic *hibakusha*, as much as those that suffered its effects, the autoplastic *hibakusha*: a contrapuntal process. And we are all *hibakusha* now. We have all been affected by the *pika*. The atomic bomb has both transformed the world and transformed humanity – at one and the same time. *Tetsuo* – through its interweaving of inversions – interpolates history as a shock to thought.

Images of thought

Such disruptions of a narrative line by traces of the *pika* and *hibakusha* engender what Adam Lowenstein calls a 'shock' which, after Walter Benjamin, can be seen as 'a means of blasting open the continuum of history'.[126] Lowenstein writes that Benjamin, in the essay 'Theses on the Philosophy of History' (1940), 'distinguishes between historical materialism and historicism as methods of inquiry into the past'.[127] One the one hand, historicism 'becomes aligned with depicting history as "eternal" and "universal" … and as "progress"', and 'the historicist merely establishes "a causal connection between various moments in history"'.[128]

Benjamin's historical materialism, on the other hand, forsakes 'historicism's "homogenous, empty time" in favour of … "*Jetztzeit*," or "time filled by the presence of the now"'.[129] In our own way, this is exactly what we have attempted in this chapter – exposing moments of *Jetztzeit*, traces of the nuclear event in the Japanese cinema, the symptoms of the impulse-image and the figures of the attraction- and inversion-image.

Jetztzeit is an essential conceptualization of the trace. For Lowenstein, critical engagements with Japanese film in the wake of the atom bomb tend to focus upon direct depictions of the atomic attacks 'over "allegorical" ones', citing Carole Cavanaugh's claim that there is a 'troubling absence of "an honest reconnection with history beyond allegory"'.[130] However, for Lowenstein, this preference happens 'without a sufficient sense of what allegory might mean in this particular context' – in the context of the Japanese cinema.[131] Linnie Blake, in *The Wounds of Nations*, explores such 'elusive and allusive' figures in Japanese horror through the spectral image of Sadako in *Ring* who appears as a 'wound'.[132] 'Multiplicitous … her naming evokes one Sasaki Sadako … a child of Hiroshima who died in 1955.'[133] Known as Sadako of the Thousand Paper Cranes, the girl suffered latent radioactive poisoning and believed that if she could make one thousand paper origami cranes she would beat the disease. For Blake, the ghost becomes 'that which will not be eradicated by American colonialism in Japan or by the Japanese refusal to acknowledge the sins of its own past'.[134] These female ghosts from the *onryou* genre (vengeful ghost stories most usually focused around young women and girls) 'evoke the horrors of Hiroshima and Nagasaki' where these figures are like blood soaking through the prematurely bound wounds of a national trauma.[135] Such are the wounds that can be seen in *Kwaidan*. Akira Mizuta Lippit, in *Atomic Light (Shadow Optics)*, sees such wounds as the 'trace'.[136] *Kwaidan* displays the trace of the unseen in the visual image, the visible and the invisible, what he describes as the 'avisual'.[137] For Lippit, such 'suspended visuality is critical to understanding a crisis initiated at the end of World War II … The destruction of Hiroshima and Nagasaki in 1945 exposed the fragility of the human surface, the capacity of catastrophic light and lethal radiation to penetrate the human figure.'[138] It is these traces that appear in *Face of Another*: 'facial disfigurement can be seen as one trope of atomic violence, a figure that destroys all figures. The end of figuration in disfiguration.'[139] These traces of the *pika* and the *hibakusha* are images which disrupt such films, and it is such symptoms and figures we have been concerned with in this chapter by way of Deleuze's impulse-image, attraction-image and inversion-image. Symptom, figure, trace, wound, shock, *Jetztzeit* – we can employ any number of terms for these spectres of impossibility which haunt the Japanese screen.

Ultimately, we can identify such spectres as images of thought – a heterogeneous assemblage of signs which create thought of the historical moment of the Japanese nuclear event by the way in which images of the *pika* and the *hibakusha* disrupt the texts from which they emerge: yakuza flicks, horror films, the avant-garde and cyberpunk. This formulation is crucial and thus requires an unfolding, for it extends the conceptual trajectory we have been developing.

Chapter 1 was concerned with establishing the conditions for an exploration of images of the nuclear event within the Japanese cinema, their distribution, intensity and heterogeneity. In the first place, we discovered the poles of the distribution of images to be the *pika* and the *hibakusha*, the bomb and the Japanese people, the nonhuman and the human. In the second place, we exposed an intensity of expression: from the direct to the indirect, and, subsequently, from such opaque engagements to those of the trace. In the third place, such a distribution of images and expression of intensities was seen to be heterogeneous, the Deleuzian cineosis describing the assemblage as a series of different types of response engendering different types of spectatorship. Chapter 2 was concerned with establishing the conditions for these cinematic images of the nuclear event as being considered ineludibly historical. We thus discovered different horizons of history arising from the cineosis. In the first place, we encountered a universal history and people's history of the action-image, oppositions which described historical realism. In the second place, this realism was revealed (earlier in this chapter) as but one pole in a greater opposition of historiographic forces, which saw its other limit the idealism of the affection-image. In the third place, between such poles, the signs of the movement-image cineosis were conceived as a nexus of combinatory forces, creating isolations (naturalism) as well as critiques of one form through another. Such critiques were foretold with the genetic signs of the small and the large in respect to their opposing action-image forms, and announced with naturalism in respect to realism and idealism. And it is just such a critique we encounter with attraction-images and inversion-images.

Except we appear to have invoked a new way of conceiving the critique. With attraction-images and inversion-images, we no longer have an image which refers us to a horizon of history, but rather to thought. History is no longer given in the image of a direct or even an indirect expression; the image is a trace, and becomes a moment of thought both for the film and for the spectator. The conceptual trajectory we have been developing is thus: image as image → image as an image of history → image as an image of thought.

It is with the first two aspects of the reflection-image – attraction and inversion – that such an extension of the conceptual trajectory is announced; and it is with the third figure – the discourse-image – that the extension becomes explicit. In other words, these images of thought need not only be considered as an arising of the trace of the nuclear event through the disruption of other narrations. Traces of the *pika* and the *hibakusha* can become the subject of the film in a film of a direct expression of the atomic attacks. In this way the trace becomes a figure of discourse, an explicit image of thought. It is the nuclear event as an image of thought that will become the focus of the remaining two chapters of this book, which will explore, in turn, various mental-images then time-images. Accordingly, images of thought will themselves be proved to be a heterogeneous assemblage. However, it is with the discourse-image that we must begin.

III. Discourse (image, history, thought)

Discourse-images

The discursive figure does not testify to the transformation of one form of the action-image by the other, as with the previous avatars of the reflection-image. Rather, it 'directly reflects its object'.[140] This, for Deleuze, manifests itself in 'a clear distinction between the two forms, rather than a complementarity'.[141] Films of the discourse-image treat the large form and the small form as pure, instead performing what might be thought of as a 'transformation on the spot'.[142] This amounts to each form reflecting upon its own structure and creating 'figures of thought'.[143] In the first instance, the discourse-image 'subjects the large form to a broadening which operates as a transformation on the spot'.[144] In the second, the discourse-image 'subjects the small form to a lengthening, a drawing-out which transforms it in itself'.[145] In this way, we reach the extreme limits of the action-image.

Accordingly, the first pole of the sign of composition is 'an extremely pure SA formula'.[146] Here, the milieu (S) is not given in-and-for-itself: 'the givens

... are not simply those of the situation [but] ... the givens of a question which is hidden in the situation'.[147] It is this hidden question ('of which there must be a complete exposition') that 'the hero must extract in order to be able to act'.[148] Thus 'the "response"' is 'more profoundly, a response to the question, or to the problem that the situation was not sufficient to disclose'.[149] It is as if possible situations are opaque. The actions of the characters do not rectify the milieu as in the large form proper, but rectify the problem the milieu obscures. The second pole of the discourse-image centres on the purity of the small form and approaches an answer to a question in another way. For Deleuze it is as if a series of distinct local events create a void which functions as an encompassing whole. As Deleuze puts it, this void 'links up the heterogeneous elements, while keeping them heterogeneous'.[150] The situation that is revealed through such links will thus be a 'very special homogeneity'.[151] The signs of composition of the discourse-image, in essence, explore questions. With regard to the small form, the discursive component is revealed in the divergent actions that surround a central void; with regard to the large form the discursive component appears through the quest of the character to understand what is hidden in the milieu. In both cases, for Deleuze, the main characteristic is that the discursive figure discovers the purest of action-image forms through the very questioning of the formulae. The signs of molar composition thus originate in the large and small forms of the action-image, and are the limit of the large and the small. The genetic sign, once again, remains unidentified by Deleuze. Yet following the procedure of the molecular inversion-image which we also utilized with regard to the attraction-image, this can be considered as a questioning and lengthening of a fundamental action-image, composite, but – albeit paradoxically – no less pure. The genetic component of the discourse-image will make any formal origin impossible to determine and the two forms will create the purest possible action-image. The monadic, dyadic and triadic levels of the discourse-image can be illustrated as in Table 3.10.

Kuroki Kazuo's *Face of Jizo* is a film of the discourse-image. The action takes place over four days in the summer of 1948. The setting is Hiroshima, or more

Table 3.10 Discourse-image

discourse-image		
molar composition		molecular genesis
limit of large form	limit of small form	limit of action-images

precisely, what was once an unpretentious family-run inn at the outskirts of the city, now – three years after the bomb – semi-derelict. Living there are Mitsue (Miyazawa Rie), a beautiful young woman in her twenties, and Takezou (Harada Yoshio), her good-natured (and more than a little iniquitous) father. *Face of Jizo* will employ traces of the nuclear event within an explicit exploration of the *pika* and *hibakusha* as a cinematic self-reflection. These traces become figures of discourse, figures that explore atomic bomb imagery and appropriate attraction-images of the genre cinema and inversion-images of the avant-garde. *Face of Jizo*, as will be seen, is a film at the very limit of the action-image creating powerful images of thought.

Face of Jizo (2004)

The skeleton of Hiroshima Prefectural Hall, above it a bruised a sky. Thunder, then lightning – a storm approaches. *Geta* sandals clip-clap on shards of broken pottery, find their way through the rubble-strewn path and weeds escaping from pavement cracks. A stumble, a cry – Mitsue runs toward the remains of her house, past the broken, diseased teeth of the burnt trees jutting from the brown, dried earth. Up the steps, through the sliding wood and glass *shoji* doors, she kicks off her clogs in the *genkan* as thunder explodes the sky. She runs from the entrance hall, screams as the lightning lights up the dining room, holding onto and hiding beneath the solid wooden column that supports the ceiling. Takezou, her father, is in the cupboard. He slides back the door and commands: 'Over here Mitsue, quick. Get this cushion on your head.' More thunder and lightning: 'Daddy, I'm scared.' They huddle in the dark security of the closet while the storm rages outside the house. 'Remember Nobu from the photo shop?' her father asks. Takezou and Mitsue reminisce how during the war Nobu would take 'racy' photos of women, and Takezou exchange them for rations with soldiers staying at their inn. Mitsue laughs. Nobu can no longer take photos: 'Every time one of his magnesium bulbs popped he couldn't get the flash of the bomb out of his head.' Kuroki cuts to an image of the *pika* in the blue sky.

Mitsue is frightened of the thunder and lightning because it is a visceral reminder of the day of the atomic bomb. Mitsue is a *hibakusha* and *Face of Jizo* tells the story of how this young woman is affected by the *pika*. Twenty-three years old, pretty, good-natured; yet living alone with her old father, caring for him after returning from the library where she works, rejecting the possibilities of love and of a life in the wake of the nuclear event. *Face of Jizo* is a masterful portrayal of the effects of the atomic bomb on the Japanese people.

It is exactly this type of Japanese atom bomb film which Lowenstein believes to be problematic. In this way, his validation of allegorical nuclear cinema is revealed as an overturning of such 'realist' direct depictions, which he sees as attempts at 'coherence' and 'intelligibility'.[152] 'Japan, like all nations, has a need to define itself to its own citizens and to the world's citizens, especially in the face of traumatic events such as Hiroshima.'[153] Thus Japan creates films focusing upon the *hibakusha* as atomic bomb victims. 'Hiroshima becomes scripted into dominant national narratives, into what Benjamin calls "the continuum of history".'[154] For Lowenstein, the 'dominant national narrative' with regards to the nuclear event is that of the 'A-bomb maiden'.[155] Lowenstein turns to Lisa Yoneyama's *Hiroshima Traces* (1999), which describes how post-Pacific War Japanese culture has occluded the era of fascism and militarism by concentrating upon the *pika* and the *hibakusha*. Furthermore, this exchange is gendered: images of pretty young women, keloid-scarred – or better still, suffering from latent radiation sickness or psychological trauma so their beauty is not compromised – replace images of heroic male soldiers implicated in the imperial project, war crimes, and, indeed, the shame of surrender. Consequently, Yoneyama writes, 'Japanese womanhood became fully implicated in sustaining the myth of national innocence and victimology'.[156] As Lowenstein concludes, 'traditional gender roles are deployed not only to provide a source of stability in the face of trauma, but to displace Japanese national responsibility for the trauma itself'.[157] Accordingly, 'the figure of woman enables a historical narrative of forgetting'.[158] This is the paradox of A-bomb maiden films (*Face of Jizo* and, we must assume, Shindo's *Children of the Atom Bomb*); they necessarily remember the nuclear event while – at one and the same time – enabling a forgetting of the full historical conditions. This, concludes Lowenstein, is 'exactly the sort of narrative that must be blasted open'.[159]

This problem is surfaced by Lowenstein as the ground for his work on allegorical Japanese nuclear cinema and the moment of *Jetztzeit*. This moment, in films that do not directly depict the nuclear event, allows the viewer to encounter the complexity of such historical forces – moments in which these traces at once escape meaning but, at the same time, invite an examination of the atomic attacks in respect to history. Accordingly, Lowenstein's analysis of Shindo's medieval horror film *Onibaba*, in which the murderous women break gendered stereotypes, capture up the forces of both of the *hibakusha* and Japanese national aggression and create a dialogue 'between victimisation and war responsibility'.[160] Similarly, Blake sees the figure of the female ghost in *Ring* (again inherently ambiguous) as creating such a dialogue – and it is this kind of confrontation encountered in *Face of Another*, in the reflection between the main narration and that of the film-within-a-film. In this way, these movies challenge the innocence of the A-bomb maiden with the ambiguities of the demon hag, killing spectre, or male anti-hero. It is such a dialogue we have encountered throughout this chapter in the films of the impulse-image, attraction-image and inversion-image, through symptoms, vults and originary worlds; through plastic and theatrical representations; through transformations of the sublime and enfeeblement. *Face of Jizo*, however, as a direct depiction of the nuclear event and as an A-bomb maiden film, appears complicit in a premature binding of the wounds of national trauma, as Blake would see it; constituting, according to Lowenstein after Yoneyama, a forgetting of history.

The limit of the small form action-image

Must every A-bomb maiden film, must every direct depiction of the nuclear event be a film of complicity? It is the use of the Deleuzian cineosis that allows us to explore the Japanese cinema of the atom bomb as a heterogeneous assemblage, and it is *Face of Jizo* that can confront such categorical identity with repetition and difference. In such a way we can discover an escape from the analyses of Blake and Lowenstein.

Face of Jizo is set over four days and the narration follows the interactions of Mitsue with her father Takezou. Mitsue wants to forget the *pika*, Takezou believes such forgetting betrays history and life. The situation that engenders this discord is the appearance of Kinsohita (Asano Tadanobu), a young researcher who has come to Hiroshima to collect artefacts relating to the bombing, and with whom Mitsue has fallen in love. Mitsue, however, attempts to reject both Kinsohita's love and any remembering of the *pika*. Kinsohita appears only in flashback, as a figure of thought. He is a trace, and a collector of trace objects. It is the effect of such traces on Mitsue that cause other painful memories to arise. And it is such figures of thought that reveal the film to be the purest of small form action-image. The crisis engendered by Kinsohita has caused the return of Takezou – the father is revealed to be the father's ghost; or rather, Mitsue is haunted by the memory of Takezou. The story thus centres entirely on one character – Mitsue – besieged by trace-images: the broken Hiroshima cityscape, her dilapidated house, the flashbacks to Kinsohita, hallucinations of her father. *Face of Jizo* is a direct engagement with the Japanese nuclear event, a film of the discourse-image at the very limit of the small form. There is the linking up of heterogeneous elements that remain heterogeneous – atom bomb film, love story, ghost movie – and these figures of thought are moments of self-reflexivity that create a special homogeneity: a paean to memory. In this way, traces of the nuclear event appear as moments of *Jetztzeit* in a direct depiction of the Japanese cinema of the atom bomb, and proliferate across the film, across the four days that the film encompasses. These traces are not simply psychological, but simultaneously historical.

When Kinoshita first comes to the library to ask for material on the *pika* for his research and to enquire about storing his collection of artefacts, Mitsue tells him: 'Even if we gather information on the bomb, the occupation forces forbid going public.' She continues: 'Besides, as an atom bomb victim myself, I am trying to forget. Nothing about what happened on that day will make a story, a picture, a poem, a novel or a subject to be studied.' This moment is complex. Kuroki cuts to an image of an American military base, aligning political and psychological repression. The monologue is conceived as a visual flashback, narrated by Mitsue to her father, the hallucination-ghost. It is self-reflexive: *Face of Jizo* attempting the very thing Mitsue believes impossible. These visual and sound images form an interweaving of discourses: American political policy which forbade any mention of the bomb or the war; Japanese complicity in such repression; and the problems of representation. Images of remembrance become traces that must be obliterated. The void must be maintained. Mitsue concludes: 'That's why we don't collect things on it. Not only that. If there were such things, we'd destroy them for good.' Such discourses weave a web of reflections upon cinematic image, history and thought.

Face of Jizo demands the void of Mitsue's forgetting be encircled by heterogeneous traces of memory. This is crystallized in the way in which Mitsue suppresses the love she feels for Kinoshita, a love that is stymied by her past: 'I mustn't fall in love with anyone … others have been denied happiness, why should I be happy?' One among these was her friend Akiko. She tells of how she met her friend's mother in the aftermath of the bomb, who screamed at her: 'What are you doing alive, when my daughter is dead?' The ghost-father responds: 'There is a name for what you have: guilt-ridden survivorist.' On the fourth day, the last day of the film, she lets Kinoshito store his artefacts at her house. Among them is a broken statue, the face of Jizo. This stone face blasts open her memory, a memory she has been trying to suppress over all others. On the day her father died she abandoned him: 'I left you and ran away.' But her ghost-father reminds her, he ordered her to leave; stuck beneath the burning house she had no chance of rescuing him, she could only have sacrificed her own life needlessly. In this way, Mitsue's attempt to suppress her memories is at the very heart of why she feels guilt and why she cannot allow herself to live life. Yet through Kinoshito's return – or rather, Kuroki's filmic return of the trace of her father, the ghost as an element of Mitsue's memory – forgetting is revealed as psychologically injurious. Mark Shilling writes: 'As a 15-year-old war plant worker, Kuroki saw his friends and colleagues blown to pieces in an air raid. Instead of staying to help the wounded, he ran to save his own skin – and carried a burden of guilt forever after. His war films, he has said, are an act of penance.'[161]

Face of Jizo explores memory as an image of thought describing the tensions between forgetting and remembering. For Lowenstein, it appears the aim of every film of the Japanese cinema of the atom bomb must be to remember and express 'Japanese national responsibility for the trauma itself'; anything but is wilful forgetting.[162] We are not concerned with such proscriptions or homogenizations – which may simply extend the mechanisms of repression they seek to disrupt. We are more concerned with what each film, in its own way, explores. The discourse-images of *Face of Jizo* are exemplary in revealing the nuclear event as an image of thought. Thus, contra Lowenstein, where 'the figure of

Figure 3.11 Mitsue encounters the face of Jizo as a trace, *Face of Jizo* (Kuroki, 2004)

woman enables a historical narrative of forgetting', the film exposes the very machinery of such forgetting, both psychological and political.[163] Far from the A-bomb maiden being deployed to 'provide a source of stability in the face of trauma', Mitsue is a locus of instabilities.[164] At the very limit of the small form action-image, the discourse-image is a reflection-image of the trace as memory. In this way, *Face of Jizo* does not so much elide histories of the nuclear event, as create indices that reveal traces. These indices form a vector describing the void, the vast reservoir of suppressed memories of the Japanese people.

Cleaving memory from such forgetting is, for Kuroki, the solution to the harms of both historical and psychological repression. An overcoming of such repression – remembering – heals wounds.

Consummation and crisis

The self-reflexivity of the discourse-image exposes the nature of traces of the nuclear event in the Japanese cinema, revealing the conceptual trajectory we have been developing over the course of this book: image as image → image as an image of history → image as an image of thought. The trace as image of thought was initially conceived in respect to the figures of attraction and inversion of the reflection-image. In these yakuza movies, horror flicks, arthouse and cyberpunk films traces of the *pika* and the *hibakusha* appeared as images of thought that disrupted a generalized forgetting of the nuclear event through complex and ambiguous figures that enacted a remembering. With attraction-images and inversion-images we encountered a breaking-through of history as an image of thought. No longer have we an image which refers us to a horizon of history; history is no longer given in the image of a direct or even an indirect expression. Rather the image is a trace, and becomes a moment of thought both for the film and for the spectator.

Reflection-images enact an incremental amplification of intensities, gradually exposing the trace as an image of thought. This was explicitly experienced in the self-reflexivity of the discourse-image, which allowed the trace to be explored in the context of a direct expression of the nuclear event in Japanese cinema through psychological memory. Yet we also saw such images of thought in the symptoms of the impulse-image, in vults and relics, as co-ordinates of an originary world. In this way, perhaps we can understand the image of thought not simply as a function of reflection-images, but of all cineotic images, a function that the reflection-image merely surfaces. After all, have we not – all along – encountered the image as engendering thought? With the affection-image of *Children of the Atom Bomb*, the face expressed externally the internal intensities of thought. Action-images such as *Godzilla* allowed us to think of the monster as emperor which in this way validated America's nuclear solution, while *Barefoot Gen* revealed the conscious and unconscious complicities of the Japanese people in the imperial project of the Pacific War. And we must foreground that these opaque and direct action-images, each in their own way, answer Lowenstein's call for an acknowledgement of 'Japanese national responsibility for the trauma itself'.[165] These films, the others we have explored, create images of thought. The reflection-image reveals every film as already an image of thought. Not so much a trajectory, then, but strata of the image: image as image ↔ image as an image of history ↔ image as an image of thought.

Cinema creates images as images of history and of thought. However, it has taken the reflection-image to expose this, and the discourse-image to take such images as the subject of the film. The final two chapters in this book extend this discovery of the discourse-image into mental-images and time-images, which reveal images of thought to be a heterogeneous assemblage. We begin, in the next chapter, with mental-images which create recollections, nightmares and symbols of the Japanese nuclear event. Mental-images not only bring the cinema of the movement-image to its completion, but at one and the same time, engender a fundamental crisis at the heart of such images.

4

Consummation (and Crisis)

The mental image would be less a bringing to completion of the action-image, and of the other images, than a re-examination of their nature and status.[1]

Mental-images

The nuclear attacks on Hiroshima and Nagasaki – these events are the very stuff of nightmarish dreams, horrific memories and apocalyptic imaginations. This chapter explores how such images are captured in the Japanese cinema of the atom bomb. The focus will be upon the films of Kurosawa Akira, who – throughout his years as writer and director – invented and propagated the *pika* and the *hibakusha* as such images of thought. Accordingly, these films can be explored through Deleuze's cineotic domain of mental-images, which capture up the perceptions, affects and actions of the movement-image in nightmares of the dream-image, memories of the recollection-image and symbolizations of the relation-image. This, as we will see, is both a consummation of the movement-image and – at one and the same time – the condition for its crisis and collapse.

Kurosawa began making films toward the end of the Pacific War, during the final suicidal throes of Japanese militarism, and was creating cinema right up to his death in the late 1990s. A politically engaged filmmaker, it is no surprise that he wrote and directed atom bomb movies. Completed just after the occupation, *I Live in Fear* (1955) tells the story of an aging Tokyo industrialist beset by thoughts of the Japanese atomic event and the possibility of a Cold War repetition to come. Many years later *Rhapsody in August* (1991), Kurosawa's penultimate film, explored the legacy of the nuclear event through the eyes of three generations of a Japanese family at the time of the forty-fifth anniversary of the Nagasaki bomb. Both these movies – in their own way – describe how the atomic attacks haunt the memories and imaginations of characters, interweaving image, history and thought. Kurosawa took this approach to an extreme in *Dreams* (1990), a film composed of eight different nightmares and dreams (supposedly his own, from across his life), two sequences of which depict post-apocalyptic scenarios. More obliquely there is *Rashomon* (1950), which can be said to be the first of Kurosawa's atom bomb movies, filmed during the American occupation and subject to the censorship regulations of the time. This medieval drama – set in a devastated milieu in the aftermath of war – can be seen as a way of exploring, through traces of the nuclear event, the very nature of memory.

Kurosawa's atom bomb films will be discussed in reference to Deleuze's cineotic domain of the mental-image. Mental-images are announced through the figures of attraction and inversion of the reflection-image – traces as filmic metaphors and allusions – carried through to figures of discourse where the trace becomes the subject of the film. In the previous chapter we saw how Kuroki's *Face of Jizo* was a discourse-image exploring repressed memories of the *pika* and the *hibakusha*. For Kuroki, such repression resulted in ill effects, conquered only through an active remembering. Kurosawa, in *I Live in Fear* (1955), approaches the question of the discursive-trace in quite a different way, through a reversal. This discourse-image film examines how a character is overwhelmed by memories of the atomic bomb, an overpowering terror that ultimately results in insanity. Surfacing and remembering the event, for Kurosawa, is not a solution in-and-of itself, but must necessarily be tempered by a forgetting. Kurosawa, in this way, uses the discourse-image to reveal thought as fundamentally problematic – a revealing that is explicitly explored in Deleuze's cineotic domain of mental-images: recollection-image films riven with pasts as flashbacks; dream-image movies overcome by hallucinations, dreams and nightmares; and relation-image cinema permeated by symbols, filmic marks of thought. Kurosawa will discover Japan and the atom bomb through each of these movement-image avatars. *Rashomon* is organized through a nexus of flashbacks, exposing cultural echoes of the defeat of Japan and the unfathomability of the American nuclear solution. The atomic nightmares of *Dreams* encounter images of the *pika* and the *hibakusha* haunting the dark depths of consciousness. *Rhapsody in August* tells how the atomic attacks retain, after nearly half a century, a presence in memorials, rituals and thought, experienced in different ways by the generations that lived through and came after the horror. Together, Kurosawa's four atom bomb films attempt to explore – but also, ultimately, to resolve – fundamental problems in the way memory, dreams and thought capture the Japanese nuclear event.

Such an analysis of mental-images brings to completion our journey through movement-images of the Japanese cinema of the atom bomb. Yet mental-images simultaneously proclaim a crisis that will allow the time-image to arise. The problems of film and thought will become the ground of cinema. The time-image – as we will see in Chapter 5 – will encourage such problems to remain unresolved and to decompose the film, destroying the co-ordinates of action, affect and perception, and in so doing creating a new cinematic semiosis. Mental-images, in distinction, explore thought within the domain of movement-images: thinking perception, thinking affect, thinking action; thinking contingent centres, thinking historical horizons; thinking the trace. Mental-images, in this way, attempt – through their various forms – to both acknowledge such problems and to bring these problems to resolution. These two domains of Deleuze's cinematic thought – mental-images and time-images – are inspired by Henri Bergson's double articulation of memory in *Matter and Memory*; it is thus via a return to Bergson that we must begin.

Bergson, memory

Bergson's initial thesis in *Matter and Memory* (as seen in Chapter 1) was of an enmeshed human in the world of matter. Perceptions of the world cause affects: external collisions cause variations in internal intensity (physical, biological, chemical). Affects, in turn, are externalized, engender action and modify the world. This is the sensory-motor trajectory: perception → affect → action. Such a trajectory immediately appears purely deterministic, disavowing agency, choice, freedom or thought. However, take the simplest of organisms, a microscopic single-cell life form, drifting in a liquid environment. Even here a perception productive of an almost instantaneous reaction (collisions, vibrations, light waves or suchlike) has no absolute determination. Perceptions can produce varied externalized reactions. Between perception and action, affect is a centre of indetermination. In slightly more complex animals, such as the human, internal intensities are multiplied through more intricate, numerous and disseminated arrays, creating the condition for more disparate responses, more possibilities of action, difference. Yet responses will also tend toward repetitions of the same, actions become habitual through selection. We thus see a dialectic of determination and indetermination.

We have already encountered, if not fully explored, such a formulation: Peirce's categories of firstness, secondness and thirdness (Chapter 3). Here we saw firstness equated with affect and secondness with action (engendered by zeroness of perception). Thirdness was described as mediating between and an encompassing of firstness and secondness, what Peirce called representational thought, which was relational, law-like.[2] The Peircian semiosis designated a complex interweaving of signs, of sign divisions and sign classes, allowing variation in relations. In Bergsonian terms, we aligned thirdness with the memory-image of the sensory-motor system. Affect, in this way, is the threshold of memory-images, the centre of indetermination an intricate interweaving of sensation and thought for the production and habituation of a diverse range of actions. On the one hand, memory-images allow the body-qua-itself to affect what it perceives by intervening in the selection of images: what (consciously or unconsciously) interests us? On the other hand, the memory-image intervenes in the affective selection of actions, allows the body-qua-itself to actualize possible reactions: what (conscious or unconscious) responses are appropriate?

Yet Bergson identifies another kind of memory, one that goes beyond and is before the memory-image (and remains unaccounted for in the Peircian schema).[3] This is 'pure memory'.[4] If the memory-image inhabits and inhibits the brain and body, pure memory is radically different. While perception produces action via affect and memory-images, the selection of perceptions and actions through affect and the memory-image is ultimately a function of pure memory. Actualization emerges from the virtual: 'the virtual image evolves toward the virtual sensation and the virtual sensation toward real movement: this movement, in realising itself, realises both the sensation of which it might have been the natural continuation and the image which has tried to embody itself in the sensation.'[5] We can express such an actualization of the virtual, of pure memory becoming memory-image (anticipating aspects of the discussion to come) as in Table 4.1.

What is this pure memory? One can say that for Bergson pure memory is no-'where'. Pure memory can be called the soul, the spirit and true thought. Do we in this way encounter dualism? Bergson admits his proposal is 'frankly dualistic'.[6] Yet this is not classical dualism, not the dualism of Descartes; the body and the mind are not two distinct substances. The brain-body is matter,

Table 4.1 Sensory-motor system and pure memory

[zeroness] firstness secondness thirdness	perception → affect → action memory-image sensory-motor system	actual	movement
[-]	pure memory	virtual	time

and matter and Bergsonian pure memory cannot exist apart from one another. Pure memory is not substance. The mind-body problem for Bergson is thus, in its own way, a kind of monism. However, neither 'a kind of dualism' nor 'a kind of monism' really captures Bergson's conceptualization; we rather encounter Bergsonian multiplicity. We encounter the body-mind as space-time: the central nervous system is in a continuous and spatial present; while pure memory is temporal, what was (and what could have been) and what (could or) will be.

Let us explore this through a radical domain of the modern scientific selectionist theory of memory. One hundred years after the publication of *Matter and Memory*, Patrick McNamara writes: 'Bergson's memory theory is "selectionist" or Darwinian in character.'[7] This selectionist memory theory describes two aspects: elements and process. First 'a generator of variation that produces an array of elements or traits which become the raw material for the selection process'; second, 'a selection process … which acts to reduce the number of elements in the initial array.'[8] Nature produces pure memory as potential and deploys it as memory-images across the central nervous system.[9] In this way, selection (actualization) is that of a reduction and habituation of possible (virtual) process-driven responses.

This conceptualization discovers a fundamental proposal. Traditional accounts see memory as being formed in response to external stimuli. McNamara writes it may appear that 'what drives the sequence of events is an external cue and then a search process'.[10] However, 'Bergson argued against this empiricist approach to memory'.[11] JZ Young comments: 'The nervous system contains a vast number of nerve cells and fibres, perhaps ten thousand million neurons in the human cerebral cortex and at least ten thousand million in the cerebellum. Moreover, each cell makes a great number of connections: there are up to 60,000 synaptic points on a large cortical neuron.'[12] Across this material network pure memory is molecular potential and virtual process. There is thus, as McNamara puts it, 'no notion of encoding or retrieval' in Bergsonian and selectionist accounts of memory.[13] There is 'no need to encode new information into the system since it already "contains," in the initial repertoire or in virtual ("generate-able") form, all the memories possible'.[14] In this way, 'most memories / rememberings are not triggered by external cues. Memory has its own rhythms and laws – its own agenda.'[15] Bergson's theory of spontaneous, or pure, memory thus has a 'non-dependence on external cues for its operations'.[16] And 'spontaneous rememberings, in fact, are the norm for human beings.'[17] Pure memory is a spontaneous flow which encounters the external world, the perception of which causes a break in that flow for the production of memory-images, affect and action. In this way 'selection is Darwinian in the sense that what is chosen is what is used'.[18] McNamara comments: 'Bergson suggested we are always steeped in a virtual infinity of images.'[19] From such a virtual, molecular infinity, selections are actualized and utilized at the 'molar behavioural level'.[20] There are, as McNamara puts it, only 'resonances' between extensive and intensive states. [21]

In summary, we can say with Bergson we encounter a double articulation of memory: memory-image (actual) and pure memory (virtual) – inseparable and in resonance. Pure memory, true thought, is virtual, processes actualized in the body and mind as the sensory-motor system, memory-images, images of thought, supporting the perception → affect → action trajectory.

This chapter and the next will explore how Bergson's double articulation of memory inspires Deleuze's cinematic time-images of pure memory and filmic mental-images of memory-images. We will begin, in this chapter, with mental-images (while the final chapter will concern itself with time-images). For Deleuze, memory-images tame pure memory, mental-images are time-images resolved through a grounding in the perception-image → affection-image → action-image trajectory. Yet still, mental-images initiate a radical and fundamental reorientation of the way in which we conceive of movement-images. Mental-images are both the consummation and crisis of the movement-image. It is such a consummation and crisis, such a problematizing and resolution, that we will explore through the Japanese atom bomb cinema of Kurosawa Akira, who invents and continually redeploys mental-images of the nuclear event.

Cineosis and cinema

Kurosawa, in *Rhapsody in August*, creates an incredible actualization of the *pika* and *hibakusha* as an image of thought. Kane (Murase Sachiko) is standing in the garden outside her house, looking toward the hills that separate her village from the city of Nagasaki. Suddenly there is a nuclear explosion, a mushroom cloud arises behind the hills; yet immediately it is obscured by a human eye, which slowly opens, and gazes down upon the valley, upon Kane. This image is complex. For Kane, now an old woman, the image appears for her and through her, on-screen. A witness to the atom bomb forty-five years before, reminded of the nuclear event by her grandchildren's questions, such memories infused by those of her long-dead brother who would repeatedly draw the *pika* as an eye. For Kurosawa, this actualization is made possible by creating it as an image

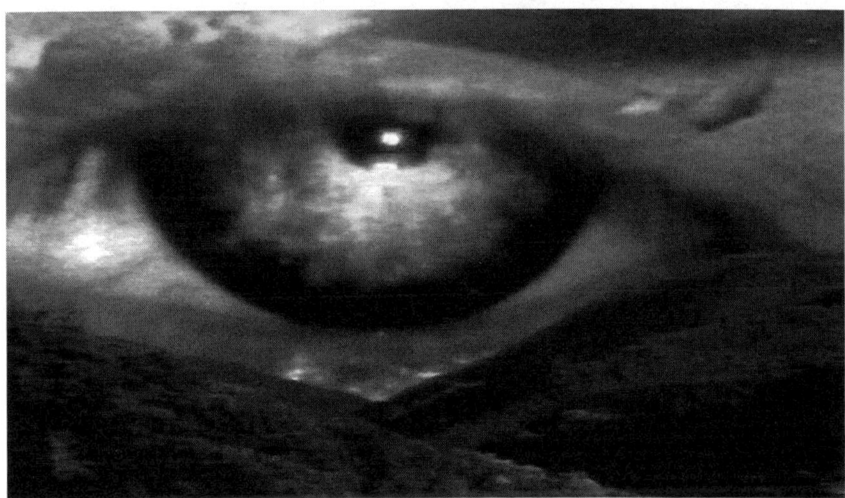

Figure 4.1 The big eye opens, superimposed upon the mushroom cloud that arises from behind the hills of Nagasaki, *Rhapsody in August* (Kurosawa, 1991)

of thought, by depicting the nuclear event through the memory-images of a *hibakusha*, and by the selection of a symbolic image of the *pika* as eye, a trace with cultural resonance. Cinematic memory, hallucination and symbolism created as an actualized image: this is the mental-image.

In Chapters 1 through 3, we have explored how cinematic images appear as perception-images, affection-images and in respect to the domain of action-images. In this chapter and the next we encounter the way in which cinematic images appear as a function of memory and thought: mental-images and time-images. Mental-images describe the way in which thought appears on-screen in respect to the sensory-motor system; while time-images describe the way in which thought is engendered through cinema as spontaneous, pure memory. From this perspective, we encounter a reversal. It has so far appeared that perception, affect and action are the primary co-ordinates of the cineosis. Now it is revealed that mental-images and time-images take primacy. Mental-images express the way in which thought appears as a memory-image, actualized memory in respect to affect, perception and action. Time-images express spontaneous thought, pure memory, memory as a process prior to actualization. In this way cinematic images of thought are both the consummation of the movement-image and its crisis. This crisis describes a loosening of the sensory-motor process which comes to fruition in the time-image, pure optical and sound images, opsigns and sonsigns, a beyond of the movement-image. Time-images – which we explore in Chapter 5 – describe thought overcoming sensory-motor organization. Mental-images – the subject of this chapter – describe thought captured within the regime of movement-images. We can express these relations as in Table 4.2.

Mental-images appear in cinema through recollection-images, dream-images and relation-images, yet are announced through the precursors of the reflection-image (filmic figures of thought), most explicitly in the discourse-image. Together, these images capture up perception-, affection- and action-images as an image of thought through the sensory-motor process as movement-images. When mental-images dominate a film we encounter cinema replete with traces, flashbacks, dreams and symbols. The atomic event in *Rhapsody in August* is such a mental-image. It is an actualization made possible by spontaneous memory, a taming of the processes of pure memory. It is captured up in traces, recollections, dreams and relations, which in turn refer us to perceptions, affects and action. This image appears to Kane as a memory of a perception through a flashback; it is overlaid with hallucination, affective memory from the insanity of her brother; and in this way creates relations of thought between the event, Kane and the various generations of her family. Simultaneously this mental-image is created by Kurosawa in the context of the film (as both a response and precursor to the events which structure the narration) and in the context of the Japanese cinema of the atom bomb (direct, indirect and trace depictions). This matrix – as we will later discover – is the most essential of mental-images, the relation-image, a complex and ambiguous symbol, and can be considered as the crowning achievement of Kurosawa's atom bomb films.

Yet in order to realize such a relation-image, Kurosawa needed to first invent mental-images of the nuclear event in all facets, as dream-images of nightmares, as recollection-images of memory, and as discourse-images of the trace. Before

Table 4.2 Movement-image and time-image after Bergson

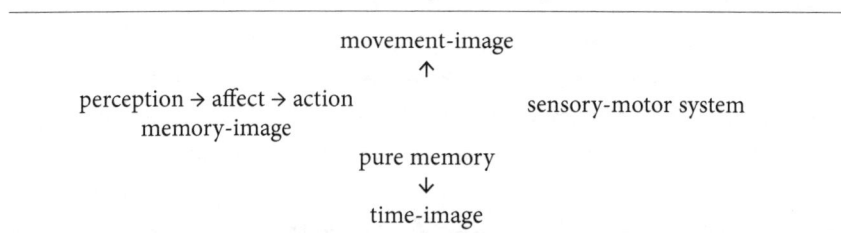

	movement-image	
	↑	
perception → affect → action		sensory-motor system
memory-image		
	pure memory	
	↓	
	time-image	

we encounter *Rhapsody in August* as relation-image, we must therefore pass through the recollection- and dream-images of *Rashomon* and *Dreams*, and – before that – the discourse-image of *I Live in Fear*. Such a trajectory will allow us to explore how Kurosawa appeared to invent the first mental-image of the atomic attacks through the discourse-image of *I Live in Fear*, a film made soon after the end of the occupation. However, our trajectory reflects the subsequent unearthing of a secret mental-image of the nuclear event prior to *I Live in Fear*, one embedded in the time of occupation censorship, the recollection-image that is *Rashomon*. It is only after taking into account the recollection-images of *Rashomon* that we can fully appreciate the discourse-images of *I Live in Fear*, and the experimental mental-images of the *pika* and the *hibakusha* in the dream-images of Kurosawa's *Dreams*. Discourse-images → recollection-images → dream-images lead us to the relation-images of *Rhapsody in August*, Kurosawa's final atom bomb film. Why devote a chapter to Kurosawa? The answer is that his atom bomb films and only his films inhabit and explore the domain of mental-images in all facets, because Kurosawa invented the mental-image of the nuclear event, and produced in these four films only mental-images of the nuclear event. In so doing, Kurosawa continually redeploys images of thought of the *pika* and the *hibakusha*, examining the Japanese nuclear event from different perspectives at different times under different conditions. Kurosawa brings the Japanese movement-images of the atomic bomb to consummation, taking them beyond a depiction as special image and beyond the idea of history as the ultimate horizon, or limit, of the Japanese nuclear event. Kurosawa foregrounds the *pika* and the *hibakusha* as images of thought, images in time, subject to redistribution and reinvention. This, as will be reflected upon toward the end of the chapter, is the very crisis of the movement-image.

I. Discourse and forgetting

I Live in Fear (1955)

A lunatic asylum: examiner of the domestic court, Dr Harada (Shimura Takashi), is talking with the institution's psychologist (Nakamura Nobuo). They sit facing one another across a wooden desk. In the background, behind a rough wire partition, patients of the communal ward (seemingly) walk aimlessly in circles; some approach the mesh, crowd together watching the two doctors. 'Perhaps we are the ones who are insane.' Perhaps, continues the psychologist, the only truly sane person is Nakajima (Mifune Toshiro). Harada makes his way to Nakajima's private cell. He is sitting calmly on the clean white sheets of his bed. They chat politely for a few moments, eventually falling into silence. Nakajima asks: 'By the way, what happened on Earth? Are there many people left?' He believes he is finally safe, has been relocated to a faraway planet, no longer living under the threat of worldwide nuclear annihilation. 'They'd better leave soon before disaster strikes.' Nakajima lifts his head, looking out his window. Through the bars he sees the sun. In abject despair, screaming – it has finally happened – the Earth is consumed by nuclear war: 'The Earth is burning, burning, burning.' Harada can do nothing. He leaves the room, the ward, and slowly descends the ramp that leads toward the asylum exit.

So ends Kurosawa's *I Live in Fear*. The film centres upon the difficulties created by ageing industrialist Nakajima Kiichi for his family, who want him 'certified of unsound mind' after developing 'a phobia about atomic and hydrogen bombs'. To avoid radioactive fallout from American testing in the

Figure 4.2 Nakajima believes the sun to be the Earth consumed by a nuclear explosion, *I Live in Fear* (Kurosawa, 1955)

Pacific, Nakajima purchased land in the Sembuku district of Akita province, northern Japan, and ordered 'a strange underground home' to be constructed for the family. However, upon hearing the Soviets are now testing to the north, he comes to believe the only safe place on Earth is South America. His family cannot contemplate leaving Japan and thus appeal to the authorities for a court order giving them control of Nakajima Foundry. Family court mediator Dr Harada is put in charge of the case. However, before Harada can make his decision, Nakajima burns down the foundry in a last desperate attempt to sever the family's ties to Japan.

I Live in Fear explores traces of the atom bomb as figures of thought. The sound of planes overhead, wind, rain and thunder, a flash of lightning, the sun in the sky – all are mistaken by Nakajima for the atom bomb. These sound and visual images occur in the world – others hear and see them too – yet only Nakajima reacts as if they are something other than what they are. Only Nakajima encounters them as traces of the atom bomb. In the previous chapter we were concerned with discovering the nature of such traces. Beginning with naturalist dramas, yakuza flicks, horror movies, cyberpunk and avant-garde cinema, we found symptoms and figures of the *pika* and the *hibakusha* saturating the mise-en-scène, appearing as allusions, metaphors, metonyms, allegories and inversions. These moments disrupted the co-ordinates of the films, appeared as moments of the shock of history. Through the discourse-image we discovered the genesis of such traces: images of thought – a memory breaking through a continuum of repression. Kuroki's *Face of Jizo*, as discourse-image, explored how the repression of the Japanese nuclear event resulted in the past haunting the present and this present ossifying future life. Kuroki believed an active remembering of the nuclear event would create the solution to the harms of such historical and psychological forgetting, such overcoming healing wounds. *I Live in Fear*, while exploring the same ground as *Jizo*, does not appear to offer such consolation.

Sato Tadao believes the film cinematically important for Japan. Kurosawa approached the atom bomb in a way no other filmmaker had – as yet – attempted, 'treating it for the first time as a psychological force devastating human life from within, rather than simply as an outer force of destruction'.[22] Yet despite such innovation, for Sato and other critics, Kurosawa's methodology necessarily failed. Stephen Prince, in his monumental *The Warrior's Camera* (1991), writes: 'Kurosawa's efforts to apply his forms to social problems in the contemporary world inevitably led to confrontations with problems of a magnitude far beyond the reformist capabilities of the individual hero.'[23] Nakajima, while acting decisively, does so as an individual and thus cannot modify the world-situation. Because of this, he goes insane. He does not discover a social solution; does not, for instance, join the Japanese anti-nuclear movement. Nakajima's catastrophe 'is a structural symptom of the deadlock that besets Kurosawa's own analysis, confined as it is to individuals and ethical questions of personal responsibility'.[24] The impasse of *I Live in Fear* is illustrative of the necessary failure of any non-social response to the question of the atom bomb. As Joan Mellen writes: 'Kurosawa falls short of counterposing to Nakajima's quixotic plan a more effective means of approaching the threat of nuclear war. Lacking this dimension, the film seems incomplete as if something remains to be said.'[25] Prince, in a wonderful formulation, sees this lack as foundational: 'with the path toward a really political analysis foreclosed, the film must repress the bomb itself, disclosing its threat connotatively.'[26] The visual and sound images must appear only as figures of thought in respect to Nakajima – they cannot be actualized on-screen. 'What makes *Record* [*I Live in Fear*] a fascinating film', for Prince, 'is its awareness of that which it represses': Nakajima's insanity and incarceration are 'evidence of the textual work of repression', ultimately the repression of the 'transindividual nature of the problem'.[27]

The consensus view would seem to be that *I Live in Fear* – through the insanity and incarceration of Nakajima – fails to propose a solution to the problem of the nuclear situation the film presents. Furthermore, this occurs because any solution which would propose the consolations of personal memory (as proffered by Kuroki's *Face of Jizo*) must necessarily fail. *I Live in Fear* not only revokes *Face of Jizo* through this impasse, but also itself. However, what if there is another way to explore *I Live in Fear*? It seems to me that by focusing purely upon Nakajima's insanity, such analyses create the very impasse they identify. *I Live in Fear*, in other words, can be seen to have a transindividual dimension if the focus is shifted. Furthermore, what is considered failure can be revaluated, making a corroboration of the consolations of individual memory possible – albeit in a radically different way than *Jizo*. Such a reading can begin with Deleuze's own engagement with Kurosawa in *Cinema 1*.[28]

Deleuze on Kurosawa

Kurosawa is a filmmaker, for Deleuze, whose movies can be encountered through the discourse-image, under the sign of the extreme limit of the large form action-image. The large form action-image describes a situation → action → new situation trajectory, where the milieu creates two lines of force in conflict, a binomial that is resolved at the end of the film. The narrative thus explores how the character becomes (or is unable to become) equal to the final required action by way of traversing a series of polynomial duels. The limit of the large form reflects upon this trajectory, makes the trajectory itself a figure of thought.[29] This is, as Deleuze puts it, 'an extremely pure SA formula' where the character 'must know all the givens before acting and in order to act'.[30] How does the milieu permeate the environment? What are the determinates, and what are the elements? How can a response – the correct response – be identified and deployed? Only then, once these givens are understood, can the character act.

The sign of limit of the large form is taken up by Kurosawa in his films and becomes the pedagogy of his vision, his ethic. This is why, for Deleuze, 'Kurosawa's films often have two clearly distinct parts: the first, a long exposition and the second when senseless brutal action begins'.[31] In the elongated first section, the character is on a quest to understand all the givens; this takes much time and 'is difficult'.[32] Only then, in the final coda, can the character act. For Deleuze, Kurosawa's films can explore this trajectory in four ways.

'In the first place,' writes Deleuze, 'the givens, of which there must be a complete exposition, are not simply those of the situation.'[33] Rather 'they are the givens of a question which is hidden in the situation, wrapped up in the situation, which the hero must extract in order to be able to act, in order to be able to respond to the situation'.[34] Thus the response 'is not merely that of action to the situation, but, more profoundly, a response to the question, or to the problem that the situation was not sufficient to disclose'.[35] 'A problem' for Deleuze 'is not an obstacle.'[36] The large form proper presents obstacles to be overcome – at the limit we encounter an insight into what is essential within the situation. Kurosawa will also explore the failure of this quest: 'he who does not understand, he who is in a hurry to act because he believes he possesses all the givens of a situation … will perish.'[37] Second, a Kurosawa film can negotiate between success and failure. Here the character appears to be on the path to destruction, but at the last moment swerves. The 'character believes it is enough to grasp the givens of a situation: he even proceeds to draw all the consequences, but notices there is a hidden question, which he suddenly understands and which changes his decision.'[38] Third, the nature of the final act can be displaced: 'instead of absorbing a situation in order to produce a response which is merely an explosive action, it is necessary to absorb a question in order to produce an action which would truly be a considered response.'[39] Kurosawa replaces the decisive brutal action with another kind of reaction, one beyond, before or other than violence.

Finally, 'a fourth case, in effect, allows us to recapitulate the whole'.[40] Some of Kurosawa's films pass through all the modifications, distributing the trajectories to various characters or even through one character at the centre of the film. *Ikiru / To Live* (1952) – which Deleuze believes 'one of Kurosawa's finest films' – is such an instance of this fourth case.[41] Watanabe Kanji (Shimura Takashi) discovers he has only a few days before he will die. At first he thinks he knows what he should do – live life to the full in the time he has left. He visits strip-joints and bars, but finds them distasteful. He tries a love affair, but once again this leaves him unfulfilled. Finally, he discovers the problem hidden in the situation, which allows him to change his path. As Deleuze puts it, 'the man understands: the givens of the question "What is to be done?" are those of the useful task to be performed'.[42] The final act of the dying man is thus a response to a question which was extracted from the situation. Watanabe remembers that, before he found out about his illness, he wanted to restore a public park devastated during the war. The crucial point is that the character's response remains personal, but is concomitantly extended into the world, for the world, a universal answer. Such is the source of Kurosawa's humanism. Just how we might define Kurosawa's humanism will be discussed in the sections that follow; as Mitsuhiro Yoshimoto comments, 'although Kurosawa's films are often discussed as films of humanism, what this ambiguous notion means is not always clear'.[43]

To Live provides us with an example of how Kurosawa creates a cinema at the limit of the large form through an interweaving of his three trajectories as a fourth. *I Live in Fear* appears a very different film from *To Live*. However, in its own way, it too is an instance of this fourth case.

The limit of the large form action-image

The most fundamental co-ordinates of the large form action-image inspire *I Live in Fear*. We traverse the trajectory of situation → action → new situation through the parallel montage that structures a conflict in the narration. This consists of the conflict between Nakajima and Harada, and becomes polynomial through the duels between each of them and their families, colleagues and associates. The situation that engenders this crisis is Japan and the atom bomb.

Yet *I Live in Fear* goes beyond the elementary co-ordinates of the large form, toward the limit. The film is a quest for the question hidden in the situation. On the one hand, Nakajima believes he has understood the situation, and rushes to act. In so doing he brings disaster upon himself, his family, and the workers dependent upon employment at the foundry. Harada, on the other hand, is in search of the givens of the question behind the situation; he is in search of the problem, which he doggedly pursues. This duel between the old industrialist and the court mediator thus explores all the modifications of Kurosawa's film-philosophy. If one man appears to act too soon, the other appears to act too late; and both appear to fail. Harada's indecision is as much to blame for the tragedy as Nakajima's decisive act. However, the disaster at the factory allows – in the final instance – Harada to have Nakajima committed. This is why the coda at the end of the film is so important, not simply to dissect Nakajima's insanity, but more importantly to show that Harada has finally discovered a response. What appeared to be interminable indecision is now resolved: Harada has swerved. Accordingly, in opposition to Nakajima's violent solution is Harada's considered response. *I Live in Fear* is constructed at the limit of the large form, and plays out Kurosawa's three trajectories between the two conflicting characters, constituting a recapitulation of the whole.

Consequently, not only must we consider Nakajima's path of destruction but simultaneously Harada's exploration of the givens. Harada – who must rule on Nakajima's sanity – spends the entire film attempting to understand what must be done. He asks his son what he thinks about the atom bomb, if he is afraid. The son replies: 'Everyone is afraid.' So, 'how can you be so calm?' The answer: 'Because there is no escape.' Another question: 'What would happen if you thought about it all the time?' The son's reply is 'you'd go crazy'. Dr Harada continues his quest as his boss loses patience with the process, freezing Nakajima's assets. Medical tests have proved Nakajima sane, but another mediator thinks him paranoid. 'Exactly, he's paranoid,' replies Harada, 'but don't we all fear the H-bomb?' Then the questions: 'Why does he feel it so acutely? What brought it to a head? Ought we not to look more closely?' Still pursuing answers, Harada visits the foundry – now burned out, a water-damaged and smoking shell. Nakajima is unrepentant; the family and the workers devastated.

Accordingly, we encounter the transindividual, social, aspect of *I Live in Fear*. The conflict between the two men explores the situation: through Nakajima's rich bourgeois family, his relations and his mistress; through Harada's middle-class relations, the governmental institutions represented by the court officials, and the workers at Nakajima Foundry. In the wake of the arson, one of the men asks: 'Master … you're saying we can go to the dogs?' The factory supports more than Nakajima's family: it supports a whole community. At first Nakajima offers to take everyone to Brazil, but then he realizes that this solution is both impossibly too large and still infinitesimally too small. Who should be saved? What can be done so all don't perish? These paradoxes finally throw Nakajima over the edge of sanity. Nakajima's collapse, both mental and physical (into wet mud and ashes) provides Harada with an understanding of what lies behind the situation.

This understanding is a function of the traces of the atom bomb in *I Live in Fear*, traces that have accumulated over the trajectory of the film. Such traces appear, on the one hand, for Nakajima as unactualized mental-images: spontaneous memory resonating with actual visual and sound traces. On the other hand, traces of the atom bomb are actualized through Harada's quest: his research, the books he reads, the interviews and conversations he has with the multitude of characters that populate the screen-space. Harada's discourse-images bring forth figures of thought and place them into direct relation with perception- and affection-images. These traces have to be torn from the milieu, their reconstitution disruptive of the continuum of the lives of the Japanese people. What Harada comes to understand is this: remembering disturbs, is not necessarily the solution to the trace. Hence the deferred – but ultimately constituted – action-image, which occurs at the extreme limit of the large form: Harada's considered response, the incarceration of Nakajima. Memory has two facets: remembering and forgetting. *I Live in Fear* promotes forgetting. In such a way, Kurosawa can be said to display an aspect of Nietzscheism with regard to the memory. Memory 'returns as a ghost and disturbs the peace', writes Nietzsche.[44] Therefore 'it seems necessary to constrain and control' memories 'if one is not oneself to perish in their conflict'.[45] 'Consider the cattle, grazing as they pass you by, this is a hard sight for man to see; for, though he thinks himself better than the animals … he cannot help envying them their happiness.'[46] The animal 'at once forgets', 'every moment really dies, sinks back into night and fog'.[47] For Nietzsche, 'it takes a great deal of strength to live and to forget'.[48]

Instead of Remember! Forget! Kuroki's *Face of Jizo* depicted how historical and psychological repression of the Japanese nuclear event resulted in harms, the past haunting the present, petrifying future life. Kuroki's solution was a reconstitution of memory at the level of the individual. *I Live in Fear* is on the side of forgetting. Repression only leads to ill effects once broken open, when what is repressed returns. Forgetting allows the human and society to function. Nakajima must be sacrificed for society; this is Harada's considered response. Accepting this difficult responsibility is Harada's heroism. The consolations of memory, in *I Live in Fear*, are to be found in active forgetting. This is Kurosawa's radical proposal.

Yet this conclusion presents a problem which we must deal with first, by way of a detour: for if Kurosawa proposes such forgetting, why the return to the subject of the atom bomb?

Blocs of sensation

Such revisitations are a significant aspect of that which makes Kurosawa's atom bomb films so interesting. What does such a return mean? We can perhaps begin to answer this no doubt complex question by considering Kurosawa as an artist, as an auteur – and, furthermore, by considering the concept of the auteur with regards to Deleuze and the cineosis.

In 1990 Kurosawa was honoured at the 62nd American Academy Awards. His response was delightful: 'I really don't feel that I have yet grasped the essence of cinema. Cinema is a marvellous thing, but to grasp its true essence is very, very difficult … from now on I will work as hard as I can at making movies, and maybe by following this path I will achieve an understanding.'[49] Prince comments that Kurosawa 'kept his word. He continued making movies and finding new directions in the medium. In his last three films, he reinvented his work.'[50] Kurosawa abandoned the discourse-image for mental-images. Prince writes: 'at its end, Kurosawa's became a cinema … not [of] action' but one 'in which activity has given way to memory.'[51] Yet Kurosawa's films had explored memory prior to his late period. We have seen this in *I Live in Fear* with memory as a factor of the discourse-image capturing up figures of thought within the action-image. And even his earliest films experiment with different forms of the image of thought. Nowhere is this seen more explicitly than in *Rashomon* with its narrative almost entirely constructed of mental-image flashbacks.

Rashomon is exemplary, for it creates a disjunction in the idea of an auteur trajectory. Prince writes, for instance, that as Kurosawa's films progressed 'his relationship to the medium, as to life, altered significantly'.[52] Thus '*Sanshiro Sugata* (1943) to *One Wonderful Sunday* (1947) show Kurosawa's developing mastery of film style'.[53] Then 'from *Drunken Angel* (1948) to *Red Beard* (1965)' (the period of *Rashomon* and *I Live in Fear*), the films 'belong to an age of heroism' where his 'cinema reflected the tasks of post-war reconstruction'.[54] 'From *Dodeskaden* (1970) to *Ran* (1985)' we encounter 'a period of melancholy and bitterness', leading to 'the final films, beginning with *Dreams* (1990)', which 'manifest a more contemplative outlook, in the twilight of life'.[55] There is nothing wrong with this account; it seems to me a practical way of grasping a whole. Indeed, it acknowledges temporality and transformation. Yet such an approach has severe limits. Temporality and transformation are subsumed within a successive trajectory which entails a homogenization within each period and problematizes aberration. This creates difficulties for the interpretive and political dimensions of film-philosophy, the film in-itself risks becoming lost in a brouhaha of hero-worship (and disappointment), and an imbroglio of generalization.

Yet is not Deleuze complicit in such auteurist narration? As we have seen, Kurosawa, for Deleuze, is a filmmaker of the discourse-image, a 'genius', his films corresponding to the sign of the limit of the large form action-image.[56] Is this not the purest form of auteurism? Deleuze does not even appear to allow for temporality and transformation, for succession and progression, let alone aberration. Sign = auteur. 'We might take Gilles Deleuze's famous two-volume typology of the signs of cinema in terms of the "great auteurs" as an extreme manifestation of this philosophy of purity', writes Dana Polan.[57] 'What he is presenting is a classification in which each director is associated in irreducible purity with a specific sign and in which any succession between directors is taken to result from a logic of signs themselves rather than from the pressures of material history.'[58] Is this the case? The first question must be what Deleuze understands by the term auteur; the second that of the relationship between auteur and sign.

'Auteur' – and 'there are other just as respectable names for other types of producers, such as editor, programmer, director, producer' – is, for Deleuze, 'a function that refers to an artwork'.[59] We may want to explore a film or films through an actor – as indeed Deleuze does in the *Cinema* books – or a cinematographer, or an editor. The author, or auteur, is just one way of creating a set. The important word is 'function'. What is this functional relationship between art and author, painter, sculptor; between film and filmmaker? In *What is Philosophy?* Deleuze and Guattari write that the artwork 'is independent of the creator through the self-positing of the created, which is preserved in itself. What is preserved – the thing or the work of art – is a bloc of sensation.'[60] In this way, it is the sensation as bloc that creates linkages: 'great creative affects can link up or diverge, within compounds of sensations that transform themselves, vibrate, couple, or split apart.'[61] A filmic bloc of sensation may be an image, a sequence, a film, or series of films. An image from this film can link to an image from that film, and so on. A filmic bloc of sensation may be a series of movies, independent of director, that conform to one sign of the cineosis (as we have seen with the Showa *Godzilla* cycle in respect to the binomial of the large form action-image). A filmic bloc of sensation may be a theme explored by an author that traverses any number of signs and images (as we have seen with regards to Shindo Kaneto and his atom bomb films of the affection-image, impulse-image and action-image). Such blocs of sensation 'account for the artist's relationship with the public, for the relation between different works by the same artist, or even for a possible affinity between artists.'[62] Such blocs link images, films, history, cinema history and cinematic thought in any number of ways.

Polan misses the essential aspect of the cineosis – the signs are little machines used to connect images and to connect films in order to produce readings. 'What we classify are signs in order to formulate a concept that presents itself as an event.'[63] Thus, while Deleuze explores Kurosawa as a filmmaker of the discourse-image, operating at the extreme limit of the large form, he does so only in respect to the films he momentarily connects and in the sense of an alliance between a name and a sign in order to begin an exploration. This is crucial. For the danger inherent in auteurism is twofold. In the first instance there is aberration: the risks being that aberrations are annulled or seen as not abiding the auteur's true path, a failure of form to explore content, or content that cannot be explored through form. Rather, every film is an aberration. Thus the second threat: evaluation. The so called aberrant movies – and certain periods of the successive trajectory of temporality and transformation – can be seen as necessarily degenerative. For instance, Prince writes of Kurosawa that 'the films after *Red Beard* notably lack the strong, striving protagonists … and the engagement with social transformation that these characters and their quests symbolised.'[64] Accordingly, Kurosawa's cinema 'was never again a populist or popular cinema, and it became increasingly didactic and remote in tone.'[65] Yet does such change necessarily entail a repudiation or betrayal of an ideal form? (And was there ever an ideal form?) Why must such a move away from popular cinema (or perhaps it was popular cinema moving away from the auteur?) be considered problematic? And can we not discover such moves, moreover, in the images and films of the creator throughout their oeuvre?

From discourse-image to mental-image

Mitsuhiro Yoshimoto writes: 'Kurosawa is not an auteur who single-mindedly pursued throughout his career, which spanned more than fifty years, a single project, whether artistic, political or otherwise.'[66] *Kurosawa* (2000) is organized through a successive trajectory – yet Yoshimoto takes every precaution. He explores each film in-and-of-itself, linking this one with that as he discovers and creates resonances. 'The complexity, contradiction, and openness of Kurosawa's work cannot be reduced to either the intention and subjectivity of an auteur, or the cultural traditions and patterns of a particular nation called Japan.'[67] Rather there are connections. Images and films link up and diverge, create mobile blocs of sensation.

For Deleuze, a filmmaker is not necessarily limited to one image, to one sign. With Kurosawa, furthermore, Deleuze creates a bloc of sensation that both diverges from the discourse-image and links up with the mental-image (and other images): 'the givens of the question in themselves implied dreams and nightmares, ideas and visions, impetuses and actions of the subjects involved.'[68] Accordingly, 'this is the origin of Kurosawa's oneirism, such that the hallucinatory visions are not merely subjective images, but rather figures of thought which discover the givens of a transcendent question, in so far as they belong to the world, to the deepest part of the world'.[69] In *I Live in Fear* the atom bomb appears as figures of thought through the discourse-image, an interweaving of traces unactualized and actualized on-screen through Nakajima's spontaneous memory and Harada's quest of examining memory-images to reveal the transcendent question. In certain other of Kurosawa's films, however, different images of thought arise and dominate. These overwhelmings appear under different conditions, in films as late as *Dreams* and *Rhapsody in August*, but also as early as *Rashomon*. In these films Kurosawa creates blocs of sensation we call mental-images, which in turn can be said to create a thematic bloc of sensation within the heterogeneous assemblage of the Japanese atom bomb cinema. And if *Dreams* and *Rhapsody in August* mark a return to the subject thirty-five years after *I Live in Fear*, *Rashomon*, made five years before, can be said to constitute the origin of Kurosawa's exploration of Japan in the wake of the nuclear event.

Through this detour on Deleuze's auteurism, we discover the essential reason for Kurosawa's return, both in *Dreams* and *Rhapsody in August* after *I Live in Fear*, and in *I Live in Fear* after *Rashomon*. The problem of memory not only cannot be silenced, but presents itself anew at different times, under different historical and material conditions. In so doing it requires, for Kurosawa, new investigations using other forms, a continual re-evaluation of the solution in respect to the time (in history, in life) in which the film was made.

II. Recollections, dreams and ahistory

Recollection-images

Mental-images describe the way in which thought is captured and actualized within the sensory-motor schema. We can approach the co-ordinates and characteristics of mental-images in terms of the Peircian semiosis, as genuine thirdness which has an in-itself and two degenerate forms relative to secondness and firstness. In this way, we have thirdness, or thought, with affect in ascendancy (relative firstness of thirdness): the dream-image, which describes nightmares, hallucinations and dreams. We have thirdness, thought, riven with action (relative secondness of thirdness): the recollection-image, which captures memory of the past for the present through flashbacks. We have thirdness in-itself, mediating the nexus of affect and action (thirdness of thirdness): the relation-image, which captures the very processes of thought as marks of the sensory-motor schema. Such tendencies show that the mental-image is not apart from the other movement-images, but rather gathers them up in thought.

We can begin with memories of the past. Recollection-images appear as flashbacks, and flashbacks depict memories, be it those of a single character or of multiple characters. Deleuze identifies two poles for the recollection-image, which correspond to the molar and molecular: these are 'destiny' and 'forking paths'.[70] For Deleuze, the flashback creates a 'closed circuit' which negotiates a trajectory 'from the present to the past, then … back to the present'.[71] With molar destiny, the link between the present and the image in the flashback creates a loop which does not stymie the sensory-motor schema, but rather bolsters, reinforces and justifies it. As Deleuze writes: 'we know very well that the flashback is a conventional, extrinsic device: it is generally indicated by a dissolve link … it is like a sign with the words "watch out! Recollection"'.[72] While Deleuze does not decompose this molar composition into its two constituent signs, we might describe these as the strong and the weak. Strong destiny would create a flashback loop without ambiguity, assigned to a character and the image would drive forward the narrative with trenchant logic. Weak destiny would describe a flashback that is more of a clue, or a theme, or a remembrance, where the content of the image is not integral to the plot, an affective link. We could also (just as Deleuze will do with dream-images, as we shall see) think of the strong and the weak in terms of technical signalling. A strong flashback will announce itself with effects such as the slow dissolve, the departure to the past and return to the present appearing without ambiguity. A weak flashback may involve simple cuts for the departure and return, and be difficult to identify. Furthermore, the strong may relate one character and their flashbacks, while the weak may have many characters and many flashbacks which – while not contradicting one another – could designate relative perspectives.

In respect to the genetic or molecular sign, we encounter flashbacks where there is 'no longer any question of an explanation, a causality or a linearity'.[73] Rather, we discover the 'fragmentation of all linearity, perpetual forks like so many breaks in causality'.[74] Deleuze writes that a recollection-image film permeated by such forks displays a 'multiplicity of circuits': 'it is not simply several people each having a flashback, it is the flashback belonging to several people'; and 'it is not just the circuits forking between themselves, it is each circuit forking within itself'.[75] In this way, the forks become 'repetitions' which 'are not accumulations'; rather, these paths 'refuse to be aligned, or to reconstitute destiny, but constantly split up any state of equilibrium … in a collection of non-linear relations.'[76] While with destiny the flashback constitutes an answer to a question which can drive the film forward, forks ask 'what happened? How have we arrived at this point?'[77] For Deleuze, this is 'perhaps the question of all questions'.[78] The crucial aspect is that forking paths do not simply depict memories, rather, they show how memory is reconstituted in the present: 'it is in the present that we make a memory, in order to make use of it … we witness the birth of memory.'[79] The monadic, dyadic and triadic levels of the recollection-image can be illustrated as in Table 4.3.

Kurosawa's *Rashomon* is a film of forking paths. What we will discover are not simply flashbacks to memories relative to the characters in the present and for the present. Rather, flashbacks disperse and proliferate; we no longer know

Table 4.3 Recollection-image

recollection-image		
molar composition		molecular genesis
strong destiny	weak destiny	forking paths

who 'owns' the flashback, or even if it is to be understood in such terms. We encounter flashbacks within flashbacks – a recounting of another's memory of someone other's recollection. Memory is, in this way, discovered as problematic. It was such a problematic that inspired *I Live in Fear*, a film Kurosawa made five years after *Rashomon*. However, with *I Live in Fear* memories appeared as a trace, as figures of thought caught up in discourse-images. With *Rashomon*, memories permeate the film, recollection-images consume screen time. Memory is no longer the subject of the film, the film itself is memory.

Rashomon (1950)

Rain cascades upon the broken bones of Rashomon Gate. It finds its way through the shattered roof, through gaping holes, missing beams and shingles torn down in the devastations of war. Crooked columns, many supporting nothing, jut at odd angles from the vast raised plinth of stone. The flooded platform is strewn with detritus; rainwater torrents over the ancient stone steps and discarded wood, creating rivulets. Smashed parts of the structure lie in the filth, lintels,

Figure 4.3 The devastated milieu of Rashomon Gate, *Rashomon* (Kurosawa, 1950)

pegs, carved ornaments. Finally, we see Rashomon Gate in silhouette against the dark, doomy sky. The once great and beautiful structure announcing entry to Kyoto is now in ruin.

Such are the opening moments of *Rashomon*. The mise-en-scène depicts a milieu of utter destruction. 'Why was an atmosphere of gloom and decay, of physical and spiritual misery, chosen as a background to the film?'[80] James F. Davidson, in 'Memory of Defeat in Japan' (1954), sees the film as a 'Japanese reflection on their defeat and occupation … overtones [of which] are present throughout the picture and come through strongly in many of its details.'[81] James Goodwin, in 'Akira Kurosawa and the Atomic Age' (1994), concurs and believes the film 'Kurosawa's response … to the unprecedented destructiveness with which the atomic age begins'; accordingly, the ruinous backdrop 'depicted as an era of devastation to Japan's cities and of threatened social chaos.'[82] All well and good, but this milieu is not that of 1945, but of the eleventh century. Yet for these critics the mise-en-scène recalls the any-space-whatevers of post-Pacific War Japanese cities in the wake of the atomic bombings, just five years previous to the film's release. It is as if the carcass of Rashomon Gate refers to the skeletal remains of Hiroshima Prefectural Hall or Nagasaki Cathedral.

The film tells the story of the rape of a woman and the death of her samurai husband. Under what remains of Rashomon Gate, sheltering from the thunderstorm, sit a woodcutter (Shimura Takashi) and a priest (Chiaki Minoru). The woodcutter heaves a sigh, repeating the mantra 'I can't understand it … I can't understand it', half to himself, half to the priest, lost in his own thoughts. A man approaches, a commoner (Ueda Kichijiro). He too is looking for somewhere to hide from the storm. Listening to the woodcutter's complaints, the commoner becomes curious, and asks what it is that is troubling him. In this way the woodcutter begins to tell a story. Kurosawa cuts to a flashback of the woodcutter walking in the forest, discovering discarded possessions which lead him to a dead samurai (Mori Masayuki). 'I ran to tell the police. That was three days ago. Today I was called to give evidence.' A wipe relocates the action to a court compound, with the woodcutter explaining what he saw. Another wipe, the priest is in the place previously occupied by the woodcutter, who now sits against the compound wall. The priest gives his testimony; and a third wipe creates a transition to the road of Yamashina, where he saw the samurai and his wife (Kyo Machiko), the wife riding a grey stallion, her husband walking alongside leading the horse. A fourth wipe: a sheriff (Kato Daisuke) and a bound bandit, Tajomaru (Mifune Toshiro) now sit in the foreground (the priest joining the woodcutter against the wall). The sheriff proudly explains how he captured Tajomaru, who had been thrown from the stolen horse, and was found in possession of the samurai's belongings. Tajomaru, however, has a different story – he was ill, and had merely climbed from the horse to rest. He then recounts what occurred in the grove, how he killed the samurai and raped his wife. At this point Kurosawa concludes the flashback, and returns us to the three men at Rashomon Gate: one circuit from the present to the past and back to the present has been completed.

Already it is clear there is a complex interweaving of recollection-images, a forking of paths. Internal to this flashback has been a complex series of events: the woodcutter in the forest; the woodcutter's testimony; the priest's testimony; and the priest's story. Has the woodcutter been speaking on behalf of himself and the priest? If so, we have moved from the reconstitution of a memory to a memory of a story told by another. Either way, Kurosawa has created ambiguous flashbacks, and flashbacks within flashbacks. Things get more complicated still. The two incompatible versions of Tajomaru's capture told by others not present at the gate were depicted as flashbacks within this recollection-image circuit. Kurosawa has, in one sequence of forking paths, conjoined memory and truth, and undermined both. And the film will go on to narrate a number of different versions of what happened in the grove.

Who is lying, who is telling the truth? Richie, in *The Films of Akira Kurosawa* (1998), analyses the narrative of *Rashomon*, attempting to resolve these multiple forks. In order to do so he has to make many assumptions about who is telling which story and has to discount as unreliable the testimony of the dead samurai given through a spirit medium. Richie's analysis is perhaps not entirely serious; even so, it is indicative of a yearning for resolution. Accordingly, the name of the film has been used to describe 'the idea of contradictory truths' and such a need to 'resolve contradictions' in Karl G. Heider's ethnographic study 'The Rashomon Effect' (1988).[83] Yet Kurosawa appears to have something else in mind. In his *Something Like an Autobiography* (1981) he writes: 'one day just before the shooting was to start, the three assistant directors Daiei had assigned me came to see me.'[84] Kurosawa is informed they find the story 'baffling' and they demand an explanation.[85] So he tells them: 'You say that you can't understand this script at all, but that is because the human heart itself is impossible to understand … if you focus on the impossibility of truly understanding human psychology and read the script one more time, I think you will grasp the point of it.'[86] For Kurosawa the film's recollection-images are reconstituted as forking paths in order to stymie any resolution to the different versions of what happened in the grove. Indeed, this is the fundamental principle of the film, and this principle ultimately allows us to consider *Rashomon* as a film of the Japanese atom bomb cinema.

Forking paths and a history

This fundamental principle has three immediate consequences pertaining to aspects of the Japanese past, present and future. The aspect of the present refers us to the mise-en-scène of the Rashomon Gate. The film was completed during the American Occupation of Japan when cinematic production was under the strict censorship of the Civil Censorship Detachment (CCD). The aim of such secret censorship (as we have seen throughout our journey in this book) was to suppress any representations of the moment or aftermath of the Pacific War and the atomic bombing of Hiroshima and Nagasaki. In this way, the eleventh-century mise-en-scène allows Kurosawa to sidestep such proscriptions and create a trace actualization of the devastated post-Pacific War milieu – a recollection-image which substitutes one present for another. Such traces permeate the film. As Yoshimoto has observed in respect to the flashback witness testimonies, 'the fact of the Occupation is most clearly registered in the absence of the magistrate in the courtyard scenes'.[87] Kurosawa films these sequences with the characters facing the camera, speaking to the magistrate and answering his questions. Yet the magistrate is never seen and never heard. 'Consistent with the overall design of the film,' concludes Yoshimoto, 'the censoring eyes of the Occupation are formally inscribed on the film's textual surface as structural absence', the CCD's aim being to erase its own existence as well as the act of censorship itself.[88] The absence of the magistrate, in this way, refers us to a substitution of presents.

The recollection-image of the present in *Rashomon* has a correlative in the forking paths of the past. Forking paths ask 'what happened?' Yet *Rashomon* provides no answer. It is this idea in-itself (rather than the actual events that occurred in the grove) that becomes the subject of the film. In this way, Kurosawa's forking paths attempt to problematize memory and through memory, history. As we saw in Chapter 2, the filmic explorations of historical forces begin in the *Cinema* books in reference to the large form action-image and Nietzsche's analysis of universal history. The large form describes the way in which situations engender actions and has three co-ordinates: the monumental creates parallels between times; antiquarian sustains traditions; and the critical judges the past. Kurosawa's forking paths expose the abuses of such historical conceptions. Once again, we discover a Nietzschean Kurosawa. As Nietzsche puts it, 'monumental history deceives'; with it 'the past itself suffers harm: whole segments of it are forgotten, despised, and flow away … and only individual embellished facts rise out of it'.[89] With antiquarian history 'man is encased in the stench of must and mould'; 'it knows only how to preserve life, not how to engender it'.[90] With critical history 'every past … is worthy to be condemned – for that is the nature of human things: human violence and weakness have always played a mighty role in them. It is not justice here that sits in judgement; it is even less mercy'.[91] It is such abuses of universal history that Kurosawa's forking paths expose. What happened during the war? How did the Japanese lose? Did it take the atom bomb for Japan to surrender? What do Hiroshima and Nagasaki mean? It is not so much that these questions are unknowable – it is not knowledge that is lacking. Rather these questions, and others, are caught up in narratives of heroism and of shame that serve the purposes – the memory (remembering and forgetting) – of those who narrate them.

This rejection of universal history is not simply the replacement of one form with another, but rather something far more radical: the ahistorical. Just as we encountered a forgetting in memory with *I Live in Fear*, we discover in *Rashomon* a primary forgetting in history. Paradoxically, such forgetting refers us to the aspect of the future; the ahistorical is, for Nietzsche, 'an atmosphere within which alone life can germinate', it is 'vital and more fundamental, inasmuch as it constitutes the foundation upon which alone anything sound, healthy and great, anything truly human, can grow'.[92] Accordingly, in *Rashomon*, Kurosawa resolves the problems of history through the future. At the end of the film – abiding by the Kurosawan formula of long exposition and short coda – the three men discover an abandoned baby. The commoner, who has asked questions and cynically dismissed the others' concerns about memory and truth, steals from the crib before running off. The woodcutter – who has had his lies exposed – takes the child as his own. This child is the final recollection-image in the film, a reference to the thousands of orphans created in the wake of the Pacific War and the atom bomb: children as the future of the nation. The Priest praises the woodcutter, absolving him of the sins of the past. The rain stops, the clouds clear and Japan bathes in a rising sun. As Yoshimoto comments, *Rashomon* not only 'underlines the man-made nature of the social chaos', but at 'the same time, what saves humans comes from themselves, too … compassion, honesty, and altruism'.[93]

'The affirmation of humanity at the final moment as a narrative pattern', continues Yoshimoto 'is similarly found in Kurosawa's other films from the same period.'[94] Can this be said of the coda in *I Live in Fear*? Both films propose a Nietzschean forgetting, *Rashomon* believes such a forgetting of history must occur in order to allow Japan to create a future free of the horrors of the past. *I Live in Fear* – made five years later, three years after the end of the American Occupation – appears to re-evaluate and modify such a position in the context of the transformations already undergone by Japan through the pressures of material history: Japan under the aegis of American imperialism, the playing out of the Korean War, the permeating fears of the Cold War. Kurosawa sustains his memory-image as one riven with problems. He still believes that a forgetting of the nuclear event is necessary for life. However, *I Live in Fear* delivers such a resolution with a heavy heart, through a binary conflict that harms all involved. A turning toward the future through forgetting (*Rashomon*) becomes a turning away from the past through an act of violent repression (*I Live in Fear*). Forgetting becomes a demanding undertaking. Forgetting the nuclear event becomes an active task, and the risk is always a return of that which must be repressed, of that which threatens the living of life, in traces, in memories – and in dreams.

Dreams (1990)

Kurosawa's *Dreams* is composed of eight sequences, eight blocs of sensation, eight nightmares and dreams. In (1) 'Sunshine Though the Rain' a little boy ventures alone and without parental permission into the woods, where he encounters a strange wedding procession. Upon returning home his mother hands him a knife, with instructions to kill himself. In (2) 'The Peach Orchard' a boy (somewhat older than the first) follows a young woman out of his house to where Japanese spirits – arranged across a tiered hillside – rebuke him, as representative of his family, for cutting down all the trees that once grew on their land. In (3) 'The Blizzard' four adventurers make their way through snow and ice. The leader watches the others collapse from cold and exhaustion before he himself succumbs. On the edge of death, he is saved by a young woman, who transforms into a demon. In (4) 'The Tunnel' a soldier heading home after the war is confronted with the ghosts of those he fought alongside and who died in action. In (5) 'Crows' a young man at a Van Gogh exhibition enters into the paintings and goes in search of the artist to talk with him.

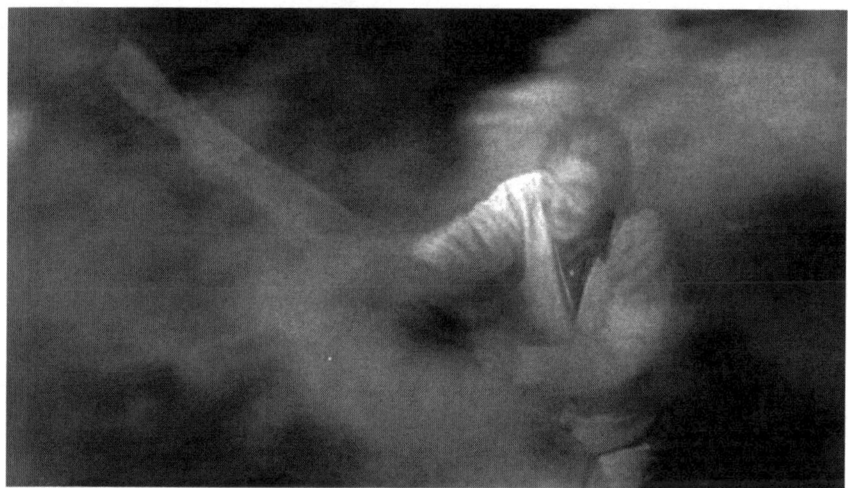

Figure 4.4 A futile attempt to beat back clouds of atomic radiation, 'Mount Fuji in Red', *Dreams* (Kurosawa, 1990)

It is (6) 'Mount Fuji in Red' and (7) 'The Weeping Demon' which directly and indirectly relate to the Japanese cinema of the atom bomb. 'Mount Fuji in Red' is divided into two parts. The first takes place at the foot of Mount Fuji – which appears as if it has turned into an active volcano. People are fleeing the cataclysm. One young man seems different from the rest; he pushes against the crowd shouting 'what's happening?' Eventually, a woman with children and a suited older man are extracted from the faceless multitude and explain. Six atomic reactors in a nuclear power plant have exploded. The scene then shifts to a barren cliff-top above the sea. Everyone has abandoned their belongings and thrown themselves into the waves below. The older man, who admits to being involved in the plant, eventually takes his own life by jumping from the cliff. The sequence ends with the young man trying to beat back the atomic radiation – clouds of coloured gas – with his coat to save the woman and her offspring. In 'The Weeping Demon' a middle-aged man is alone in a post-apocalyptic world. He walks with purpose but without direction through this environment, eventually meeting a *hibakusha*-like demon. The demon conducts a tour of this world, through a land devastated by the *pika*, to where great mutated dandelions grow. The man is then invited to see the place where all the demons live. They are now cannibals, feasting upon one another.

The sequences which explicitly reference the nuclear situation – and concomitantly, *Dreams* – are almost universally disparaged. David Desser

Figure 4.5 A post-apocalyptic world, giant dandelions and ravaged humanity, 'The Weeping Demon', *Dreams* (Kurosawa, 1990)

believes the film demonstrates that Kurosawa was 'senile'.[95] A more generous view comes from Goodwin: 'Kurosawa takes the legacy of human and natural destruction to nightmarish extremes in imagining an apocalypse.'[96] In this way, the two sequences describe 'conditions of resignation, powerlessness, and empty rhetoric' which can 'be understood as aspects of an absurdist predicament in the atomic age'.[97] However, 'without question, *Dreams* lacks the dialogic interaction among possible truths and courses of action that are contained in *Record* [*I Live in Fear*]'.[98] *I Live in Fear*, for Goodwin, displays Kurosawa's mastery of the 'dialogic' form; its purpose is to 'render the exploration into humanity and society through a constant interaction of meanings, meanings that are often in contradiction and competition with one another'.[99] While 'Nakajima may be shown to adopt a monologic position', there is a 'larger, dialogic context' in the 'experiences of Dr Harada'.[100] With *Dreams*, such interactions are lacking. Goodwin reports that the film was funded by accident, Kurosawa's finished script – written without, as was usual, collaboration – being mistaken for an initial draft.[101] Prince similarly displays an ambivalent attitude toward *Dreams*, seeing the film as having no 'structural unity'.[102] 'The film is a collection of eight vignettes that are loosely ordered according to the issues they examine.'[103] Accordingly, there are 'no structural features that determine this ordering, and the vignettes could be reshuffled into a different order'.[104] *Dreams* is 'nonnarrative'; it lacks 'the holistic design possessed by Kurosawa's narrative works. It does not have the strengths which narrative proffers.'[105]

Such criticisms, it seems to me, arise when a film is viewed within an auteurist framework which, while acknowledging temporality and change, sees a director as creating an ideal personal form and having a unitary way of working. The aberration becomes a betrayal. Yet there is another way – every film as aberration: explore the film in-itself, as well as the breaks and flows between this film, that film and other films, images and signs. We can see with both Goodwin and Prince a nostalgia for an ideal Kurosawan form and approach. Such evaluation immediately limits an exploration of the value of *Dreams* in-itself. For Goodwin the relinquishing of the dialogic form of discourse-images results in simplicity; for Prince the turning away from a unitary structure results in disharmony. Yet perhaps, between such simplicity and disharmony, we encounter a 'paradox' that is an 'affirmation'; and perhaps this paradox will allow us to explore the film as a vital cinematic composition.[106] Perhaps this paradox will allow us to see 'Mount Fuji in Red' and 'The Weeping Demon' as vital contributions to the Japanese cinema of the atom bomb, and – at the same time – as developing the trajectory Kurosawa explored in *Rashomon* and *I Live in Fear*.

Dream-images

We must begin with the claim that the film relinquishes narration for the nonnarrative. Such an assertion is fundamental with regards to the Deleuzian cineosis, which does not acknowledge such a distributive binary. Rather, we could say that a film is a bloc of sensation where the nonnarrative is a function of narration; narration a function of the nonnarrative: an interweaving of narration and nonnarrative elements – as Deleuze puts it in *Logic of Sense*, 'a play of sense and nonsense, a chaos-cosmos'.[107] 'Narration', for Deleuze, 'is never an evident given of images, or the effect of a structure which underlies them; it is a consequence of the visible images themselves, of perceptible images in themselves, as they are initially defined for themselves.'[108] Narration arises from the images and signs of cinema. Cinema is not an effect of narration; cinema creates narrations – it creates narrations of many different types, no type more worthy or philosophical than another. We should not mourn the passing of Kurosawa's discourse-images for dream-images. We should rather celebrate his exploration of new forms. We should listen to Kurosawa, who sees dreams as 'the fruit of pure and earnest human desire'.[109] 'I believe', says Kurosawa, 'a dream is an event created in the uninhibited brain of a sleeping person, emanating from an earnest desire which is hidden in the bottom of his heart while awake.'[110]

Deleuze begins to sketch out such dream-images with reference to Bergson. The 'dreamer is not at all closed to the sensations of the external and internal world'; rather, the connection between these sensations and the images produced are simply very weak.[111] In this way, the sensory-motor schema has loosened, but not relinquished, its grip on the dreamer. Deleuze writes that 'the dream represents the largest visible circuit or "the outermost envelope" of all circuits', an aspect of the perimeter of the sensory-motor schema.[112] Is the dream something from the past, occurring in the present? Is the dream possibility for the future? Is the dream a fantasy, creating a nexus of the past, present, future; the possible and impossible? It can be all of these things, yet through it we encounter thought as affect. The crucial aspect, thus, is how the dream appears in relation to the film as a whole, and Deleuze designates a dyadic polarity of the dream-image as being the explicit and the implicit dream.[113] Implicit dreams correspond to the molecular, while explicit dreams correspond to the molar – and have, as always, two signs of composition. The monadic, dyadic and triadic levels of the dream-image can be illustrated as in Table 4.4.

Deleuze designates the poles in the sign of composition of the dream-image 'according to their technical production'.[114] The first pole is complex and 'proceeds by rich and overloaded means'.[115] The filmmaker will use strange colours and sounds, slow-motion, unusual objects, strange situations, superimpositions – in other words, all the possibilities of camera and post-production effects at their disposal. The other pole is the 'restrained'.[116] A simple cut may suffice. All there is to indicate the dream may be the closing of the eyes and the dream in-itself may appear as real as the real world outside the dream. Thus, signs of the rich present the dream or hallucination without ambiguity, while signs of the restrained engender a question: is this or is this not a dream, a hallucination, a nightmare? Either way, in the signs of composition, the dream appears as actualized images in the film's space-time. Dream-time is an anomaly

Table 4.4 Dream-image

dream-image		
molar composition		molecular genesis
rich dreams	restrained dreams	movement of world

which the dreamer enters and from which they will emerge. Both the rich and the restrained are explicit dreams, are expressed on-screen as a dream-image and appear for a character or characters, a function of individual or group subjectivity. Within the narrative of the film these dreams appear as affective thought of the past and present inextricably interweaving and orientated toward the future as portents, omens and premonitions with regard to the plot. Accordingly, for Deleuze, 'whichever pole is chosen, the dream-image obeys the same law … each image actualizes the preceding one and is actualized in the subsequent one, to return in the end to the situation which set it off.'[117]

In distinction to the signs of composition of the explicit dream, Deleuze offers up the implied dream as the genetic sign, a 'movement of world'.[118] In this dream-image it is not the character that succumbs to the dream, but rather the whole world which becomes a dream. No longer is the character engendered by the situation, moving through the landscape to be caught up in dreams if only to return; but rather, dreams engender the world, landscapes are any-space-whatevers that move around a dreamer. The whole film is a dream and describes 'the limit of the largest circuit', the extreme outlying edge of the sensory-motor schema.[119] Kurosawa's *Dreams* is such a movement of world: eight nightmares and dreams from the life of a dreamer, appearing without the frame of the one who dreams. The dreamer never goes to sleep, the dreamer never awakes – the dreamer only traverses dream-worlds.

Movement of world and contemplation

The movement of world in *Dreams* is a complex interweaving of images: the domain of thought capturing up affection-images, backgrounds appearing as any-space-whatevers. For Deleuze, the any-space-whatever 'has one of its points of origin … in the experimental cinema which breaks with the narration of actions and the perception of determinate places'.[120] As the genetic sign of the affection-image, any-space-whatevers are related to the genetic sign of the perception-image, where there is a proliferation of images without an actual centre. 'If the experimental cinema tends towards a perception as it was before men (or after), it also tends towards the correlate of this, that is, towards an any-space-whatever released from its human co-ordinates.'[121] Just as we discovered a nonhuman perception, we discover nonhuman affects, where faces, bodies, colours, sounds and words are subsumed within and as part of the mise-en-scène. Such any-space-whatevers have 'two states': 'deconnection' and 'emptiness' – the deconnection between elements, and the emptying of the frame and shot.[122] In *Dreams* deconnection occurs between the blocs of sensation of each sequence. As Deleuze puts it, such dream backgrounds constitute a 'plurality of worlds' where 'every world and every dream is shut in on itself, closed up around everything it contains … and becomes pure description of the world which replaces situation'.[123] Concomitantly, there is an emptying out within each bloc: the endless sunlit woods; the manicured surfaces of the bare orchard and tiered hillside; the pure white of the snowstorm; the interminable darkness of the tunnel; the surreal coloured landscapes of Van Gogh's Arles; the crowds and dust beneath Mount Fuji; the coloured clouds of radioactive gas on the cliff-top; and the barren earth and weird flowers of the post-apocalyptic wasteland.

Yet – through the dream-image and movement of world – these disconnected and emptied-out any-space-whatevers link up and a centre is created within and across them. For Goodwin, there are resonances between the spaces: the 'demons, shrieking in pain and howling in aggression' are the 'antithesis to the procession of dancers at the wedding of foxes in the first episode'; and the gigantic dandelions 'appear as a grotesque distortion of the passionate intensity of the sunflowers in the famous Van Gogh canvas, seen in episode five'.[124] For Prince, as we saw above, there is no necessary ordering to these 'vignettes'. Yet a connection lies in 'a recurring character who appears in the dream blocs. This character is Kurosawa's surrogate, who embodies the director's presence inside the various dreams.'[125] The disconnected and emptied-out any-space-whatevers that provide the mise-en-scène of the dreams are caught up in a web of dream-images which emanate from a dreamer and place the dreamer as an actualized centre within and across each. We thus want to go much further than Goodwin and Prince and say that not only are there resonances between the dreams, and not only does an actual centre appear in *Dreams*, but it is this centre which gives an essential order and trajectory to the film, and it is this centre that creates the flow of narration. As Deleuze puts it, there is 'no longer simply movement of world, but passage from one world to another, entry into another world, breaking in and exploring'.[126]

First, the centre occupies what appears as an empty space. Any-space-whatevers become dreams through the dreamer. The dreamer who walks through the dreams is named I. This naming of the character collapses auteur and character, filmmaker and film into an affective assemblage. This is no surrogacy. The film creates 'depersonalized and pronominalized movement'.[127]

Pronominalized movement in the sense of the subject being replaced by a simple pronoun – I (first person) – a cinematic anaphora where the meaning of the pronoun is reliant upon Kurosawa; depersonalized movement in the sense of Kurosawa looking upon himself as if from afar, as if looking upon another. Second – and as a consequence – the centre connects that which is disconnected. *Dreams* follows Kurosawa from boyhood through youth to adulthood and (as we will see) old age; and this following occurs through Japanese culture: the fairy-tale dimensions of childhood, the mythic realm of youth, then adulthood and history – the brutal aftermath of war with the returning of soldiers to Japan.

Yet, if we have seen how the emptied-out, deconnected any-space-whatevers are both filled and connected by and through a centre – at one and the same time – the centre becomes fragmented through such a deconnection between spaces and the emptying-out of space similarly disperses that centre.

First, I becomes Is: child-Kurosawa; youth-Kurosawa; wartime-Kurosawa; artist-Kurosawa. Kurosawa becomes fragmented. This is seen most powerfully in the final sequence, (8) 'Village of the Watermills'. A middle-aged I is wandering through beautiful landscapes when he comes across a village with no name. There he meets an old man who tells of how his heart was broken when young by a wonderful woman. Today that woman is being buried. The old man evinces no resentment and no sense of loss. We should celebrate life he says, and finishes with a hearty laugh. 'It's good to be alive.' The film ends with the old man joining the parade of the funeral procession, music playing, people dancing. 'Village of the Watermills' is a Kurosawan coda. It could be said that the seven previous dreams are all nightmares (even the Van Gogh sequence is haunted by fear, the cutting off of the ear, the sense of time slipping away, the terror of crows). Through these nightmares, fear has been continually embodied in the form of demons, yet the nature of the demon is transformed by the age of the Is and the social spaces through which the Is wander. Fox and tree spirits; a woman in white; ghosts of soldiers; then remnants of the apocalypse to come: 'Are you a demon?' asks I/Kurosawa in 'The Weeping Demon'. 'I suppose so, I used to be human.' It is in this penultimate dream that memory as fear is at its most intense, projected into the future as powerful hallucination, as portent and omen. 'Long ago this place was a beautiful field of flowers,' weeps the demon-*hibakusha*, 'then those nuclear bombs, those missiles turned it into a desert.' Only the final dream-coda is untouched by fear. In 'Village of the Watermills' Kurosawa is both I and the old man – the old-Kurosawa contemplating a life of fear.

John Gray, in *Straw Dogs* (2002), observes that 'action preserves a sense of self-identity that reflection dispels. When we are at work in the world we have a seeming solidity.'[128] 'Action gives us consolation', yet in *Dreams* actions no longer emerge from situations and situations no longer create actions.[129] In a movement of world the world moves around the dreamer: 'it is not the idle dreamer who escapes from reality. It is practical men and women, who turn to a life of action as a refuge.'[130] 'Can we imagine a life that is not founded on the consolations of action?' asks Gray.[131] 'Can we not think of the aim of life as being simply to see?'[132] Kurosawa, in *Dreams*, achieves such a seeing – and in the final dream dreams a reconciliation with a life of fear.

I Live in Fear used the duel and dialogic form, the large form action-image at its limit, to create a complex interweaving of contradictions. *Rashomon* achieved its power through the interactions of the forking paths and the concomitant tension between the unfathomability of history and the possibilities of the future. In *Dreams* it is the disconnection, connection and fragmentation between worlds which create interactions and contradictions of meanings. The coda of *Dreams* is thus very different from that of Kurosawa's previous atom bomb films. No longer must history and memory be subjected to a turning away from the past in preference for future actions; no longer should history and memory be actively repressed in order to sustain life. Rather, that which haunts the imagination can be accommodated through contemplation. In time, the trauma of the Japanese nuclear event can be borne without fear, and without resentment.

Yet there is a second, far more radical, aspect to such contemplation. If a disconnection between spaces fragments the centre, the centre is in this way dissipated through an emptying out. In *Dreams* Kurosawa discovers a wonderful formula, or rather becomes fully conscious of a hidden formula that had always inhabited his images of thought; something that was hidden in all his films; that permeates cinema. With the mental-image, the spectator must become an active participant in the film. Mental-images 'no longer conceive … of the constitution of a film as a function of two terms – the director and the film to be made – but as a function of three: the director, the film and the public which must come into the film, or whose reactions must form an integrating part of the film.'[133] What we encounter in *Dreams* is the creation of multiplicities through the deconnection and emptying out of the dreams and the fragmentation of Is which invite the spectator to enter into the film and to contemplate the blocs of sensation. This potential of cinema that Kurosawa discovered in *Dreams* (which

Kurosawa discovered in cinema) was exploited to its fullest in *Rhapsody in August*, creating powerful mental-images of the atom bomb as a way of implicating the spectator in the nuclear event.

III. Relation and implication

Rhapsody in August (1991)

Kane gathers her four grandchildren around her. She tells them a 'spooky' story about the youngest of her ten or so brothers – she finds it difficult to recall exactly how many brothers she has, their order of birth, and all their names. Suzukichi, however, she remembers well, him being 'slightly weak in the head'. This brother spent his days shut away from the family, closeted in his room. Come night-time, 'when the moon came up', he would sneak out and swim in a waterfall not far from the farmhouse where Kane still lives. Shinjiro (Isaki Mitsunori), the younger of two boys, asks what Suzukichi was doing in his room. Drawing pictures of an eye, Kane responds. 'Like this' – pointing to her own eye. As long as there was paper to be had, he would sketch out such a symbol on the page. Shinjiro takes up a piece of chalk and quickly draws a white outline on the playroom blackboard. 'Just like that!' she says. Then pausing, the

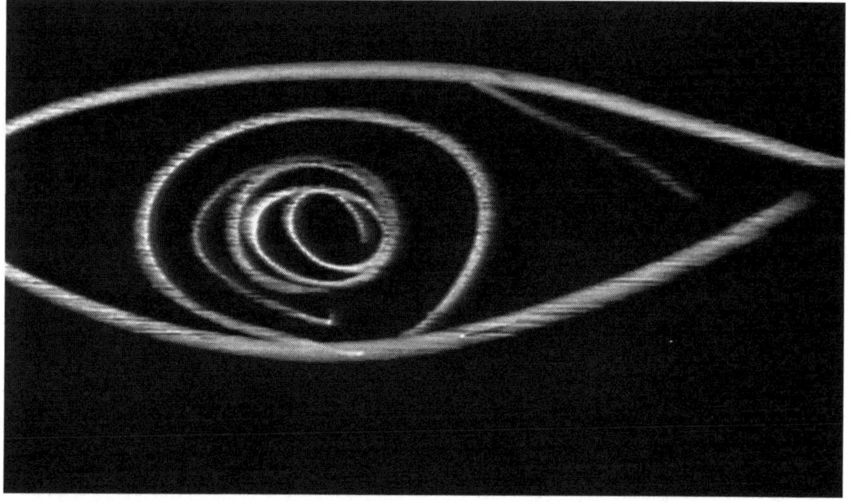

Figure 4.6 The eye as symbol, *Rhapsody in August* (Kurosawa, 1991)

robust old lady slowly puts on her glasses and studies Shinjiro. 'You certainly look like Suzukichi.' A provocation: his sister and cousins howl with laughter, and soon the children are all fighting.

The four grandchildren are staying with Kane during the summer vacation. Tami (Otakara Tomoko) and Shinjiro, a teenage girl and her younger brother, are cousins with Tateo (Yoshioka Hidetaka) and Minako (Suzuki Mieko), a teenage boy and his younger sister. Kane's son Tadao (Igawa Hisashi) is visiting family in Hawaii, so has asked his mother to take care of Tami and Shinjiro; Kane's daughter Yoshie (Negishi Toshie) has sent Tateo and Minako to join their grandmother and cousins for the holiday. The children spend their time teasing Kane mercilessly (most usually about her bland cooking) and finding ways to annoy each other. However, a letter arrives from Hawaii, from Tadeo. He and his wife Machiko (Kayashima Narumi) have encountered – and it is never clear if this was the intended reason for the trip or not – one of Kane's older brothers. Suzujiro travelled to America during the Taisho democratic period of the 1920s, stayed there, married, and built up a successful business. Now he is dying, and would dearly love to see his sister before either of them passes on. This letter from Hawaii has a ripple effect – Kane, at first, cannot remember a brother called Suzujiro, or so she claims. So the children start asking her about the family, her husband and her brothers. Memories surface, slowly, and Kane tells stories as these memories return. For instance, one night while off swimming in the waterfall, Suzukichi nearly drowned. Kane remembers that a water imp came and got her, to help save the young man. Kane's stories capture their imaginations and the next day they all go in search of the waterfall. As they sit down and unpack their picnic, they are disturbed by a snake as it skims across the top of the pool toward where they picnic. As they flee, Shinjiro says to the others 'Did you see that snake's eyes? Those eyes are …'

It is in this way we encounter a very powerful image of thought. Kurosawa cuts before Shinjiro finishes speaking. It is unclear if the edit interrupts these words, or if the image that follows replaces them, Shinjiro unable to speak. Kurosawa cuts from a close-up of the snake to a shot of the chalk eye drawn on the blackboard, before cutting back to a close-up of the waterfall. During this succession of images, the audiotrack is manipulated so that the noise of the waterfall is heightened in the sound design, drowning out all else. This is where Kurosawa ends the scene, and in doing so displays his mastery of cinematic mental-images: snake → eye → waterfall, overlaid with the deafening and unending sound of crashing water. The question is, of course, to what does this obscure triad refer, what is snake + eye + waterfall? It might be said to be the visual equivalent of a riddle: what has the deadly bite of a snake, gazes at you, and has the power of a waterfall? Tateo thinks the eye represents Suzukichi's fear of being looked at by people; Shinjiro will declare the eye is that of a snake. Kane, however, knows different. Her husband died in the atomic bombing of Nagasaki city forty-five years before. She and Suzukichi were at the farmhouse; as they watched, the atom bomb exploded on the other side of the hills separating the city from the village. 'Those eyes were not snake eyes,' whispers Kane, 'those eyes were the *pika*.' What has the deadly bite of a snake, gazes at you, and has the power of a waterfall? Kurosawa is conjuring up the spectre of impossibility: the atom bomb. The images that follow are startling. Behind the Nagasaki hills there is a nuclear explosion, yet immediately it is obscured with a human eye, which slowly opens, and looks down upon the valley. It is a vision only Kane sees, but one she claims to have shared with her brother on the day of the bomb.

These images appear as actualized thought; cinematic thought is made possible through actualized images in the very materiality of screen space-time. Thought is made possible by the editing between images and connecting of images on the screen: the eye on the blackboard, the eye of the snake, the eye of the *pika* above the mountains; the eye in-itself, the eyes through the eye-series, the eye as part of the snake–waterfall series. These are images of thought. These are relation-images.

The relation-image

A film of the relation-image will make thought a specific sign of the movement image. No longer will perception, affect or action dominate, rather thought will prevail by the actualization of special images. Deleuze puts it thus: 'it is an image which takes as its object, relations, symbolic acts, intellectual feelings.'[134] The first sign of composition is the 'mark'.[135] As Deleuze puts it: 'in accordance with the natural relation, a term refers back to other terms in a customary series such that each can be "interpreted" by the others: these are marks.'[136] It requires at least three mark images to create such a logical sequence. However 'it is always possible for one of these terms to leap outside the web and suddenly appear in conditions which take it out of series', writes Deleuze.[137] This leaping outside of the web is the second pole of the sign of composition, the 'demark'.[138] In the demark series, then, it is as if three images are both of a sequence but one of them is simultaneously awry. For Deleuze, if marks and demarks constitute the poles of the sign of composition through natural relations, the genetic sign is a 'symbol', an 'abstract relation'.[139] As Deleuze puts it, 'demarks are clashes of natural relations (series) and symbols are nodes of abstract relations'.[140] Thus 'demarks and symbols can converge … a single object … can, according to the images in which it is caught, function as a symbol'.[141] The monadic, dyadic and triadic levels of the relation-image can be illustrated as in Table 4.5. Crucially for Deleuze, the function of a symbol is to 'implicate the spectator in the film'.[142] A symbol is a figure of thought which must be interpreted. And the symbol, the genetic sign of the relation-image (the relation-image being the purest of mental-images) is the general condition of all mental-images. With mental-images 'actions, affections, perceptions, all is interpretation, from beginning to end'.[143]

It is relation-images that structure *Rhapsody in August*. Marks (in a series of three) traverse the film: Tadeo's three letters from Hawaii; the three telegrams from their Japanese-American cousin Clark; the three taxis bringing the middle generation of the family to Kane's house and the three taxis taking them away. It is the series of three marks that allows the relation-image to emerge, for the relation-image is Peirce's purest thirdness, capturing up the firstness of affection-images and the secondness of action-images. *Rhapsody in August* explores thirdness in a number of ways. It appears in the very relationship between characters. The grandmother expresses the affection-image, she is one alone, often shot in silence, or praying. Then there are the grandchildren, embodying action, running riot round the house, fighting each other in polynomial duels, entering into a binomial with the grandmother. But then there is a third element in this family drama: Kane's children, the parents of the grandchildren. During the first part of the film it might seem they are absent, but this is not the case. The very first scene involves a letter from them, inviting Kane and the grandchildren to Hawaii. Their absence, then, is purely a physical one, not structural. Indeed, they do not even constitute a visual absence as they appear on-screen through photographic images sent with the letter. Kurosawa even takes care to frame the photos as photogrammes, and not as objects held

Table 4.5 Relation-image

relation-image		
molar composition		molecular genesis
mark	demark	symbol

in the grandmother's and children's hands. Thus, the confrontation between grandmother and grandchildren as action-image – as a duel – is superseded by thirdness, the relation-image. It is Tadeo's trip to Hawaii, the discovery of Clark (also of the second generation) which introduces memories, hallucinations and thought into the film.

This organization of threes also appears in *Rhapsody in August* with regard to the perception-image. In other words, perception-images are transformed into relation-images, the transformation reorientating the signs of perception toward thought. This is clear from a sequence in the film when the children visit Nagasaki and encounter three sets of atom bomb memorials. The first memorial is the schoolyard where their grandfather died. There, preserved in a quiet corner, is a melted iron climbing frame. The camera explores the twisted metal, traversing its curves and angles. After this flowing, liquid sequence the children visit the Nagasaki city centre. What follows is a sequence of shots showing stone statues. There is a series of solid, statically filmed images, close-ups of stone faces damaged by the bomb. Or almost – there are eight images in total, the final shot that of a headless statue: a demark as part of the series of marks. There is then a cut from the headless statue to the top of a war memorial and thus begins the third memorial sequence. These are objects not produced by the devastation of the atom bomb, but gifts to Japan from foreign powers: 'Portugal … Czechoslovakia … Italy … Poland … Bulgaria … The USSR … China … Brazil … Cuba … Holland.' The camera freely flows over the first few, while the final few are captured as static, solid images. This combination of liquid and solid perception-images mediates between the climbing frame (liquid) and the stone heads (solid). The first two memorial sequences are the remnants of the atom bomb, the climbing frame captured in the act of liquidizing, melting. The heads are solid stone, broken by the force of the blast. The mediating sequence of the foreign monuments sets up a gaseous relationship between the three series.

Rhapsody in August is structured through and through by thirdness, by marks and demarks organizing perception-, affection- and action-images. Yet at the centre is the eye, passing through marks and beyond the demark to become symbol. To present affection-images or action-images of the atom bomb is not enough; to present the atom bomb in flashbacks or nightmares, through recollection-images or dream-images is not enough – or perhaps too much. In conversation with Gabriel García Márquez, Kurosawa said: 'I have not filmed shocking realistic scenes which would prove to be unbearable and yet would not explain in and of themselves the horror.'[144] Rather Kurosawa creates relation-images to 'convey ... the type of wounds the atomic bomb left in the heart of our people'.[145] The eye is not the *pika* but the *pika* is the eye (*pika* becomes eye); and the eye as symbol gazes out of the screen, a symbol which must be read. Such reading implicates the spectator in the film.

Symbols and spectators

We critics, theorists and philosophers who encounter *Rhapsody in August* are spectators. When Tami, Minako and Shinjiro visit the foreign war memorials, Richie writes: 'little Shinichiro notices monuments from Czechoslovakia, Poland, Bulgaria, China, Cuba and the USSR and says with surprise that there is none from America, Tami responds, "Naturally. It was Americans that *dropped* the bomb".'[146] For Richie, this scene points toward anti-Americanism within the film by way of ignoring the wider historical issues surrounding the gifting of these memorials. Richie's enunciation of the list is thus crucial to his analysis. Stephen Prince echoes Richie's concerns, writing: 'montage shows the memorials contributed by other nations, and a substantial number of these are from the former Eastern Bloc and other communist countries.'[147] Bernstein and Ravina claim that in Kurosawa's film 'the bomb exists outside history', that the film is so focused on 'Japanese-American relations it ignores the complex political motivations for other countries to send memorials'.[148] Bock goes even further, commenting: 'America's complete responsibility for nurturing and protecting Japan in the post-war era is never acknowledged, nor is the fact that Japan forced America into the war.'[149] Yet as Yoshimoto points out, these critics omit to mention the non-Communist countries' memorials that Kurosawa films; accordingly their analyses become a ploy to obscure the point being made, that there is no American monument. Bock's analysis is indicative of the simplification of the political co-ordinates expressed through the mark-series of monuments, where the absent American memorial becomes a demark through Shinichiro's question and a symbol through Tami's response. It is not that Kurosawa fails to place the symbol within a socio-historic framework so much as the symbol exposes the social-historic framework of the critic. The symbol must be interpreted, and through interpretation the spectator is implicated within the film.

Relation-images are not only constituted through the visual image; they can also arise through sound, through music or through the voice. Richie comments: 'When Tami says, "We couldn't even guess how the A-bomb victims felt … we never stopped to think," the effect is ludicrously weak.'[150] Such exegesis, for Richie, 'is not good artistic policy', it is 'too simplistic a statement', it is 'inadequate for its horrific subject'.[151] Yet Tami's words are a complex enunciation, delivered in voice-over: 'that day we kept walking all over the town because we wanted to know more about the bomb.' Voiced from the future to the past, interjecting the present, the voice-framing acts as a commentary. Such commentary appears as a demark to the marks of the children's dialogues in the present. Tami's words answer nothing; they are a call for thought. Such complex audio relation-images inspire the most virulent of critical responses with the arrival of the children's American uncle Clark (Richard Gere). Contemporary (American) reviews at the time are incredulous: 'the children are initially anxious about [Clark's] visit, but he … apologises for the atomic attack 45 years ago', and 'the old woman forgives all when he apologises to her for the bomb'.[152] For Yoshimoto, it is quite clear that Clark does not apologize for the atom bomb. Rather, he simply apologizes for his family insisting Kane come to Hawaii at the time of the annual remembrance service. Yet perhaps Yoshimoto is being too defensive here. Or rather, Yoshimoto's defence of the film, it appears, is his own interpretation of ambiguous relation-images. The conversation between Kane and Clark, the latter speaking only rudimentary Japanese, is difficult for them both. To my mind it remains unclear exactly what Clark is apologizing for; indeed, if he is clear himself. Understanding this point is absolutely crucial to the film. Clark is not simply American, but Japanese-American. In this we see the full impact of the relation-image as a mediating term. Clark is of the middle generation, arrives in the third taxi and lives in Hawaii, an island midway between Japan and the American mainland. He is the third human term in the ruse of the dichotomy between America and Japan. Earlier in the film one of the children is overheard by Kane: 'Grandma doesn't like America … after all Grandpa was killed by the bomb.' The children initially adopt the position they believe to be Kane's. But Kane responds: 'It was a long time ago that I felt bitter about America … now I neither like nor dislike America … it was because of the war … the war was to blame … during the war many Japanese died … and so did many Americans.' For Kane the atom bomb was not simply the result of the duel between the Japanese and the USA; rather, war itself becomes the third term, a relation-image.

Relation-images, marks, demarks and symbols permeate the film through visual and sound images. Take the relation-image of the rose. Tateo has been fixing an old organ. He practises with Schubert's 'Heidenröslein' ('Rose on the Heath'). When Clark arrives it is finally able to be played in tune and all the children sing the song. During the Nagasaki atomic bomb memorial service at the village shrine, Clark notices a red rose. Then, toward the end of the film, Kane hears that her long-lost brother has died before she could see him. She becomes forgetful and distracted, eventually disappearing during a thunderstorm. The family chase after her, and the film ends with series of slow-motion images, each family member shot on their own running through the rain. These images are overlaid with 'Heidenröslein,' and as Kane struggles onwards, 'a gust of wind turns her umbrella inside out, making it look like a rose'.[153] For Yoshimoto this image changes her from an ailing old woman into 'a brave warrior whose struggle against the rain and wind transforms her into an allegorical icon affirming the dignity and preciousness of life'.[154] Yet the rose is an ambiguous symbol in the film. 'Heidenröslein' tells of a boy who picked a rose, and of the rose pricking the boy. The rose at the shrine is covered with ants (ants using roses to farm aphids as a live food supply). The rose is an ambiguous symbol, open to interpretation. Could it not be that Kane's initial refusal to remember her older brother and then her insistence that she remain at Nagasaki until after the memorial service constitute a Kurosawan critique of memory – the refusal to remember the living in preference to a remembering of the dead? Is it this realization that sends her over the edge? Does not the coda of *Rhapsody in August* resonate with that of *I Live in Fear*? Has Kane fallen into insanity just as Nakajima did? Is it memories and memorials that are important? Is it the living and life? In the final instance, the permeation of *Rhapsody in August* by symbols stymies any resolution. It is left open for interpretation.

Impure anarchic multiplicities

Implicating the spectator in the film is the discovery of the mental-image – an always there in Kurosawa's atom bomb films. In *Dreams* the potential of space for the spectator is created between the deconnection of elements and the emptying out of environments. Yet it is the affirmations of colour that invite the spectator in: we encounter trees almost purple; flowers through a cacophony of pigments; sky as clear as glass; grass beyond green. The surface of white in the snow; the depth of black in the tunnel; Van Gogh's colours transposed onto the landscape – painted onto bridges and buildings, onto the very characters themselves. 'Colour is dream, not because the dream is in colour, but because colours … are given a highly absorbent, almost devouring, value', writes Deleuze.[155] Accordingly, 'this means that we have to insinuate ourselves, to let ourselves become absorbed, without at the same time losing ourselves or being snatched away'.[156] In *I Live in Fear* traces of the atom bomb appear as figures of spontaneous thought: the sound of planes overhead, wind, rain and thunder, a flash of lightning, the sun in the sky. All are mistaken by Nakajima for the atom bomb, only Nakajima reacts as if they are something other than what they are – yet the spectator must react with him. In *Rashomon* one of the most fundamental aspects of the film is the way in which Kurosawa shoots the testimonies of the woodcutter, the priest, the wife and the medium/husband at the court compound. These characters are all filmed looking into the camera; the magistrate is never seen. It is as if the audience is being asked to assume this role. In this way the spectator becomes implicated in the film. Yoshimoto puts it this way: 'as if to compensate for the lack of the reverse shot, the film shows instead the woodcutter and the priest, who sit silently in the background of the courtyard as witnesses to the testimonies. Because of their position and the direction of their look, the woodcutter and the priest become the mirror image of the film's audience.'[157]

Figures of thought, movements of world, forking paths, symbols – each of these narrations are created through the mental-image to which they refer: discourse-images, dream-images, recollection-images and relation-images. In each case the spectator becomes an integral component within that structure: there is no longer simply a dialogue between the filmmaker and the film. This is the consummation of the movement-image.

Yet *Rhapsody in August* goes further than *Rashomon, I Live in Fear* and *Dreams*. All of Kurosawa's previous atom bomb films explored the same problems of memory and history, and in the final coda each proposed a solution: a turning away from the past and a turning toward the future; forgetting/repression; the abandonment of resentment through contemplation. *Rhapsody in August* interweaves these themes through its relation-images, through its marks, demarks and symbols – yet Kurosawa replaces the coda-resolution with the open-coda, tempting the spectator with the allure of interpretation. The author and the film no longer provide closure. This indicates a crisis in the movement-image. In *Cinema 2* Deleuze returns to Kurosawa and articulates this crisis. Kurosawa 'shows us characters constantly seeking the givens of a "problem" which is even deeper than the situation in which they find themselves caught: in this way he goes beyond the limits of knowledge, but also the conditions of action. He reaches a purely optical world, where the thing to be is a seer.'[158] In this way, 'sensory-motor situations have given way to pure optical and sound situations to which characters, who have become seers, cannot or will not react so great is their need to "see" properly what there is to the situation.'[159] This is not so much a beyond of the movement-image, but rather the disintegration of its co-ordinates, the delinking of affection-images, action-images and mental-images, the collapse of perception-images to discover pure optical and auditory signs. *Rhapsody in August* was able – through the genetic sign of the relation-image – to create opaque symbols within the framework of the movement-image. When a film becomes overwhelmed by such opsigns and sonsigns we encounter the time-image, anarchic multiplicities. In such a way the Japanese cinema of the atom bomb becomes one of an equivocity of the image, a disjunctive unfolding of narration, and a retention and dispersal of narrative discord.

5

Impure Anarchic Multiplicities

It will have destroyed every model of the true so as to become creator and producer of truth: this will not be a cinema of truth but the truth of cinema.[1]

Time-images

Cinema is movement and time. Time is riven with difference: paradoxes, disjunctions and discords. When movement subordinates time, it attempts to resolve such difference, to create a seamless flow through an image and from one image to another. Some films, however, reverse the subordination and preserve difference. Deleuze calls these time-images. This chapter identifies time-images of the Japanese cinema of the atom bomb, exploring them through a new series of signs, a new cineotic moment describing the indeterminacy of an image, the disjunctive unfolding of narration, and the retention and dispersal of narrative discord. Together, these processes confound recognition and truth, creating a new image of cinematic thought. Each film discussed in this chapter, accordingly, describes indeterminate images of the *pika* and *hibakusha*, disturbs narrations and histories capturing up the Japanese nuclear event, and creates the atomic attacks on Hiroshima and Nagasaki as a discordant moment in thought.

Smearing the screen black, Sekigawa Hideo's *Hiroshima* (1953) depicts the immediate aftermath of the *pika* in one of the most harrowing sequences in cinematic history – an apocalyptic chaos where the *hibakusha* wander zones of nuclear destruction. Imamura Shohei's *Black Rain* (1989) describes the experiences of a family of *hibakusha* through a complex interweaving of codes of tragedy and comedy across two disparate space-times. Despite many differences, these films are both based upon *hibakusha* testimonies and both question – in their own way – the very possibility of capturing the *pika* within human understanding. Oshima Nagisa's *The Pacific War* (1968) and (another, earlier) Imamura film, *A History of Postwar Japan as Told by a Bar Hostess* (1970), exploit the permeable boundaries between fiction and documentary to explore history and truth. Imamura's film initially appears as documentary, recording a personal narrative in conjunction with Japanese history over the years since the nuclear event. However, the documentary reveals itself as manipulation. *The Pacific War* attempts something far chancier. The film is composed entirely of newsreel footage of Japan's imperial, fascist and militarist past, displaying as-is images from the war years leading up to the atomic attacks. Finally, Kiriya Kazuaki's *Casshern* (2004) is a science-fiction epic utilizing twenty-first century cinematic digital technology to conduct an almost imperceptible thought experiment, the continuation of the Pacific War where the atomic event becomes an indeterminate historical un/happening.

These films will be explored through Deleuze's taxonomy of the time-image. As was seen in Chapter 4, the time-image is promised through the crisis of the movement-image – announced with the arrival of mental-images. Mental-images exposed memory, imagination and understanding as the very ground of cinema: perception, affect and action reconceived as an image of thought. Such images of thought were revealed as fundamentally problematic – the ambiguities of recollections, the uncertainties of nightmares and dreams, the opacity of symbolic relations. Yet being of the domain of movement-images, mental-images discovered different ways of resolving such problems. The time-image, in distinction, will sustain and propagate such ambiguities, uncertainties and opacities – in this way creating opsigns and sonsigns, pure optical and sound images. From these fundamental cinematic signs, a whole new cineotic arises. Hyalosigns describe an indeterminacy of the image; chronosigns organize narration according to non-linear and serial trajectories; and noosigns create narrative discords between bodies and the world. In their simultaneity these images are lectosigns, images that necessarily require a reading (do not simply need to be seen). If the movement-image was concerned with how the heterogeneity of cinematic images are tamed, then time-images are concerned with how a film retains such heterogeneity. In this way, time-images create an intensive perspectivism which disavows any alignment of film image with historical truth: *Casshern* through a conceiving of the moment of the atomic event as indeterminate; *A History of Postwar Japan* and *The Pacific War* through an undermining of narration and the horizons of history; *Black Rain* and *Hiroshima* through the retention and dispersal of narrative discord. Each of the films explored in this chapter are 'anarchic multiplicities', perspectival archives, compositions of stratigraphic signs that attempt to problematize depictions of the Japanese nuclear event.[2]

Time-images destroy the co-ordinates of the movement-image: its centres, its historical conceptions and its figures of thought. The aim of this chapter, accordingly, is to extend the domain of the Japanese cinema of the atom bomb through the diversity of time-images. In so doing, we reveal the fundamental nature of the cinematographic event, as image, as image of history, and as image of thought. To begin this task it will first be necessary to describe Deleuze's syntheses of time. These syntheses, as explicated in the second chapter of *Difference and Repetition* (1968), not only provide the philosophical foundation of the time-image, but also inspire the co-ordinates of that cineosis.[3]

Deleuze, syntheses of time

Difference and Repetition can be seen as an attempt to set free an alternative 'image of thought' by confronting the concept of identity.[4] Identity, for Deleuze, reconstitutes the same at the expense of difference, annulling difference in-itself. Identity co-opts difference at a level of the difference between things. Difference in-itself is a foregrounding of internal difference and creates connections through the repetition of differences. Repetition for-itself is thus never the repetition of the same. Things, bodies and masses are heterogeneous assemblages. Such is the overturning of identity through difference and repetition, taking these concepts 'together rather than separately'.[5]

A body-mass, for example, exists through spatial stability and temporal fusion: spatial in that it is an organic gathering of the matter of the universe; temporal in that a body-mass fundamentally perseveres in some way in the present, past and future, a synthesis of time. Spatial cohesion creates identity; while the temporal reveals a fundamental difference and repetition. As Henry Somers-Hall writes, *Difference and Repetition* critiques the idea of identity in 'thinkers from Plato, Aristotle, Descartes, Leibniz and Kant, through to Heidegger' by way of an 'alternative conception of philosophy … in relation to an alternative tradition of thinkers'[6] – philosophers such as Nietzsche and Bergson, both of whom have managed, 'at least partially', to 'free themselves' from a classical image of thought.[7] The new image of thought thus foregrounds temporality.

First, a body-mass is temporal through the contraction (synthesis) of different instants into a present. Second, a body-mass is temporal because it resonates within compacted (synthesized) moments as a past. Third, a body-mass is temporal through a continual re-encountering (synthesizing) of the permeable wall of the future. Each of these syntheses is a perspective of (and not on) time, thus simultaneous. As Jay Lampert writes, 'there exist nine forms of the present, past, and future'.[8] In this way a body-mass is complex temporal nexus prior to being located spatially in the universe, before consciousness, an active synthesis.[9]

We are – once again – encountering a Deleuzian taxonomy. As Somers-Hall comments, *Difference and Repetition* displays 'Deleuze's love of taxonomy', a love for the 'proliferation of distinctions, each of which plays a subtle role in the development of the argument as a whole'.[10] These four syntheses can be illustrated as in Table 5.1.

The first synthesis of time, the 'originary synthesis', is that of the 'lived, or living, present'.[11] It is passive, an ever-present now, a 'succession' or 'repetition of instants'.[12] This succession negotiates the flow of future instants into past instants. So, for Deleuze, the first passive synthesis has the present in ascendancy and 'to it belong both the past and the future' as facets of the present.[13] This contraction of time both foresees the future and preserves the past but only inasmuch as it gives 'direction to the arrow of time'.[14] The past is a form of the present through 'retention', a reservoir of instants synthesized from the present.[15] The future is a form of the present as an 'expectation', that the next now will follow the one before.[16]

The first passive synthesis extends itself in two ways; on the one hand into an active synthesis of 'psycho-organic memory and intelligence (instinct and learning)'.[17] Here the past as retention becomes a 'reflective past of representation' and the future as expectation becomes a 'reflexive future of prediction'.[18] Active synthesis is thus 'superimposed upon and supported by the passive synthesis'.[19] There are then two types of the successive present: the first passive

Table 5.1 Deleuze's syntheses of time

syntheses	dimensions		
active synthesis	sensory-motor system perception → affect → action [memory-image]		
first passive synthesis (present)	retention past of the present	habit present of the present	expectation future of the present
second passive synthesis (past)	memory past of the past	providence present of the past	reminiscence future of the past
third impassive synthesis (future)	experience past of the future	metamorphosis present of the future	caesura future of the future

synthesis of the present ('the primary habits that we are') and the active psychological present ('the sensory-motor habits that we have [psychologically]'), perceptions, affects, impulses, actions, reflections and memory-images.[20]

On the other hand, the first passive synthesis (the now) extends itself toward a second passive synthesis (memory). 'The paradox of the present', writes Deleuze, is to 'constitute time while passing the time constituted', thus a 'necessary conclusion … there must be another time in which the first synthesis of time can occur'.[21] Deleuze contrasts the first and second passive syntheses in this way: if the first is the 'foundation' of time, the second is 'ground'.[22] This is the pure past – memory as the 'pure, general, *a priori* element of all time'.[23] This domain is riven with paradox. The past's relationship with the present is one of domination, the simultaneities of the past a comet's tail to a present as focalization. We can call this present of the past 'fate'.[24] The future of the past is 'reminiscence', and – Deleuze makes this clear – this reminiscence is an 'involuntary', spontaneous happening.[25] This is where the power of the future (of the past) lies, in the infinite levels of a pure past.[26]

That we have a passive synthesis of the present (the now) and the past (memory) indicates a synthesis of the future. Yet, as Nathan Widder comments, 'Deleuze never refers to the third synthesis … as passive'.[27] Nor does he refer to it as active. Rather, this third synthesis could be described, as Deleuze puts it in *Logic of Sense*, as 'impassive', allowing 'the active and the passive to be interchanged more easily, since it is neither one nor the other'.[28] If the first synthesis of succession threatens consistency and the second synthesis of memory threatens to close up upon itself, it is a third synthesis that 'fractures' this line and closure.[29] It is a 'caesura'.[30] Or to put it another way, time is fundamentally a caesura which is susceptible to closure and consistency through memory and succession. If the first passive synthesis constituted the ground, the second the foundation, the third has 'overturned its own ground'.[31] And just as with the first and second, the third is also a perspective on the whole of time: the past of the future appearing as the 'experience' of time; the present of the future as 'metamorphosis', the possibility of change.[32] These futures create novelty in the present through a variable past: freedom, of a kind – one that fractures passive and active syntheses alike.

Such are the differences and repetitions of temporality beneath the surface of the sensory-motor system. In *Cinema 2* Deleuze is inspired by these passive and impassive syntheses to create the semiotic infrastructure of the time-image cineosis.

Cineosis and cinema

Along the thoroughfare, upon pavements, walking the streets, across bridges – the people converge on and pass beyond the skeletal remains of Hiroshima Prefectural Hall, thousands upon thousands, children and adults. These images of the present dissolve. The Hiroshima dead arise. Boys, girls, men and women burnt black, emerging through cinematic superimposition from the rivers where they drowned, from devastated city ruins that describe the aftermath of the nuclear event. It is not enough to say that the people in the present are reconstituting in thought those who have died in the past. Rather, this sequence describes a simultaneity of time: the past of the dead; the present of the living. Yet there is another, secret, dimension – a future of a people to come. This final simultaneity is the virtual component of the actual present and the actualized past, and remains virtual in that neither present nor past cohere; and in consequence of a resistance to actualization. There is a cut to black before any promise of the future. Sekigawa Hideo creates, across these final few moments of *Hiroshima*, a time-image.

Figure 5.1 Succession – the people of the living present, *Hiroshima* (Sekigawa, 1953)

Figure 5.2 Memory – the people as the dead of the past, *Hiroshima* (Sekigawa, 1953)

Figure 5.3 Caesura – the people to come, of the future, *Hiroshima* (Sekigawa, 1953)

The emergence of the time-image is signalled by a crisis of the movement-image, a collapse of its co-ordinates into opsigns and sonsigns. In previous chapters we saw how Deleuze's movement-image taxonomy, inspired by Bergson's sensory-motor schema, created a nexus of cinematic signs describing flows of perception → affect → action, creating characters, emotions and situations. However, we also exposed a beyond of the movement-image. This was conceived through Bergson's concept of memory, seen as having two aspects different in kind. There was the memory-image, which engendered a sensory-motor image of thought as the mental-image. And there was pure memory, thought as process. Pure memory, for Deleuze, guaranteed another kind of cinema: the time-image. Thus the relationship between the movement-image and the time-image, with respect to Bergson, was equivalent to that of the sensory-motor system/memory-image and the processes of pure memory.[33] However, we can also describe this relationship through Deleuze's syntheses of *Difference and Repetition*. On the one hand the sensory-motor system/memory-image of the movement-image correspond to an active synthesis. On the other hand, the time-image corresponds to temporal syntheses.[34]

The time-image cineosis begins with opsigns and sonsigns, pure visual and auditory images that will link up according to the three temporal syntheses. The first passive synthesis creates cinematic hyalosigns. Hyalosigns are images that appear in the now, describe the present. In this way, 'the actual is cut off from its motor linkages' and will instead explore 'the coalescence of an actual image and its virtual image'.[35] This hyalosign is crystalline, connections occurring on each facet, describing a living present, the past as retention and the future as expectation. 'What we see … in the crystal', writes Deleuze, 'is time'; a 'double movement of making presents pass, replacing one by the next while going towards the future, but also preserving all the past, dropping it into an obscure depth'.[36] Hyalosigns thus create time-images at the level of image, description as indeterminacy.

Chronosigns 'no longer concern … description, but narration'.[37] Chronosigns create narrations by disrupting the temporal flow of images, disrupting the order of time, resisting continuity, the strategy one of 'a series of powers, always referring to each other and passing into one another'.[38] The chronosign thus refers to the second passive synthesis of time: the pure past; the present as radical fate, and the future as a force of reminiscence as a becoming. Chronosigns are narrations that 'shatter the empirical continuation of time, the chronological succession, the separation of before and after'.[39] In this way narration 'becomes fundamentally falsifying' and 'ceases to be truthful, that is, to claim to be true'.[40] As Deleuze puts it, 'this is not a simple principle of reflection or becoming aware: "Beware! This is cinema"'.[41] Narration is disjunctive and a 'source of inspiration'.[42]

Noosigns can be seen to correspond with the impassive synthesis. This third synthesis is a 'caesura' exploring the future as an 'empty form of time'.[43] Noosigns 'force … us to think'.[44] While hyalosigns are descriptions and chronosigns are narrations, noosigns involve the story articulated through bodies and the mise-en-scène. Thought (our thought, the spectator's thought) is not engendered as a consequence of a given, actual sensory-motor linkage between the character and the situation, but rather through the absence, or virtual resonance, of such relationship. In the absence of an actual link and in the constitution of virtual relinkage, thought becomes us. The noosign will accordingly explore the three simultaneities of the impassive synthesis: the past as experience of time, the present as metamorphosis, and the future as caesura. Noosigns, in this way, are the retention and dispersal of narrative discord.

The five time-image films explored in this chapter are composed of opsigns and sonsigns – and each will be seen to create descriptive images as hyalosigns, narrations as chronosigns and narratives as noosigns. However, any time-image film can be said to embody a principle: indeterminate image, disruptive narration, dispersive narrative. *Casshern* will be explored as indeterminate images or hyalosign; *The Pacific War*, *A History of Postwar Japan* and *Black Rain* as disruptive narrations or chronosigns; and *Hiroshima* as dispersive narrative or noosign.

Noosigns, chronosigns and hyalosigns are narrative, narration and description – composed from opsigns and sonsigns – the zeroness (0) of the time-image. Concomitantly, hyalosigns, chronosigns and noosigns are simultaneities appearing as a lectosign: a film that demands not only to be seen, but requires a reading. Time-images can thus be considered 'a finite composite sensation … opening onto the plane of composition that restores the infinite to us, = ∞'.[45] Such lectosigns (∞) are the object 'of a fundamental encounter'.[46] Simon O'Sullivan, glossing this statement from *Difference and Repetition*, writes that with an object of recognition 'our knowledge, belief and values are reconfirmed. We, and the world we inhabit, are reconfirmed as that which we already understand our world and ourselves to be'.[47] The time-image lectosign is an encounter which stymies any reconfirmation of our beliefs, understandings and values. Deleuze comments: 'Noël Burch put it very well when he said that, when images cease to be linked together "naturally" … grasping them "requires a considerable effort of memory and imagination, in other words, a reading".'[48] 'What we call reading' time-images 'is the stratigraphic condition … To read is to relink instead of link … a new Analytic of the image.'[49] The three time-images, their sensations (opsigns and sonsigns) and reading (lectosigns), can be illustrated in reference to the temporal syntheses as in Table 5.2.

The final moments of *Hiroshima* are a lectosign, a composition arising from the sensations of opsigns and sonsigns organized through hyalosigns, chronosigns and noosigns. The images of the people – *hibakusha* dead, alive and to come – are descriptions putting actual and virtual into powerful relation. From hyalosign to hyalosign, narration is disjunctive constituting chronosigns of the present, past and future. The final cut is an unactualized virtual future creating an image of cinematic thought for the spectator, a noosign, the unthought of the film. Such a composition of time-images is thus a cinematic event escaping recognition and creating an encounter.

This chapter will read a number of such encounters: *Black Rain* and its subtle perspectivism; *A History of Postwar Japan* and its ungrounding of memory; *The Pacific War* and its fracturing of history. Yet we begin with a time-image produced nearly sixty years after the atomic bombing of Hiroshima and Nagasaki. *Casshern* describes the nuclear event through indeterminacy, makes it imperceptible, and in so doing creates a disturbing thought experiment.

Table 5.2 Time-images and the three passive and impassive syntheses of time

syntheses		**images / dimensions**	
0 opsigns and sonsigns			
first passive synthesis		hyalosigns (present) – description	
	retention (past)	habit (present)	expectation (future)
second passive synthesis		chronosigns (past) – narration	
	memory (past)	fate (present)	reminiscence (future)
third impassive synthesis		noosigns (future) – narrative	
	experience (past)	metamorphosis (present)	caesura (future)
			lectosigns ∞

I. Indeterminacy of the image

Casshern (2004)

Casshern – a resurrected/reanimated Azuma Tetsuya (Iseya Yusuke) – stands at the edge of the precipice, his silver armour rent, soaked in blood. The blood is not only his own. Behind him, in the ruins of the Neoroid castle, lie the dead. Among them his lover Luna (Aso Kumiko), killed by his own father. 'I wasn't able to stop the fighting': these words – Tetsuya's thoughts rendered as voiceover – are accompanied by strange archaic symbols in gold skimming across the screen. Luna rises; gently speaks Tetsuya's name as an image appears of a young boy and girl, maybe ten years of age. Casshern turns, Luna approaches: 'this', she whispers, 'isn't the real me.' Another image of the boy and the girl, Tetsuya and Luna in fecund parkland, smiling. Black-and-white documentary footage from the twentieth century: figures pass before a burning coffin; the fuselage of a bomber; an aircraft carrier at sea. Tetsuya and Luna embrace, the fire-gilded sky behind them. Documentary images: the German army of World War One; a battlefield of tree stumps and barbed wire; soldiers firing rifles from a trench. On the plateau below the castle, among the debris of the Neoroids' destroyed android army, thousands of twenty-first-century soldiers are dead or dying. Documentary images: African refugees; the Middle East, bodies on broken pavements; an army marching; two dead children, one with little red rubber boots; an army on parade, swords and rifles. Tetsuya and Luna, lying together on a haystack, laughing. There are images of the characters from the film in

Figure 5.4 Tetsuya resurrected as Casshern and not-the-real Luna, *Casshern* (Kiriya, 2004)

Figure 5.5 An imaginary temporal moment, *Casshern* (Kiriya, 2004)

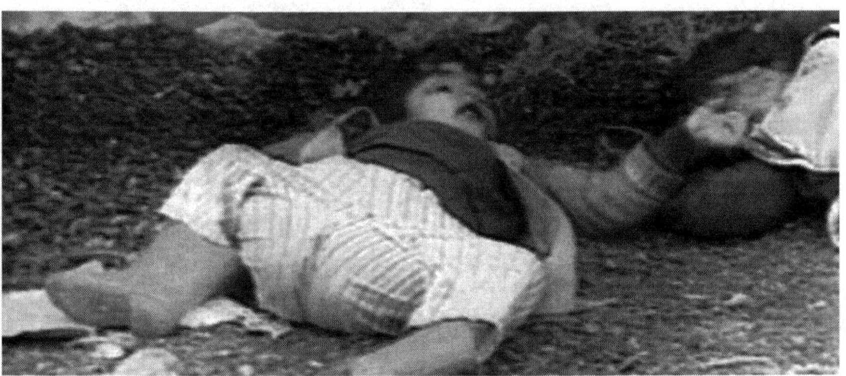

Figure 5.6 Documentary footage, dead children from an undisclosed conflict, *Casshern* (Kiriya, 2004)

family photos or home video footage – images which appear to be from an alternate reality. Documentary footage: a dead adult swathed in robes clinging to a dead baby; a dead baby in a little makeshift coffin; an American bomber unleashing its load; two dead children, one in the arms of the other …

The final moments of Kiriya's *Casshern* are a cascade of indeterminacy. Images realized through the grainy filmstock of documentary footage; the high-definition, computer-generated, putrid colours at the castle; the dark and dirty expressionism of the high plateau battlefield; naturalistic 16mm home movies. Accompanied by synthesized piano and strings, the words spoken by Tetsuya and Luna (sometimes as direct utterances, sometimes in voiceover) are cryptic, ambiguous, and oblique: 'Now I understand. We harm something through our very existence. That's what living is all about.' The documentary footage is presented through hyper-rapid montage, staccato images of war, suffering and death: conflicts and nationalities can be assumed, but only by the quality of the filmstock, clothing, backgrounds, weapons. Images from the castle and the high plateau appear in slow motion, highly stylized and rendered with CGI, reminiscent of a computer game. There is something poignant about this sequence – the music, the words and the images. However any emotional response is complex: the words are poetic, yet banal and inane; the interweaving of real and fictional suffering appears exploitative. Has Kiriya gone too far?

This final sequence of *Casshern* – and as we will see, the entire film – is a cascade of indeterminate images. Deleuze calls such images pure optical and auditory images, or opsigns and sonsigns. Opsigns and sonsigns are constituted through the collapse of the movement-image cineosis. This collapse and constitution can be described in both technical and taxonomic registers.

Cascades of pure optical and auditory images: opsigns and sonsigns

Let us begin with the technical components of cinema: frame, shot, montage, colour and sound. Movement-images attempt to orientate the spectator within the frame. Opsigns endeavour to create disorientations through saturation and rarefaction; geometrical and physical manipulations; unnatural camera angles. Through 'saturation' or 'rarefaction' the frame is overloaded and complicated with elements, or undergoes an emptying out.[50] Through 'geometrical or physical … limitation' landscapes and bodies are fragmented and anomalous relations created between elements.[51] Through strange camera angles point-of-view becomes inexplicable (in the movement-image, tilts and cants indicate a disturbed psychological or social state).[52] Such disorientations are the conditions of a re-theorization of the out-of-field. The out-of-field creates a presence through non-presence. With movement-images such presence is in the service of continuity: the glance off-screen to connect space; the body part in close-up which always supposes the rest of the body; the landscape and sky in a wide shot that connects to world and universe. This out-of-field is a 'closed system' in the sense that it creates a 'homogeneous continuity'.[53] In contrast, with opsigns the out-of-field does not exist outside the frame, but rather, as Deleuze puts it, 'insists' or 'subsists' within the frame.[54] It points to 'a more radical Elsewhere, outside homogeneous space and time'.[55] It 'works as a pictorial frame which isolates a system'.[56] In this way, the radical out-of-field creates a direct relationship with the whole, and 'the whole is the Open', the virtual.[57] The frame turns in upon itself.

Once the frame is in motion (frame → frame → frame and so on) we encounter the shot. The shot is thus in-time and in-movement: a nexus of movement of camera and movement of elements over time. In the movement-image, the nexus is rational. The camera moves with necessity, elements move with inevitability and obligation. From shot to shot: montage. In the movement-image there is continuity from 'shot to montage and from montage to shot'.[58] Cuts on movements create invisible montage, and even when visible, montage creates rational links between images. In this way the spectator is caught up in the flow of images, in the flow of movement through an image and between images. With the shot as opsign we may encounter a reduction in length to escape perception (hyper-rapid editing). We may encounter the deep focus allowed by depth of field with elements traversing different planes. We may encounter the extension of the shot over a protracted period of time (the long take), and this shot describing less and less movement. Nothing happens: the spectator must encounter the image in-and-for-itself rather than simply see it in order to understand what will come next. In this way everything happens: the shot encounters 'the insisting / subsisting out-of-field'.[59] Opsigns, accordingly, 'no longer asks how images are linked' but rather 'what does the image show?'[60] Montage evokes 'false continuity': jump-cuts disrupt flows and spatial conventions are dissembled, shot-reverse shots disappear in favour of more nebulous connections between characters.[61] Essentially, 'there is no longer an alternative between montage and shot', and movement no longer dominates, setting time free.[62]

The final component of the opsign is colour. Deleuze opposes the coloured image of the movement-image with the colour-image of the time-image.[63] The former tends toward invisibility through a determination of elements. With the latter colour becomes visible: we encounter 'surface-colour of the great uniform tints'; 'the atmospheric colour which pervades all others'; and 'the absorbent characteristic' where one colour infects all others.[64] In this way even the black-and-white image can become a colour-image (even during the black-and-white era): black, white or grey envelops all.

From opsigns to sonsigns: for Deleuze, as others before, there is no such thing as a silent cinema – the coming of the sound film simply integrated pre-existing sound elements. Music from the orchestra pit or platform had always 'found itself subject to a certain obligation to correspond to the visual image, or to serve descriptive, illustrative and narrative ends'.[65] Speech had always appeared (internally) as intertitles and (externally) through the use of narrators, particularly in Japan through *benshi* performances. Integration served to strengthen continuity with regard to the movement-image. Visual images and sound images were inextricably linked, it being difficult to judge where one ended and the other began. As Deleuze points out, such 'sound components are separate only in the abstraction of their pure hearing'; in effect 'they are a … dimension of the visual image' and 'they all form together one single component, a continuum'.[66] However, sonsigns attempt to disrupt the continuum. Music can be suppressed: the film becomes truly silent. Sound effects can be removed, thus reducing the spatial out-of-field. Unexpected music and sound effects can be employed. The voice can be, as Michel Chion puts it, 'denaturalised' using 'theatrical speech', 'textual speech' (where the voice overloads the visual image), and 'decentering' (where the visual images overload the sound images).[67]

Such may be some of the technical strategies for the dissolution of movement-images and the constitution of opsigns and sonsigns. Yet we can simultaneously describe such dissolution-constitution in taxonomical terminology, the collapse of the links between sensory-motor images and the disintegration of their internal dynamics. In the movement-image, such internal dynamics and linkages are established by the perception-image. Perception-images describe the creation of a special image, a contingent centre (usually a character) that will establish a concomitant relation with all other images in the film. In the first instance then, perception-images organize subjective and objective perception. These are the dyadic co-ordinates of molar and molecular organization, described through solid perception and gaseous perception, and moving from one to the other through the liquid. Thus the three levels of movement-image perception – the monadic (the image), dyadic (molar and molecular) and triadic (solid, liquid, gaseous). Images, sequences and the film will each be dominated by solid or liquid or gaseous perception, organizing subjective and objective relations which will sustain – in the second instance – affection-images, action-images and mental-images. Affection-images traverse the special image with emotion, on a face, across bodies or through the mise-en-scène. Action-images organize the way this contingent centre defines or is derived from a determined situation and how that situation can be reconfigured by acts from the centre. Finally, mental-images capture up perception-, affection- and action-images with respect to the special image as flashbacks, dreams and symbolic relations, describing the processes of thinking, imagination and memory.

The collapse of the internal dynamics of the perception-image will thus destroy these co-ordinates of the movement-image. As Deleuze puts it, 'the distinction between subjective and objective … tends to lose its importance'.[68]

'Not because they are confused', but because 'we do not have to know'.[69] Here we encounter 'a principle of indeterminability, of indiscernibility', perception-images become opsigns and sonsigns, pure audio-visual signs, and this principle will effect each of the other movement-images through extension and from within. With the affection-image 'a purely optical or sound situation becomes established in … "any-space-whatever"'.[70] Centres diffuse into the mise-en-scène, and the mise-en-scène, in turn, becomes disconnected and empties out. Accordingly, action-images can no longer create determined situations, and links between situation and action, action and situation become fragile, are barely constituted. Here we encounter 'the dispersive situation, deliberately weak links, the voyage form', a reflection on clichés and an overriding 'condemnation of plot'.[71] Finally, we 'no longer know what is imaginary or real, physical or mental'.[72] Dreams merge with world and the world with dreams; flashbacks no longer place the past in respect to the present for the future; and images of thought permeate the screen. Everything is indiscernible. Everything is opsigns and sonsigns, pure audio-visual indeterminability.

Casshern as a cascade of indeterminate images is composed of opsigns and sonsigns constituted through technical processes which enact a dissolution of the movement-image: pure audio-visual images, any-space-whatevers, dispersive situations, weak links; reflections upon and inversions of clichés – and in this way we witness a dissolution of the plot and proliferation of ambiguities of real and imaginary, mental and physical. It is through such indeterminacy that *Casshern* will capture up the atomic attacks of Hiroshima and Nagasaki within a troubling thought experiment. However, before we can go on to explore this aspect of the film, it is necessary to go beyond a description of *Casshern* in terms of the crisis and collapse of movement-images. For to define opsigns and sonsigns as such is to approach them only by way of their destructive characteristic: this is just a potential. Opsigns and sonsigns form stratigraphic fibres: relink. Relink, but retain their textures of indeterminacy. And it is through such relinkages that opsigns and sonsigns create radical powers.

Hyalosigns

Hyalosigns are descriptions in-themselves, the first relinkage of opsigns and sonsigns, images encountered in the present retaining indeterminacy. As Deleuze comments, 'the indiscernibility of the real and the imaginary, or of the present and the past, of the actual and the virtual, is definitely not produced in the head or the mind, it is the objective characteristic of certain existing images'.[73] This indiscernibility arises as these 'existing images … are by nature double'.[74] This doubling occurs through a relinkage of the image with itself and concerns 'the actual image and its virtual image' constituting 'the smallest internal circuit'.[75] In so doing the hyalosign performs a 'double movement of making presents pass, replacing one by the next while going towards the future, but also preserving all the past, dropping it into an obscure depth'.[76] Hyalosigns, in this way, refer to the first passive synthesis of time which describes the ever-present now as succession negotiating the flow of future instants into past instants. The presentness of the present thus has a past of the present as retention and a future of the present as expectation. In the hyalosign these dimensions designate three types of image that compose actual and virtual circuits.

The present (of the present) is an actual image describing a mirroring: 'two facing mirrors', 'oblique mirrors, concave and convex mirrors and Venetian mirrors', a 'palace of mirrors'.[77] Here bodies and backgrounds appear multitudinous – and in this way the actual propagates indiscernibility enacted by the virtual linkages between elements. The past of the present, retention, creates an exchange of actual and virtual: one image becomes opaque as another becomes limpid, the limpid actualized in the present corresponding to an opaque retention of the past as virtual image. Mirrors and the limpid and opaque concern the structure of hyalosigns, but a third component describes the genetic process. Here actual and virtual appear as seed and environment. The present can be a seed, the future a virtual environment in relation to that seed, an expectation: a virtual succession which subsists or insists within the seed image. Reciprocally, an actualized environment may refer to a virtual seed. Either way, one is 'pure virtuality' in respect to the other in that 'it does not have to be actualised'.[78] The hyalosign, its dual poles of structure and process, and its three component images, can be illustrated as in Table 5.3.

With *Casshern*, we can begin at the level of the hyalosign in-itself in order to delineate the image in the present as description. Take the permeating battle-sequences: when Tetsuyo-Casshern faces Neoroid leader Burai (Karasawa

Table 5.3 Hyalosign

hyalosign		
crystalline structure		genetic process
mirrors face-to-face	limpid and opaque	seed and environment

Toshiaki) and his machine-army for the first time: *anime*, CGI and live action are overlaid within the frame and shots, connecting through hyper-rapid montage. Sometimes backgrounds plummet into an almost infinite deep focus describing thousands upon thousands of machines; sometimes backgrounds appear as matt-black plane-surfaces upon which Tetsuyo-Casshern and Burai operate in isolation. The music traversing the visual image is used not to heighten affects or effect, but rather appears in-itself as parallel accompaniment. Such procedures are replicated throughout the fight and battle scenes of the film. The piano, strings and choirs of 'Divine Will'; the heavy metal of The Black Horn's 'Requiem'; Ludwig van Beethoven's 'Moonlight': symphonies, electronica, rave, metal and ballads. These sequences are like music videos. Accordingly, they have no need to orientate the spectator visually with regard to subject and object positions. They are, as Deleuze puts it, 'spectacle, in accordance with the demands of a pure optical and sound perception'.[79] In this way *Casshern* is vital in its visceral descriptions, creating a dynamic image in the present that will create mirror images, the limpid and opaque, and seeds and environments.

Early on in the film Tetsuya's corpse is returned from the battlegrounds of Zone 7 where he has died. Being the son of eminent state scientist Professor Azuma (Terao Akira), his body is treated with great deference, the coffin lying in state in the atrium of his father's vast laboratory. Another Tetsuya crawls on top of the coffin, looking in upon his own corpse: glass between them, faces separated by a screen which connects the two. As Deleuze puts it, with mirror images 'the actual and the virtual image co-exist', entering 'into a circuit which brings us constantly back from one to the other; they form one and the same "scene"'.[80] Tetsuya is dead / Tetsuya is alive; and while it is simple to identify the dead and the alive, this simultaneity creates an indeterminacy, a virtual relinkage that 'immediately extends into the opaque-limpid, the expression of their exchange'.[81] Such exchange both precedes and supersedes this mirror image. As Tetsuya dies on a battlefield, a Tetsuya visits his blind and dying mother Midori (Higuchi Kanako) and a Tetsuya visits the sleeping Luna. These 'alive' Tetsuyas are not (or not only) dream-images, hallucination and nightmare – but autonomous incarnations of son and lover. Tetsuya appears for himself as much as for others, these moments do not appear simply as Luna's and Midori's points-of-view. Later, as Professor Azuma submerges his dead son's body in the fluid that will resurrect him, another Tetsuya stands looking on pleading to be allowed to remain dead. Such exchanges between Tetsuyas as limpid-opaque extend outwards toward his embodiment of the mythic Casshern: 'when the virtual image becomes actual, it is then visible and limpid ... but the actual image becomes virtual in turn, referred elsewhere, invisible, opaque, shadowy.'[82] After his reanimation which brings with it powers beyond the human, Tetsuya will adopt the name of the mythical god-figure worshipped by the people of Zone 7, a people the Japanese are in process of annihilating, a people reduced to body-parts out of which Dr Azuma creates the Neoroids. In this way, just as mirror images develop into the limpid and the opaque (present to past), so they extend into the seed and the environment (present to future): 'expression moves from the mirror to the seed.'[83] The perspective thus shifts from the past as retention to future as expectation. In the opening moments of the movie, as the camera traverses the sky above the clouds, a giant statue appears – a winged figure cut through by a bolt of lightning penetrating its spine. This statue is an embodiment of the mythical, opaque Casshern. Yet this statue is a seed image of a new Casshern yet to arise, the reanimated Tetsuya. Such a trajectory is essential to the indeterminacy of the film, for the lightning bolt is grasped by the hands of the statue, arms reaching back over its shoulders – and it is unclear if this Casshern is welcoming or attempting to repel the power which is given. It is a lightning bolt that will activate the reanimating fluid that enacts the transformation of dead Tetsuya into the alive Casshern.

In considering *Casshern* as composed of hyalosigns, we can begin to see how the relinking of its cascade of opsigns and sonsigns constitutes a collapse of the sensory-motor system (the movement-image). We encounter a dispersive situation, weak links between images, a voyage form, a consciousness of clichés and the condemnation of plot. Kiriya's *Casshern* is based upon the Japanese television series of the same name, yet series and subsequent film are very different. The tagline of the former is 'Kyasshan ga yaraneba, dore go yaru?' – 'If Casshern doesn't do it, who will?' In the television series Casshern is conceived as a superhero, engendered by the situation and through whose actions the situation is always resolved. In Tetsuya's film Casshern is radically impotent, powerfully powerless. 'If Casshern doesn't do it, who will?' – as Deborah Shamoon puts it – 'when it comes to transcending human nature and ending warfare, perhaps no one.'[84] Thus, for Shamoon, as the film 'lurches toward its inevitable apocalyptic' conclusion we encounter 'a bleak ending.'[85] Casshern-Tetsuya at the edge of the precipice, silver armour rent, soaked in blood, surveying the thousands dead: 'I wasn't able to stop the fighting ... not only that, but I averted my gaze from all the suffering.' Casshern-Tetsuya has resolved nothing; he is a seer traversing a path of pure spectacle.

A spectacle of the imperceptible

It is the nature of this spectacle, these hyalosigns, that refers us to Japanese history, the atomic attacks on Hiroshima and Nagasaki and the Pacific War, and a new image of thought of the *pika* and the *hibakusha*. We can begin with the seed and the environment. 'The seed is on the one hand the virtual image which will crystallise an environment which is at present amorphous; but on the other hand the latter must have structure which is virtually crystallisable, in relation to which the seed now plays the role of actual image': (virtual) seed ↔ (actual) environment and/or (actual) seed ↔ (virtual) environment.[86]

In the first place: (virtual) seed ↔ (actual) environment. As the film begins it is declared: 'After fifty years of bitter warfare, the Greater Eastern Federation has defeated the European Union and taken control of almost all of the Eurasian continent.' This is an alternative world of the present, a world in which, as Dr Azuma pronounces in a speech to the fascist-militarist complex, Japan 'is, with ever increasing momentum, establishing a co-prosperity sphere in Eurasia.' Such is the environment of the film. Japan is now the Greater Eastern Federation, a supreme imperialist war-machine. In such a scenario we seem to have encountered counter-factual fiction. Mark Lawson writes: 'The second world war is such a pivotal event in human history that generations have inevitably speculated about what might have happened had the momentum swung slightly another way.'[87] 'With counter-factual fiction,' Lawson continues, 'you pull out one thing and the rest unravels.'[88] Such speculative narratives, however, depend upon a modification of an historical event. With *Casshern* – and this is the essential point – it is never clear what event is modified. The actual environment of the present refers to a virtual seed of the past which cannot be determined; we encounter a dispersed situation which instead generates a series of questions. Did the nuclear event of Hiroshima and Nagasaki happen? If it did, what explains the rise of the Greater Eastern Federation? Did Japan fight on, resist surrender and somehow triumph in a fifty-year war? Or if it did not happen, why? Did the Japanese not bomb Pearl Harbor? Did the Americans not enter the war? The virtual seed image of the actualized environment – its centre – is indeterminate, a virtual absence/presence which insists and subsists within the environment of *Casshern*.

The atomic bombing of Hiroshima and Nagasaki thus appears as a virtual component of the actual images in a very special way. We can compare this virtual aspect with Ito's documentary *The Effects of the Atomic Bomb on Hiroshima and Nagasaki* (Chapters 1 and 3). In *Effects*, while the atomic bomb was never depicted the *pika* appeared as a virtual centre in every moment of the film, which was organized through gaseous perception-images: devastated any-space-whatevers of the cities, and the images of the *hibakusha* in the wards of the makeshift hospitals. Yet *Effects*, with its unequivocal socio-temporal placement and its clear lines of force, corresponded exactly to the sign of the milieu of the large form action-image: an empirical, purely historical realist account of the Japanese nuclear events. With *Casshern* everything is different, the virtual is not determined but indeterminate. There are two aspects to this indetermination. In the first place, this concerns hyalosign genesis: the correlation between the actual image (environment) and the atomic event as virtual image (seed), this link posing problematic and unanswerable questions. In the second place, this concerns the indeterminacy of the compositions (mirrors; limpid-opaque): for instance, the dead original humans of Zone 7 that become Neoroids arising from the resurrection soup, these images resonant visual traces of the *hibakusha*. Yet these images remain indeterminate. Shamoon, in a wonderful exegesis, sees these Neoroids in the context of Japanese war crimes, writing: 'the name Zone 7 is a reference to the notorious Unit 731 in Manchuria, where during the war Japanese scientists carried out vivisection and other experiments on thousands of men, women, and children. Among the experiments were attempts to amputate and reattach limbs and internal organs.'[89] Furthermore, 'the name of the official who funds Azuma's lab, Naito, is also a reference to the second-in-command at Unit 731, Lieutenant Colonel Naito Ryoichi … The Original Humans literally embody the lands and cultures of the Greater East Asia Co-Prosperity Sphere, which Imperial Japan intended to use as raw materials to sustain itself.'[90] For Shamoon, the film thus is 'the expression of collective guilt over Japanese wartime atrocities, in this case, vivisection and the slaughter of civilians.'[91] In *Casshern*, neither the *pika* nor the *hibakusha* are the centre, they appear as a virtual absence/presence with the absence/presence of the Japanese military and their enemies during the Pacific War.

In the second place: (actual) seed ↔ (virtual) environment. In the final moments of *Casshern*, (dead-alive) Luna and Tetsuya-Casshern embrace and kiss. Light pours from their bodies. Tetsuya-Casshern, Luna and the battlefield dead become light and all join as one. This light breaks free from the Earth's atmosphere, traverses planets, moons, asteroids and stars, the galaxy, and collides with a distant planet. The energies of the dead and dying creating, it would appear, a seed of future life, a spark of life to come. Thus, reciprocally, the nuclear event simultaneously appears as an actual seed of a virtual environment. The light that is generated from the carnage on Earth encounters a virgin planet, a nuclear event on a new world as genesis. Is this a rebirth of the Japanese into difference: the lightning bolt of life engendering a year zero and the chance to start again? Is this the way to understand the atomic attacks on Hiroshima and Nagasaki? Or is this moment a rebirth to be a repetition of the same? The future is not a given. The future is rather an expectation: an indeterminate matrix of expectations. Thus, alongside Shamoon's analysis that the film has a bleak ending, we must also see the film as describing in this actual seed a virtual environment which Tetsuya-Casshern articulates in this way: 'this is where we must start from … Hope' – an escape from the succession of the same.

From seed to environment and environment to seed, through mirrors and the limpid and opaque, *Casshern* links its actual images with the *pika*, the *hibakusha*, the Japanese military and the atrocities of the Pacific War. It is a film of encounter, not recognition. In *Difference and Repetition* Deleuze writes: 'each faculty – perception, memory, imagination, understanding' has 'its own particular given and its own style, its particular ways of acting upon the given. An object is recognised, however, when one faculty locates it as identical to that of another, or rather when all the faculties together relate their given and relate themselves to a form of identity in the object.'[92] Accordingly, 'recognition thus relies upon a subjective principle of collaboration of the faculties for "everybody"'.[93] The encounter 'is not the given but that by which the given is given.'[94] It is in this way we encounter the imperceptible: 'it is imperceptible precisely from the point of view of recognition.'[95] Hyalosigns create descriptions which escape recognition, *Casshern* escapes a given image of the *pika* and the *hibakusha*, a given image of history becomes problematic. *Casshern* retains difference in-itself within the film, generating multiple perspectives on the images and in relation to history as a new image of cinematic thought. It is such a new image of cinematic thought that will be explored in two documentary films which explicitly depict the histories that preceded and succeeded the nuclear event: Oshima's *The Pacific War* and Imamura's *A History of Postwar Japan as Told by a Bar Hostess*. However, these films, depicting real historical events with found-footage, will need to supplant an indeterminacy of the image with a disjunction between images, with disjunctive narration.

II. A disjunctive unfolding of narration and history

Chronosigns

If hyalosigns concern description, chronosigns concern narration, the assemblage of hyalosignic images. And if hyalosigns suppose a succession of images through the present, chronosigns suppose an amassing of images in a pastness, a reservoir of heterogeneous connections. As Deleuze puts it in *Cinema 2*, this second time-image creates a narration of 'non-chronological time' from the 'pre-existence of a past in general'.[96] In this way, chronosigns refer to the second passive synthesis of time from *Difference and Repetition*, the pure past. With the second synthesis time is produced in relation to the past, and it is this past that describes the consummate dimensions of temporality yielding the present and future. The present of the past appears as a prism of fate, while the future of the past appears as creative reminiscence. The three dimensions of the second synthesis give rise to the three images of the chronosign.

We necessarily begin with narration dominated with the pastness of the past, the chronosign as an encounter with a pure past. Here we confront a 'coexistence' of 'sheets of the past'.[97] Such an organization of images concerns a narration exploring an 'infinity of levels'.[98] The film resists the flow of the succession of images through the present, replacing such an organization with leaps between circles of the past, from one sheet to another. Each sheet is a sequence of the past in reference to all others in the narration. In this way the film is composed of many past times. Deleuze puts it this way: 'Between the past as pre-existence in general and the present as infinitely contracted past there are … all the circles of the past constituting so many stretched or shrunk regions, strata, and sheets.'[99] Through its narration, the film may present each sheet in an order of time where it is the relative past of the one succeeding it, and the relative future of the one preceding it. The crucial point is that each sheet has 'its own characteristics, its "tones," its "aspects," its "singularities," its "shining points" and its "dominant themes"'.[100] At the most extreme the film may resist all linearity, instead leaping from sheet to sheet through connections which reveal secret temporal flows. In such a way sheets of the past create a narration capturing the pastness of the past.

Peaks of the present are the second type of chronosign. Here we encounter the present through its pastness, through the infinity of pasts which create the present. In this way narration will create different versions of the present.

As Deleuze puts it, with peaks of the present 'narration will consist of the distribution of different presents to different characters, so that each forms a combination that is plausible and possible in itself, but where all of them together are "incompossible"'.[101] This type of chronosign similarly disrupts the order of time as did sheets of the past, giving 'narration a new value, because it abstracts it from all successive action'.[102] Narration appears in the repetitions of the different presents. In this way past(s) dominate(s) the present(s). This is the past as the fate of the present – not in the sense of prescribed fate (a retroactive now which depends upon linear trajectory) but rather in the sense of 'setting time free'.[103] Accordingly, at its most extreme peaks of the present may construct a narration that repeats the same moment several times, each repetition different in-itself. Fate is freedom. And freedom is choice, the choice between 'inextricable differences'.[104]

Peaks of the present and sheets of the past discover the pure past in the past and in the present. Yet this pure past can also be said to be a dimension of the future. This third chronosign is no longer concerned with an exploration or disruption of the order of time. Rather, it reveals (and in this way is the genesis of) the procedures of sheets and peaks by way of an enunciation of the pure past in reference to the future. Memory is spontaneous, reminiscence is creative. The reconstitution of the past always occurs as a reminiscence for the future in the present. While sheets and peaks concerned the order of time – that is, 'the coexistence of relations or the simultaneity of the elements internal to time' – the third concerns the series of time.[105] Thus, we encounter 'a series of powers, always referring to each other and passing into one another'.[106] Here before and after are a becoming; 'instead of separating them: its paradox is to introduce an enduring interval into the moment itself'.[107] The film reveals the fundamental perspectival nature of time. Not the different perspectives of different times; not different perspectives on the same time, but rather how the event as it is in-itself is fundamentally perspectival. As Deleuze puts it, such perspectivism is 'not defined by variation of external points of view on a supposedly invariable object (the ideal of the true would be preserved)'.[108] Rather 'the point of view' is 'internal', is 'presented as the metamorphosis of one and the same thing in the process of becoming'.[109] Narration is no longer concerned with creating truth but is 'fundamentally falsifying'.[110] Deleuze comments: 'If we take the history of thought, we see that time has always put the notion of truth into crisis. Not that truth varies depending upon the epoch. It is not the simple empirical content, it is the form or rather the pure force of time which puts truth into crisis.'[111]

This is the power of the false of the chronosign. The power of the false destroys the notion of truth in-itself, destroys the idea that somehow the truth can be discovered in the event. This is the power acknowledging all images as false. Truth is created, and this is what powers of the false describe: 'this will not be a cinema of truth but the truth of cinema.'[112] The chronosign, its dual poles of order and series, and its three component images can be illustrated as in Table 5.4.

Chronosigns, the non-chronological organization of time through the disruption of order and the serialization of images, create very powerful strategies of narration. Such strategies unearth the indiscernibility of time in an event, how time is layered, incompossible, and how it is fundamentally falsifying. Chronosigns thus not only refer us to narration, but also to history. With the hyalosign, history appeared as opaque to the limpid present, an indiscernible mirror image, a virtual environment or seed. With chronosigns history permeates the narration, for chronosigns are the past in general. Yet history will appear as an infinity of sheets, an incompossibility of peaks, and as powers of the false. In the discussion that follows, we will consider two Japanese documentaries which use chronosigns capturing up the atomic bombings of Hiroshima and Nagasaki within Japanese history. Oshima's *The Pacific War* utilizes the sheets of the past through a composition of newsreel footage of Japan's imperialist, fascist and militarist past, the nuclear event concluding the film. Imamura's *A History of Postwar Japan as Told by a Bar Hostess* begins with the nuclear event, going on to explore the occupation and post-occupation period, using peaks of the present to interweave the political and personal. Both these films undermine the documentary format through chronosigns and thus reveal the power of false, a disrupting of history and truth. Imamura's *Black Rain*, with which we will conclude this section, creates such chronosigns in a fiction film, forming an interweaving of sheets, peaks and powers as impure anarchic multiplicities in two time-spaces: 1945 Hiroshima and 1950 Ujina. As we will see, *Black Rain* ultimately explores, through a perspectival nexus of *hibakusha* experiences, a disjunctive unfolding of narration and history, a disjunction between narration and history, between truth and history.

Table 5.4 Chronosign

chronosign		
order of time		series of time
sheets of the past	peaks of the present	powers of the false

The Pacific War (1968)

Oshima's *The Pacific War* is composed entirely from existing archival visual and sound information: from the attack on Pearl Harbor in December 1941 to the atom bomb in August 1945. It is thus a very particular kind of documentary, what Mark Freeman describes as a 'compilation' or 'found' film, 'films created from … pieces and fragments of other films'.[113] The use of such archival material has three imperatives. The first involves the source: Oshima used only visual and sound images originally distributed and sanctioned by the Japanese authorities. We thus encounter newsreels and reportage, government proclamations and state propaganda. The second imperative involves composition: Oshima used the material as-is, raw footage. He did not record a voice-over commentary to explicate the images, to pass judgement. Oshima makes these first two imperatives clear; a title announces: 'All parts of this motion picture were filmed during the Pacific War. All narration, sound and music were recorded by the Japanese at that time. Films purchased from abroad are presented as dubbed by the Japanese at that time. This is a record of the Pacific War as we the Japanese people experienced it.'[114] The film begins with the successful attack on Pearl Harbor and Japan's territorial gains across the Pacific, eventually alluding to the shift in fortunes beginning a year later with the American bombing of Tokyo and Japanese defeats in the battles of the Solomons (August 1942) and Guadalcanal (February 1943). The second half of the film traces the downfall of the militaristic imperial regime: the desperation of sustaining the war to reticent surrender in the wake of the nuclear attacks on Hiroshima and Nagasaki.

Yet, there is a third, hidden, imperative: the choice and organization of material. This, in a sense, returns us to and overwrites the first two imperatives. In other words, it is through such a process of selection and connection that Oshima creates the narration of *The Pacific War*.

In this move from the first two procedures to the reversals of the third we discover the way in which Oshima uses chronosigns. In the first instance, this is sheets of the past: 'between the past as pre-existence in general and the present as infinitely contracted past.'[115] The schema of *The Pacific War* may appear simple: found footage of the historical past presented as-is in a continuum. Things are more complex than this. On the one hand, there is no centre. The images are not organized around a historical figure for which all the other images of the film exist. Nor, indeed, are the images organized around a singular event which will be explained through other events which are positioned in relation to it. These sheets/sequences are not even organized around a question. Rather, what we encounter are sequences, each of which encompasses an event which appears as a sheet of the past in respect to the statement in the introductory title. On the other hand, the introductory title appears as a present (a now at the edge of the past) to which each of the sheets refer. Each sequence is a sheet of the past which has its impetus in relation to a statement of procedure: the two manifest imperatives and their oblique reversal.

Two reciprocal questions arise, which are in fact two aspects of the same question: how are sheets of the past related to recollection-images, and why are these sheets not recollection-images? It will be remembered (from Chapter 4) that recollection-images are flashbacks. They are engendered as psychological moments, the memory of a past event brought into the present, for the present, to ensure the movement towards the future. In this way, despite a circling from the present to the past back to the present, this detour retains the flow of the sensory-motor schema, placing affect and action at the service of a mental-image. Sheets of the past, however, operate differently. They may entail the use of the flashback, yet if they do so, they bring to the flashback a new value. Equally, however, sheets of the past may entirely relinquish their need for recollection-images. Indeed, such a move from use to renunciation can be seen, according to Deleuze, as a 'rigorous progression' in the creation of sheets by filmmakers who have explored their function over a number of films.[116] Deleuze positions this creation of cinematic sheets of the past in reference to Bergson who 'distinguished two main instances': in the first case 'the past recollection may still be evoked in an image, but the latter is now useless, because the present from which the evocation set off has lost its motor-extension which would make the image usable.'[117] Secondly, 'the recollection can no longer be evoked in an image, although it persists in a region of the past.'[118] In *The Pacific War*, Oshima seems to have created his sheets of the past at the very moment between these two poles.

In an early film by Oshima, *Nihon no yoru to kiri / Night and Fog in Japan* (1960), the present of a wedding creates the impetus for what initially appears as recollection-images. These past images are complex formations and pass through any number of procedures, ultimately surrendering any individual psychological co-ordinates to become manifestations of memory in general, 'the overtaking of psychological memory towards a world-memory.'[119] Furthermore, these images of the past are not used in the present (as arguments or disclosures) for a sensory-motor trajectory. The recollection-image formula is reversed:

flashbacks are not engendered for the present, but the present becomes a staging ground for various leaps into the past, sheets of the past are the focus of the film. *The Pacific War* is both far simpler and more complex. The moment of the present is reduced to the introductory title which immediately entails a leap into the past. What then of this leap into the past and the subsequent images from 1941 to 1945, from Pearl Harbor to Hiroshima and Nagasaki? Is not such a trajectory a continuum? Deleuze writes that 'these regions of past' may have 'a chronological course', however each of the sheets 'in themselves, and in relation to the actual present' are 'all coexistent, each containing the whole … in one form or another'.[120] Each of these sheets 'has what Bergson calls "shining points," singularity,' and 'each collects around these points the totality'.[121] In short, with sheets of the past non-chronological narration does not necessarily require a non-linear organization. Rather, it means a stymieing of necessity, of cause and effect. A disruption of the flow of images of the sensory-motor schema: from perception to affect and from affect to action, images joined in logical cohesive sequence, where the prior image presupposed the following, and the current image prepares us for what is to come caught in a network of mental relations. Sheets, simply put, organize the past as regions, 'each with its own accents or

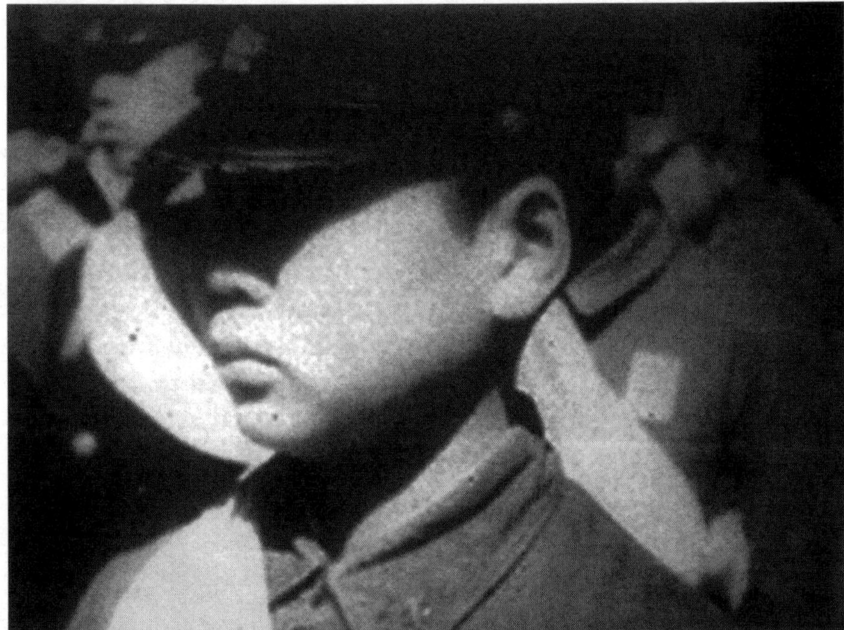

Figure 5.7 Boy soldiers, *The Pacific War* (Oshima, 1968)

potentials', each marking 'critical moments'.[122] 'Each sheet of past … calls up all the mental functions simultaneously: recollection, but equally forgetting, false recollection, imagination, planning, judgement.'[123]

This is what we get with *The Pacific War*: a series of sequences, a series of sheets of the past. Early in the film there is a proclamation from the Imperial Headquarters by the Departments of the Army and Navy: 'We announce the final results confirmed by the air bombers and photographic reconnoitring party. It is confirmed that the American Pacific Fleet and Air Force in Hawaii were annihilated. Just last spring, the U.S. commissioned new 35,000-ton battleships, the *North Carolina* and the *Washington*, which gave them 18 major ships designed to gain world mastery.'[124] The communiqué continues: 'Nine of these 18 major ships were put to death at this one battle. Not only have the U.S. ambitions collapsed, but they have been downgraded to a second- or third-class naval nation.'[125] The Japanese enter Malaya, Thailand and Singapore. There are celebrations outside the Imperial Palace. Towards the end of the film boy soldiers are seen signing up and the *kamikaze* pilots take to the skies above the Philippines. Each of these sequences has its own consistency: propaganda announcement, imperial proclamation, newsreel reportage. Each appears as singularity. Reciprocally, 'the brain is the set of non-localizable relations between all these sheets, the continuity which rolls them up and unrolls them like so many lobes, preventing them from halting and becoming fixed in a death-position'.[126] In this way the sheet that refers us to the atomic bombing of Hiroshima and Nagasaki appears in a strange way. The events are mentioned, but not depicted (no official Japanese footage of the moment existing). They are events which appear alongside the firebombing of Tokyo and the invasion of Okinawa. The moment of the atomic bomb is not the logical conclusion of the Pacific War but just one experience of the Japanese people, as rendered through *The Pacific War*. The atomic bomb is no longer a centre. As Deleuze says in respect to another film, it 'is not another film about war, to glorify or attack it. It films the categories of war, which is something quite different.'[127]

It is in this way that sheets of the past as the order of time have their foundation in the series of time, the serial organization of the 'genesign.'[128] This is the powers of the false, which puts into question the notion of truth. Before we go on to explore this aspect, it will be helpful to see how another filmmaker leads us to powers of the false in respect to the Japanese cinema of the atom bomb, this time from the perspective of the second co-ordinate of the order of time, peaks of the present.

A History of Postwar Japan as Told by a Bar Hostess (1970)

It is as if Shohei Imamura's *A History of Postwar Japan*, made two years after Oshima's film, confronts *The Pacific War* to complement it, but skewing and expanding its procedures. Whereas Oshima's film ends with the atomic bombings of Hiroshima and Nagasaki, Imamura takes this as his starting point. He thus presents a series of sequences on-screen leading from the nuclear event up to the present day of the film, the occupation and early to late post-occupation periods. Echoing Oshima, Imamura's film operates under the three imperatives, yet in a completely different way. Oshima's film was composed of sanctioned Japanese material as-is, reversed through selection and connection which in-itself operated as a hidden commentary. Imamura reworks this procedure. While he presents found images as-is, Imamura films a screen within the mise-en-scène upon which these images are projected. And just as Oshima reworked the relationship between the image and commentary, so too does Imamura – yet again, in a completely different way. As *Postwar Japan* opens, Etsuko Akaza, beehived hairdo, in sixties miniskirt and plunging top, is seated between the camera and the screen, watching the images as a film within a film, listening to the soundtrack, commenting upon it, and responding to questions and prompts from Imamura himself, who sits to one side of the camera. The commentary has been integrated into the film, yet violently exposed as commentary. The first sequence projected refers to the atomic bombing of Hiroshima and Nagasaki, which happened when Etsuko was fifteen years of age. Yet Etsuko would rather focus upon her own life stories. We encounter other sequences, the surrender of Japan, General MacArthur's arrival in Japan, the Allied occupation, the return of prisoners of war, the independence of Japan, the Korean War, student protests during the sixties: the whole process behind the liberal democratic post-war reconstruction of Japan. These moments are interspaced by cutaways to her family, through which we get to know Etsuko, revealed as a bar hostess and sometime prostitute. Imamura, in searching for a character to provide the commentary, found Etsuko in a Yokosuka *gaijin* bar: 'it was the kind of place where no one had any family outside the bar itself ... Scorning Japan and the Japanese, they seek the company of strangers, only to find GIs or American sailors.'[129] She talks of her survival through prostitution, her good times with the 'Yank tricks' and her friends, her sadness at getting older. She calls the Americans 'gentlemen', commenting upon their kindnesses to both her and her friends. In this way, the official narratives are commented

Figure 5.8 Etsuko Akaza, *A History of Postwar Japan as Told by a Bar Hostess* (Imamura, 1970)

upon in an oblique way; some she remembers well, some she doesn't, sometimes she disagrees with the official version of history on-screen: 'It never happened like that!' she screams at the screen. At the end of the film we discover her in preparation to leave Japan for America with her new soldier boyfriend.

With *Postwar Japan*, we find ourselves in 'a direct time-image of a different kind from the previous one: no longer the coexistence of sheets of the past, but the simultaneity of peaks of the present'.[130] The sequences of official history from the past, being not directly put on-screen, but filmed on a screen, occur in this way in the present of the film; similarly, Etsuko is in the present, reconstituting the past as dialogue. We here encounter many paradoxes of the present: the past as the foundation of the present, and reciprocally, this present in relation to itself (as present), to the past of this present and to this present's future. The crucial point, however, is that 'time is revealed inside the event, which is made for the simultaneity of these three implicated presents'.[131] It is thus 'the possibility of treating the world or life, or simply a life or an episode, as one single event'.[132] This is the incompossible, the simultaneity of different presents 'where the inexplicable is thereby maintained and created'.[133] Each simultaneous sequence in the present is torn open and dispersed. It is as if we encounter a wave formation generated by two sources, with Imamura – his film – as a third, a third object causing a break in the flow between the on-screen projections and the memories of the bar hostess. We do not arrive at the truth of the events, but rather at the truth of memory and history in respect to the present.

Once again, as with *The Pacific War*, *A History of Postwar Japan* discovers the order of time as having its foundation in the series of time, the serial organization of the genesign, powers of the false, but through the simultaneity of peaks of the present. The concern is not the atomic attacks on Hiroshima and Nagasaki as the event which began everything: this does not hang over the documentary-trajectory. To this end, toward the conclusion of the film Imamura reveals a third procedure: it becomes apparent that the prostitute is also an actress. Etsuko has been rehearsed, the film shot over a number of weeks. Yet, reciprocally, it seems clear that the prostitute is not an actress, that her being an actress is also a role. Such a complex interaction of forces plunges the film into an abyss from which truth cannot escape. These are the powers of the false.

From sheets to peaks to powers: chronosigns 'are thus connected with each other and interpenetrate.'[134] Jasper Sharp, in his commentary of *A History of Postwar Japan*, has put it this way: 'it's been hinted elsewhere that the film is in fact faked', yet this is of 'secondary importance to the message that Imamura is trying to get across. It merely serves to underscore the point that fiction is arguably a more potent and truthful way of approaching historical events than documentary.'[135] Accordingly, 'by eschewing all pretensions of realism and objectivity falsely engendered by the documentary format, it can come closer to the heart and the spirit of what it is trying to portray than by limiting itself to a "realistic" perspective.'[136] While we can agree that the film undermines 'all pretensions of realism', contra Sharp, the reverse is also the case, fiction ungrounded by documentary. What then of truth? Imamura writes of *A History of Postwar Japan* and his other films of this period, that they are 'essentially documentaries', where 'I tried to reveal some hidden truth about real life. That's why I made them semi-fiction.'[137] What is this semi-fictional truth? In another Imamura documentary, *Ningen Johatsu / A Man Vanishes* (1967), one of the participants asks just this question: 'What is truth?' Imamura replies: 'I don't know.' He then claps his hands and shouts 'set', upon which the mise-en-scène of a tea room is dismantled, revealing the characters as actors in a vast studio space. In a programme note, Imamura writes: 'You think this set is a kind of truth because it looks like a nice, comfortable room: but it's not – it's a fiction built in a film studio.'[138] Truth is thus a construct of the narration, and would not be created 'if the film weren't being made'.[139] For Imamura, the crucial aspect is always to unground and reveal the creation of truth. This is the truth of Imamura's cinema. In *Postwar Japan*, this approach reveals such a truth in respect to history. Allan Casebier comments upon Etsuko's 'groundless denials of motion picture scenes showing events she has lived through'.[140] It is as if through the bar hostess, the historical on-screen images undergo an overt forgetting and becoming. As Gilles Laprévotte has written, Imamura 'seems to have adopted a type of counter-history', where 'the social schism revealed in the film' is that 'the barmaid is hardly interested in the destiny of her country of origin'.[141] Such is the present as fate.

Powers of the false

It is in this way that we encounter the powers of the false. Deleuze writes that 'having lost its sensory-motor connections, concrete space ceases to be organised according to tension and resolutions of tension, according to goals, obstacles, means or even detours'.[142] Accordingly, 'a new status of narration follows … Narration ceases to be truthful, that is, to claim to be true, and becomes fundamentally falsifying. This is not at all a case of "each has its own truth," a variability of content. It is a power of the false which replaces and supersedes the form of the true.'[143] To create such powers of the false, 'the images must be produced in such a way that the past is not necessarily true'.[144] This is what Imamura does, creates images through peaks of the present to undermine the notion of truth in respect to history. Why is this important? For Deleuze, 'truthful narration is developed organically, according to legal connections in space and chronological relations in time'.[145] Such movement-image narration will thus refer to judgements.[146] Thus, when powers of the false are released through time-images such a system of judgement will break down.

Take Oshima's *The Pacific War*, which presents Japanese fascist, militaristic and imperialist images as-is through a process of selection and connection of sheets of the past. Maureen Turim is right to say that 'the idea was to avoid strategies of standard Occupation counterpropaganda, on the one hand, and leftist and particularly communist propaganda, on the other, which typically offered didactic explications of Japanese militarism underscoring lies and deceptions'.[147] Yet this procedure is dangerous: 'one could argue that in its self-imposed restrictions, it does not adequately place these propaganda pieces in a broader context that would reveal their full horror.'[148] The rape of Nanking, the creation of the co-prosperity sphere to procure oil and gas reserves for Japan, the suppression of Japanese resistance to the war effort – 'if one does not understand' or 'know' of these things 'such a strategy could simply feed latent militarist nostalgia.'[149] Oshima does not present a balanced view; there are no counter arguments to Japanese militarism, no voice-overs commenting upon the horrors of the fascist past from the peace of the democratic present. In this way Oshima does not present a documentary film within the co-ordinates of the sensory-motor experience; instead the spectator is left with more questions than answers, the gaps are chasms into which the brain plunges and generates immense powers of thought – sensations of pride as much as shame, loss as much as gain. Between counter-emotional polarities generated by the purest mise-en-scène of found images, Oshima offers the opportunity for thought. Oshima provides powerful co-ordinates of the brain to allow the possibility for thought in the spectator, which the film does not think in-and-for-itself.

Turim's final take on the film is that 'the contradictions it shows could be seen as largely narcissistic and woefully inadequate to the lessons that one might hope the Japanese should learn from the war.'[150] Yet a lesson is not what is at stake. Oshima, in an essay entitled 'The Error of Mere Theorization of Technique' (1967) written the year before he made *The Pacific War*, questions the problem of representation with regards to war and the atom bomb. Oshima asks, in response to Japanese films about the atom bomb (and indeed the return by the US of Ito's *Effects*), 'what does this state of things signify?'[151] While Oshima saw in *Effects* a 'resistance' to war, and the return of the film as having a 'positive significance' for Japan, he was also aware of a problem; movement-images that describe the milieu of war and the atom-bomb 'make the people of Japan accept war as an everyday matter.'[152] This prevalence of images of the war and the atom bomb is intentional: 'these overflowing images of war – including the tragic, painful and even meaningless ones – are intended to penetrate our consciousness.'[153] For Oshima, 'once they have become the stuff of everyday life, we will probably accept the tragic, the painful, and the meaningless.'[154] Oshima is acknowledging the problem in the use of images of the *pika* and *hibakusha*. For Oshima, constructing the Japanese people as victims of the atom bomb or heroes that avert another apocalypse misses the point. These films are complicit in simply getting the spectator to accept and not think about the event. These films present pre-thought, pre-digested images of horror and war. What is there to do? asks Oshima. He replies, 'almost nothing, except to become accomplices in the state of things?'[155] Thus, in making *The Pacific War*, Oshima is becoming an accomplice. Oshima's method is to make the viewer such an accomplice. As Deleuze writes, 'falsifying narration … shatters the system of judgement because the power of the false (not error or doubt) affects the investigator and the witness as much as the person presumed guilty'.[156] Crucially, 'the system of judgement becomes definitively impossible, even and especially for the viewer'.[157] For Turim, Oshima risks his audience not experiencing the system of judgement implicit in the text. It seems to me that through using powers of the false, Oshima rather makes the viewer an accomplice of history. Oshima, in *The Pacific War*, and Imamura, in *A History of Postwar Japan* – each in their own way – create cinematic powers of the false which undermine the system of judgement that says a presentation of history can be truthful.

Both Oshima and Imamura would revisit Japanese history and the Pacific War in the 1980s through fiction films, though in very different ways: Oshima with *Merry Christmas Mr Lawrence* (1983), which depicted the war from the point of view of the enemy; Imamura with *Black Rain* (1989), which would once again explore the post-war situation, this time through the explicit portrayal of the atomic bombing of Hiroshima. We thus leave Oshima in our wake for Imamura's time-images of the nuclear event, chronosigns in respect to a fiction film.

Black Rain (1989)

'If a rainbow appears now, a miracle will occur.' Old Shizuma Shigematsu (Kitamura Kazuo) is speaking out loud, standing looking out over the village toward the hills. 'It won't be an ominous white rainbow, but a beautiful coloured one.' A few minutes earlier: a field ambulance halts on the potholed dirt path that runs alongside a small unplanted field. Two medics, carrying between them a stretcher of clean white cloth sewn on to two wooden poles, run across the field. When they reach Shigematsu's stone-built house, they let themselves in. Yuichi (Ishida Keisuke), a young man dressed almost in rags, pushes past them. In his arms he carries Yasuko (Tanaka Yoshiko), a beautiful young woman. Yasuko is pale, barely conscious. Yuichi runs out of the door, through the garden and across the field. When Yuichi reaches the ambulance, the medics – who have now caught up with him – help get Yasuko inside. 'You'll be all right', he says to her, again and again. He strokes her forehead, hair and neck. Yasuko's eyes look at Yuichi, her only possible response. The ambulance rumbles away, begins the long journey back to the rural island's small hospital. Shigematsu stands outside his house, watching as his dying niece and her fiancé disappear along the hard scrabble road that winds up through the hills that surround the village. The ambulance kicks up clouds of dirt behind it, and soon that is all that marks its progress. The film ends with Shigematsu waiting for his miracle.

Black Rain is set in two time-spaces: 1945 Hiroshima and 1950 Ujina, a small village on a nearby island in the Setonaikai Inland Sea.

In 1945, Yasuko is in Ujina, moving her family's possessions from Hiroshima. Her uncle, Shigematsu – with whom she has lived since her mother's death – is in the city, on his way to work. It is the morning of 6 August. As Yasuko is drinking tea with people from the village, as her uncle is boarding the train for the office, the atomic bomb is dropped. In Ujina this is experienced as a blinding white light, and, in the distance, the slow, silent formation of a mushroom cloud. In Hiroshima, at the train station, the explosion tears through the building and carriages. Many people die, many are blinded and burnt. Shigematsu, however, makes it back to the family house where he and his wife Shigeko (Ichihara Etsuko) prepare to abandon the city. Meanwhile, Yasuko and some villagers row from the island to the mainland. On the way, fat black raindrops start to fall, staining their clothes and faces like ink. Yasuko finds Shigematsu and Shigeko

Figure 5.9 Shigematsu awaits the colourful rainbow, *Black Rain* (Imamura, 1989)

just as they are ready to leave. As the firestorms rage, the family begin a horrific journey through the centre of Hiroshima, and the epicentre of the atomic bomb.

In 1950 Shigematsu and Shigeko are attempting to find Yasuko a husband. But, there are rumours that she is a *hibakusha*. These rumours, from who-knows-who, have already caused two proposals to be terminated. Accordingly, Shigematsu sets about trying to prove Yasuko is in good health, in the first instance taking his niece to the island hospital to get a certificate. However, the certificate only serves to raise the suspicions of her current fiancé, and once again the arrangement falls through. Shigematsu has another idea. The diaries Yasuko and he have from that time will prove she was not in the city when the bomb was dropped. So he and his wife set about copying out relevant passages for the match-maker. Yet, even as they do so, they realize Yasuko being caught in the black rain may well be taken as proof that she, if not currently showing symptoms, will one day succumb to radiation sickness.

Black Rain cuts between these two time-spaces of 1950 Ujina and 1945 Hiroshima, from one to the other and back again, throughout the film.

John T. Dorsey and Naomi Matsuoka comment that *Black Rain* has 'faced criticism … from those who believe' the film 'showed too much gruesome detail and from those who believe', conversely, 'it did not show enough; from those who favour strong political statements and from those who prefer that art have nothing to do with politics'.[158] Dorsey and Matsuoka themselves believe the film

Figure 5.10 Shigematsu, Yasuko and Shigeko make their way through rubble and bodies, *Black Rain* (Imamura, 1989)

prefers 'understatement and irony to direct statements'.[159] On the one hand, *Black Rain* 'intentionally understate[s] the case in depicting the destruction of Hiroshima'.[160] On the other hand, while 'there is a generalised criticism of both America and Japan', Dorsey and Matsuoka see such 'criticism as subdued … presenting it indirectly, by dealing with it humorously, dismissing the question as a matter of common sense'.[161] They conclude, as the world 'face[s] the dangers of nuclear war on a global scale … one may wonder whether the understatement prized by … Imamura may not in fact invite a contrary response, not a recognition of what is left unsaid, but a tacit acceptance of the unacceptable'.[162] Furthermore, 'one may wonder if there is a politics of understatement, a reserve which unwittingly serves the interests of those who would dwarf Hiroshima [and Nagasaki] with a nuclear apocalypse'.[163]

Such an analysis is possible, as Dorsey and Matsuoka see *Black Rain* as a movement-image, as being composed of 'traditional narrative techniques' that allow Imamura 'to control the material, to place it in the context of the knowable, the manageable'.[164] For instance, the film 'uses traditional narrative structures beginning with his decision to make the film in black and white. He uses flashbacks and voice-overs to treat the destruction of Hiroshima based on the diary format with flashbacks. For the present he uses a technique similar to third person narration.'[165] It is here we can intervene in order to begin a reappraisal of the film at the level of narration, through sheets, peaks and powers. It seems to me the black-and-white image, the voice-over and flashback in-themselves are not traditional tools of the movement-image. All depends upon deployment. *Black Rain* uses these tools to create time-images.

'How can we die without knowing the truth?'

Let us begin with the black-and-white image. It is not clear why Dorsey and Matsuoka believe absence of colour to be a foundation of traditional narration. Indeed, the use of black-and-white has its *raison d'être* in the closing moments of the film: the im/possibility of the appearance of a colourful rainbow. Yet it is through flashback and the voice-over that Imamura creates his sophisticated time-images. The opening sequence of the film, for instance, is set in 1945: Yasuko in Ujina and Shigematsu in Hiroshima. Both these threads appear in the present, with voice-overs from each of the characters. Yasuko is in the back of a truck, surrounded by packing cases: 'I took a day off to pack up our belongings … My aunt's best formal kimono. Other things too.' Shigematsu is catching the train: 'A hot morning, I hurried to Yokogawa station to go to the factory where I worked.' After the atomic bomb is dropped, the voice-overs end, these threads enter into parallel montage and eventually converge when Yasuko joins Shigematsu and his wife at the family home, and all three begin their nightmare walk through the destroyed, burning city. This line of narration ends – abruptly – when the three see a man, blinded by the *pika*, in a first-storey window: 'Where's Hiroshima?', he shouts, 'It's disappeared.' The man falls to his death. Cut to 1950 Ujima: Yasuko and Shigematsu at the hospital for their check-up, securing the certificate of good health for Yasuko. It appears as if we have moved from one present to another via a great ellipsis. However, as the film continues in 1950 Ujina, after Yasuko's third attempt at marriage has failed, Shigematsu and Shigeko will pick up the diaries. Shigematsu reads and copies his own, his wife reads and copies Yasuko's. This copying out initiates a return to 1945: the three family members witness a melted boy, trying to convince his brother that he is his brother; a woman holding her charred baby; the broken city littered with the dead and dying.

There are here some very complex manipulations of time and memory. In the first instance, the dual threads that began the film now appear retroactively as visual and sound images (flashback and voice-over) from the accounts of the diaries, read and copied by Shigematsu and Shigeko. They appear as memories reconstituted via the written word, not directly from the memory of a subject – particularly in the case of Yasuko's testimony, which comes via Shigeko's reading. In the second instance, when these dual threads dovetail, it remains unclear which diary is the reference point: Shigematsu's? Yasuko's? An amalgam of both? As Shigematsu states: 'I'll copy my diaries too. I'll put them with hers. We'll make an accurate record.' And the same is true of the 1945 sequence that is returned to following this statement. Rather than the flashback sequence appearing in a traditional way, a past in respect to a present, we encounter a very complex arrangement of pasts, presents and futures, of analepsis and prolepsis, of time and memory. We encounter here very subtle, very beautifully intertwined sheets of the past. The film is organized in such a way that the beginning is dominated by images of 1945, but as it progresses, images from 1950 are in ascendancy. Yet throughout, 1950 intercuts with 1945, and 1945 with 1950. These interactions are negotiated in a number of diverse ways. Shigematsu attends a funeral in 1950 and false continuity carries over to 1945. Similarly, as funerals occur in 1950, Imamura uses a wipe to jump from one to another, performing a temporal but not spatial cut, a leap referred to in a voice-over which is enunciated from the future of both events: 1950 now appears as a past to a voice-over in some undefined present.

These sheets of the past, in short, are constituted in any number of ways – one of the most extreme examples being the sheets which appear in reference to Yuichi, the young traumatized ex-soldier who will eventually become Yasuko's fiancé. Each time he hears a vehicle passing on the road that runs alongside his shack, he becomes an anti-tank combatant, his body becomes a sheet of the past. Throwing himself onto the dirt, he attempts to push the small bag he believes to be explosives under a bus, or car or motorbike: 'Mission accomplished!' These sheets initially appear as comedic, yet somehow transform into a terrible reconstitution of a suffering mind. Yasuko asks him how he came to be this way. As he begins to tell her the story, Imamura transforms the workshed where Yuichi obsessively chisels his rough little sculptures into a battlefield. The mise-en-scène becomes a filmset (reminiscent of the moment in *A Man Vanishes* where Imamura claps his hands, or in *Postwar Japan* where the bar hostess is transformed into an actress). The soundtrack is overdubbed with sonsigns of war: gunshots, mortar fire, explosions. The natural ambient light is revealed as a studio construct, the shed plunged into darkness, Yuichi captured in a spotlight that tracks him as he crawls between the sculptures, now the bodies of his dead and dying comrades. It is as if the images of the past that traverse his brain have become the mise-en-scène. And at one and the same time, he is in the present, narrating his own traumatic memories of killing Americans, and seeing the members of his battalion killed. In this way, Imamura creates very powerful images not only of the atomic bomb, but of the Pacific War. The film is run through with history and time: each night when Shigematsu sets the clock by the radio news, we encounter the Korean War. The final time this happens, we hear how the Americans are once again contemplating using the atomic bomb.

This is as much to say that Imamura weaves a surface of presents, a series of peaks of the present: the Pacific War, the nuclear event, the occupation and the Korean War saturate the mise-en-scène, different characters and their events describing different moments. Such characters proliferate. There is Fumiko (Tateichi Mayumi), who returns to the island from Fukuyama, escaping some kind of involvement with the black market and prostitution – only to be sought out by a yakuza. There is the mother of Fumiko, also called Fumiko (Sawa Tamaki), who seems to have had – and is still having – affairs with most of the village men (any of which could have been the father of the daughter). There is the old grandmother, who mistakes everybody for someone else. There is the village soothsayer, with her mystic objects and messages from beyond the grave. There are the three old men, contemporaries of Shigematsu, *hibakusha* all, who spend their days taking it easy, fishing in the village pond for carp and shooting the crap. From comedy to tragedy, an interweaving of tones: as one of the old fellows faces death from the latent radioactive sickness that has at last manifested itself, he asks: 'How can we die without knowing the truth?' But that is exactly what Imamura allows. *Black Rain* will not permit the appearance of a colourful rainbow. In this way we move from orders of time to the series of time. The sheets of the past and peaks of the present are powers of the false: a series of encounters with different characters, tones, themes, spaces and times. It is a film which decentres the atomic attack both temporally and spatially; allows it to inhabit memories and bodies, allows it to be forgotten and repressed; disperses its meaning back into the Pacific War and forward into the Korean War.

'Everyone tells me that *Black Rain* is so calm and restrained compared with my previous films,' says Imamura, 'but I think I'm just making films that are more suitable for a man of my age.'[166] These chronosigns are subtle, sophisticated – or, as Dorsey and Matsuoka would have it, understated. Let us take as an example a consistent criticism of the film. Dorsey and Matsuoka write: 'One is occasionally tempted to believe that the title of Imamura's film should be "A Marriage for My Niece," … Yasuko sometimes seems to be playing the main role in the film.'[167] Maya Morioka Todeschini concurs. Imamura 'desires[s] to denounce the bomb', his 'intention [being] to construct a genuinely compassionate portrait of [a] female survivor.'[168] *Black Rain* is thus '"woman-centred" and sympathetic to women', however, this 'does not mean that' that it 'give[s] credit to the complexities of *hibakusha* women's experiences'.[169] The film fails to give 'much weight to the heroine's subjective experiences of suffering' and 'provides little narrative space for the victims'.[170] In other words, with regard to Yasuko 'there is no hint of despair or rebellion, or even ambivalence', and the focus upon Yasuko means the diverse experiences of the *hibakusha* – men as much as women – are elided.[171]

However, as we have seen, Todeschini's claims seem hard to maintain. Yasuko is beautiful and stoic, but when her third marriage proposal fails, she is found in tears. When her hair begins to fall out, an external sign of her beauty fading, she looks at the strands with fascination. It is never clear exactly what these reactions mean. A crucial moment in the film is when it is revealed – in a very subtle way – that it is Yasuko herself spreading the rumours of her own sickness

Figure 5.11 Yasuko's black hair begins to fall out, *Black Rain* (Imamura, 1989)

in order to escape potential marriages she does not want. In this way she steps outside of tradition, eventually becoming engaged to a man of a lower caste, who like her is suffering in the wake of the Pacific War. Yasuko is composed of rebellions, silences, stoicism, weaknesses. Finally, the film is neither simply Yasuko-centred or woman-centred. The narration will focus as much upon the efforts of Shigematsu to fulfil his duty toward his niece. But even this is to efface the multitude of characters that inhabit the screen: Yuichi, his mother, the wonderful mother and daughter Fumikos, the three old carp fishermen, Shigematsu's wife (who will also die during the film), her mother, the soothsayer. It is between these characters that the narration unfolds.

Black Rain is a perspectival archive, an interweaving of characters, anarchic multiplicities. Such are powers of the false, which reveal the film to be a creation of differences and repetitions. These powers ultimately lead us beyond the description of hyalosigns and the narration of chronosigns to narratives and noosigns: 'as we shall see,' writes Deleuze, 'a third element now intervenes, which is the story, distinct from description and narration.'[172]

III. Narrative, discord, event

Noosigns

Powers of the false suppose a third time-image. This is the noosign. The noosign in turn refers – as we saw at the beginning of this chapter – to a third synthesis of time. If the first passive synthesis was that of the living present through succession, and the second passive synthesis that of memory of a pure past, the third synthesis encounters the future as open. This is the caesura. The first synthesis was the foundation of time, the second the ground, and the third will incur a fundamental ungrounding. It is this impassive synthesis that fractures that which the passive syntheses engender, that which is achieved in active synthesis: a binding linearity of continuity and an encircling of the past as closure. The third synthesis is thus impassive in that it ungrounds active and passive syntheses alike. It will do so through synthesizing the present and the past with the openness of the future, the past appearing as (infinite) experience and the present as metamorphosis (conditions of change).

With respect to the time-image, which takes the three temporal syntheses as its inspiration, noosigns supersede hyalosigns and chronosigns. While hyalosigns are in the present (the now as a succession of future to past) and chronosigns capture the past (memory for the present and future), noosigns are orientated toward the future (as thought ungrounding present and the past). For Deleuze this cinematic trajectory is that of description (hyalosigns) → narration (chronosigns) → narrative (noosigns), where narrative is the story arising from the narration and description thereof. And just as with hyalosigns and chronosigns, the noosign will have three components, arranged as two elements of composition in respect to the genetic moment to which the temporal synthesis corresponds. Deleuze names the poles of genesis (future) and composition (present and past) as world and the body, and the three signs corresponding to these poles as a cinema of the brain, the body of gest and the body of attitude. The noosign, its dual poles and three component images can be illustrated as in Table 5.5.

Table 5.5 Noosign

	noosign	
body		world
body of attitude	body of gest	cinema of the brain

The formula of the noosign will take some unfolding. How will the past and the present refer us to bodies, and what are bodies of attitude and gest? How is a future captured in film, concomitantly as an image of the brain and an image of the world? In what way are all three components aspects for the future and in what way does this future correspond to thought? And finally, how do all these aspects refer to the narrative of a film? In answering these questions we will not only unfold the noosign, but explore the most fundamental aspects of the time-image cineosis.

We can begin with the movement-image (active synthesis, the sensory-motor system, organic co-ordinates). This cineosis described the perception → affect → action trajectory, where the world engendered bodies with internal intensities and external behaviours grounded upon psychological memory (recollections, imagination and thought). The crisis in the action-image and the concomitant collapse of the movement-image enacted a delinkage of these co-ordinates, creating pure optical and sound situations, opsigns and sonsigns. Yet the time-image cineosis was constituted through a relinkage. This relinkage, however, was a composition of opsigns and sonsigns in such a way that they retained the very crisis and collapse that gave birth to them. This required the film to be organized through purely temporal (and not organic) co-ordinates. In the first place, hyalosigns are the image as description relinked to the next image exposing the virtual. In the second place, there are chronosigns as non-chronological narration, a relinkage of sequences through series. In this way we can say that the image as description is in the present: what is happening? That narration is an unfolding in respect to images in the past: what has happened? Consequently, the story being constituted is in the future: what will happen? Thus, in the third place, noosigns are discordant narratives encountered in thought in respect to indeterminate description and disjunctive narration. And not simply as the film plays out, but – even more so – after the film has finished and the lights come up. A thinking of the time-image film (a necessity due to the indeterminacy of the image and the disjunctive unfolding of the narration) that is always to come. As Deleuze puts it in *Cinema 2*, the story will 'replace filmstock, in a virtual film which now only goes on in the head'.[173] And it will always be a rethinking, if a thinking occurs at all, as the temporality of the images and narration render the narrative eternally discordant: a problem without solution, 'problematic and problematizing'.[174] The noosign, in this way, is the condition of the new image of cinematic thought.

It is, furthermore, the storytelling function of the noosign that constitutes an abstraction of the image and narration as discordant thought of the world and its bodies. In truth, bodies and worlds are all there ever was. Hyalosigns composed bodies and world in mirrors, through the limpid-opaque and from seed to environment; and chronosigns through sheets of the past, peaks of the present and powers of the false. Yet with hyalosigns and chronosigns bodies and world subsisted in image and narration; it takes the narrative function of the noosign to set them free.

We can, once again, consider this aspect of noosigns in contrast to movement-images. The aim of time-image cinema, for Deleuze, 'is not to reconstitute a presence of bodies, in perception and action, but to carry out a primordial genesis of bodies'.[175] In other words, 'the body is initially caught in quite a different space, where disparate sets overlap and rival each other, without being able to organise themselves according to sensory-motor schemata. They fit over each other, in an overlapping of perspectives which means that there is no way to distinguish them even though they are distinct and incompatible.'[176] This is a world, therefore, appearing 'before action'; a body which 'does not, as in action-image, allow itself to be determined in relation to goals and means which would unify the set, but is dispersed in "a plurality of ways of being present in the world," of belonging to sets, all incompatible and yet coexisting'.[177] In other words, the world and bodies are a heterogeneous assemblage (that the movement-image attempts to organize through the sensory-motor schema, positioning the body as a direct response to the situation, and feelings and thoughts of that body as a function of the action to come). The time-image, as revealed through the noosign, retains the heterogeneity of bodies and the world.

With noosigns, therefore, we encounter in thought a series of disjunctions: the disparate states of the body in-itself; the dissonance between bodies in their distinct states; and the discord between these bodies and the world, the world in-itself as absonant. This formula refers us to the three aspects of the noosign. First aspect: the attitude of the body, its differences, postures in the present. Second aspect: the connection between these disparate states, from present to past, the 'gest which links' attitudes.[178] This is the body and bodies as a repetition of differences. 'It is a cinema of bodies which has broken all the more with the sensory-motor schema through action being replaced by attitude, and supposedly true linkage by the gest which produces … [time-image] story-telling.'[179] Third aspect: the relation between attitude-gest and world which appears through the mise-en-scène as an image of the brain. As Deleuze puts it, 'the internal sheets of memory and the external layers of reality will be mixed up, extended, short circuited and form a whole moving life, which is at once that of the cosmos and the brain'.[180] In this way, 'thought no longer appears on the screen as function of the body: flashbacks, symbols and dreams, but rather is strictly identical to every image – it is cerebral space'.[181]

Noosigns are the fundamental encounter with a film as a new, discordant time-image of cinematic thought, an image of thought of bodies and world as a heterogeneous assemblage, as pure difference and repetition. As D. N. Rodowick comments, such 'thinking or thought is defined not by what we know but by the virtual or what is unthought. To think, Deleuze argues, is not to interpret or to reflect.'[182] Interpretation and reflection are that which are made possible by chronosigns and hyalosigns, and brought to fruition in movement-images. 'Rather than making thought visible,' with time-images, and through the noosign, 'visibility is perforated by the incoherence and inchoate quality of thought.'[183]

Image, thought, event

In describing the time-image as a cinematic trajectory of indeterminate description (hyalosigns) → disjunctive narration (chronosigns) → discordant narrative (noosigns) we do so only in respect to the cineotic. These time-images are rather a nexus – an interweaving stratum of the nine elements that compose the three time-images and the nine dimensions of temporal syntheses. It is this entwining of indeterminacies, disjunctions and discords of the present, past and future that allows us to consider a time-image film as a direct image of thought. We thus encounter the formula: cinematic time-image ↔ inchoate quality of thought.

Immediately, a final question appears before us: how should we consider the link between the time-image, the temporal syntheses and history? With the movement-image we progressively uncovered (Chapters 1 through 3) the cineotic trajectory: cinematic movement-image → image of history → image of thought. Yet (as was seen at the conclusion of Chapter 3 and explored in Chapter 4) this trajectory was also ultimately revealed as an interlacing stratum of images: cineotic image ↔ image of history ↔ image of thought. Thus, just as the cineosis of the movement-image can be contrasted with the cineosis of the time-image, and just as the organic image of thought is distinguished from the new discordant quality of thought, the image of history will encounter its own crisis, collapse and rebirth. This is history renewed as the event.

As a way of preparing to explore the event, we can reiterate and extend Nietzsche's analysis of historical practices in 'On the Uses and Disadvantages of History for Life', an analysis which we have turned and returned to throughout our discussions of movement-images. It will be remembered (from Chapter 2) that Nietzsche saw reflective history as a stratigraphic nexus of aspects which captured up the past in the present for the future (which Deleuze linked with the realism of the large form action-image). These aspects were the forces of monumental, antiquarian and critical history which established analogies between moments of the past, moments to be preserved and engendering an ethic. Subsequently, we expanded the categories and approaches of history as we encountered further domains of the movement-image. On the one hand we moved from realism to idealism: from the objective empiricism of the large form to the small form and people's history, the cosmic cycles of impulse-images, and the subjective idealism of affection-images. On the other hand, the gradations of and isolations between realist and idealist history were reflected upon and entered thought as historical shock, discourse and memory. History was not given, but revealed as a process of remembering and forgetting. Indeed, it was through such processes (in Chapter 4) that we re-encountered Nietzsche: history needed and depended upon ahistory. To free oneself from the yoke of an overpowering historical past required a forgetting, and such forgetting was a living in the present, being with the animals, an unachievable state as a pure perspective, yet a necessary impurity to live for the future. In such a way we encountered mental-images as the acknowledgement of such a double movement, remembering tempered with forgetting, forgetting allowing selection and memory.

Yet Nietzsche discovers a third perspective: in addition to the historical and ahistorical, the suprahistorical. Nietzsche writes: 'Ask your acquaintances if they would like to relive the past ten or twenty years … they will all answer No.'[184] The question is, what do they mean by 'No'? Nietzsche continues: 'Some may perhaps be consoling themselves: "but the next twenty will be better" … Let us call them historical men; looking to the past impels them towards the future and fires their courage to go on living.'[185] Such is the annealing of the historical with the ahistorical. However, 'the No of the suprahistorical man … sees no salvation in the process … rather, the world is complete and reaches its finality at each and every moment'.[186] This suprahistorical perspective comes from the future – not as a reconstitution of the remembered, not as such a reconstitution passing through a forgetting, but as that which is beyond past and the present, and brought back to unground the present and the past. It is the suprahistorical perspective that will become, in Nietzsche's later texts, what Henry Somers-Hall calls the 'esoteric doctrine' of the eternal return.[187] And it is this doctrine that will inspire Deleuze's conceptual frameworks of the third impassive synthesis, the noosign and the event.

For Somers-Hall, Deleuze's third synthesis proves to be a powerful deployment of Nietzsche's eternal return. 'What returns', writes Somers-Hall, 'cannot be actual states of affairs', cannot be active synthesis.[188] Nor can such recurrence be engendered through the passive syntheses of succession and coexistence; rather, succession and coexistence are 'different ways of presenting the same underlying form of time', a presenting re-presented in active synthesis as realized linearity and closure.[189] The first and second passive syntheses are instead 'both expressions of the same ontologically prior temporal form, which in itself is neither successive nor coexistent'; and this prior temporality is the eternal return, 'the pure and empty form of time … which bifurcates itself into' succession and coexistence, 'the field of intensive difference that is the future'.[190] 'Repetition occurs not because the same forms repeat, but because the same field of intensive difference engenders these different forms. What returns, therefore, is the pure form of time.'[191] Nathan Widder extends this conception of 'the third synthesis, understood as eternal return' into a consideration of history; or rather, of the event, which 'concerns only the future'.[192] The event is thus the field of intensive difference that both engenders historical memory and allows historical forgetting. 'For Deleuze,' concludes Widder, 'the event's eventness necessarily locates it in the future, the event enters history from the future.'[193]

It is such a consideration of the pure open future as the eternal return that inspires the time-image noosign as a cinematic conceptualization of narrative as event. We thus encounter the strata-formula: cinematic time-image ↔ pure event ↔ inchoate quality of thought. Deleuze puts it very well in *Logic of Sense*. Events 'bear exclusively upon problems and define their conditions'; however, 'we do not say that the problem is thereby resolved; on the contrary, it is determined as a problem'.[194] The event is the encounter which 'perplexes', writes Deleuze in *Difference and Repetition*.[195] A film 'forces it[self] to pose a problem: as though the object of encounter, the sign, were the bearer of a problem – as though it were a problem'.[196] The event in time-image cinema ungrounds history through the noosign, creating a problematic cerebral space of world and bodies which retains and propagates discord. From encounter to eternal return, to impassive synthesis, to noosigns, as Paul Patton comments in 'Events, Becoming and History' (2009), Deleuze (and Deleuze with Guattari) explored the idea of the event in many ways. Such explorations were 'experiments in which the same issues and concepts are taken up and reworked'.[197] 'Deleuze does say that he has tried, in all his books, to discover the nature of events'; however, as Patton concludes, 'he does not say that he has succeeded or that he has arrived at a final theory.'[198] In the same way, we can consider films of the time-image, films of the noosign, as being attempts – each in their own way – to discover the nature of events. And we can consider noosigns of the Japanese cinema of the atom bomb as exploring the eventness subsisting within the nuclear attacks. In the final film of this book we will encounter the first perhaps to do so, the first time-image of the Japanese cinema of the atom bomb, Sekigawa Hideo's *Hiroshima*.

***Hiroshima* (1953)**

Black then white frames in quick succession: a sustained intense light. A woman covers her eyes. Buildings collapse, dust, smoke, fire. Such is the moment of the *pika* in Sekigawa's *Hiroshima*. Twelve seconds of cinema with as many shots, brutal hyper-rapid montage giving on to a lingering image of the formation of the mushroom cloud. After this, the screen, for a whole hour, is smeared black: a broken city with burnt bodies and dark shadows – a chaos of images. Young schoolgirls caught in a destroyed building call for Komehara (Yumeiji Tsukioka), their teacher, 'Sensei, Sensei'. A mother crawls through the tiles of her broken house, clothes torn, covered in blood. She calls for her child, 'Michiko, Michiko'. At a crèche, the teacher regains consciousness to see all the little ones dead, bodies cooked. The mother wanders away from her broken home to search for her child; at the house the child emerges from the rubble. Yukio (Yoshi Kato) tries to free his wife. As the fire storm consumes his neighbourhood he attempts to find help. But the people that pass are burnt, blind, barely conscious, hallucinating, terrified or insane. No one will stop. His wife burns to death. At the boys' school, the children are trapped under their desks, many dead. People traverse the rubble-strewn streets like zombies through the smoke. A burnt and skinned toddler stands screaming as people stumble heedlessly past. A soldier is ranting in madness. Komehara has gathered those girls still alive, and they help each other through the streets, leading and dragging the blind and disabled. People are taking to the river. Dead babies, bloated and burnt black, are carried with the flow. Komehara and the girls enter the water, they cling to each other. They sing. Then, one by

Figure 5.12 A burnt child stands crying in the ruins, people pass by, *Hiroshima* (Sekigawa, 1953)

Figure 5.13 The girls slowly allow themselves to be taken by the river water, *Hiroshima* (Sekigawa, 1953)

one, a child slips beneath the water, glides away. One after another … their friends looking on … joining them. This cinematic moment is one of the most devastating ever captured on film. The song is now sung by a lone voice. Then silence.

This sequence of *Hiroshima* is the purest of noosigns creating a discordant narrative event. The *hibakusha* appear as bodies of attitude, the *pika* having severed the sensory-motor link between the world and the characters. The sequence begins with images of Hiroshima describing a city under the sway of militarism at the end of the war. Callisthenics at school and the army parade ground mirror each other. An officer strikes a schoolchild who has not come to attention smartly enough. Formalized alternate parallel montage shows marching girls and marching soldiers, both groups working side by side on building defences against the anticipated land invasion by the Americans. The atom bomb explodes, the screen fades to black, and such links between situation and action are immediately severed. Afterwards bodies display attitudes: a woman in debilitating shock sitting holding a dead child; a crazed soldier running, screaming 'banzai' at an indeterminate foe; a mother looking for a child; a child looking for its mother; a baby crying, alone in rubble. Deindividualized states: pure states of terror, hallucination, confusion, fear, loss. Together these states, or attitudes, are moments of pure experience, multiplicities. As the day extends and becomes days, states link, assemble as a vast gest. Stories begin, end suddenly, branch out, are curtailed by death. Heterogeneous storylines map the horror: burnt and blind people walking the streets, people looking for family, a weeping child, the people sheltering in caves and factories. Soldiers going insane. People trying to escape the city in overcrowded boats, boats overturning, and people drowning; makeshift hospitals spontaneously forming where the *hibakusha* gather. Here is year zero. The social conditions have collapsed, all differentiations – gender, age, caste, class – are annulled. Here are the *hibakusha*.

Such are noosigns of the body and bodies: not deployed in action, but wandering a narration of terror, encountering pure descriptions of horror; and even if nascent actions do appear to be forming, they are stymied, people look for others and arrive too late or find them dead. The nuclear event is not staged in order to be overcome, it is a happening. What is the nature of this happening? It is a series of any-space-whatevers, broken buildings ravaged by fire, river water carrying the dead, hospitals, a sea of burnt bodies, dark caves of human fear. It is the mise-en-scène as chaos, the world as an inchoate image of thought. Nothing can be resolved. Nicholas Vroman has called the film a 'tapestry'.[199] This is an apt description, a flat intense surface of the purest noosigns – as Deleuze has it, a 'cerebral space'.[200] It is a sequence of film that problematizes image and narration, creates a narrative without solution. This is no history, it is a pure event.

Ungroundings

Yet we must immediately challenge such a reading of the film. Richie writes that *Hiroshima* 'contains two interwoven and contrasting sections: first, a well-made, dramatically moving, documentary-like reconstruction of the explosion … second, a statically filmed, tedious, polemic filled tract'.[201] *Hiroshima* is bookended by two very different, and much shorter, episodes – and we must assume Richie is conjoining these in what he calls the second section, for he continues to describe scenes occurring in both, scenes 'in which Americans … are reported to have said that the bomb was nothing more than a simple scientific experiment, and that the Japanese were nothing more than experimental animals … and ending with scenes of American tourists busy buying souvenir bones of persons killed in the explosion'.[202] These initial and final episodes constitute, for Richie, a historicizing of the nuclear event. *Hiroshima* ultimately presents a totalizing historicist understanding of the atomic bomb, one which simultaneously resonates with Pacific War period fascist-militarism and aligns with post-war anti-occupation radical communism.[203] Such a nexus of seemingly disparate political positions is achieved, according to Richie, by way of a pervasive anti-Americanism. In other words, despite the event of the *pika-hibakusha* sequence as extended centre, the first and final episodes ultimately historicize by subsuming it within movement-images. Richie's critique is important. The first episode focuses upon a young female student called Michiko (Reiko Matsuyama) who succumbs to latent radiation poisoning during a history lesson on the atomic bomb. As Michiko dies, Sekigawa creates a dissolve, a flashback to the *pika-hibakusha* sequence which thus appears to be a recollection-image of the student. With the final episode, which emerges from the *pika-hibakusha* sequence, the focus is upon Hideo, a street child, begging, forming a gang and ultimately pillaging the mass graves of the Hiroshima dead, collecting skulls to sell to American military. It is as if the event-sequence has created a situation which will coalesce to engender Hideo's action-images. Sekigawa seems to have created, in the first episode, an encircling of the past as closure in respect to the passive synthesis of coexistence; and in the second episode, a binding of the linearity of the passive synthesis of succession. In such a way the noosign *pika-hibakusha* event is tamed, framed within movement-images and historicized.

However, it seems to me we encounter exactly the opposite procedure. That is to say, Sekigawa performs an ungrounging of the passive syntheses of succession and coexistence. Richie, in conceptually conjoining the first and final episodes, performs a sleight of hand that disavows the actuality of the organization of images and narration. The noosigns of the central sequence instead permeate the film. This is not to say, of course, that history does not become captured in the film. Paul Patton puts it well: history is 'a surface phenomenon', the 'molar … processes that unfold in linear time'.[204] Events – in contrast – 'unfold in history'.[205] 'The point is not to oppose' event and history 'but to distinguish between them and to show that there are "all kinds of correlations and movements back and forth"'.[206] And here we have what is essential: Deleuzian (film-)philosophy and the time-image cineosis 'is experimental thought' and such 'experimentation is not historical', yet '"without history experimentation would … lack… any initial conditions"'.[207] Sekigawa's *Hiroshima* is such an experiment; the central sequence of noosigns enact an indeterminacy of description and a disjunction of narration in the first and final episodes that resist a framing within the movement-image and unground a determining of historical co-ordinates.

The film begins with an any-space-whatever, wisps of cloud in the sky coalesce as a voiceover describes the circumstances of the atom bomb: the bombardment of Pearl Harbor and the nuclear attacks on Hiroshima/Nagasaki. As the voice continues with this history lesson, clouds part and land is revealed. The camera slowly zooms in on Hiroshima until a cross-fade discloses a classroom, the students within listening to a lecture – yet the lecture comes from the radio. This beautifully choreographed opening sequence illustrates the way in which a totalizing given is disavowed. The situation, as a cinematic extra-diegetic voice-over, appeared objective, as-is, in the position of truth. As a radio broadcast the veracity of the voice is immediately weakened, revealed as a version of events sanctioned by SCAP and the CCD, propagated by the Japanese government. Such procedures are then multiplied; the students, inspired by Michiko's radio-active sickness, each stand and tell of their own experience of post-war Japan. Sekigawa visually explores their monologues through a series of disparate images: some documentary, some enacted for the film. *Hibakusha* begging in the street; characters of despair and nihilism at the pachinko machines; girls and women dating the American military: these are personal experiences, but ones Sekigawa uses to map the diverse social situation of the Japanese people.

The first episode thus performs a series of displacements and disjunctions. Indeed, such disjunctions appear with regard to the trajectory of the first episode into the central sequence. The flashback of the dying Michiko is constituted in death, will escape her subjectivity to encompass the creation of all Hiroshima *hibakusha*. Furthermore, it will never enact a return, the flashback dissipates and remains open. Of an entirely different nature is the passage from the *hibakusha-pika* sequence to the present through the incremental focusing in upon Hideo. Here the linearity of continuity that may appear to be constituted is stymied by being shot in serial form, leaping from one zone to another, exploring the life of a street child at different times during the occupation, a whole series of disconnected events.

Such an ungrounding of coexistence and succession also occurs with respect to the future. After Hideo's arrest, the forces that have threatened linearity encounter a fundamental caesura. Along the thoroughfare, upon pavements, walking the streets, across bridges, the people of Hiroshima gather, thousands upon thousands, children and adults. These images dissolve. The Hiroshima dead then arise, boys, girls, men and women burnt black, emerging from the rivers where they drowned, from devastated city ruins that describe the aftermath of the nuclear event. This final simultaneity creates virtual linkages between actualized present and actualized past, and remains virtual in that neither present nor past cohere; and in consequence of a resistance to actualization. There is a cut to black before any image of the future. The future is unconstituted by *Hiroshima*, and in such a way retains the problematizing power of the event, a power that has been constructed through the noosigns that fracture linear flows, resist closure for the open and create a discordant narrative.

It is as if the dispersed centre of the film, the cerebral space, is a black hole which disrupts the very possibility of closure and linearity, coexistence and succession being sustained as open and fractured. In this way, both the first episode and the last are in the present, but two indeterminate presents, a disjunctive narration leading into and away from the past which appears as discordant narrative through the extended noosign sequence at centre of the film. Noosigns not only create and permeate the *pika-hibakusha* sequence that constructs this extended centre, but also structure the entire film. *Hiroshima* sustains the eventness of the event of the atomic attacks on Japan; it creates it as an inchoate image of thought through the film for the spectator, a radical encounter, an encounter that both escapes and problematizes historical representation.

Lectosigns: The impower of the time-image

Noosigns, chronosigns and hyalosigns are narrative, narration and description – composed from opsigns and sonsigns, the zeroness of the time-image. Concomitantly, hyalosigns, chronosigns and noosigns are simultaneities appearing as a lectosign, the plane of composition that restores to us the infinite. Such lectosigns are the object of the encounter, images that must not simply be seen, but time-images which require reading. As we saw at the beginning of this chapter, Deleuze commented: 'Noël Burch put it very well … when images cease to be linked together "naturally" … grasping them "requires a considerable effort of memory and imagination, in other words, a reading".'[208] We have described the conditions for such readings: noosigns sustaining narrative discord, disrupting the threat of the linear binding of hyalosigns and the encircling and closure of chronosigns, ungrounding history through a direct presentation of the inchoate quality of thought. Such are the conditions; we have yet to designate consequences. Put simply, we have yet to ask the question, what guarantees are there that what we call a time-image will be considered as such a lectosign?

With *Hiroshima*, Richie's critical procedure allowed for the silencing of discord, disjunction and indeterminacy. Indeed, we have encountered such silencings at every juncture. For Dorsey and Matsuoka, as well as for Todeschini, *Black Rain* was a narration of understatement unequal to the horrors of the atomic bomb. Sharp saw *A History of Postwar Japan* as the triumph of fiction over documentary rather than the radical disintegration of such *a priori* categories; and Turim saw the strategies of *The Pacific War* as an inadequate representation of and reflection upon the wartime actions of the Japanese. What of *Casshern* with its impotent spectacle? For Shamoon the film was ultimately linear and conclusive, a bleak apocalypse with no caesura, without an opening into indeterminacy, disjunction and discord. Indeed, a consideration of *Casshern* can become an exemplar of such silencings which are echoes of the eternal prognosis: the death of cinema. Not that films will cease to be conceived, produced, created and consumed. But that cinema will no longer experiment and challenge. *Casshern* is a twenty-first-century genre picture (sci-fi) and revels in spectacle (inspired by music videos): how can such a film be said to confound recognition and truth, create a new image of cinematic thought? 'Every music video you see is a kind of implementation of all the critiques of continuity and of illusory space', and every cinematic innovation will be 'sucked into the mass or else it will never be seen'.[209] So proclaims Burch, turning away from the possibilities of cinema that requires reading, of the possibilities of Deleuze's time-image declared some twenty years previously. Burch's proclamation is not simply nostalgia for a moment when cinema was radical, but a re-evaluation of the conditions and consequences of film: 'to modify a perception of the world is an undertaking which is absolutely doomed to failure.'[210] Cinema is – and always was – dead: the death of cinema as eternal prognosis.

Yet perhaps such a prognosis is symptomatic of fatigue. In *Anti-Oedipus*, Deleuze and Guattari write that the object of encounter – or time-image – is 'a pure dispersed and anarchic multiplicity'.[211] Yet 'to be sure, one can always establish or re-establish some sort of links … organic links … psychological and axiological links – the good, the bad – that finally refer to the persons or to the scene from which the elements are borrowed; structural links between the ideas or the concepts apt to correspond to them'.[212] In other words, we can always turn away from an encounter; we are always apt to betray a time-image: for while the conditions can be created, the consequences are not guaranteed. All a time-image filmmaker can create is an indeterminacy of the image and a disjunctive narration that attempts to sustain narrative as a discordant image of thought. As Deleuze writes in *Cinema 2*, appropriating a statement from the painter Paul Klee, time-image filmmakers 'can do no more'.[213]

What guarantees can *Casshern* offer that we will see it as a thought experiment on the necessity of the atomic attacks on Japan? What guarantees can *The Pacific War* and *A History of Postwar Japan* offer that we will encounter them as critiques of historical truth? What guarantees can *Black Rain* and *Hiroshima* give that we will appreciate them as questioning – each in their own way – the very possibility of capturing the moment of the *pika* and the experiences of the *hibakusha* within human understanding? We answer: none. The conditions of the time-image do not give guarantees, the film as lectosign is not a consequence of time-images. There is here no cause and effect. Nothing is given. It is exactly the opposite procedure. This is the impower of the lectosign. Yet this impower is the very opportunity to open ourselves up to an encounter. An act of will. We must, in other words, turn toward the time-image to discover within it the eventness of the event and the inchoate quality of thought, to encounter the truth of cinema.

Conclusion: Spectres of Impossibility

The usefulness of theoretical books on cinema has been called into question…[1]

The spectre of impossibility

How can a film capture, express, depict such an event as the atomic attacks on Hiroshima and Nagasaki? How can cinema do justice to the *pika* and the *hibakusha*? How can the Japanese nation make movies that explore the moment of the nuclear event, that explore the antecedents, the consequences? We have, after Abé Mark Nornes, described the Japanese screen as being haunted by the spectre of impossibility. Yet we have, over the course of this book, discovered a heterogeneous assemblage of films, cinematic masterpieces that have – each in their own way – found the will and means to overcome such a spectre. We have discovered movement-images and time-images of the Japanese cinema of the atom bomb.

Cinematic territories and critical processes

The trajectory of this book has been taxonomic. This may have appeared a strange procedure. Perhaps we are more used to books on cinema that are organized along an historical timeline, around a director or group of directors, through genres or by themes. Yet the cineotic methodology has not precluded these organizations. Indeed, the relationship is far more complex than that. On the one hand, when we limited our domain to a national cinema, when we selected an event within that dominion, these choices came before the cineosis. On the other hand, the cineosis has allowed, when forces aligned and the time was right, for explorations of certain themes, genres, directors, in and through cinema history. In other words, as Floyd Merrell has asked, 'is thought even possible without taxonomies?'[2] Working with a national cinema, focusing upon an event, selecting genres, themes and so on, also involves taxonomic choices. Nonetheless, shadowing Deleuze's cinematic semiosis and using it to structure this book has allowed a reversal to occur. It has provided a denaturalized foundation. It has allowed such taxonomic choices to be foregrounded as problems, problems which are not so much awaiting a solution, but problems in-themselves. One of the fundamental aims of this book has been the proposal that cinema is a heterogeneous assemblage. Using the Deleuzian cineosis is productive of such a proposal, and has permitted an encounter with each film in order to de- and re-connect it with other films, with history and with philosophy. Merrell puts it wonderfully: 'A taxonomy can at least serve a preliminary stage on the arduous road of enquiry leading toward a model of generation.'[3] Generating what? Thought – or writing, or storytelling, as you prefer: a dramatization.

This methodology has, furthermore, another aspect, one central to Deleuze's cinema-philosophy. This is the question of a film in-itself: the value of a film. This point can be clarified through a counter-example. In *The Philosophy of Motion Pictures* (2008), Noël Carroll writes: 'Isn't it overwhelmingly obvious that movies can be categorised? We have lots of motion picture categories, indeed, many that are perfectly unobjectionable, such as suspense, horror, structural films, melodrama, mysteries, thrillers, trance films, action films …'[4] So, take any film, Carroll writes; 'you said that it is good; I said that it is bad'.[5] Who is right? For Carroll such an evaluation becomes possible through the conjunction of taxonomy and debate. Carroll invokes what he calls a 'pluralistic-category approach'.[6] If our films are in the same category, then deciding which one is best can be decided upon through debate. However, what if they are not of the same category? The 'pluralistic-category approach to motion picture evaluation has to be supplemented', and the categories themselves can be placed in a hierarchy.[7] Carroll writes: 'an overall evaluation – a.k.a. an "all-things-considered judgement" – of a motion picture should take into account not only the movie's success or failure by its own (category-relative) lights, but the value or disvalue of the purpose or purposes to which the category is committed.'[8] This approach not only appears as good and common sense, but will be familiar to us all from our own post-movie-watching experiences, on the way home through the night or in a bar or coffee or tea house. We judge, and in order to judge, we must compare this film to that film. A lot of fun can be had this way. Carroll provides a sophisticated philosophical argument to validate such an approach to cinema. And while it may be 'our evaluative debates may go unresolved', so be it.[9]

The crucial point here, for Carroll, is that no film has value in-itself; it can only be evaluated through the debates ensuing from pluralistic approach and its supplement. This book, and the Deleuzian approach it foregrounds, takes a different path. We have not been concerned with evaluating the films explored. This is not the purpose of the Deleuzian cineosis, as we see it. We have rather been concerned with the value of a film. Of course there are good and bad films. But we challenge any cinema theory of evaluation: this is the abyss.

Value is something entirely different. The Deleuzian taxonomy, as I see it, rather believes a film to have value for how it creates a problem and attempts either to resolve or sustain it. The cineosis is a machinic toolbox to conjoin a film with a conception of history, with a philosophical procedure, with another film or other films that extend an argument, an experiment, a discovery. What is the value of the film from the point of view of what we can do with it, what connections we can make? The cineosis is a network of regimes, avatars, images, polarities, functions and signs availing themselves to different filmic, historical and philosophical conceptions. Film theory, in this sense, is not evaluative. Making a film is a creative endeavour and 'theory too is something which is made, no less than its object'.[10] For Deleuze, 'theory is itself a practice'.[11] Every film is carved from matter and puts in play virtual forces. Every great film is an effort of will, created by filmmakers (directors, actors, cinematographers and so on) over any number of months or years. This Deleuzian approach does not expend energies in finding clever ways to uncover how a film fails (as every film can be looked upon in such a way if we so wish). And we disregard what we consider films of no or little value (no matter how wrong we may be, no matter if we have no ground for such a turning away, no matter if we later – with time – change our mind). Either way, we do not invite the interminability of evaluative debate. Concomitantly, our task has been to confront critical approaches which attempt such evaluations, evaluations which intend to silence what we consider great cinema, evaluations that say this film is the same as all these other films, is worse or better than that film, and evaluations which propagate the idea a film can either succeed or fail in truthfully representing or recreating the verisimilitude of an event.

Cineosis, cinema, event

We have, in this book, brought the Deleuzian taxonomy and the cineotic approach to the Japanese cinema of the atom bomb. Our proposal was that there is such a cinema worthy of this name, composed of many masterpieces and constituting a heterogeneous assemblage of films. This Japanese cinema of the *pika* and *hibakusha* is composed of documentaries, dramas, monster movies and science-fiction films, constituted through classical realist and social-realist codes, modernist exegeses and post-modernist spectaculars. This cinema has attempted to explain the nuclear event, to resolve and rectify it, to problematize it – seen it as explaining everything and nothing. The atomic attacks on the cities and peoples of Hiroshima and Nagasaki have appeared through direct, indirect and trace depictions as an objective moment, as a subjective experience, through cinematic figures, memories and thoughts. The Japanese nuclear event has appeared as a centre, has been pushed to the periphery, has been captured up in history and escaped history. This is what we mean by a heterogeneous assemblage of films: affection-images, impulse-images, action-images, reflection-images, mental-images and time-images.

Yet there is one last secret to this heterogeneous assemblage. It must not be believed that from movement-images to the time-image Deleuze is exploring films in order to overcome the former with the latter. 'It is not a matter of saying the modern cinema of the time-image is "more valuable" than the classical cinema of the movement-image. We are talking only of masterpieces to which no hierarchy of value applies.'[12] Yet time-images reveal something fundamental, and such films of the nuclear event reveal the fundamental nature of the Japanese cinema of the atom bomb. Time-images are a heterogeneous assemblage in-themselves. Yet from movement-image to time-image, across all the images and signs, through all the virtual conceptual connections, the Japanese cinema of the atom bomb is itself a heterogeneous assemblage, a bloc of sensation that appears as a perspectival archive, an anarchic multiplicity. Impure: giving rise to moments of an encircling of the past as closure and a binding of the linearity of succession, taming the event, framing it within movement-images and historicizing; yet, at the same moment, enacting an indeterminacy of description and a disjunction of narration, resisting such captures of movement-images, ungrounding the determinations of history. This is the truth of the Japanese cinema of the atom bomb. The heterogeneous assemblage, a mosaic, is a cinematic time-image, a dramatization, cinematization that describes indeterminate images of the atomic attacks on Hiroshima and Nagasaki; that disturbs narrations and histories that capture up the Japanese nuclear event; that creates the moment of the *pika* and the experiences of the *hibakusha* as a discordant moment in thought.

Notes

Introduction

1 Gilles Deleuze, *Cinema 2: The Time Image*, trans. Hugh Tomlinson and Robert Galeta (Minneapolis: University of Minnesota Press, 2001), 209.

2 Tsuyoshi Hasegawa, *Racing the Enemy: Stalin, Truman and the Surrender of Japan* (Cambridge, Massachusetts and London, England: The Belknap Press of Harvard University Press, 2005), 180; 201; Donald Richie, '"*Mono no aware*": Hiroshima in Film', in *Hibakusha Cinema: Hiroshima, Nagasaki and the Nuclear Image in Japanese Film*, ed. Mick Broderick (London and New York: Kegan Paul International, 1996), 20; Ashley Smith, 'The Occupation of Japan', *International Socialist Review* 29 (2003): accessed January 21 2013, http://www.isreview.org/issues/29/japan_occupation.shtml

3 David M. Desser, 'Japan: An Ambivalent Nation, an Ambivalent Cinema', in *Hiroshima: A Retrospective, Swords and Ploughshares*, IX, No. 3–4 (1995), 15: accessed January 21 2013, http://acdis.illinois.edu/publications/207/publication-HiroshimaARetrospective.html; Richie, '"*Mono no aware*"', 28.

4 This neologism indicates Deleuze's cinematic images and signs are a semiotic: cinema + semiosis = cineosis. The term was created to support my online cineosis project. See David Deamer, *Cineosis blog* (2010–): accessed January 21 2013, http://cineosis.blogspot.com; and David Deamer, *Cineosis* (2010): accessed January 21 2013, http://cineosis.com. The term was first used in print with David Deamer, 'A Deleuzian cineosis: cinematic syntheses of time', *Deleuze Studies*, 5 (2011).

5 Ronald Bogue, *Deleuze on Cinema* (New York and London: Routledge, 2003), 104.

6 Deleuze, *Cinema 2*, 29.

7 *Pika* literally means flash, referring to the intense light of the atom bomb; from, and sometimes appears as, *pikadon*, where *don* refers to the sound of the explosion, the blast, the boom. *Pika* tends to be the more everyday usage.

8 Abé Mark Nornes, 'The Body at the Centre – *The Effects of the Atomic Bomb on Hiroshima and Nagasaki*', in *Hibakusha Cinema: Hiroshima, Nagasaki and the Nuclear Image in Japanese Film*, ed. Mick Broderick (London and New York: Kegan Paul International, 1996), 122.

9 Theodor W. Adorno, 'Cultural Criticism and Society', in *Prisms*, trans. Samuel Weber and Shierry Weber (Cambridge, Massachusetts: MIT Press, 1986), 34.

10 Theodor W. Adorno, *Negative Dialectics*, trans. E. B. Ashton (New York: Seabury Press, 1973), 362.

11 John T. Dorsey and Naomi Matsuoka, 'Narrative Strategies of Understatement in *Black Rain* as a Novel and a Film', in *Hibakusha Cinema: Hiroshima, Nagasaki and the Nuclear Image in Japanese Film*, ed. Mick Broderick (London and New York: Kegan Paul International, 1996), 203.

12 Ibid., 203.

13 Ibid., 203.

14 E. Ann Kaplan and Ban Wang, 'Introduction: From Traumatic Paralysis to the Force Field of Modernity', in *Trauma and Cinema: Cross-Cultural Explorations*, ed. E. Ann Kaplan and Ban Wang (Hong Kong: Hong Kong University Press, 2008), 8.

15 Ibid., 8.

16 Ibid., 8.

17 Ibid., 8.

18 Ibid., 9–10.

19 Ibid., 10.

20 Ibid., 15; 9.

21 Adam Lowenstein, 'Allegorizing Hiroshima: Shindo Kaneto's *Onibaba* as Trauma Text', in *Trauma and Cinema: Cross-Cultural Explorations*, ed. E. Ann Kaplan and Ban Wang (Hong Kong: Hong Kong University Press, 2008), 147–8.

22 Ibid., 146.

23 Gilles Deleuze, *Cinema 1: The Movement-Image*, trans. Hugh Tomlinson and Barbara Habberjam (London: The Athlone Press, 2002), x.

24 Deleuze, *Cinema 1*, xiv.

25 Nornes, 'The Body at the Centre', 120–59.

26 James Goodwin, 'Akira Kurosawa and the Atomic Age', in *Hibakusha Cinema: Hiroshima, Nagasaki and the Nuclear Image in Japanese Film*, ed. Mick Broderick (London and New York: Kegan Paul International, 1996), 178.

27 See Joseph L. Anderson and Richie, *The Japanese Film: Art and Industry* (Princeton, New Jersey: Princeton University Press [1959] 1982), 218–19; and Richie, *A Hundred Years of Japanese Film* (Tokyo; New York; London: Kodansha International, 2001), 149–50.

28 See Sato Tadao, *Currents in Japanese Cinema*, trans. Gregory Barrett (Tokyo: Kodansha International, [1982] 1987), 197–200. Sato's book is a compendium of various Japanese writings, although according to the translator most of the text – including the short section on atom bomb films – comes unedited from *Nihon eiga shiso-shi* (known in English as *A Theoretical History of Japanese Film*; or *Thought and Image in Japanese Film*; or *History of the Intellectual Currents in Japanese Film*, 1970). Also see Noël Burch, *To the Distant Observer: Form*

and Meaning in the Japanese Cinema (Berkeley and Los Angeles: University of California Press, 1979), 283.

29 Richie, "'*Mono no aware*'", 20–37.

30 Ibid., 23.

31 Ibid., 22.

32 Ibid., 36.

33 Jerome F. Shapiro, *Atomic Bomb Cinema: The Apocalyptic Imagination on Film* (New York and London: Routledge, 2002), 274.

34 Ibid., 352.

35 Anderson and Richie, *The Japanese Film*, 14.

36 Richie, *Japanese Cinema: Film Style and National Character* (London: Secker & Warburg, 1971), 7.

37 Richie, *A Hundred Years of Japanese Film*, 11.

38 Ibid., 11.

39 Ibid., 17.

40 Ibid., 17.

41 For a wonderful overview of these and other historical filmic experimentations see Mark Cousins, *The Story of Film* (London: Pavilion Books, 2004).

42 Ibid., 85–6, 89.

43 David Desser, *Eros plus Massacre: An Introduction to the Japanese New Wave* (Bloomington and Indianapolis: Indiana University Press, 1988), 6.

44 Ibid., 13.

45 Ibid., 13.

46 Burch, *To the Distant Observer*, 12.

47 Ibid., 14.

48 Ibid., 16–17.

49 Ibid., 17.

50 Ibid., 16.

51 Ibid., 27.

52 Ibid., 27.

53 *Desser, Eros plus Massacre*, 14.

54 Burch, *To the Distant Observer*, 11.

55 Ibid., 12.

56 David Martin-Jones, *Deleuze and World Cinemas* (London and New York: Continuum, 2011), 11.

57 Ibid., 11–12.

58 Ibid., 12.

59 Ibid., 16.

60 Ibid., 11.

61 Ibid., 11.
62 Deleuze, *Cinema 1*, 211.
63 Deleuze, *Cinema 2*, 19.
64 Ibid., 215–24; 220; 196.
65 Martin-Jones, *Deleuze and World Cinemas*, 11.
66 Deleuze, *Cinema 2*, 41.
67 Ibid., 270.
68 Lúcia Nagib, 'Towards a Positive Definition of World Cinema', in *Remapping World Cinema: Identity, Culture and Politics in Film*, eds Stephanie Dennison and Song Hwee Lim (London and New York: Wallflower Press, 2006), 30–7.
69 Ibid., 35.
70 Ella Shohat and Robert Stam, *Unthinking Eurocentrism: Multiculturalism and the Media* (London and New York: Routledge, 1994), 256; 289; 328.
71 Sato, *Currents in Japanese Cinema*, 20.
72 Ibid., 20.
73 Ibid., 32.
74 Ibid., 32.
75 Ibid., 32.
76 Ibid., 32.
77 Desser, *Eros plus Massacre*, 16.
78 Ibid., 16.
79 Deleuze, *Cinema 1*, ix.
80 Gilles Deleuze, *Difference and Repetition*, trans. Paul Patton (London and New York: Continuum, 2004), xiv–xv.
81 Ibid., xv.
82 Ibid., xv.
83 Ibid., xv.
84 Ibid., xv.
85 Gilles Deleuze and Félix Guattari, *What is Philosophy?*, trans. Graham Burchell and Hugh Tomlinson (London and New York: Verso, 2009), 197.
86 Ibid., 197.
87 Ibid., 197.
88 Ibid., 197.
89 Emilie Bickerton, *A Short History of* Cahiers du cinéma (London and New York: Verso, 2009), 81. See Jean-Luc Comolli and Jean Narboni, 'Cinema/Ideology/Criticism', in *Film Theory and Criticism*, eds Leo Braudy and Marshall Cohen (New York and Oxford: Oxford University Press, 2004), 812–19.
90 Ibid., 64–5.
91 Bickerton, *A Short History of* Cahiers du cinéma, 81.

92 Gilles Deleuze and Félix Guattari, *Anti-Oedipus: Capitalism and Schizophrenia*, trans. Robert Hurley, Mark Seem and Helen R. Lane (London and New York: Continuum, 2003), 106.

93 Ibid., 106.

94 Deleuze, *Cinema 2,* 280.

95 Deleuze and Guattari, *Anti-Oedipus,* 106.

96 Ibid., 106.

97 Gilles Deleuze, 'The Brain Is the Screen: An Interview with Gilles Deleuze', trans. M. T. Guirgis, in *The Brain Is the Screen: Deleuze and the Philosophy of Cinema*, ed. G. Flaxman (Minneapolis/London: University of Minnesota Press, 2000), 367.

Chapter 1

1 Gilles Deleuze, *Cinema 1: The Movement-Image*, trans. Hugh Tomlinson and Barbara Habberjam (London: The Athlone Press, 2002), 66.

2 Henri Bergson, *Matter and Memory*, trans. N. M. Paul and W. S. Palmer (New York: Zone Books, 1991), 20.

3 Ibid., 10.

4 Ibid., 9.

5 Ibid., 25.

6 Ibid., 17.

7 Ibid., 28.

8 Ibid., 28–9.

9 Ibid., 36.

10 Ibid., 17–18.

11 Ibid., 30.

12 Abé Mark Nornes, 'The Body at the Centre – *The Effects of the Atomic Bomb on Hiroshima and Nagasaki*', in *Hibakusha Cinema: Hiroshima, Nagasaki and the Nuclear Image in Japanese Film*, ed. Mick Broderick (London and New York: Kegan Paul International, 1996), 122–3.

13 Ibid., 122–3.

14 Ibid., 122–3.

15 R. J. C. Butow, *Japan's Decision to Surrender* (Stanford: Stanford University Press, 1954), 248.

16 Ibid., 248.

17 Nornes, 'The Body at the Centre', 122–3.

18 Ibid., 122–3.

19 Kogawa Tetsuo and Tsurumi Shunsuke, 'When the Human Beings are Gone…',

trans. Maya Todeschini, in *The Japan/America Film Wars: World War II Propaganda and Its Cultural Contexts*, eds Abé Mark Nornes and Fukushima Yukio (New York: Gordon and Breach, 1994), 165.

20 Ibid., 167.
21 Ibid., 167.
22 Ibid., 167.
23 Ibid., 169; 167.
24 Ibid., 169.
25 Kyoko Hirano, 'Depiction of the Atomic Bombings in Japanese Cinema during the U.S. Occupation Period', in *Hibakusha Cinema: Hiroshima, Nagasaki and the Nuclear Image in Japanese Film*, ed. Mick Broderick (London and New York: Kegan Paul International, 1996), 108–9.
26 Ibid., 121; 134.
27 Kyoko Hirano, *Mr. Smith Goes to Tokyo: Japanese Cinema under the American Occupation, 1945–1952* (Washington and London: Smithsonian Institution Press, 1992), 60.
28 Ibid., 60.
29 Hirano, 'Depiction of the Atomic Bombings,' 134.
30 Ibid., 134.
31 Kogawa and Shunsuke, 'When the Human Beings are Gone…', 167.
32 Ibid., 182.
33 Ibid., 182.
34 Ibid., 177.
35 Ibid., 177.
36 Ibid., 177.
37 Nornes, 'The Body at the Centre', 127.
38 Ibid., 127.
39 Ibid., 129.
40 Ibid., 135–6.
41 Ibid., 136.
42 Ibid., 140.
43 Ibid., 140.
44 Ibid., 140.
45 Ibid., 136.
46 Ibid., 137.
47 Ibid., 136.
48 Ibid., 140–1.
49 Ibid., 141.
50 Deleuze, *Cinema 1*, 69.

51 Ibid., 69.
52 Ibid., 62.
53 Ibid., 62.
54 Anna Powell, *Deleuze and Horror Film* (Edinburgh: Edinburgh University Press, 2005), 213.
55 Gilles Deleuze and Félix Guattari, *Anti-Oedipus: Capitalism and Schizophrenia*, trans. Robert Hurley, Mark Seem and Helen R. Lane (London and New York: Continuum, 2003), 320.
56 Bergson, *Matter and Memory*, 199.
57 Deleuze, *Cinema 1*, 84.
58 Ibid., 76.
59 Ibid., 60–1.
60 Ibid., 85.
61 Ibid., 84.
62 Ibid., 84.
63 Gilles Deleuze, 'The Actual and the Virtual', trans. Eliot Ross Albert, in Gilles Deleuze and Claire Parnet, *Dialogues II*, trans. Hugh Tomlinson and Barbara Habberjam (New York: Columbia University Press, 2002), 148.
64 Ibid., 151.
65 Ibid., 148; 149; 152.
66 Deleuze, *Cinema 1*, 85.
67 Ibid., 85.
68 Ronald Bogue, *Deleuze on Cinema* (New York and London: Routledge, 2003), 75.
69 Deleuze, *Cinema 1*, 81.
70 Ibid., 81.
71 Nibuya Takashi, 'Cinema/Nihilism/Freedom', trans. Hamaguchi Koichi and Abé Mark Nornes, in *The Japan/America Film Wars: World War II Propaganda and Its Cultural Contexts*, eds Abé Mark Nornes and Fukushima Yukio (New York: Gordon and Breach, 1994), 128.
72 Nornes, 'The Body at the Centre', 148–9.
73 Ibid., 9.
74 Ibid., 150.
75 Hirano, 'Depiction of the Atomic Bombings', 111.
76 Monica Braw, *The Atomic Bomb Suppressed: American Censorship in Occupied Japan* (New York and London: East Gate, 1991), 27–8.
77 Ibid., 29.
78 Ibid., 133.
79 Ibid., 133.
80 Hirano, 'Depiction of the Atomic Bombings', 104.

81 Ibid., 110.
82 Ibid., 110.
83 Ibid., 111.
84 Ibid., 113.
85 Ibid., 113.
86 Ibid., 111.
87 Ibid., 112.
88 Richie, '"*Mono no aware*": Hiroshima in Film', in *Hibakusha Cinema: Hiroshima, Nagasaki and the Nuclear Image in Japanese Film*, ed. Mick Broderick (London and New York: Kegan Paul International, 1996), 23.
89 Ibid., 25.
90 Ibid., 22.
91 Ibid., 22.
92 Ibid., 22.
93 Ibid., 23–4.
94 Ibid., 22.
95 Isolde Standish, *A New History of Japanese Cinema: A Century of Narrative Film* (New York and London: Continuum, 2006), 190.
96 Ibid., 190.
97 Ibid., 189.
98 Ibid., 192.
99 Ibid., 192.
100 Deleuze, *Cinema 1*, 88, 90.
101 Ibid., 90–1.
102 Ibid., 87.
103 Ibid., 87.
104 Ibid., 87.
105 Ibid., 105.
106 Ibid., 92.
107 Gilles Deleuze, *Cinema 2: The Time Image*, trans. Hugh Tomlinson and Robert Galeta (Minneapolis: University of Minnesota Press, 2001), xi.
108 Deleuze, *Cinema 1*, 122.
109 Ibid., 120.
110 Ann Kibbey, *Theory of the Image: Capitalism, Contemporary Film and Women* (Bloomington and Indianapolis: Indiana University Press, 2005), 135.
111 Ibid., 135.
112 Ibid., 135–6. Original source: Charles Sanders Peirce, *Collected Papers of Charles Sanders Peirce: Volume III & IV*, eds Charles Hartshorne and Paul Weiss (The Belknap Press of Harvard University Press: Cambridge, Massachusetts, 1974), 4.447.

113 Kibbey, *Theory of the Image*, 136.

114 Ibid., 136.

115 Deleuze, *Cinema 1*, 116.

116 Kibbey, *Theory of the Image*, 136.

117 Noël Burch, *To the Distant Observer: Form and Meaning in the Japanese Cinema* (Berkeley and Los Angeles: University of California Press, 1979), 283.

118 Ibid., 283.

119 Deleuze, *Cinema 1*, 141.

120 Ibid., 154–5.

121 Ibid., 141.

122 Ibid., 141.

123 Ibid., 154.

124 Ibid., 151.

125 Ibid., 151.

126 Ibid., 151.

127 Ibid., 152.

128 Ibid., 153.

129 Ibid., 153.

130 Ibid., 154.

131 Ibid., 158.

132 Ibid., 143–4

133 Ibid., 144.

134 Ibid., 144.

135 Ibid., 144.

136 Richie, '"*Mono no aware*"', 28.

137 Ibid., 30.

138 Deleuze, *Cinema 1*, 144.

139 I have previously discussed *Godzilla* in respect to the genetic sign of the large form action-image; see David Deamer, 'An Imprint of *Godzilla*: Deleuze, the Action-Image and Universal History', in *Deleuze and Film*, eds David Martin-Jones and William Brown (Edinburgh: Edinburgh University Press, 2012), 18–36.

140 Chon A Noriega, 'Godzilla and the Japanese Nightmare: When *Them!* Is U.S.', in *Hibakusha Cinema: Hiroshima, Nagasaki and the Nuclear Image in Japanese Film*, ed. Mick Broderick (London/New York: Kegan Paul International, 1996), 64.

141 Ibid., 71,

142 Samara Lea Allsop, '*Gojira / Godzilla*', in *The Cinema of Japan and Korea*, ed. Justin Bowyer (London: Wallflower Press, 2004), 71.

143 Jerome F. Shapiro, *Atomic Bomb Cinema: The Apocalyptic Imagination on Film* (New York and London: Routledge, 2002), 275.

144 Ibid., 275.
145 Ibid., 275.
146 Ibid., 276
147 Allsop, '*Gojira / Godzilla*', 69.
148 Ibid., 69.
149 Noriega, 'Godzilla and the Japanese Nightmare', 60.
150 Richie, '"*Mono no aware*"', 29.
151 Ibid., 29.
152 Ibid., 30.
153 Marius B. Jansen, *The Making of Modern Japan* (Cambridge, Mass.: The Belknap Press of Harvard University Press, 2002), 669.
154 Damian Sutton, 'Philosophy, Politics and Homage in *Tears of the Black Tiger*', in *Deleuze and Film*, eds David Martin-Jones and William Brown (Edinburgh: Edinburgh University Press, 2012), 52.
155 Ibid., 52.
156 Ibid., 47.
157 Ibid., 48; 50.
158 Ibid., 50–1.
159 Ibid., 48.
160 Ibid., 52.
161 Ibid., 52.
162 Ibid., 52.
163 Richie, '"*Mono no aware*"', 29.
164 Jansen, *The Making of Modern Japan*, 671.
165 Richie, '"*Mono no aware*"', 29.

Chapter 2

1 Gilles Deleuze, *Cinema 1: The Movement-Image*, trans. Hugh Tomlinson and Barbara Habberjam (London: The Athlone Press, 2002), 163.
2 Friedrich Nietzsche, 'On the Uses and Disadvantages of History for Life', in *Untimely Meditations*, ed. Daniel Breazeale, trans. R. J. Hollingdale (Cambridge: Cambridge University Press, 2006), 67.
3 Craig Lundy, 'Deleuze's Untimely: Uses and Abuses in the Appropriation of Nietzsche', in *Deleuze and History*, eds Jeff Bell and Claire Colebrook (Edinburgh: Edinburgh University Press, 2009), 192.
4 Ibid., 192
5 Deleuze, *Cinema 1*, 149.

6 Ibid., 63.
7 Nietzsche, 'On the Uses and Disadvantages of History for Life', 91.
8 Ibid., 91.
9 Ibid., 92.
10 Ibid., 67.
11 Ibid., 69.
12 Ibid., 70.
13 Ibid., 73.
14 Ibid., 76.
15 Ibid., 77.
16 Deleuze, *Cinema 1,* 148.
17 Ibid., 149.
18 Ibid., 149.
19 Ibid., 148.
20 Ibid., 148.
21 Ibid., 148.
22 Jerome F. Shapiro, *Atomic Bomb Cinema: The Apocalyptic Imagination on Film* (New York and London: Routledge, 2002), 273.
23 Lord Russell of Liverpool, *The Knights of Bushido: A Short History of Japanese War Crimes* (London: Greenhill Books, 2005), 1.
24 Ibid., 42–3.
25 Ibid., 43.
26 Ibid., 43.
27 Ibid., 43.
28 Chon A. Noriega, 'Godzilla and the Japanese Nightmare: When *Them!* Is U.S.', in *Hibakusha Cinema: Hiroshima, Nagasaki and the Nuclear Image in Japanese Film,* ed. Mick Broderick (London/New York: Kegan Paul International, 1996), 65.
29 Ibid., 65.
30 Ibid., 65–6.
31 Deleuze, *Cinema 1,* 150.
32 Ibid., 149.
33 Ibid., 150.
34 Ibid., 150.
35 Ibid., 151.
36 Marius B. Jansen, *The Making of Modern Japan* (Cambridge, Mass.: The Belknap Press of Harvard University Press, 2002), 277.
37 Ibid., 278.
38 Ibid., 285.
39 Ibid., 287.

40 Ibid., 440.
41 Ibid., 440.
42 Richie, '"*Mono no aware*": Hiroshima in Film', in *Hibakusha Cinema: Hiroshima, Nagasaki and the Nuclear Image in Japanese Film*, ed. Mick Broderick (London and New York: Kegan Paul International, 1996), 30.
43 Ibid., 30.
44 Ibid., 30.
45 Deleuze, *Cinema 1,* 160.
46 Ibid., 161.
47 Ibid., 168.
48 Ibid., 163.
49 Julien Vincent, 'The Sociologist and the Republic: Pierre Bourdieu and the Virtues of Social History', *History Workshop Journal* Issue 58 (2004): 139.
50 Ibid., 139.
51 Pierre Bourdieu, *Distinction: A Social Critique of the Judgement of Taste*, trans. R. Nice (London: Routledge, 1984), 101.
52 Pierre Bourdieu, *Outline of a Theory of Practice*, trans. R. Nice (Cambridge: Cambridge University Press, 1977), 86.
53 Ibid., 86.
54 Pierre Bourdieu, *The Rules of Art*, trans. S. Emanuel (Cambridge: Polity Press, 1992), 66.
55 Ibid., 66.
56 Susan J. Napier, *Anime – From* Akira *to* Princess Mononoke*: Experiencing Contemporary Japanese Animation* (New York: Palgrave, 2000), 165.
57 Ibid., 165.
58 Ibid., 165.
59 Ibid., 162.
60 Ibid., 165.
61 Ibid., 165.
62 Ibid., 162.
63 Ibid., 167.
64 Ibid., 167.
65 Deleuze, *Cinema 1,* 163.
66 Ibid., 164.
67 Ibid., 162.
68 Ibid., 161.
69 Ibid., 161–2.
70 Ibid., 162.
71 Ibid., 178.

72 Phillip Brophy, *100 Anime: BFI Screen Guides* (London: BFI Publishing, 2005), 158.
73 Deleuze, *Cinema 1*, 168.
74 Ibid., 168.
75 Freda Freiberg, '*Akira* and the Postnuclear Sublime', in *Hibakusha Cinema: Hiroshima, Nagasaki and the Nuclear Image in Japanese Film*, ed. Mick Broderick (London/New York: Kegan Paul International, 1996), 94.
76 Ibid., 94.
77 Deleuze, *Cinema 1*, 159. In this way 'the pair of object and emotion thus appears in the action-image as its genetic sign'. Ibid., 158.
78 Freiberg, '*Akira* and the Postnuclear Sublime', 101.
79 Ibid., 101.
80 Ibid., 100–1.
81 Ibid., 101.
82 Ibid., 101.
83 Gilles Deleuze and Félix Guattari, *Anti-Oedipus: Capitalism and Schizophrenia*, trans. Robert Hurley, Mark Seem and Helen R. Lane (London and New York: Continuum, 2003), 29.
84 Ibid., 29.
85 Ibid., 29.
86 Ibid., 30.

Chapter 3

1 Gilles Deleuze, *Cinema 1: The Movement-Image*, trans. Hugh Tomlinson and Barbara Habberjam (London: The Athlone Press, 2002), 178.
2 It is clear Deleuze is familiar with Peirce, and with Peirce scholarship of the time. For instance, he gives a sound, short overview of the *Pragmatism and Pragmaticism* semiotic schema – from categories to sign divisions and classes – as part of the recapitulation early in *Cinema 2*, even including a version of the nine sign divisions table in an endnote. See Gilles Deleuze, *Cinema 2: The Time Image*, trans. Hugh Tomlinson and Robert Galeta (Minneapolis: University of Minnesota Press, 2001), 30–3; 287 n10. Furthermore, both *Cinema* books also contain a number of references and endnotes, indicating a familiarity with Gérard Deledalle's commentaries. See Deleuze, *Cinema 1*, 227 n13; 231 n14; 232 n6, and Deleuze, *Cinema 2:* 2001: 287 n12. For Deledalle see Gérard Deledalle, *Charles S. Peirce's Philosophy of Signs: Essays in Comparative Semiotics* (Bloomington and Indianapolis: Indiana University Press, 2000).

3 Charles Sanders Peirce, *Collected Papers of Charles Sanders Peirce: Volume V & VI*, eds Charles Hartshorne and Paul Weiss (Cambridge, Massachusetts: The Belknap Press of Harvard University Press, 1974), CP 5.13.

4 Charles Sanders Peirce, *Collected Papers of Charles Sanders Peirce: Volume I & II*, eds Charles Hartshorne and Paul Weiss (Cambridge, Massachusetts: The Belknap Press of Harvard University Press, 1965), CP 2.227.

5 Peirce comments on Bergson in respect to his proposed book on his phenomenology (which would include the semiotic): 'I feel confident the book would make a serious impression much deeper and surer than Bergson's, which I find quite too vague' (Peirce 1966a: 428). Peirce never completed this task. See Charles Sanders Peirce, *Collected Papers of Charles Sanders Peirce: Volume VII & VIII*, ed. Arthur W. Burks (Cambridge, Massachusetts: The Belknap Press of Harvard University Press, 1966), 428.

6 Peirce gives three different accounts of the semiosis over a 40-year period. T. L. Short insists that in this theory of signs many elements are incompatible. Peirce himself comments: 'All that you can find in print of my work on logic are simply scattered outcroppings here and there of a rich vein of which remains unpublished. Most of it I suppose has been written down; but no human being could ever put together the fragments. I could not do so myself.' Yet attempts have been made, starting with Paul Weiss and Arthur Burks and more recently Albert Atkins. Atkins sees 'three broadly delineable accounts: a concise Early Account from the 1860s; a complete and relatively neat Interim Account developed through the 1880s and 1890s and presented in 1903; and his speculative, rambling, and incomplete Final Account developed between 1906 and 1910.' The final account of the semiosis indicates 59,049 different sign divisions, or as Peirce puts it, '59,049 difficult questions to carefully consider', which, he says, he will leave to others to answer. See T. L. Short, 'The Development of Peirce's Theory of Signs', in *The Cambridge Companion to Peirce*, ed. Cheryl Misak (Cambridge University Press, Cambridge, 2004), 214–40. Paul Weiss and Arthur Burks, 'Peirce's Sixty-Six Signs', in *The Journal of Philosophy*, vol. 42, no. 14, 1945, 383–8. Albert Atkin, 'Peirce's Theory of Signs', in *The Stanford Encyclopedia of Philosophy*, ed. Edward N. Zalta (Winter Edition, 2010), accessed November 12 2011, http://plato.stanford.edu/archives/win2010/entries/peirce-semiotics/. Peirce, *Collected Papers: Volume I & II*, CP 2: introductory quote. Peirce, *Collected Papers: Volume VII & VIII*, CP 8.343.

7 Peirce, *Collected Papers: Volume V & VI*, CP 5.66.

8 Ibid., CP 5.66.

9 Ibid., CP 5.66.

10 Peirce, *Collected Papers: Volume I & II*, CP 2.228.

11 Ibid., CP 2.243.

12 Peirce, *Collected Papers: Volume V & VI*, CP 5.68–72.
13 Peirce, *Collected Papers: Volume I & II*, CP 2.254–63.
14 For a full exegesis of the Peircian semiosis and Deleuzian cineosis, see David Deamer, 'A Deleuzian Cineosis: Peirce, Semiosis and Movement-images,' forthcoming.
15 Deleuze, *Cinema 2*, 32.
16 Ibid., 31.
17 Deleuze continues: 'perception will not constitute a first type of image in the movement-image without being extended into the other types ... perception of action, of affection.' Ibid., 31.
18 Ibid., 31–2.
19 Ibid., 32.
20 Henri Bergson, *Matter and Memory*, trans. N. M. Paul and W. S. Palmer (New York: Zone Books, 1991), 133.
21 Ibid., 80.
22 Deleuze, *Cinema 1*, 123.
23 Deleuze, *Cinema 2*, 32.
24 Deleuze, *Cinema 1*, 160.
25 Deleuze, *Cinema 2*, 31–2.
26 Joan Mellen, 'Kaneto Shindo', in *The Naked Island, Masters of Cinema book #12* (Eureka Video, 2005), 16. See also Joan Mellen, *Voices from the Japanese Cinema* (New York: Liveright, 1975), 110.
27 Mellen, 'Kaneto Shindo', 16.
28 Ibid., 16.
29 Daisy Bowie-Sell, 'Susanne Rostock on *The Naked Island*', in *Telegraph*, June 2 2012, accessed June 6 2013, http://www.telegraph.co.uk/culture/film/film-blog/9307342/Susanne-Rostock-on-The-Naked-Island.html
30 Ibid.
31 Richie, *A Hundred Years of Japanese Film* (Tokyo; New York; London: Kodansha International, 2001), 150.
32 Ibid., 274.
33 Acquarello, 'The Naked Island', in *The Naked Island, Master of Cinema book #12* (Eureka Video, 2005), 7.
34 Ibid., 7.
35 Ibid., 7.
36 Ibid., 7.
37 Adam Lowenstein, 'Allegorizing Hiroshima: Shindo Kaneto's *Onibaba* as Trauma Text', in *Trauma and Cinema: Cross-Cultural Explorations*, eds E. Ann Kaplan and Ban Wang (Hong Kong: Hong Kong University Press, 2008), 145.
38 Shindo Kaneto, *The Naked Island* (Eureka Video, 2005), Shindo's commentary.

39 Ibid.
40 Émile Zola, 'The Experimental Novel', in *The Experimental Novel and Other Essays*, trans. Belle M. Sherman (New York: Haskell House, 1964), 53–4.
41 Ibid., 26.
42 Ibid., 31.
43 Ibid., 52.
44 Ibid., 2.
45 Ibid., 2, footnote.
46 Ibid., 40.
47 Ibid., 54.
48 Shindo, *The Naked Island*, Shindo's commentary.
49 Zola, 'The Experimental Novel', 25.
50 Ibid., 25; 26.
51 Deleuze, *Cinema 1,* 123.
52 Ibid., 123.
53 Ibid., 123.
54 Ibid., 123.
55 Ibid., 123.
56 Ibid., 123.
57 Ibid., 127.
58 Ibid., 127–8.
59 Ibid., 124; 123.
60 Ibid., 128.
61 Ibid., 130.
62 Ibid., 130.
63 Quote from Shindo on DVD jacket. Unattributed, *The Naked Island* (Eureka Video, 2005), DVD jacket.
64 Deleuze, *Cinema 1,* 123–4.
65 Ibid., 124.
66 Ibid., 137.
67 Harriet Gilliam, 'The Dialectics of Realism and Idealism in Modern Historiographic Theory', in *History and Theory* vol. 15, no. 3, 1976, 231.
68 Ibid., 231.
69 Ibid., 232.
70 Ibid., 232.
71 Ibid., 233.
72 Ibid., 233.
73 Ibid., 234.
74 Ibid., 234.

75 Ibid., 234.

76 Ibid., 233.

77 Søren Kierkegaard, *Concluding Unscientific Postscript* (Cambridge: Cambridge University Press, 2009), 144.

78 Ibid., 143.

79 Peirce, *Collected Papers: Volume V & VI*, CP 5.66.

80 Deleuze, *Cinema 1,* 134.

81 Ibid., 136.

82 Mircea Eliade, *The Myth of the Eternal Return* (New York: Bollingen Foundation Inc, 2005), 17.

83 Deleuze, *Cinema 1,* 125.

84 Ibid., 124.

85 Ibid., 124.

86 Ibid., 126.

87 Deleuze, *Cinema 2,* 33.

88 In the glossary at the end of *Cinema 1* Deleuze puts it thus: the figure is a 'sign which instead of referring to its object, reflects another; or which reflects its own object, but by inverting it; or which directly reflects its object'. Deleuze, *Cinema 1,* 218.

89 Pierre Fontanier, *Les figures du discourse* (Malesherbes: Champs classiques, 2009), 77; 109. My own translation.

90 Ibid., 79; 87; 99; 105; 111; 123; 143.

91 Ibid., 221.

92 Ibid., 283; 323; 359; 403.

93 Deleuze, *Cinema 1,* 183.

94 Ibid., 183.

95 Ibid., 183.

96 Ibid., 183.

97 Tom Mes, *Agitator. The Cinema of Takashi Miike* (Godalming: FAB Press, 2003), 178.

98 Ibid., 178.

99 Ibid., 179.

100 Ibid., 179.

101 Ibid., 178.

102 Deleuze, *Cinema 1,* 183.

103 Ibid., 182.

104 Ibid., 182.

105 Ibid., 182.

106 Ibid., 182.

107 Ibid., 183.

108 Ibid., 183.

109 Jay McRoy, 'Introduction', in *Japanese Horror Cinema*, ed. Jay McRoy (Honolulu: University of Hawai'i Press, 2005), 3.

110 Ibid., 3.

111 Deleuze, *Cinema 1*, 184.

112 Ibid., 184.

113 Ibid., 185.

114 Ibid., 185.

115 Ibid., 185–6.

116 Ibid., 186.

117 Yamamoto Taro, 'Poem', trans. Richie in Unattributed, *Screendance: The State of the Art Conference Proceedings*, trans. Richie (Durham, NC: American Dance Festival, Duke University, July 6–9 2006), accessed July 3 2007 http://www.videodance.org.uk/pages/Proceedings.doc

118 Unattributed, *Screendance: The State of the Art Conference Proceedings* (Durham, NC: American Dance Festival, Duke University, July 6–9 2006), accessed July 3 2007 http://www.videodance.org.uk/pages/Proceedings.doc

119 Andrew Grossman, '*Tetsuo / The Iron Man and Tetsuo 2 / Tetsuo 2: Body Hammer*', in *The Cinema of Japan and Korea*, ed. Justin Bowyer (London: Wallflower Press, 2004), 140.

120 Ibid., 141.

121 Ibid., 140–1.

122 Ibid., 141.

123 Ibid., 141.

124 Ibid., 144–5.

125 Ibid., 145.

126 Lowenstein, 'Allegorizing Hiroshima', 149.

127 Ibid., 148.

128 Ibid., 148.

129 Ibid., 148.

130 Ibid., 146; 147.

131 Ibid., 146.

132 Linnie Blake, *The Wounds of Nations: Horror Cinema, Historical Trauma and National Identity* (Manchester: Manchester University Press, 2008), 59.

133 Ibid., 59.

134 Ibid., 59.

135 Ibid., 52.

136 Akira Mizuta Lippit, *Atomic Light (Shadow Optics)* (Minneapolis, London: University of Minnesota Press, 2005), 2.

137 Ibid., 2.
138 Ibid., 2.
139 Ibid., 118.
140 Deleuze, *Cinema 1,* 218.
141 Ibid., 192.
142 Ibid., 192.
143 Ibid., 190.
144 Ibid., 192.
145 Ibid., 192.
146 Ibid,. 188.
147 Ibid., 189.
148 Ibid., 189.
149 Ibid., 189.
150 Ibid., 194.
151 Ibid., 194.
152 Lowenstein, 'Allegorizing Hiroshima', 159.
153 Ibid., 159.
154 Ibid., 159.
155 Ibid., 159.
156 Ibid., 149.
157 Ibid., 150.
158 Ibid., 150.
159 Ibid., 150.
160 Ibid., 150.
161 Mark Shilling, 'Life after the bomb', in *Japan Times* August, 4, 2004; republished in *The Asia-Pacific Journal: Japan Focus,* accessed June 6 2013, http://www.japanfocus.org/-Mark-Schilling/1731
162 Lowenstein, 'Allegorizing Hiroshima', 150.
163 Ibid., 150.
164 Ibid., 150.
165 Ibid., 150.

Chapter 4

1 Gilles Deleuze, *Cinema 1: The Movement-Image,* trans. Hugh Tomlinson and Barbara Habberjam (London: The Athlone Press, 2002), 205.
2 Charles Sanders Peirce, *Collected Papers of Charles Sanders Peirce: Volume V & VI,* eds Charles Hartshorne and Paul Weiss (Cambridge, Massachusetts: The Belknap Press of Harvard University Press, 1974), CP 5.66.

3 Gilles Deleuze, *Cinema 2: The Time Image*, trans. Hugh Tomlinson and Robert Galeta (Minneapolis: University of Minnesota Press, 2001), 33.
4 Henri Bergson, *Matter and Memory*, trans. N. M. Paul and W. S. Palmer (New York: Zone Books, 1991), 133.
5 Ibid., 131.
6 Ibid., 9.
7 Patrick McNamara 'Bergson's *Matter and Memory* and Modern Selectionist Theories of Memory', in *Brain and Cognition* 30 (1996): 215.
8 Ibid., 216.
9 Ibid., 216.
10 Ibid., 222.
11 Ibid., 222.
12 Ibid., 216.
13 Ibid., 220.
14 Ibid., 220.
15 Ibid., 222.
16 Ibid., 222.
17 Ibid., 222.
18 Ibid., 223.
19 Ibid., 223.
20 Ibid., 230.
21 Ibid., 220.
22 Sato Tadao, *Currents in Japanese Cinema*, trans. Gregory Barrett (Tokyo: Kodansha International, [1982] 1987), 199.
23 Stephen Prince, *The Warrior's Camera: The Cinema of Akira Kurosawa,* revised and expanded edition (Princeton: Princeton Univerity Press, 1991), 156.
24 Ibid., 168.
25 Joan Mellen, *The Waves at Genji's Door* (New York: Pantheon Books, 1976), 203.
26 Prince, *The Warrior's Camera*, 168.
27 Ibid., 168.
28 Deleuze, *Cinema 1*, 186–92.
29 Ibid., 190.
30 Ibid., 188.
31 Ibid., 188.
32 Ibid., 188.
33 Ibid., 189.
34 Ibid., 189.
35 Ibid., 189.
36 Deleuze, *Cinema 2*, 176.

37 Deleuze, *Cinema 1*, 189.
38 Ibid., 190.
39 Ibid., 190.
40 Ibid., 191.
41 Ibid., 191.
42 Ibid., 191.
43 Mitsuhiro Yoshimoto, *Kurosawa: Film Studies and Japanese Cinema* (Duke University Press, 2000), 425 n3.
44 Friedrich Nietzsche, 'On the Uses and Disadvantages of History for Life', in *Untimely Meditations*, ed. Daniel Breazeale, trans. R. J. Hollingdale (Cambridge: Cambridge University Press, 2006), 61.
45 Ibid., 78.
46 Ibid., 60.
47 Ibid., 61.
48 Ibid., 76.
49 Prince, *The Warrior's Camera*, 343.
50 Ibid., 343. When Kurosawa spoke these words, *Dreams* had already been completed.
51 Ibid., 324.
52 Ibid., 293.
53 Ibid., 293.
54 Ibid., 293.
55 Ibid., 293.
56 Deleuze, *Cinema 1*, 189.
57 Dana Polan, 'Auteur Desire', *Screening the Past*, 12, uploaded March 2001, accessed March 15 2013, http://www.latrobe.edu.au/www/screeningthepast/firstrelease/fr0301/dpfr12a.htm, 12.
58 Polan, 'Auteur Desire', 12.
59 Gilles Deleuze, 'The Brain Is the Screen: An Interview with Gilles Deleuze', trans. M. T. Guirgis, in *The Brain Is the Screen: Deleuze and the Philosophy of Cinema*, ed. G. Flaxman (Minneapolis/London: University of Minnesota Press, 2000), 370.
60 Gilles Deleuze and Félix Guattari, *What is Philosophy?*, trans. Graham Burchell and Hugh Tomlinson (London and New York: Verso, 2009), 163–4.
61 Ibid., 175.
62 Ibid., 175.
63 Deleuze, 'The Brain Is the Screen', 368.
64 Prince, *The Warrior's Camera*, 343.
65 Ibid., 344.
66 Yoshimoto, *Kurosawa*, 375.

67 Ibid., 376.

68 Deleuze, *Cinema 1*, 190.

69 Ibid., 190.

70 Deleuze, *Cinema 2,* 48; 53.

71 Ibid., 48.

72 Ibid., 48.

73 Ibid., 49.

74 Ibid., 49.

75 Ibid., 49.

76 Ibid., 49.

77 Ibid., 50.

78 Ibid., 50.

79 Ibid., 52.

80 James F. Davidson, 'Memory of Defeat in Japan: A Reappraisal of *Rashomon*', in *Rashomon*, ed. Richie (New York: Grove Press, 1969), 162.

81 Ibid., 159.

82 James Goodwin, 'Akira Kurosawa and the Atomic Age', in *Hibakusha Cinema: Hiroshima, Nagasaki and the Nuclear Image in Japanese Film*, ed. Mick Broderick (London and New York: Kegan Paul International, 1996), 178.

83 Karl G. Heider, 'The Rashomon Effect: When Ethnographers Disagree', in *American Anthropologist*, new series, vol. 90, no. 1 (Mar. 1988), 74; 78.

84 Kurosawa Akira, *Something Like an Autobiography*, trans. Audie E. Bock (New York: Vintage Books, 1983), 183.

85 Ibid., 183.

86 Ibid., 183.

87 Yoshimoto, *Kurosawa,* 189.

88 Ibid., 189.

89 Nietzsche, 'On the Uses and Disadvantages of History for Life', 71; 70–1.

90 Ibid., 74; 75.

91 Ibid., 76.

92 Ibid., 63.

93 Yoshimoto, *Kurosawa,* 183.

94 Ibid., 184.

95 David Desser, '*Madadayo*: No, Not Yet, for the Japanese Cinema', *Post Script* 18, no. 1, Fall 1998, 58.

96 Goodwin, 'Akira Kurosawa and the Atomic Age', 196.

97 Ibid., 196.

98 Ibid., 195.

99 Ibid., 191.

100 Ibid., 191.
101 Ibid., 195–6.
102 Prince, *The Warrior's Camera*, 303.
103 Ibid., 303.
104 Ibid., 303.
105 Ibid., 304; 303.
106 Gilles Deleuze, *Logic of Sense*, trans. Mark Lester with Charles Stivale, ed. Constantin V. Boundas (London: The Athlone Press, 2004), 3.
107 Ibid., 3.
108 Deleuze, *Cinema 2,* 27.
109 Prince, *The Warrior's Camera*, 303.
110 Ibid., 303.
111 Deleuze, *Cinema 2,* 56.
112 Ibid., 56.
113 Ibid., 59.
114 Ibid., 58.
115 Ibid., 58.
116 Ibid., 58.
117 Ibid., 58.
118 Ibid., 59.
119 Ibid., 59.
120 Deleuze, *Cinema 1*, 121–2.
121 Ibid., 122.
122 Ibid., 120.
123 Deleuze, *Cinema 2,* 63.
124 Goodwin, 'Akira Kurosawa and the Atomic Age', 194.
125 Prince, *The Warrior's Camera*, 303.
126 Deleuze, *Cinema 2,* 63.
127 Ibid., 60.
128 John Gray, *Straw Dogs: Thoughts on Humans and Other Animals* (London: Granta Books, 2003), 194.
129 Ibid., 194.
130 Ibid., 194.
131 Ibid., 194.
132 Ibid., 199.
133 Deleuze, *Cinema 1*, 202.
134 Ibid., 198.
135 Ibid., 203.
136 Ibid., 203.

137 Ibid., 203.
138 Ibid., 218.
139 Ibid., 218.
140 Ibid., 218.
141 Ibid., 205.
142 Ibid., 205.
143 Ibid., 200.
144 Goodwin 'Akira Kurosawa and the Atomic Age', 196.
145 Ibid., 196.
146 Richie, *The Films Of Akira Kurosawa* (Berkeley/Los Angeles/London: University of California Press, 1996), 224.
147 Prince, *The Warrior's Camera*, 320.
148 Yoshimoto, *Kurosawa*, 366.
149 Ibid., 366.
150 Richie, *The Films Of Akira Kurosawa*, 224.
151 Ibid., 224.
152 Yoshimoto, *Kurosawa*, 367–8.
153 Ibid., 371.
154 Ibid., 371.
155 Deleuze, *Cinema 2,* 63.
156 Ibid., 63.
157 Yoshimoto, *Kurosawa*, 188.
158 Deleuze, *Cinema 2,* 176.
159 Ibid., 128. See also 169.

Chapter 5

1 Gilles Deleuze, *Cinema 2: The Time Image*, trans. Hugh Tomlinson and Robert Galeta (Minneapolis: University of Minnesota Press, 2001), 151.
2 Gilles Deleuze and Félix Guattari, *Anti-Oedipus: Capitalism and Schizophrenia*, trans. Robert Hurley, Mark Seem and Helen R. Lane (London and New York: Continuum, 2003), 324.
3 For a fuller (earlier) exegesis of the Deleuzian cineosis in respect to the three syntheses, see David Deamer, 'A Deleuzian Cineosis: Cinematic Semiosis and Syntheses of Time', in *Deleuze Studies*, vol. 5.3, 2011: 358–82.
4 Gilles Deleuze, *Difference and Repetition*, trans. Paul Patton (London and New York: Continuum, 2004, 164.
5 Ibid., xiii.

6 Henry Somers-Hall, *Deleuze's Difference and Repetition* (Edinburgh: Edinburgh University Press, 2013), 2
7 Ibid., 2.
8 Jay Lampert, *Deleuze and Guattari's Philosophy of History* (London and New York: Continuum, 2006), 8.
9 Ibid., 100.
10 Somers-Hall, *Deleuze's Difference and Repetition*, 2.
11 Deleuze, *Difference and Repetition*, 91.
12 Ibid., 91.
13 Ibid., 91.
14 Ibid., 91.
15 Ibid., 91.
16 Ibid., 91.
17 Ibid., 93.
18 Ibid., 92.
19 Ibid., 92.
20 Ibid., 95.
21 Ibid., 100.
22 Ibid., 100.
23 Ibid., 101; 103–4.
24 My translation: Deleuze writes 'C'est ce qu'on appelle un destin', and the translator of the English edition renders it – quite rightly – 'This is what we call destiny'. I have translated this as 'fate' to distinguish between this and the sign of composition of the recollection-image, which Deleuze also calls 'destin' and appears as 'destiny' in English. See Gilles Deleuze, *Différence et répétition* (Paris: Épiméthée, Presses Universitaires de France, 2011), 113; Deleuze, *Difference and Repetition*, 105; Deleuze, *Cinema 2*, 48; and Gilles Deleuze, *Cinéma 2: L'image-mouvement* (Paris: Les Éditions de minuit, 2010), 68.
25 Deleuze, *Difference and Repetition*, 107.
26 Ibid., 105.
27 Nathan Widder, 'Deleuze on Bergsonian Duration and Nietzsche's Eternal Return', in *Time and History in Deleuze and Serres*, ed. Bernd Herzogenrath (London and New York: Continuum, 2012), 145 n8.
28 Gilles Deleuze, *Logic of Sense*, trans. Mark Lester with Charles Stivale, ed. Constantin V. Boundas (London: The Athlone Press, 2004), 10.
29 Deleuze, *Difference and Repetition*, 109.
30 Ibid., 111.
31 Ibid., 111.
32 Ibid., 112.

33 It is worth noting that, for Peirce – whom we aligned with the Bergsonian sensory-motor system in Chapter 3 – sees no beyond of thirdness (aligned to Bergson's memory-image and Deleuze's mental-image). See Deleuze, *Cinema 2,* 33.

34 There are a few precursors with regards to the question of the cineosis and the three syntheses: see D. N. Rodowick, *Gilles Deleuze's Time Machine* (Durham and London: Duke University Press, 1997), 127; David Martin-Jones, *Deleuze, Cinema and National Identity: Narrative Time in National Contexts* (Edinburgh: Edinburgh University Press, 2006), 60–2; Richard Rushton, 'Passions and Actions: Deleuze's Cinematographic Cogito', in *Deleuze Studies*, vol. 2.2, 2008: 121; Joe Hughes, 'Schizoanalysis and the Phenomenology of Cinema', in *Deleuze and the Schizoanalysis of Cinema*, eds Ian Buchanan and Patricia MacCormack (New York: Continuum, 2008), 15–26; and Patricia Pisters, 'Synaptic Signals: Time Travelling through the Brain in the Neuro-Image', in Deleuze Studies, vol. 5.2, 2011: 261–74. For a commentary on these precursors, see Deamer, 'A Deleuzian Cineosis', 358–82.

35 Deleuze, *Cinema 2,* 127.

36 Ibid., 87.

37 Ibid., 127.

38 Ibid., 133.

39 Ibid., 155.

40 Ibid., 131.

41 Ibid., 131.

42 Ibid., 131.

43 Deleuze, *Difference and Repetition*, 111; 108.

44 Deleuze, *Cinema 2,* 189.

45 Gilles Deleuze and Félix Guattari, *What is Philosophy?*, trans. Graham Burchell and Hugh Tomlinson (London and New York: Verso, 2009), 197.

46 Deleuze, *Difference and Repetition*, 176.

47 Simon O'Sullivan, *Art Encounters Deleuze and Guattari: Thought Beyond Representation* (London: Palgrave Macmillan, 2006), 1.

48 Deleuze, *Cinema 2,* 245.

49 Ibid., 245.

50 Gilles Deleuze, *Cinema 1: The Movement Image*, trans. Hugh Tomlinson and Barbara Habberjam (London: The Athlone Press, 2002), 12.

51 Ibid., 13.

52 Ibid., 15.

53 Ibid., 17; 16.

54 Ibid., 17.

55 Ibid., 17.
56 Ibid., 16.
57 Ibid., 17.
58 Deleuze, *Cinema 2,* 42.
59 Deleuze, *Cinema 1,* 28.
60 Deleuze, *Cinema 2,* 42
61 Ibid., xi.
62 Ibid., 42.
63 Deleuze, *Cinema 1,*117–18.
64 Ibid., 118.
65 Ibid., 238.
66 Ibid., 235.
67 Michel Chion, *Audio-Vision: Sound on Screen*, trans. Claudia Gorbman (New York: Columbia University Press, 1994), 170.
68 Deleuze, *Cinema 2,* 7.
69 Ibid., 7.
70 Ibid., 5.
71 Deleuze, *Cinema 1*, 207.
72 Deleuze, *Cinema 2,* 7.
73 Ibid., 69.
74 Ibid., 69.
75 Ibid., 69.
76 Ibid., 87.
77 Ibid., 70.
78 Ibid., 79.
79 Ibid., 84.
80 Ibid., 84.
81 Ibid., 70.
82 Ibid., 70.
83 Ibid., 74.
84 Deborah Shamoon, 'If Casshern Doesn't Do It, Who Will?', in *Mechademia 4: War/Time*, ed. Frenchy Lunning (Minneapolis: University of Minnesota Press, 2009), 326.
85 Ibid., 326.
86 Ibid., 74.
87 Mark Lawson, 'What would you have done?', *Saturday Guardian*, December 8, 2012, 12.
88 Ibid., 12.
89 Shamoon, 'If Casshern Doesn't Do It, Who Will?', 326.

90 Ibid., 326.
91 Ibid., 326.
92 Deleuze, *Difference and Repetition*, 169.
93 Ibid., 169.
94 Ibid., 176.
95 Ibid., 176.
96 Deleuze, *Cinema 2,* 127; 99.
97 Ibid., 99.
98 Deleuze, *Difference and Repetition*, 105.
99 Deleuze, *Cinema 2,* 99.
100 Ibid., 99.
101 Ibid., 101.
102 Ibid., 101.
103 Ibid., 102.
104 Ibid., 105.
105 Ibid., 155.
106 Ibid., 133.
107 Ibid., 155.
108 Ibid., 143.
109 Ibid., 143.
110 Ibid., 131.
111 Ibid., 130.
112 Ibid., 151.
113 Mark Freeman, 'A Guide to the Study of Documentary Films', Mark Freeman Films, accessed January 1, 2008, http://www-rohan.sdsu.edu/~mfreeman/resources.php?content_id=11
114 Translation taken from Maureen Turim, *The Films of Oshima Nagisa: Images of a Japanese Iconoclast* (Berkeley: University of California Press, 1988), 226.
115 Deleuze, *Cinema 2,* 99.
116 Ibid., 110.
117 Ibid., 110.
118 Ibid., 110.
119 Ibid., 274.
120 Ibid., 105–6.
121 Ibid., 106.
122 Ibid., 106.
123 Ibid., 124.
124 Translation taken from Turim, *The Films of Oshima Nagisa*, 226.
125 Deleuze, *Cinema 2,* 226.

126 Ibid., 124; 125.

127 Ibid., 186.

128 Ibid., 275.

129 Max Tessier (with Audie Bock and Ian Buruma), 'Interview with Shohei Imamura', trans. Ian Buruma, in *Shohei Imamura*, ed. James Quandt (Toronto: Toronto International Film Festival Group, 1997), 65.

130 Deleuze, *Cinema 2,* 101.

131 Ibid., 100.

132 Ibid., 100.

133 Ibid., 101.

134 Ibid., 155.

135 Jasper Sharp, '*History of Postwar Japan as Told by a Bar Hostess*', Midnight Eye, accessed June 6, 2013, http://www.midnighteye.com/reviews/history-of-postwar-japan-as-told-by-a-bar-hostess/

136 Ibid.

137 Imamura Shohei and Michel Ciment, 'Traditions and Influences', trans. Stéphane Erviel and Mark Cousins, in *Shohei Imamura*, ed. James Quandt (Toronto: Toronto International Film Festival Group, 1997), 130.

138 Allan Casebier, 'Images of Irrationality in Modern Japan: The Films of Shohei Imamura', in *Shohei Imamura*, ed. James Quandt (Toronto: Toronto International Film Festival Group, 1997), 91.

139 Ibid., 92.

140 Ibid., 98.

141 Gilles Laprévotte, 'Shohei Imamura: Human, All Too Human', trans. Lara Fitzgerald, in *Shohei Imamura*, ed. James Quandt (Toronto: Toronto International Film Festival Group, 1997), 105.

142 Deleuze, *Cinema 2,* 128–9.

143 Ibid., 131.

144 Ibid., 132.

145 Ibid., 133.

146 Ibid., 133.

147 Turim, *The Films of Oshima Nagisa*, 225.

148 Ibid., 234.

149 Ibid., 233.

150 Ibid., 234.

151 Oshima Nagisa, 'The Error of Mere Theorization of Technique', in *Cinema, Censorship, and the State: The Writings of Nagisa Oshima, 1956–1978*, trans. Dawn Lawson, ed. Annette Michelson (Cambridge, Mass / London: MIT Press, 1992), 144.

152 Ibid., 144; 145.

153 Ibid., 145.

154 Ibid., 145.

155 Ibid., 145.

156 Deleuze, *Cinema 2,* 133.

157 Ibid., 139.

158 John T. Dorsey and Naomi Matsuoka, 'Narrative Strategies of Understatement in *Black Rain* as a Novel and a Film', in *Hibakusha Cinema: Hiroshima, Nagasaki and the Nuclear Image in Japanese Film*, ed. Mick Broderick (London and New York: Kegan Paul International, 1996), 204.

159 Ibid., 204.

160 Ibid., 204.

161 Ibid., 219.

162 Ibid., 220.

163 Ibid., 220.

164 Ibid., 220.

165 Ibid., 220.

166 Nakata Toichi, 'Shohei Imamura: Interviewed by Toichi Nakata', trans. Toichi Nakata, ed. Tony Rayns, in *Shohei Imamura*, ed. James Quandt (Toronto: Toronto International Film Festival Group, 1997), 123.

167 Dorsey and Matsuoka, 'Narrative Strategies of Understatement', 215.

168 Maya Morioka Todeschini, '"Death and the Maiden": Female Hibakush as Cultural Heroines and the Politics of A-bomb Memory', in *Hibakusha Cinema: Hiroshima, Nagasaki and the Nuclear Image in Japanese Film*, ed. Mick Broderick (London and New York: Kegan Paul International, 1996), 222–52; 223.

169 Ibid., 223.

170 Ibid., 235.

171 Ibid., 239.

172 Deleuze, *Cinema 2,* 135.

173 Ibid., 215.

174 Deleuze, *Logic of Sense,* 64.

175 Deleuze, *Cinema 2,* 201.

176 Ibid., 203.

177 Ibid., 203.

178 Ibid., 198.

179 Ibid., 276.

180 Ibid., 209.

181 Ibid., 211.

182 Rodowick, *Gilles Deleuze's Time Machine*, 198.

183 Ibid., 191.

184 Friedrich Nietzsche, 'On the Uses and Disadvantages of History for Life', in *Untimely Meditations*, ed. Daniel Breazeale, trans. R. J. Hollingdale (Cambridge: Cambridge University Press, 2006), 65.

185 Ibid., 65–6.

186 Ibid., 66.

187 Somers-Hall, *Deleuze's Difference and Repetition*, 81.

188 Ibid., 83.

189 Ibid., 82.

190 Ibid., 82; 83.

191 Ibid., 83.

192 Widder, 'Deleuze on Bergsonian Duration and Nietzsche's Eternal Return', 141; 143.

193 Ibid., 143–4.

194 Deleuze, *Logic of Sense*, 64; 65.

195 Deleuze, *Difference and Repetition*, 176.

196 Ibid., 176.

197 Paul Patton, 'Events, Becoming and History', in *Deleuze and History*, eds Jeffrey A. Bell and Claire Colebrook (Edinburgh, Edinburgh University Press, 2009), 34.

198 Ibid., 34.

199 Nicholas Vroman, 'Review: *Hiroshima*', *JFilm Pow-wow*, accessed January 6, 2013, http://jfilmpowwow.blogspot.co.uk/2011/09/review-hiroshima.html

200 Deleuze, *Cinema 2*, 211.

201 Richie, '"*Mono no aware*": Hiroshima in Film', in *Hibakusha Cinema: Hiroshima, Nagasaki and the Nuclear Image in Japanese Film*, ed. Mick Broderick (London and New York: Kegan Paul International, 1996), 25.

202 Ibid., 25.

203 Ibid., 25.

204 Patton, 'Events, Becoming and History', 50.

205 Ibid., 50.

206 Ibid., 50.

207 Ibid., 50.

208 Deleuze, *Cinema 2*, 245.

209 Clive Myer, 'Playing with toys by the wayside: an interview with Noël Burch', in *Journal of Media Practice*, vol. 5.2, 2004: 77; 79; 72.

210 Ibid., 78–9.

211 Deleuze and Guattari, *Anti-Oedipus*, 324.

212 Ibid., 324.

213 Deleuze, *Cinema 2*, 224.

Conclusion

1 Gilles Deleuze, *Cinema 2: The Time Image*, trans. Hugh Tomlinson and Robert Galeta (Minneapolis: University of Minnesota Press, 2001), 280.
2 Floyd Merrell, *Semiosis in the Postmodern Age* (West Lafayette, Indiana: Perdue University Press, 1995), 92.
3 Ibid., 92.
4 Noël Carroll, *The Philosophy of Motion Pictures* (Malden, MA / Oxford / Victoria: Blackwell Publishing, 2008), 208.
5 Ibid., 209.
6 Ibid., 209.
7 Ibid., 219.
8 Ibid., 220.
9 Ibid., 223.
10 Deleuze, *Cinema 2,* 280.
11 Ibid., 280.
12 Gilles Deleuze, *Cinema 1: The Movement Image*, trans. Hugh Tomlinson and Barbara Habberjam (London: The Athlone Press, 2002), x.

Select Bibliography

Acquarello, 'The Naked Island', in *The Naked Island (Masters of Cinema #12)*, Eureka Video, 2005), 4–9.

Allsop, Samara Lea, '*Gojira / Godzilla*', in J. Bowyer (ed.), *The Cinema of Japan and Korea*, London: Wallflower Press, 2004, 63–72.

Anderson, Joseph L. and Richie, Donald, *The Japanese Film: Art and Industry*, Princeton, New Jersey: Princeton University Press, [1959] 1982.

Bergson, Henri, *Matter and Memory*, N. M. Paul and W. S. Palmer (trans.), New York: Zone Books, 1991.

Bickerton, Emilie, *A Short History of* Cahiers du cinéma, London and New York: Verso, 2009.

Blake, Linnie, *The Wounds of Nations: Horror Cinema, Historical Trauma and National Identity*, Manchester: Manchester University Press, 2008.

Bogue, Ronald, *Deleuze on Cinema*, New York and London: Routledge, 2003.

Bourdieu, Pierre, *Outline of a Theory of Practice*, R. Nice (trans.), Cambridge: Cambridge University Press, 1977.

—*Distinction: A Social Critique of the Judgement of Taste*, R. Nice (trans.), London: Routledge, 1984.

—*The Rules of Art*, S. Emanuel (trans.), Cambridge: Polity Press, 1992.

Braw, Monica, *The Atomic Bomb Suppressed: American Censorship in Occupied Japan*, New York and London: East Gate, 1991.

Brophy, Philip, *100 Anime: BFI Screen Guides*, London: BFI Publishing, 2005.

Burch, Noël, *To the Distant Observer: Form and Meaning in the Japanese Cinema*, Berkeley and Los Angeles: University of California Press, 1979.

Butow, R. J. C., *Japan's Decision to Surrender*, Stanford: Stanford University Press, 1954.

Carroll, Noël, *The Philosophy of Motion Pictures*, Malden, MA / Oxford / Victoria: Blackwell Publishing, 2008.

Casebier, Allan, 'Images of Irrationality in Modern Japan: The Films of Shohei Imamura', in *Shohei Imamura*, James Quandt (ed.), Toronto: Toronto International Film Festival Group, 1997, 89–100.

Chion, Michel, *Audio-Vision: Sound on Screen*, C. Gorbman (trans.), New York: Columbia University Press, 1994.

Cousins, Mark, *The Story of Film*, London: Pavilion Books, 2004.

Davidson, James F., 'Memory of Defeat in Japan: A Reappraisal of *Rashomon*', in D. Richie (ed.), *Rashomon*, New York: Grove Press, 1969.

Deamer, David, 'Cinema, Chronos/Cronos: Becoming an Accomplice to the Impasse of History', in J. A. Bell and C. Colebrook (eds), *Deleuze and History*, Edinburgh: Edinburgh University Press, 2009, 161–87.

—'A Deleuzian Cineosis: Cinematic Semiosis and Syntheses of Time', *Deleuze Studies*, 5.3, 2011, 358–82.

—'An Imprint of *Godzilla*: Deleuze, the Action-Image and Universal History', in D. Martin-Jones and W. Brown (eds), *Deleuze and Film*, Edinburgh: Edinburgh University Press, 2012, 18–36.

Deledalle, Gérard, *Charles S. Peirce's Philosophy of Signs: Essays in Comparative Semiotics*, Bloomington and Indianapolis: Indiana University Press, 2000.

Deleuze, Gilles, *Bergsonism*, H. Tomlinson and B. Habberjam (trans.), New York: Zone Books, 1991.

—'The Brain Is the Screen: An Interview with Gilles Deleuze', M. T. Guirgis (trans.), in G. Flaxman (ed.), *The Brain Is the Screen: Deleuze and the Philosophy of Cinema*, Minneapolis / London: University of Minnesota Press, 2000.

—*Cinema 2: The Time Image*, H. Tomlinson and R. Galeta (trans.), Minneapolis: University of Minnesota Press, 2001.

—'The Actual and the Virtual', E. R. Albert (trans.), in Gilles Deleuze and Claire Parnet, *Dialogues II*, H. Tomlinson and B. Habberjam (trans.), New York: Columbia University Press, 2002, 148–52.

—*Cinema 1: The Movement-Image*, H. Tomlinson and B. Habberjam (trans.), London: The Athlone Press, 2002.

—*Difference and Repetition*, P. Patton (trans.), London and New York: Continuum, 2004.

—*The Logic of Sense*, M. Lester with C. Stivale (trans.), C. V. Boundas (ed.), London: The Athlone Press, 2004.

Deleuze, Gilles and Guattari, Félix, *Anti-Oedipus: Capitalism and Schizophrenia*, R. Hurley, M. Seem and H. R. Lane (trans.), London and New York: Continuum, 2003.

— *What is Philosophy?*, G. Burchell and H. Tomlinson (trans.), London and New York: Verso, 2009.

Desser, David, *Eros plus Massacre: An Introduction to the Japanese New Wave*, Bloomington and Inadianapolis: Indiana University Press, 1988.

—'Japan: An Ambivalent Nation, an Ambivalent Cinema', *Hiroshima: A Retrospective, Swords and Ploughshares*, IX, no. 3–4, 1995. < http://acdis.illinois.edu/publications/207/publication-HiroshimaARetrospective.html > [accessed 21 January 2013].

Dorsey, John T. and Matsuoka, Naomi, 'Narrative Strategies of Understatement in *Black Rain* as a Novel and a Film', in M. Broderick (ed.), *Hibakusha Cinema: Hiroshima, Nagasaki and the Nuclear Image in Japanese Film*, London and New York: Kegan Paul International, 1996.

Eliade, Mircea, *The Myth of the Eternal Return*, New York: Bollingen Foundation Inc., 2005.

Eno, Brian and Schmidt, Peter, *Oblique Strategies: Over One Hundred Worthwhile Dilemmas* (5th Edition), Opal Ltd. < www.enoshop.co.uk > 2001.

Fontanier, Pierre, *Les figures du discourse*, Malesherbes: Champs classiques, 2009.

Freeman, Mark, 'A Guide to the Study of Documentary Films', *Mark Freeman Films* < http://www-rohan.sdsu.edu/~mfreeman/resources.php?content_id=11 > [accessed 1 January 2008].

Freiberg, Freda, '*Akira* and the Postnuclear Sublime', in M. Broderick (ed.), *Hibakusha Cinema: Hiroshima, Nagasaki and the Nuclear Image in Japanese Film*, London and New York: Kegan Paul International, 1996, 91–102.

Gilliam, Harriet, 'The Dialectics of Realism and Idealism in Modern Historiographic Theory', *History and Theory*, vol. 15, no. 3, 1976, 231–56.

Goodwin, James, 'Akira Kurosawa and the Atomic Age', in M. Broderick (ed.), *Hibakusha Cinema: Hiroshima, Nagasaki and the Nuclear Image in Japanese Film*, London and New York: Kegan Paul International, 1996, 178–202.

Gray, John, *Straw Dogs: Thoughts on Humans and Other Animals*, London: Granta Books, 2003.

Grossman, Andrew, '*Tetsuo / The Iron Man* and *Tetsuo 2 / Tetsuo 2: Body Hammer*', in J. Bowyer (ed.), *The Cinema of Japan and Korea*, London: Wallflower Press, 2004, 139–50.

Hasegawa, Tsuyoshi, *Racing the Enemy: Stalin, Truman and the Surrender of Japan*, Cambridge, Massachusetts and London, England: The Belknap Press of Harvard University Press, 2005.

Heider, Karl G., 'The Rashomon Effect: When Ethnographers Disagree', *American Anthropologist*, new series, vol. 90, no. 1, 1988, 73–81.

Hirano, Kyoko, *Mr. Smith Goes to Tokyo: Japanese Cinema under the American Occupation, 1945–1952*, Washington and London: Smithsonian Institution Press, 1992.

—'Depiction of the Atomic Bombings in Japanese Cinema during the U.S. Occupation Period', in M. Broderick (ed.), *Hibakusha Cinema: Hiroshima, Nagasaki and the Nuclear Image in Japanese Film*, London and New York: Kegan Paul International, 1996, 103–19.

Imamura, Shohei and Ciment, Michel, 'Traditions and Influences', S. Erviel and M. Cousins (trans.), in J. Quandt (ed.), *Shohei Imamura*, Toronto: Toronto International Film Festival Group, 1997, 129–31.

Jansen, Marius B., *The Making of Modern Japan*, Cambridge, Massachusetts: The Belknap Press of Harvard University Press, 2002.

Kaplan, E. Ann and Wang, Ban, 'Introduction: From Traumatic Paralysis to the Force Field of Modernity', in E. A. Kaplan and B. Wang (eds), *Trauma and Cinema: Cross-Cultural Explorations*, Hong Kong: Hong Kong University Press, 2008, 1–22.

Kibbey, Ann, *Theory of the Image: Capitalism, Contemporary Film and Women*, Bloomington and Indianapolis: Indiana University Press, 2005.

Kierkegaard, Søren, *Concluding Unscientific Postscript*, Cambridge: Cambridge University Press, 2009.

Kogawa Tetsuo and Tsurumi Shunsuke, 'When the Human Beings are Gone…', M. Todeschini (trans.), in A. M. Nornes and Y. Fukushima (eds), *The Japan / America Film Wars: World War II Propaganda and Its Cultural Contexts*, New York: Gordon and Breach, 1994), 160–71.

Kurosawa, Akira, *Something Like an Autobiography*, A. E. Bock (trans.), New York: Vintage Books, 1983.

Lampert, Jay, *Deleuze and Guattari's Philosophy of History*, London and New York: Continuum, 2006.

Laprévotte, Gilles, 'Shohei Imamura: Human, All Too Human', L. Fitzgerald (trans.), in J. Quandt (ed.), *Shohei Imamura*, Toronto: Toronto International Film Festival Group, 1997, 101–6.

Lawson, Mark, 'What would you have done?', *Saturday Guardian*, 8 December 2012, 12.

Lippit, Akira Mizuta, *Atomic Light (Shadow Optics)*, Minneapolis, London: University of Minnesota Press, 2005.

Lord Russell of Liverpool, *The Knights of Bushido: A Short History of Japanese War Crimes*, London: Greenhill Books, 2005.

Lowenstein, Adam, 'Allegorizing Hiroshima: Shindo Kaneto's Onibaba as Trauma Text', in E. A. Kaplan and B. Wang (eds), *Trauma and Cinema: Cross-Cultural Explorations*, Hong Kong: Hong Kong University Press, 2008, 145–62.

Martin-Jones, David, *Deleuze, Cinema and National Identity: Narrative Time in National Contexts*, Edinburgh: Edinburgh University Press, 2006.

—*Deleuze and World Cinemas*, London and New York: Continuum, 2011.

McNamara, Patrick, 'Bergson's Matter and Memory and Modern Selectionist Theories of Memory', *Brain and Cognition* 30, 1996, 215–31.

McRoy, Jay, 'Introduction', in J. McRoy (ed.), *Japanese Horror Cinema*, Honolulu: University of Hawai'i Press, 2005, 1–11.

Mellen, Joan, *Voices from the Japanese Cinema*, New York: Liveright, 1975.

—*The Waves at Genji's Door*, New York: Pantheon Books, 1976.

Merrell, Floyd, *Semiosis in the Postmodern Age*, West Lafayette, Indiana: Perdue University Press, 1995.

Mes, Tom, *Agitator. The Cinema of Takashi Miike*, Godalming: FAB Press, 2003.

Myer, Clive, 'Playing with toys by the wayside: an interview with Noël Burch', *Journal of Media Practice*, vol. 5.2, 2004, 71–80.

Nagib, Lúcia, 'Towards a Positive Definition of World Cinema', in S. Dennison and S. H. Lim (eds), *Remapping World Cinema: Identity, Culture and Politics in Film*, London and New York: Wallflower Press, 2006, 30–7.

Nakata Toichi, 'Shohei Imamura: Interviewed by Toichi Nakata', T. Rayns (ed.), T. Nakata (trans.), in J. Quandt (ed.), *Shohei Imamura*, Toronto: Toronto International Film Festival Group, 1997, 107–24.

Napier, Susan J., *Anime - From* Akira *to* Princess Mononoke: *Experiencing Contemporary Japanese Animation*, New York: Palgrave, 2000.

Nibuya Takashi, 'Cinema / Nihilism / Freedom', K. Hamaguchi and A. M. Nornes (trans.), in A. M. Nornes and Y. Fukushima (eds), *The Japan / America Film Wars: World War II Propaganda and Its Cultural Contexts*, New York: Gordon and Breach, 1994, 124–9.

Nietzsche, Friedrich, 'On the Uses and Disadvantages of History for Life', in *Untimely Meditations*, D. Breazeale (ed.), R. J. Hollingdale (trans.), Cambridge: Cambridge University Press, 2006, 57–124.

Noriega, Chon A., 'Godzilla and the Japanese Nightmare: When Them! Is U.S.', in M. Broderick (ed.), *Hibakusha Cinema: Hiroshima, Nagasaki and the Nuclear Image in Japanese Film*, London and New York: Kegan Paul International, 1996, 54–74.

Nornes, Abé Mark, 'The Body at the Centre - *The Effects of the Atomic Bomb on Hiroshima and Nagasaki*', in M. Broderick (ed.), *Hibakusha Cinema: Hiroshima, Nagasaki and the Nuclear Image in Japanese Film*, London and New York: Kegan Paul International, 1996, 120–59.

O'Sullivan, Simon, *Art Encounters Deleuze and Guattari: Thought Beyond Representation*, London: Palgrave Macmillan, 2006.

Oshima, Nagisa, 'The Error of Mere Theorization of Technique', D. Lawson (trans.), in A. Michelson (ed.), *Cinema, Censorship, and the State: The Writings of Nagisa Oshima, 1956–1978*, Cambridge, Massachusetts / London: MIT Press, 1992, 144–58.

Patton, Paul, 'Events, Becoming and History', in J. A. Bell and C. Colebrook (eds), *Deleuze and History*, Edinburgh: Edinburgh University Press, 2009, 33–53.

Peirce, Charles Sanders, *Collected Papers of Charles Sanders Peirce: Volume I & II*, C. Hartshorne and P. Weiss (eds), Cambridge, Massachusetts: The Belknap Press of Harvard University Press, 1965.

—*Collected Papers of Charles Sanders Peirce: Volume VII & VIII*, A. W. Burks (ed.), Cambridge, Massachusetts: The Belknap Press of Harvard University Press, 1966.

—*Collected Papers of Charles Sanders Peirce: Volume III & IV*, C. Hartshorne and P. Weiss (eds), Cambridge, Massachusetts: The Belknap Press of Harvard University Press, 1974.

—*Collected Papers of Charles Sanders Peirce: Volume V & VI*, C. Hartshorne and P. Weiss (eds), Cambridge, Massachusetts: The Belknap Press of Harvard University Press, 1974.

Polan, Dana, 'Auteur Desire', *Screening the Past*, 12, 2001, < http://www.latrobe.edu.au/www/screeningthepast/firstrelease/fr0301/dpfr12a.htm > [accessed 15 March 2013].

Powell, Anna, *Deleuze and Horror Film*, Edinburgh: Edinburgh University Press, 2005.

Prince, Stephen, *The Warrior's Camera: The Cinema of Akira Kurosawa* (revised and expanded edition), Princeton: Princeton Univerity Press, 1991.

Richie, Donald, *Japanese Cinema: Film Style and National Character*, London: Secker & Warburg, 1971.

—*The Films of Akira Kurosawa*, Berkeley / Los Angeles / London: University of California Press, 1996.

—'"*Mono no aware*": Hiroshima in Film', in M. Broderick (ed.), *Hibakusha Cinema: Hiroshima, Nagasaki and the Nuclear Image in Japanese Film*, London and New York: Kegan Paul International, 1996, 20–37.

—*A Hundred Years of Japanese Film*, Tokyo / New York / London: Kodansha International, 2001.

Rodowick, D. N., *Gilles Deleuze's Time Machine*, Durham and London: Duke University Press, 1997.

Sato Tadao, *Currents in Japanese Cinema*, G. Barrett (trans.), Tokyo: Kodansha International, 1987.

Shamoon, Deborah, 'If Casshern Doesn't Do It, Who Will?', in F. Lunning (ed.), *Mechademia 4: War/Time*, Minneapolis: University of Minnesota Press, 2009, 323–6.

Shapiro, Jerome F., *Atomic Bomb Cinema: The Apocalyptic Imagination on Film*, New York and London: Routledge, 2002.

Sharp, Jasper, 'History of Postwar Japan as Told by a Bar Hostess', *Midnight Eye* < http://www.midnighteye.com/reviews/history-of-postwar-japan-as-told-by-a-bar-hostess/ > [accessed 6 June 2013].

Shohat, Ella and Stam, Robert, *Unthinking Eurocentrism: Multiculturalism and the Media*, London and New York: Routledge, 1994.

Smith, Ashley, 'The Occupation of Japan', *International Socialist Review* 29, 2003, < http://www.isreview.org/issues/29/japan_occupation.shtml > [accessed 21 January 2013].

Somers-Hall, Henry, *Deleuze's Difference and Repetition: A Philosophical Guide*, Edinburgh: Edinburgh University Press, 2013.

Standish, Isolde, *A New History of Japanese Cinema: A Century of Narrative Film*, New York and London: Continuum, 2006.

Sutton, Damian, 'Philosophy, Politics and Homage in *Tears of the Black Tiger*', in D. Martin-Jones and W. Brown (eds), *Deleuze and Film*, Edinburgh: Edinburgh University Press, 2012, 37–53.

Todeschini, Maya Morioka, '"Death and the Maiden": Female Hibakusha as Cultural Heroines and the Politics of A-bomb Memory', in M. Broderick (ed.), *Hibakusha Cinema: Hiroshima, Nagasaki and the Nuclear Image in Japanese Film*, London and New York: Kegan Paul International, 1996, 222–52.

Turim, Maureen, *The Films of Oshima Nagisa: Images of a Japanese Iconoclast*, Berkeley: University of California Press, 1988.

Widder, Nathan, 'Deleuze on Bergsonian Duration and Nietzsche's Eternal Return', in B. Herzogenrath (ed.), *Time and History in Deleuze and Serres*, London and New York: Continuum, 2012, 127–46.

Yoshimoto, Mitsuhiro, *Kurosawa: Film Studies and Japanese Cinema*, Duke University Press, 2000.

Zola, Émile, *The Experimental Novel and Other Essays*, B. M. Sherman (trans.), New York: Haskell House, 1964.

Select Filmography

Akira (Otomo Katsuhiro, Japan, 1988)
Barefoot Gen (Masaki Mori, Japan, 1983)
Bell of Nagasaki, The (Oba Hideo, Japan, 1952)
Black Rain (Imamura Shohei, Japan, 1989)
Casshern (Kiriya Kazuaki, Japan, 2004)
Children of the Atom Bomb, The (Shindo Kaneto, Japan, 1952)
Dead or Alive (Miike Takashi, Japan, 1999)
Dreams (Kurosawa Akira, USA/Japan, 1991)
Effects of the Atomic Bomb on Hiroshima and Nagasaki, The (Ito Sueo, Japan, 1946)
Face of Another, The (Teshigahara Hiroshi, Japan, 1966)
Face of Jizo, The (Kuroki Kazuo, Japan, 2004)
Ghidorah, the Three-Headed Monster (Honda Ishiro, Japan, 1964)
Godzilla (Honda Ishiro, Japan, 1954)
Godzilla vs. Mechagodzilla (Fukuda Jun, Japan, 1974)
Hiroshima (Sekigawa Hideo, Japan, 1953)
History of Postwar Japan as Told by a Bar Hostess, A (Imamura Shohei, Japan, 1970)
I Live in Fear (Kurosawa Akira, Japan, 1955)
King Kong vs. Godzilla (Honda Ishiro, Japan, 1962)
Kwaidan (Kobayashi Masaki, Japan, 1964)
Lucky Dragon No. 5 (Shindo Kaneto, Japan, 1959)
Man Vanishes, A (Imamura Shohei, Japan, 1967)
Naked Island, The (Shindo Kaneto, Japan, 1960)
Nausicaa of the Valley of the Wind (Miyazaki Hayao, Japan, 1984)
Navel and A-Bomb (Hosoe Eikoh, Japan, 1960)
Night and Fog in Japan (Oshima Nagisa, Japan, 1960)
Pacific War, The (Oshima Nagisa, Japan, 1968)
Rashomon (Kurosawa Akira, Japan, 1950)
Rhapsody in August (Kurosawa Akira, Japan, 1991)
Ring (Nakata Hideo, Japan, 1998)
Terror of Mechagodzilla (Honda Ishiro, Japan, 1975)
Tetsuo (Tsukamoto Shinya, Japan, 1988)
To Live (Kurosawa Akira, Japan, 1952)

Index